The English
Royal Family of Amer

C000156490

ALSO BY MICHAEL A. BEATTY

County Name Origins of the United States
(McFarland, 2001; paperback 2012)

The English Royal Family of America, from Jamestown to the American Revolution

MICHAEL A. BEATTY

McFarland & Company, Inc., Publishers

Jefferson, North Carolina, and London

The present work is a reprint of the illustrated case bound
edition of The English Royal Family of America, from
Jamestown to the American Revolution, *first published
in 2003 by McFarland.*

LIBRARY OF CONGRESS CATALOGUING-IN-PUBLICATION DATA

Beatty, Michael A., 1935–
The English royal family of America,
from Jamestown to the American Revolution / by Michael A. Beatty.
p.   cm.
Includes bibliographical references and index.

ISBN 978-0-7864-7383-0

softcover : acid free paper ∞

1. Great Britain — Kings and rulers — Biography.
2. Great Britain — History — Tudors, 1485–1603.   3. Great Britain — History —
Stuarts, 1603–1714.   4. Great Britain — History — 18th century.
I. Title.
DA28.1.B39   2012   929.7'2 — dc21   2003001322

BRITISH LIBRARY CATALOGUING DATA ARE AVAILABLE

© 2003 Michael A. Beatty. All rights reserved

*No part of this book may be reproduced or transmitted in any form
or by any means, electronic or mechanical, including photocopying
or recording, or by any information storage and retrieval system,
without permission in writing from the publisher.*

Cover images © 2012 PhotoSpin and PhotoDisc

Manufactured in the United States of America

*McFarland & Company, Inc., Publishers
Box 611, Jefferson, North Carolina 28640
www.mcfarlandpub.com*

To Carol Haynes Beatty,
my wife and my best friend

CONTENTS

KING CHARLES II (1630–1685)

KING JAMES II (1633–1701)

WILLIAM AND MARY

QUEEN ANNE (1665–1714)

KING GEORGE I (1660–1727)

KING GEORGE II (1683–1760)

KING GEORGE III (1738–1820)

PREFACE

My present great interest in the English royal family certainly had a long gestation period. When I was a boy, about four years old, my parents took me to the airport in New York City, where we then lived, to see the English King, and some of his family, arrive for a visit to the United States. King George V died when I was only one year old, and his eldest son, Edward, abdicated before being crowned, so the English King whom I saw walk on the red carpet must have been King George VI.

The reader will detect a certain vagueness here, but there were reasons for it. The Great Depression was just ending and my parents made it a habit to spend their "quality time" with me at attractions that were essentially free of charge. Cold or not, the annual Macy's Thanksgiving Day parade was a must-see event, and other months featured countless visits to the Bronx Zoo and the American Museum of Natural History in Manhattan.

So it is difficult for me to recall whether my parents considered the visit of the King of England to our neighborhood (we then lived in Queens) to be a truly noteworthy event. Probably its greatest attraction was its admission price (free — we were just outside a chain link fence). I know that for me, personally, the King and his family were fine enough, but my greatest interest was the box of Cracker Jacks in my hand and the certainty that a prize of some sort awaited me at the bottom of that box.

It was not too many months or years later that some genuine interest in England and its royal family came to me by way of stamp collecting. I took this hobby up at an unusually early age, possibly as a safe activity for me during my recuperation from a fractured skull. Baseball games on the radio and interesting little pieces of paper from all over the world to mount in my stamp album: those were my recreations as I recovered.

Since England was the first nation to use postage stamps, they have taken the not unreasonable position that there is no need to put the name of their country

1

on their postage stamps, although it might be well for copycat nations to insert their country names to avoid confusion. The mischief that inspired the British to avoid putting a national name on their postage stamps gave rise to a more subtle form of identification; i.e., Great Britain and its colonies tended to insert the image of the reigning monarch on their stamps.

If my stamp collection was my initial inspiration, genuine interest in England's royal family came to me as a byproduct of my need to know just who was who among them in order to write my earlier book, *County Name Origins of the United States*. During my research for that book I constructed my own genealogical charts, showing kings and queens, their spouses, parents, siblings and children, with some emphasis on titles of nobility, such as "duke of York and Albany." Birth and death years were also vital for those informal reference charts. The material on those charts has proved useful again in the present work.

America's first permanent European colonists came from England. For about a century and a half, these colonists considered themselves to be Englishmen and were proud of if it. England's royal family truly was "the English royal family of America" until the era of the American Revolution.

Selecting just who should and who should not be included in a book of biographies of members of "The English Royal Family of America…" involves some judgment calls.

The settlements of Sir Walter Ralegh were established during the reign of Queen Elizabeth I, so that monarch has been selected to start the compilation, even though Ralegh's settlements in America failed to survive.

The last monarch to be included must be King George III, for it was during his reign that the shots "heard 'round the world" were fired at Lexington and Concord, and it was from that monarch that the thirteen British colonies declared their freedom in our nation's Declaration of Independence. Thus the royal family members to be found in the present work include all of the monarchs, their spouses, and legitimate children from Elizabeth I through George III, even though a number of these persons died after 1776, and two of these children were born after 1776. Occasional mention (rather than biographical sketches) appears for illegitimate children of the monarchs and mistresses.

Several of the legitimate children of these monarchs came to the throne themselves. To avoid duplication of biographical material, these children will first be mentioned in the chapter devoted to their parent who was the monarch. A proper biographical sketch will then be presented for each of these children in the chapter devoted to each in his or her capacity as monarch.

Michael A. Beatty
Ft. Myers, Florida
January 2003

Queen Elizabeth I

Queen Elizabeth I acceded to the throne of England on November 17, 1558. Her coronation took place at Westminster Abbey on January 15, 1559, and she ruled England until her death on March 24, 1603. She never married, nor did she have any children.

1. *Queen Elizabeth I (1533–1603)*

Elizabeth's father, King Henry VIII (1491–1547), had been a practicing Roman Catholic in good standing with the Church until he decided to divorce his first wife, Catherine of Aragon (1485–1536), and marry Ann Boleyn (1507–1536). The King was unable to secure approval of that divorce from the Roman Catholic Church, and the imperious King answered this papal insolence by breaking with Rome and establishing his own church, the Church of England (*Ecclesia Anglicana*).

Elizabeth was born to King Henry VIII and his second wife, Anne Boleyn, on September 7, 1533, at Greenwich Palace. Elizabeth was well educated, spoke some six languages and was well read in both Latin and Greek.

The Roman Catholic Church had refused to recognize Elizabeth's father's divorce and his remarriage and had therefore classified Elizabeth as illegitimate while she was still in the womb. More surprisingly, both civil and church leaders in England were slow to accept the legitimacy of the marital activities of King Henry VIII and his changes concerning the conduct of worship services. An act of parliament declared Elizabeth to be illegitimate and removed her from the line of succession to the English throne, although she was later reinstated.

Elizabeth did not directly succeed her father to the English throne. Upon the death of Henry VIII in 1547, Elizabeth's nine-year-old half-brother, Edward VI

(1537–1553), took the throne. He was succeeded (for nine days) by Jane Grey (1537–1554), and then in 1553 Elizabeth's half-sister, Queen Mary I (1516–1558), took the throne. Throughout her reign, Queen Mary I devoted herself to restoring the Roman Catholic Church as the Church of England. While Queen Mary reigned, Elizabeth's life was frequently in grave danger. However the Queen's sense of justice coupled with Elizabeth's own sharp wits kept Elizabeth alive and, upon Mary's death on November 17, 1558, Elizabeth acceded to the throne she would hold for almost half a century.

Apparently Elizabeth's strongest personal views concerning religion involved lengthy sermons and married clergymen, and in both cases Elizabeth disdained them. Although it is doubtful that Elizabeth personally was particularly pious or even held strong personal beliefs concerning theological matters, the circumstances surrounding her birth and the threats against her, both foreign and domestic, were such that matters of a religious nature dominated much of her reign. She had been raised as a Protestant and as the Queen, Elizabeth arranged for the repeal of Roman Catholic legislation enacted during the reign of the Catholic Queen Mary I. In 1559 Elizabeth was declared the supreme governor of the English Church. In 1570 the Pope excommunicated Elizabeth from the Roman Catholic Church and declared her subjects absolved of their allegiance to her. During Elizabeth's reign, when military matters seemingly overshadowed religion, the warfare almost always stemmed from religious tension — primarily tension between Roman Catholicism and Protestantism.

The Catholic-Protestant contention was not the only religious issue to vex Queen Elizabeth. Puritans within England were a semi-constant source of irritation with their own preferences and demands, and the Calvinist influence drifting down from Scotland also complicated Elizabeth's balancing act. As Queen, Elizabeth insisted upon the appearance of conformity by her subjects to the established Church of England. Elizabeth's decisions and actions in matters of faith were usually, at least to her, in the best interests of England. Since Elizabethan England had no tradition of separation of church and state, as we have today in America, it is not difficult to see how Queen Elizabeth may have genuinely felt that freedom to disobey the established order on religious matters was a direct threat to the monarch's primacy in civil affairs. That logic notwithstanding, it is a fact that the measures Elizabeth took against the Catholics within her realm were abhorrent. For example, they were forbidden to attend Mass, and Roman Catholic priests were tortured, drawn and quartered and subjected to other incivilities.

Another aspect of Elizabeth's personality that impacted much of her reign was her personal relationships (or lack of them) with men. Elizabeth never married, and our state of Virginia was named in honor of her, since she was often called the "Virgin Queen" and the first attempt to found an English colony here was during her reign. Actually, it is likely that Elizabeth lost her virginity when she was still in her teens. Nevertheless, Elizabeth carefully refrained from marrying, for she knew that in those days of male domination, taking on a husband would mean sharing her power, and this she had no intention of doing. However, she managed to portray herself as a potential mate with such success that she developed "being available" into an art form. As with religion, in Elizabeth's heart she believed that what was best for Elizabeth, vis-à-vis marriage, was also best for England.

The question of succession beyond Elizabeth's reign was a thorny one. Mary, Queen of Scots (1542–1587) claimed to be the rightful Queen of England. When Elizabeth contracted smallpox in October of 1562, and was thought to be dying, there was much discussion concerning a successor. Although Elizabeth mentioned a preference on this subject when she recovered from that illness, in later life she avoided the topic, perhaps because she realized that once a successor was identified, he or she would claim at least a portion of the focus Elizabeth demanded for herself. As for the lovely Mary, Queen of Scots, events in Scotland forced her to make her home in England. In spite of Mary's involvement in several plots against the Queen, Elizabeth tolerated Mary's presence in England until her association with the Babington plot. Mary, Queen of Scots was tried, convicted, and, in 1587, she was beheaded. That Elizabeth allowed this execution to occur is rated by most as quite appropriate under the circumstances, but there are some who consider this a blot on Elizabeth's otherwise distinguished career.

Despite the fact that Queen Elizabeth's financial resources were limited, England became involved in important military actions during her reign. Spain had become rich from raiding the gold and silver mines of Mexico and Peru in the New World, and Spanish military might began to grow to dangerous proportions. With Queen Elizabeth's approval, England's famed naval tactician, Francis Drake (–1596) engaged in predatory piracy against the ships of Catholic Europe, primarily those of Spain. Drake's naval actions were largely successful and impaired Spain's military might to a degree. However, in 1580 Spain conquered Portugal and the Spanish king, Philip II (1527–1598), who once had sought Elizabeth's hand in marriage, now ruled the entire, very Catholic, Iberian Peninsula. King Philip II was determined to crush European opposition to Catholicism. Toward that end, King Philip attempted to put down a revolt in the Low Countries. Queen Elizabeth's sympathies were divided about that revolt. On the one hand, she was reluctant to give aid and comfort to encourage rebellion against established leaders, but, in 1585, Elizabeth accepted the need to aid the Dutch. Aided by the English, the Low Countries were at least partially successful in their revolt against Spain.

Meanwhile Spain continued to develop its naval armada. In the spring of 1587, Francis Drake conducted a brilliant and successful raid on Cadiz. Nevertheless, Spain was able to assemble a remarkable fighting force to invade England. When the Spanish Armada set sail in May 1588, it represented the largest military expeditionary force in history. The armada consisted of a fleet of some 130 ships manned by 8,000 sailors. King Philip's plan was to land some 40,000 troops on England's southeastern coast. Theoretically the Spanish troops, once ashore, would be joined by disgruntled English Catholics, and Protestantism would be swept from England. Spain's hope for significant aid from disgruntled English Catholics was probably unrealistic. On the other hand, their help might not have been needed had Spain been able to successfully put its enormous army on English soil, but that never happened.

The defeat of the Spanish Armada and preservation of Elizabeth's Protestant rule of England was a noteworthy achievement, indeed. Those sharing credit for that achievement included England's Lord High Admiral Charles Howard (–1624), who commanded a fleet of only some 40 first rank warships in defeating the Spanish Armada at sea. Queen Elizabeth is to be credited for the remarkably inspiring words that she gave to her fighting men and even more for her good sense in giving Admiral Howard wide powers of discretion. In contrast, the Spanish commander, Alonso Perez de Guzman, Duke of Medina-Sidonia (1550–1615), was hamstrung by precise and inviolable instructions from home. Credit must also be given to the weather. Gales first forced the Spanish Armada to return to northern Spain before they launched their attack. Then, in naval encounters in which the English generally prevailed, strong winds prevented the armada from regrouping to continue the battle, and the Spanish vessels were forced to retreat to Spain via the northern tip of Scotland. About half of the Spanish vessels and two-thirds of their men failed to reach home: a stunning victory for England.

Elizabeth's romantic adventures represent an interesting study in themselves. Her flirtations and courtships were numerous, beginning in her teens and lasting into old age, and a number of her courtships were prompted by their political advantage. Some of Elizabeth's potential mates were members of powerful European royal families, and essentially all who courted her became well known as suitors by the time she was done with them. And done with them she was, one by one, in all cases, for she had no intention of letting any man capture her or her kingdom. However, Elizabeth was outwardly free in her tender moments with the opposite sex, and vanity and enjoyment of the game prevented her ever calling a halt to romance itself.

When she was still an infant, Elizabeth was courted as a wife for the political gain that marriage to the daughter of England's ruling king, Henry VIII, might bring. Before her second birthday a proposal was made and pursued with some determination that she marry the youngest son of the King of France. The prospective groom, himself, was not yet 14 years old. Although nothing came of this proposal, it resulted more from good luck than good management. Betrothals of royal children were then common in Europe.

When Princess Elizabeth was only 13 years old, Thomas Seymour (–1549) made a bid for her hand in marriage, but was denied it by the royal court. In 1547 Seymour secretly married Elizabeth's stepmother, the Queen-dowager, Catherine Parr (–1548), in whose household Elizabeth was living; Seymour made the most of this propinquity to flirt with Elizabeth—perhaps more than flirt. Several accounts indicate that during this period Elizabeth had "a few youthful indiscretions" with him. Some sources mention a rumor that was bruited about that she had been made pregnant by Seymour. If so, the fetus miscarried, for it is certain that no child was born to Elizabeth then, or ever. This incident taught Elizabeth to keep a lower profile in her adventures with the opposite sex. During the following decade Elizabeth set her sights on preserving her life and then her path to the throne. She engaged in serious scholarship and developed self-discipline.

England desired a clear line of succession to the throne. Experience had taught that a clouded line of succession spelled potential adversity for the nation. During the period that Elizabeth's Catholic half-sister, Mary I, reigned, Elizabeth prudently refrained from presenting herself as defiantly Protestant (or anti–Catholic), thus spreading wide the nets for potential mates on the largely Catholic European continent. During this period, England itself was not a great world power and it was ripe for plucking by a more dominant continental power. Capturing Elizabeth's hand in marriage was viewed as a route to that end. An early candidate was King Philip II (1527–1598) of Spain, who had been King Consort to England's Queen Mary I. Prospects of that union soon died, but prolonged negotiations ensued for Queen Elizabeth to marry Charles, Archduke of Austria (1500–1558). Although these negotiations lasted longer, they came to nothing. A representative of Crown Prince Eric of Sweden came to London in search of a royal match, and although Eric possessed the advantage of being a Protestant (or, more to the point, he was not a Catholic), Elizabeth kept out of reach. There was, of course, no shortage of Englishmen willing to take the Queen's hand in marriage, but the next contender of consequence was from abroad, Henry, Duke of Anjou, a brother of the king of France. Elizabeth and the Duke allowed negotiations to proceed and then gracefully watched them fizzle. Another contender was the youngest prince in the royal French family, Francois, Duke of Alencon. Although Elizabeth held genuine affection for Alencon, in the end she dismissed him as a possible mate. He proved to be Elizabeth's last royal suitor from Europe.

History has taken a lively interest in the romances of Queen Elizabeth I. Elizabeth lived long and reveled in attention from suitors, even after marriage was no longer likely. Among the Queen's English favorites, some of whom were involved with the Queen during her declining years, were Robert Dudley, Earl of Leicester (–1588), Sir Christopher Hatton (1540–1591), Sir Walter Ralegh (–1618) and Robert Devereux, Earl of Essex (1566–1601).

In assessing Elizabeth's effectiveness as England's sovereign, all objective observers give her very high marks. She managed to keep control of England in English hands and she won the hearts of the English people. Under Elizabeth, the seeds of the British Empire were sown with establishment of the East India Company and initial steps towards building colonies in North America. Elizabeth's success in maintaining and strengthening the Anglican Church as the Church of England — in the face of threats from the Roman Catholic Church on the European continent and domestic challenges from Puritans and Calvinists—was remarkable.

Queen Elizabeth died on March 24, 1603. An advertisement in a recent (2001) *New York Times Book Review* for a biography of the Queen carries a tidy summary of her achievement: "The CEO who managed history's greatest corporate turnaround. In 1558 Elizabeth I inherited a business in trouble — a nation near bankruptcy, ripe for invasion, torn by religious dissension, and bereft of pride. By the end of her reign, England was the most prosperous and powerful nation in Europe."

KING JAMES I

King James I acceded to the throne of Scotland on July 24, 1567, as King James VI of Scotland. He acceded to the throne of England on March 24, 1603, upon the death of Queen Elizabeth I. His name was thenceforth styled King James I of England and King James VI of Scotland. James' English coronation took place at Westminster Abbey on July 25, 1603, and he ruled England until his death on March 27, 1625. He had only one wife, Anne of Denmark and Norway (1574–1619). Although James was bisexual, and actually preferred men to women, he performed his duty to the royal line of succession. He and Anne produced seven named children and one unnamed son. Only three of these children survived beyond infancy.

2. *King James I (1566–1625)*

James was the only son of the lovely Mary, Queen of Scots (1542–1587) and her second husband, Henry Stuart, Lord Darnley (1546–1567). James was born while his mother was Queen of Scotland, and at his Roman Catholic baptism, he was christened Charles James. The name Charles was chosen to honor the infant's godfather, King Charles IX (1550–1574) of France. The name James honored Scotland's former King of Scots, James V (1512–1542), who was the baby's grandfather. When James' mother was forced to abdicate her Scottish throne, the thirteen-month-old infant acceded to the throne as James VI, King of Scots. Although his parents had been married by a Roman Catholic priest, and James himself had been baptized as a Catholic, he was subjected, in his youth, to a rigid Calvinist (i.e., Presbyterian) upbringing, which was not to his taste.

During James' childhood, a succession of regents ruled Scotland in his stead. James, himself, became nominal ruler of Scotland when he was twelve years old, but in 1582 he was kidnapped by Ultra-Protestant barons. In 1583 the King was rescued from the Ultra-Protestants and, in June of that year, at the age of seventeen, was finally of an age to assume the reigns of government. The King soon felt obliged to put the defiant and independent Scottish Presbyterians in their place. Leaders of that church had been espousing a doctrine that would sweep away all traces of episcopacy and place the King subservient to the Presbyterian Church. In 1584 James prevailed over these Presbyterians, and the so-called Black Acts of that year affirmed the right of the Scottish crown to appoint bishops.

James had grown up surrounded by the male sex. Nubile young women were excluded from his presence by strictures of the Presbyterians. Having had little contact with female society, James had developed a sexuality that favored male companionship over that of the opposite sex. Opinions vary on just how far young James went in his homosexual explorations. Some sources indicate that nothing beyond youthful groping occurred, but a majority of sources indicate that James' sexual preferences had been established in practice long before he set out to acquire a wife. But, it was a woman that he must have as his wife if he would leave an heir to the Scottish throne and this he felt obliged to do.

The woman who was to be James' wife was Princess Anne (1574–1619), a daughter of King Frederick II (1534–1588) of Denmark and Norway. James was so anxious for this marriage that he settled for a small cash dowry, the Orkney Islands and the Hebrides Islands; i.e., the Danish crown relinquished its claim to these islands in favor of Scotland. The marriage was first done by proxy in 1589, when Anne was just fourteen years old. Young Anne and her wedding party then set sail from Denmark for Scotland, but the party was driven back by violent storms. Instead, James traveled to Scandinavia where the royal marriage was performed in person. Both of Anne's parents were Lutherans and this thoroughly Protestant background had been a factor in Anne's selection as a mate, because James wanted to avoid offending the Protestant Queen Elizabeth I, of England. Petronelle Cook's work entitled *Queen Consorts of England* tells us that it was not until the honeymoon couple returned to Scotland that Anne found that James was bisexual.

In England the childless Queen Elizabeth was getting older but refused to allow discussion of a possible successor in her presence. A statesman who had gotten himself placed close to the Queen, Sir Robert Cecil (1563–1612), opened secret negotiations with King James VI of Scotland about his acceding to the English throne when Elizabeth died. James had coveted the English throne for years, but had been more sensible and patient than his Catholic mother, Mary, Queen of Scots, in his efforts to attain it. Attain it he did, when he was proclaimed King of England on March 24, 1603, upon the death of Queen Elizabeth I. The official grounds for his accession were based on his status as the senior surviving descendant of England's King Henry VII (1457–1509). Enthusiastic English crowds met the new king's entourage as he proceeded south to claim his second crown, a popularity that would wear thin in short order. During the trip James imperiously ordered that an English thief be executed without trial. The execution did not take place. Perhaps the new King did not even care that his action was illegal in England, for he firmly believed in the "Divine Right of Kings" and had even defended this notion of government in two treatises (one in 1598, the other in 1599).

When James was crowned King of England at Westminster Abbey on July 25, 1603, he achieved by peaceful means that which England's King Edward I (1239–1307) had tried to accomplish through force of arms: the union of Scotland with England. James' title as monarch of Scotland remained James VI, but his English title was King James I. The new English King would soon harangue the English parliament to officially name his kingdom Great Britain, but they demurred. "Britain" or names similar to it had been used as place names for portions of the British Isles as early as 345 B. C. by Aristotle (384–322 B. C.), and later, about 50 B. C., by Julius Caesar (100–44 B. C.)

James fancied himself a philosopher with firm ideas on a variety of topics ranging from the "Divine Right of Kings" to the evils of both witchcraft and tobacco smoking.

In England, country gentlemen were relied upon to maintain a balance with the old nobility and to handle local government. James, bounding upon this scene and claiming the "Divine Right of Kings," had credibility problems. The first English parliament called by the new King immediately raised the question of conflict between parliamentary privilege and royal prerogative. James imperiously brushed aside these questions as personal insults and breaches of good manners. During his reign the King would often fret about irritations caused by parliament. The very existence of the House of Commons annoyed him no end; James had been accustomed to the Scottish parliament which had a vastly different structure than its English counterpart. However, the King was shrewd enough to compromise with the English parliament when he had to, in order to obtain funds.

Large-scale imports of gold and silver from the mines of Mexico and Peru in the New World by Spain had raised that nation to a military power of consequence, but, under Queen Elizabeth I, the Spanish Armada had been defeated and military threat to England was averted. However, the importation of these precious metals to Europe had resulted in serious inflation. James' predecessor on the English throne had postponed a day of reckoning on economic matters through frugal, even parsimonious, management of finances. However, England's new King was a spendthrift and the Scottish friends who had come south with him spent money at alarming rates. The English tradition held that taxes could be imposed only by consent of parliament. In an early confrontation with parliament over money, James won a skirmish when judges ruled that the King could raise certain customs duties as he wished. These customs duties were a major traditional source of money for the English crown, but when parliament questioned the validity of the judges' ruling, James increased tensions by debating the issue in terms of the technicalities of royal prerogative.

Another early crisis to king and country was the so-called "Gunpowder Plot." The stage was set for this by Queen Elizabeth I, who had been excommunicated by the Roman Catholic Church. Her annoyance at this was understandable, but she took rather extreme retaliation against Roman Catholics in her realm, forbidding them to attend Mass, having Catholic priests tortured, drawn and quartered and subjected to other incivilities. When James in Scotland was being courted as the potential monarch of England, by design or inadvertence, he encouraged English Catholics to believe that far better days would be theirs, were he to come to the English throne. He disappointed England's Catholics, and a militant element among them, led by Guy Fawkes (1570–1606), conspired in the so-called "Gunpowder Plot," to set fire to and blow up the new king, and parliament with him. The plot failed and only served to increase anti–Catholic sentiment in England.

A bright spot, early in James' reign in England, was the founding of Jamestown in England's colony of Virginia in North America. Jamestown became, in 1607, the site of the first permanent English settlement in America. In December 1606, a party had left England to establish a profitable colony for investors here. In May 1607, they selected a site on the lower James River, in Virginia, where ships could be moored in six fathoms of water. They named their settlement Jamestown in honor of the reigning King of England, James I.

Another significant accomplishment of King James I was the publication in 1611 of the King James Version of the *Holy Bible*. In Europe, generally, leaders of both church and state had resisted both translation and publication of the *Holy Bible*. The stated reasons for this resistance were diverse, but generally boiled down to fear that if the masses had access to the word of God themselves, what need would they have for priests or heads of state? Protestant leaders had begun to relent on this before the time of James I and even the Roman Catholic Church permitted a 1609 translation into English from Latin of the Old Testament. However, it was not until publication of *The King James Bible* in 1611 that English-speaking Protestants began to have convenient access to the *Holy Bible*. The 1611 work resulted from the combined efforts of some 50 scholars, but credit must be given to King James I for allowing and encouraging their work. Among Protestants, the King James version had no serious competition until 1885, and even that was simply a revised version of the King James. It was not until the 20th century that English language Protestant Bibles were produced which represented marked departures from the King James versions.

In 1612 King James and Queen Anne lost their eldest son, Henry, Prince of Wales (1594–1612), to typhoid. On February 14 of the following year, their eldest surviving child, Princess Elizabeth (1596–1662), married Frederick V (1596–1632), Elector of the Palatinate, in Germany. The wedding was held in England, and the King and Queen spared no expense in producing an extravagant wedding. Afterwards it was expected that the newlyweds would spend the rest of their lives in

Germany, leaving little more than a footnote to remember their appearance in English history.

This expectation was short of the mark for two important reasons: (1) It was a grandson of Elizabeth and Frederick V who returned to England one hundred years later (in 1714) from Continental Europe, to rule England as King George I (1660–1727). His descendants have ruled England to this day. England's current reigning monarch, Queen Elizabeth II (1926–), is a product of this line. (2) Princess Elizabeth's new husband, Frederick, soon became a focal point of Europe's Thirty Years' War. Bohemian Protestants revolted against the Roman Catholic Habsburgs and chose Frederick as King of Bohemia in 1619. European Catholics struck back, and in 1620 Frederick and the Bohemians were utterly defeated in the battle of White Mountain, near Prague. By 1623, Frederick had also been deprived of the Lower Palatinate, his territories on the Rhine. So brief was his rule that he is known as the "Winter King." King James I of England was pressed to intervene on behalf of his daughter, Elizabeth, the "Winter Queen"; however, King James was essentially a pacifist and he failed to intervene. For the remainder of King James' reign, England was a nation on the verge of war with Catholic Europe.

Many Puritans in the England of King James were dissatisfied with the degree of religious freedom afforded them. In 1620 a small band of these English Puritans, called Pilgrims, landed in New England and founded the first permanent settlement of Europeans in New England.

After the death of James' son, Prince Henry, the king's eldest surviving son and heir to the throne became Prince Charles (1600–1649), who later succeeded his father on the throne as King Charles I. During the period that Prince Charles was heir apparent, he became involved in a convoluted effort to marry into the Spanish royal family. He even visited Europe in disguise, the object of his pursuit being Princess Maria, Infanta of Spain (–1646). That marriage effort failed; however, it was but one prong of King James' unsuccessful efforts to secure help from Catholic Spain on behalf of his daughter, Elizabeth.

King James had desired to obtain a good marriage for his heir, Charles, and late in 1624, shortly before the king's death, both King James and Prince Charles ratified a marriage agreement under which Charles would marry Princess Henrietta (1609–1669) of France, daughter of the former French king, Henry IV (1553–1610) and sister of the present French monarch, King Louis XIII (1601–1643). King James' hands were so crippled with arthritis that he had difficulty signing the ratification agreement.

Early in March 1625, King James became ill following a hunting expedition at Theobalds. His illness was described "as ordinary and moderate tertian ague," a type of fever, which generally followed a three-day cycle. But the King did not recover, and collapsed, ending his days speechless. He may have suffered a convulsion due to porphyria, or perhaps a stroke. He died on March 27, 1625, robbed of dignity by the filth of dysentery.

3. *Queen Anne (1574–1619)*

Anne was the only spouse of King James I of England, VI of Scotland (1566–1625). She was born December 12, 1574, to King Frederick II (1534–1588) of Denmark and Norway and his wife Sophia, daughter of Ulric III, Duke of Mecklenburg. Her father was an orthodox Lutheran and a vigorous advocate of that faith. Anne's maternal grandfather, the Duke of Mecklenburg, was a Lutheran Bishop, so Anne assayed heavily in orthodox Lutheran ancestry. Anne was the second oldest of the seven children born to the King and Queen of Denmark and Norway. Both of her parents were patrons of science; they gave support to the famous astronomer Tycho Brahe (1546–1601). Brahe and his observatory were very useful to Johannes Kepler (1571–1630) in his work leading to Kepler's three revolutionary laws of planetary motion. Anne's mother also devoted her own time to the study of astronomy, chemistry and other sciences. Although Anne received a good enough education, she inherited none of her mother's interest in scholarship, preferring frivolity. In Leeds Barroll's *Anna of Denmark, Queen of England*, published in 2001, an attempt is made to convince us that Anne was not merely frivolous and idle, but a strong-willed person capable of asserting her prerogatives as Queen Consort. Even granting generous motivations behind the lifestyle which Anne chose, it is difficult to conclude that she was a serious person; but so what. Life would be dull indeed if we did not have light-hearted and frivolous souls among us to bring some fun to our lives.

Anne's father, King Frederick II, was involved in serious struggles with Sweden, and these struggles hardened him into an absolute and despotic monarch. Thus, Anne's childhood served to prepare her for ranting about the "Divine Right of Kings," or concepts resembling it. This preparation would become useful as the wife of King James (1566–1625).

By 1585, agents of King James (1566–1625), then King of Scotland, had begun negotiations concerning a possible marriage to one of the daughters of King Frederick II (1534–1588). Ownership of the Orkney and Shetland Islands had been a point of friction between Scotland and Denmark and Norway. It was suggested in the marriage negotiations that a marriage to one of King Frederick's daughters might satisfactorily resolve at least the Orkney Islands issue, if they were given to Scotland as part of a dowry. However, England's Queen Elizabeth I made it known that she was not enthusiastic about the idea of a marriage linking the throne of Scotland with that of Denmark and Norway. Although King James of Scotland was not subservient to the Queen of England, he had no desire to offend her because he already had hopes to be her successor. In 1587 the mother of King James, Mary Queen of Scots (1542–1587), was tried, convicted and beheaded in England. She had been in captivity in England for some years, but, with her execution, the mood in Scotland changed. Appeasing Queen Elizabeth of England no longer held great priority. Accordingly, the Scottish King allowed negotiations for his Danish bride to proceed, and it was decided that the Danish princess who would be his bride was Princess Anne. Although King James was bisexual and actually preferred men to women, during this bride selection period, apparently James' heterosexual side was aroused and for a time he sent love poems to the Princess and fondly gazed at pictures of her at night.

By the time that King James had decided upon Princess Anne for his bride, he had become so anxious for her hand in marriage that he settled for a small cash dowry and the Orkney Islands and the Hebrides Islands. The marriage was first done by proxy in 1589, when Anne was just fourteen years old. Young Anne and her wedding party then set sail from Denmark for Scotland, but the party was driven to the Scandinavian Peninsula by violent storms. King James believed in the powers of witchcraft, in general, and he believed that, in this specific instance, witchcraft had been employed to kill Princess Anne by Francis Stewart Hepburn, Earl of Bothwell (–1624). King James traveled to Scandinavia, where he and Anne were united in marriage in person at Oslo in November 1589. They had planned an early return to Scotland, but once again stormy weather frustrated their plans. They spent the winter in Denmark, and a second marriage ceremony was held in January 1590. The royal honeymoon couple finally set sail for Scotland, and arrived in May 1590. It was then that the 15-year-old bride first learned that her husband was bisexual. (Despite this major handicap, the royal couple performed their duty to the line of succession. James and Anne produced seven named children and one unnamed son. However, only three of these children survived beyond infancy.)

Anne was crowned as the Queen Consort of Scotland's King James VI in May 1590, at Holyrood Palace, Edinburgh. (Several sources give the coronation date as May 17. However, one source says that May 17 was initially selected but, since it was the Lord's Day, the ceremony was deferred until May 19.)

There were those in Scotland who viewed the new Queen Consort with suspicion. The stern Calvinists (Presbyterians) of Scotland found Anne's Lutheran background suspect and, when word got out that she actually had some Catholic sympathies, the suspicions were greatly compounded. The King was inclined toward religious tolerance, and even when Anne's interest in Catholicism increased, King James allowed it.

Even the best of marriages requires some trial and error and compromises, but Anne's marriage also carried the burden of her husband's sexual preferences. When Queen Anne failed to become pregnant promptly, her popularity in Scotland suffered. In 1594 the royal couple's first child, Prince Henry (1594–1612), was born. This birth of a male heir to the Scottish throne brought Anne some popularity, but the marriage relationship was imperfect at best. One source tells us that the marriage "...remained stable until 1593 when Anne was pregnant. After the birth, they fell out over the upbringing of the heir, though they still went on to have two more sons and four more daughters."

On March 24, 1603, England's Queen Elizabeth I died, and King James VI of Scotland was named to succeed her. When news of his accession to the English throne reached James, Anne was pregnant, so James left Queen Anne in Scotland for his trip to England. Anne's pregnancy ended in May 1603, at Stirling Castle, in

Scotland, when an unnamed son was stillborn. She then joined her husband in England, and they were crowned together at Westminster Abbey on July 25, 1603. The King's English title was King James I, but he continued to rule Scotland as King James VI.

King James inherited an economic situation in England that was grim. Large-scale imports of gold and silver from the mines of Mexico and Peru by Spain had resulted in serious inflation. James' predecessor on the English throne, Queen Elizabeth I, had postponed a day of reckoning on economic matters through frugal, even parsimonious, management of finances. However, England's new King and his Queen Consort were spendthrifts. Together with their Scottish friends who had come south to England, they spent money at alarming rates. This was money the King did not have, because English tradition held that taxes could be imposed only by consent of parliament, and the English parliament did not wish to impose them. However, King James and Queen Anne gained access to some funds to finance their irresponsible spending through a favorable ruling by judges concerning the raising of customs duties, a traditional source of money for the English crown.

King James and Queen Anne had no difficulty in finding extravagances on which to expend the enlarged royal purse. A favorite pleasure of Queen Anne's was "masques." Generally these masques were similar to amateur theatrical productions and Queen Anne appeared as a performer, herself, in some of them. The first known masque performed during the reign of King James and Queen Anne was in October 1603. At that time the royal family had temporarily moved to Winchester because of a plague. When the Queen's nine-year-old son, Prince Henry (1594–1612), arrived at Winchester, the Queen and her ladies performed a private masque for the young Prince.

Queen Anne did not invent these "masques." They had been known in Continental Europe before her time and court masques were also held in England during the reign of Queen Elizabeth I. Although Queen Anne did not invent the masques, her name has become associated with them because she held them often, viewing them as opportunities to celebrate her royal status. While Queen Anne lived, masques were held frequently and little expense was spared in making them lavish.

Masques were held for a variety of purposes such as the celebration of Christmas, weddings and the births of children. This form of courtly entertainment varied and could involve instrumental music, songs and dancing, as well as words spoken by actors and actresses. Some famous masques were produced for Queen Anne by collaboration between England's first poet laureate, Ben Jonson (1572–1637), and the architect Inigo Jones (1573–1652).

In 1612 King James and Queen Anne lost their eldest son, Henry, Prince of Wales (1594–1612), to typhoid. This grave loss caused only a bit of a lull in the calendar of masques. On February 14 of the following year, their eldest surviving child, Princess Elizabeth (1596–1662), married Frederick V (1596–1632), Elector of the Palatinate, in Germany. The wedding was held in England and the King and Queen spared no expense in producing an extravagant wedding.

Another extravagance of Queen Anne's was the Queen's House, at Greenwich, London. Work on the Queen's House was begun in 1616 for Queen Anne, although it remained unfinished at the time of her death. It was completed for Queen Henrietta (1609–1669), the Queen Consort of Anne's son, King Charles I (1600–1649).

Most of the children of King James and Queen Anne were born before James became King of England. Their last two children were born in England after James had become the nation's king, but neither of them survived infancy. Both were daughters. The first was Princess Mary (1605–1607), and the second was Princess Sophia (1606–1606) who was born on June 22, 1606, and died the following day.

Queen Anne and King James came to live more or less separate lives, and certainly the homosexual inclinations of the King contributed to this marital arrangement. Anne had been well aware of the king's interest in the male sex for years. About 1593 James had written "A Satire Against Woemen," which described the fair sex as vain, unable to keep secrets and being full of "talke and clatters." When James left Scotland in 1603 to claim his new throne in England, he brought James Hay (–1636) with him and made him master of the royal wardrobe. In time, Hay was made a baron, viscount Doncaster and Earl of Carlisle. When the King tired of James Hay, he replaced him with Philip Herbert (1584–1650), Earl of Montgomery and Earl of Pembroke. Queen Anne also had to endure the king's relationship with a more serious rival for his affections, Robert Carr (–1645). This favorite of the King was also given titles of nobility. In due course he became viscount Rochester and Earl of Somerset. Queen Anne developed a warm hatred for Robert Carr and, to displace him, she took the extraordinary measure of encouraging the King to become attached to a different homosexual lover. He was George Villiers (1592–1628), who acquired titles of nobility (Duke of Buckingham, among them) and real power in the administration of King James I. It is not surprising, then, that Queen Anne enjoyed her separate residence from the king's and that she also took pleasure in traveling around England.

A topic that is clouded in doubt is Catholicism and Queen Anne. We know that she held sympathies toward that faith and that her husband was generally tolerant of those sympathies. From this we should certainly not conclude that Queen Anne was in league with Catholics in Continental Europe to return England to the Church of Rome. Some infer that this was the case from the fact that her son Charles (1600–1649) was permitted to pursue marriage negotiations into the very Catholic royal family of Spain. However, Queen Anne was not the driving force behind those marriage negotiations, and there is no evidence to link her to a plot to restore Catholicism to England. Indeed, even evidence concerning Anne's personal spiritual orientation is mixed. Perhaps Queen Anne found the mysteries surrounding God and theology a bit overwhelming and never resolved her inner conflicts on the topic.

Queen Anne died at Hampton Court Palace on March 4, 1619. Her husband was a hypochondriac (with some justification during those unsanitary and medically-challenged times), but he was also superstitious. As a result, King James never paid a visit to Queen Anne while she was on her deathbed, nor did he even attend her funeral. However, King James was genuinely saddened by Anne's death. She was buried with all appropriate honors at Westminster Abbey.

4. *Prince Henry, Prince of Wales (1594–1612)*

Henry was the first child born to King James VI of Scotland (1566–1625), later King James I of England, and his consort, Queen Anne (1574–1619). He was born at Stirling Castle in Scotland on February 19, 1594, and baptized with much pomp and ceremony on August 30, 1594. The infant Prince's given names were Henry Frederick, in honor of his paternal grandfather, Henry Stuart, Lord Darnley (1546–1567) and his maternal grandfather, King Frederick II (1534–1588) of Denmark and Norway.

Henry would accumulate a number of titles, foremost among them Prince of Wales, the hereditary title reserved since medieval times for the male heir apparent to the English throne. This title was bestowed upon Prince Henry on June 4, 1610, seven years after his father's accession to the throne of England. On that same day he was made earl of Chester. He had earlier been titled Duke of Cornwall. In Scotland Prince Henry had accumulated titles aplenty. There he had been named Prince of Scotland, great (or high) steward of Scotland, Duke of Rothesay, earl of Carrick, Lord of the Isles and baron (or knight) of Renfrew.

Young Prince Henry's parents had a rather unsatisfactory marriage relationship, largely as a result of the bisexual orientation of his father. One of the first serious arguments between King James and Queen Anne concerned the raising of their first-born child, Prince Henry. King James had Henry placed under the guardianship of John Erskine, Earl of Mar (1558–1634). Queen Anne objected to this arrangement, but the King overruled her. The reason(s) for the King's action in this instance are uncertain and various sources attribute the decision to various causes. Some stress the fact that Queen Anne had been showing leanings toward Catholicism, while others cite friction between Queen Anne and the powerful Scottish chancellor, Sir John Maitland (–1595). Some sources attribute the decision to put the baby in the care of a guardian to the general tension that had been building between King James and Queen Anne since the honeymoon, a tension due to King James' sexual preference for men over women. Leeds Barroll's *Anna of Denmark: Queen of England* tells us that the appointment of Mar as guardian "…was predictable, even routine, since his father and grandfather had served as royal guardians before him." Mar was a widower in 1594, when he was appointed as the baby's guardian, but Mar's mother, Annabel Murray, the dowager Countess of Mar, was appointed to assist in nursing and keeping the child. The true reason was known only to King James himself, but it seems reasonable to conclude that the personal safety of the heir to the throne of Scotland was a compelling consideration. King James' father had been murdered and his mother Mary, Queen of Scots (1542–1587), had been beheaded in England in 1587. These were perilous days to be in the line of succession on the island of Great Britain and the King knew it.

Queen Anne was greatly offended to have her first-born child taken from her to be raised by others. When King James left Scotland to accept the crown of England in 1603, Queen Anne made a strenuous effort to secure custody of Prince Henry. However, King James had earlier given written instructions that Prince Henry was not to be released to the custody of his mother until he reached the age of 18. Mindful of the King's admonition, those having custody of Prince Henry refused to turn him over to his mother. Queen Anne was pregnant in 1603, at the time of this unsuccessful confrontation, and according to some sources, it was distress over her failure to gain custody of Prince Henry that caused Queen Anne's pregnancy to end in May 1603, when an unnamed son was stillborn. The King then relented and permitted Queen Anne to bring Prince Henry to England with her.

When Prince Henry was six years old, Adam Newton (–1630), a wise tutor, was selected to guide the Prince's education. That education was thorough, including both dead and living languages, music, arts and theology. The Prince also received a thorough course in physical education including exercise, archery and the wearing of combat armor. An appropriate education for a Renaissance prince but more to the point, appropriate for the first-born son of the scholarly King James. Prince Henry sent letters to his father in the Latin language with some regularity and, by his ninth birthday, he was well enough versed in Latin to read Phaedrus, Terence and Cicero. However, although Prince Henry was diligent in his studies, he never matched his father as a scholar.

King James was never happier than when he was lecturing or giving advice and he showered advice upon his son, Henry. Prince Henry was a good son in the sense that he took to heart the advice from his father, but the Prince never could bring himself to display warmth and affection to his father. Respectful, but distant, was Prince Henry's conduct toward King James.

When Prince Henry arrived in England with his mother, and sister, Princess Elizabeth (1596–1662), he immediately won the hearts of the English people. He was a handsome young man, which contrasted with the drab figure of his father. But, more to the point, since Queen Elizabeth I never married, England had been without a royal family for half a century. England's most recent male heir to the throne had been Prince Edward (1537–1553), who had come to the throne as King Edward VI in 1547. King James on many occasions demonstrated his desire to best Prince Henry or put him down. In 1605 he refused to allow the M. A. degree to be bestowed on the Prince. Although the King permitted Prince Henry to establish a court of splendor, one has the impression that this was more an expression of the spendthrift habits of the King and Queen than any desire of the King's to see Prince Henry shine. When the Prince was 17 years old he asked the King allow him to preside over the council. The King declined, perhaps jealous of the trappings that the Prince of Wales had already accumulated. (One source tells us that Prince Henry's household staff consisted of 400 to 500 persons.)

Because of an increase in plague, when Prince Henry arrived in England, his party avoided London and went first to Windsor Castle on the Thames, in Berkshire. He was later sent to Oatlands in Surrey, because of plague fears.

In 1604 Queen Anne proposed that Prince Henry marry the Infanta, Princess Anne, of Spain, the eldest daughter of the Spanish King, Philip III (1578–1621). At that time, Princess Anne was heir to the Spanish throne. However, King Philip III demanded that for this to happen, Prince Henry would first have to come to Spain to be educated in the Roman Catholic faith. The marriage negotiations broke down over this issue and, although they were renewed in 1605, and again in 1607, nothing came of the scheme. Prince Henry's role in this was that of a silent and obedient son. Had these marriage negotiations proceeded further than mere talk, there is reason to suspect that Prince Henry would have rebelled. Henry was thoroughly Protestant and anti–Catholic and his hostility to the Church of Rome was greatly increased by the unsuccessful "Gunpowder Plot" of 1605.

In England, Sir Thomas Chaloner (1561–1615) was appointed as Prince Henry's governor, while Adam Newton was his schoolmaster. From 1603 to 1604, a small academy of aristocratic youths were assembled to act as classmates for the Prince, but the arrangement fell apart as most of the young men went off to universities. Prince Henry, himself, attended Magdalen College at Oxford and matriculated from that institution in August 1605.

While Prince Henry listened, with respect, to the views of his father, those dealing with proper kingly behavior and "Divine Right of Kings" must have seemed suspect in contrast to the boorish and drunken behavior that his father presented in public. Henry also noted, with disfavor, his father's habit of appointing men of no skill or ability to important positions because they had endeared themselves to the king.

A letter from the French ambassador to England, dated October 31, 1606, described the Prince and his habits in some detail. The letter describes a young man who is never idle, but who prefers physical activity to scholarship. After studying two hours each day, the letter observed, Prince Henry then customarily engaged in vigorous outdoor activity, such as riding horses (but not hunting), "tossing the pike or leaping or shooting with the bow, or throwing the bar, or vaulting, or some other exercise of that kind." The ambassador also described the Prince as fond of tennis "…and at another Scots diversion very like mall."

Other sources reveal that Prince Henry was physically rugged and well schooled in martial arts. He was also thoroughly Protestant and a stickler for high moral standards and gentlemanly and chivalrous conduct. While not a scholar of the first rank himself, Prince Henry respected scholarship and was devoted to men of learning. The Prince also loved to endear himself to the English public, which annoyed the King no end. Roy Strong's 1986 biography, entitled *Henry, Prince of Wales and England's Lost Renaissance,* remarks quite frankly on the King's jealousy of his heir: "To the King, terrible though it may seem, the premature death of the Prince was to come almost as a relief."

Prince Henry took an active interest in military affairs, particularly navigation and the navy. The master shipwright, Phineas Pett (1570–1647), encouraged Henry in this interest in seamanship. In 1607 the Prince reactivated plans to colonize Virginia in the New World. Both Queen Anne and Prince Henry were admirers of the earlier Virginia colonizer, Sir Walter Ralegh (–1618), who King James I had imprisoned in the Tower. Prince Henry is quoted as lamenting, "Only my father would keep such a bird in such a cage."

Henry was devout in his religious life and three times each day he withdrew to pray. The Prince expected all members of his court to engage in regular prayer and he forbade swearing in his presence. To enforce this rule, court members who swore were required to place a fine in a box. The monies thus accumulated were given to the poor.

In October 1612, Prince Henry contracted the typhoid, which would take his life. During Henry's final illness the King visited him only once. Looking over our shoulders four centuries, it is hard to know what to make of this aloofness. We know that King James was a hypochondriac (with some justification during those unsanitary and medically-challenged times), but he was also superstitious and reluctant to look too closely at death, lest the view hasten his own demise. On the other hand, the King had allowed himself to become jealous of his son and heir apparent. After Prince Henry died on November 6, 1612, and was buried at Westminster Abbey, the King and Queen allowed little mourning to interfere with their calendar of extravagant masques. As soon as a decent time interval had elapsed (i.e., on February 14, 1613) they held an extravagant wedding for their daughter, Princess Elizabeth (1596–1662), who wed Frederick V (1596–1632), Elector of the Palatinate, in Germany.

There is little doubt that if Prince Henry had lived and succeeded his father as King of England, he would have made a more effective king than did his younger brother, Charles, who acceded to the throne as King Charles I (1600–1649) on March 27, 1625. If Henry had lived, perhaps England would have been spared its Civil War and lost monarchy.

5. *Princess Elizabeth (1596–1662)*

Princess Elizabeth was born in August 1596 (various dates are given by different sources, including August 15, 16 and 19). Elizabeth was the first daughter (and second child) born to King James VI of Scotland (1566–1625), later King James I of England, and his consort, Queen Anne (1574–1619). The princess was born in Scotland, but once again, we have disputes, this time concerning the location of her birth. Some sources say Falkland Castle, others favor Dunfermline. Her baptism took place on November 28, 1596. Queen Elizabeth I (1533–1603) of England was the infant's godmother and namesake, although she did not attend the ceremony in person, but sent as her proxy England's ambassador in Scotland, Robert Bowes (–1597).

Following the custom established for the royal couple's first-born child (and, indeed, the customary practice in Scotland at the time for young members of the royal family), Elizabeth was given to the care of guardians. They were Alexander Livingstone and his wife, Helen (or Helenor) Livingstone. Alexander Livingstone (–1622) was later made Earl of Linlithgow. The matter of greatest interest concerning the Livingstones was the religious climate in which Princess Elizabeth would be raised. At that time in Scotland, the dour Presbyterian denomination was preeminent, and it retains that rank today. The Livingstones had altogether too much Roman Catholicism about them for the local Scottish Presbyterians. The Catholicism was centered on Helen's side of the family, and for many day-to-day matters, it was Helen, rather than Alexander, who had real custody of the Princess. There was much furor about the arrangement from the Presbyterian authorities, but nothing came of it. Princess Elizabeth remained in the care of the Livingstones and, when a second daughter arrived in 1598 (Princess Margaret, born December 24, 1598), she was also placed in the Livingstones' care. Sadly, Princess Margaret's life (1598–1600) was cut short.

In 1603 England's Queen Elizabeth I died, and King James VI of Scotland was named to succeed her on the English throne as King James I. When news of his accession to the English throne reached King James, his consort, Queen Anne, was pregnant, so James left Anne in Scotland for his trip to England. The pregnancy ended in May, 1603, at Stirling Castle in Scotland, when an unnamed son was stillborn. Queen Anne then joined her husband in England, bringing with her their two eldest children, Prince Henry (1594–1612) and Princess Elizabeth.

The woman who would be Princess Elizabeth's English governess had been chosen and she met Princess Elizabeth on her journey from Scotland at Berwick-upon-Tweed, in northern England. The governess was Frances Fitzgerald, Countess of Kildare. She was a widow of Henry Fitzgerald, Earl of Kildare, and she married Henry Brooke (1594–1619), who was titled baron Cobham. Two plots to deprive James of his English throne, the Main plot and the Bye plot, occurred in 1603. Both of the plots fizzled, but Baron Cobham, the new husband of Princess Elizabeth's governess, was associated with one of these plots. It was decided that Princess Elizabeth must be removed from this household for her safety. These fears were well founded. These were perilous days to be in the line of succession on the island of Great Britain. In 1605 the famous Gunpowder Plot to blow up the King, and parliament with him, failed. Under one variation of the Gunpowder Plot, Princess Elizabeth was to have been seized and placed on England's throne as a Roman Catholic Queen, styled Queen Elizabeth II. The Gunpowder Plot was a miserable failure. By then new guardians were in charge of the Princess. They were Lady Anne Harington and her husband, John Harington, Baron Harington of Exton (–1613). The Haringtons served faithfully in their duties and lived with Princess Elizabeth at Combe Abbey almost continuously, until the end of 1608. After Elizabeth's marriage, the Haringtons accompanied her to Heidelberg.

During her residence with the Haringtons at Combe Abbey, Princess Elizabeth was educated with Anne Dudley, a niece of the Haringtons. Anne became an intimate friend of the Princess and also accompanied Elizabeth to Germany, where she served in her household as lady of honour.

In September 1610, a proposal arrived from King Charles IX (1550–1611) of Sweden, that King James consider for Princess Elizabeth's hand in marriage, the Swedish King's son, Prince Gustavus Adolphus (1594–1632). Queen Anne was not enthusiastic about that idea. Her father, King Frederick II (1534–1588) of Denmark and Norway, had engaged in a deathly struggle with Sweden. A second proposal arrived toward the end of 1611, which Queen Anne did fancy. It was a proposal that Princess Elizabeth wed King Philip III (1578–1621) of Spain. The Spanish King had recently become a widower and was in need of a wife and consort. However, this would involve marriage into the very Catholic royal family of Spain. Princess Elizabeth's elder brother, Henry, Prince of Wales, was now a staunch defender of the Protestant faith and he denounced the idea. King James had his own reasons for disliking the proposal and, in early 1612 he concluded a treaty alliance with the German Protestant princes. In due course it was arranged that Princess Elizabeth would wed Frederick V (1596–1632), Elector of the Palatinate, in Germany. In October 1612, Frederick came to England in hope of marrying Princess Elizabeth. Against the idea was Elizabeth's mother, Queen Anne, but allied in favor of the marriage were the King, the Prince of Wales and Princess Elizabeth, herself, who had come to favor the Protestant cause enthusiastically. Although romance and personal preferences mattered little when the high stakes game of royal marriage was played, Elizabeth became fond of her prospective German bridegroom. It was reported that Elizabeth "lykes him well."

When Prince Henry fell ill, Princess Elizabeth was forbidden to visit her elder brother for fear of contagion. Wedding plans were put in abeyance, and they were delayed still further when Henry died suddenly on November 6, 1612. Princess Elizabeth had lost her favorite sibling.

In *The Winter Queen: The Story of Elizabeth Stuart*, Josephine Ross provides this cheerful note: "The marriage arranged for reasons of state had turned out to be a love-match, and the two young people brought together by religion and politics had formed a relationship which was to prove deep and enduring. They were of the same age, they were healthy and good-looking and their mutual passion for horses and hunting was only one of the tastes which they had in common. Frederick had entered Elizabeth's life at a fortunate moment; his presence had served to soften the blow of her adored brother's death and sorrow had strengthened their dependence on one another from the outset."

Princess Elizabeth's wedding was preceded by an elaborate and costly betrothal ceremony on December 27, 1612. By then Frederick had been invested as a knight of the garter and encumbered by so many titles that he is referred to in one citation as, "The High and Mighty Prince Frederick, by the Grace of God, Count Palatine of the Rhine, Arch-Sewer of the Holy Roman Empire, Duke of Bavaria and Knight of the Most Noble Order of the Garter."

On February 14, 1613 Princess Elizabeth married Frederick V, Elector of the

Palatinate. The wedding was held in England and the spendthrift King and Queen spared no expense in producing an extravagant wedding for their only daughter who survived infancy. The wedding ceremony itself was held in Chapel Royal, at Whitehall. Surviving contemporary accounts of the wedding ceremony contain the words "verye riche" at frequent intervals. Even the spendthrift King was amazed to learn how much debt had accumulated for the wedding and its trappings.

Afterwards it was expected that the newlyweds would spend the rest of their lives in Germany, leaving little more than a footnote to remember their appearance in English history. This expectation was short of the mark for two important reasons: (1) It was a grandson of Elizabeth and Frederick V who returned to England one hundred years later (in 1714) from Continental Europe, to rule England as King George I (1660–1727). His descendants have ruled England to this day. England's current reigning monarch, Queen Elizabeth II (1926–), is a product of this line. (2) Princess Elizabeth's new husband, Frederick, soon became a focal point of Europe's Thirty Years' War. Bohemian Protestants revolted against the Roman Catholic Habsburgs and chose Elizabeth's husband, Frederick, as King of Bohemia in 1619. European Catholics struck back, and in 1620 Frederick and the Bohemians were utterly defeated in the battle of White Mountain, near Prague. By 1623 Frederick had also been deprived of the Lower Palatinate, his territories on the Rhine. So brief was his rule that he is known as the "Winter King." King James I of England was pressed to intervene on behalf of his daughter, Elizabeth, the "Winter Queen"; however, King James was essentially a pacifist and he failed to intervene. For the remainder of King James' reign, England was a nation on the verge of war with Catholic Europe.

After a brief honeymoon in England, the newlyweds sailed for Continental Europe in April 1613. Frederick left his bride for a leisurely tour of Europe and went on to Heidelberg to conduct certain affairs of state. The amorous Frederick returned to meet Elizabeth in route and they arrived together to be formally received by Frederick's family at Heidelberg Castle on June 17, 1613.

Elizabeth had been pregnant during her travels over the rough European roads and on January 2, 1614, she gave birth to the couple's first child, Frederick Henry (1614–1629). A second son, Charles Louis, was born in December 1617, and the couple's eldest daughter, Elizabeth, was born a year later, in late 1618. Thus Elizabeth's first child was born before her 18th birthday and she continued to demonstrate her fecundity on a regular basis. In 1619 Frederick and Elizabeth became King and Queen of Bohemia, and in December of that year, the son who would be Elizabeth's favorite, Prince Rupert (1619–1682), was born in Prague. By 1620, events in Europe had begun to go badly for Elizabeth and her husband, but even when she entered her thirties, neither age nor anxiety over political affairs impaired her childbearing ability. In September 1627, her tenth baby was born, a healthy boy who was named Philip. By January 1629, Elizabeth was recovering from the birth of yet another child, Princess Charlotte.

The complete list of the children of Elizabeth and Frederick is a long one:

Prince Frederick Henry (1614–1629)
Prince Charles Louis (1617–1680)
Princess Elizabeth (1618–1680)
Prince Rupert (1619–1682)
Prince Maurice (1620–1654)
Princess Louise (1622–1709)
Prince Louis (1623–1624)

Prince Edward (1624–1663)
Princess Henrietta (1626–1651)
Prince Philip (1627–1650)
Princess Charlotte (1628–1631)
Princess Sophia (1630–1714)
Prince Gustavus (1632–1641)

The child who was destined to be of continuing interest to England was Sophia (1630–1714), the last daughter, because she married Ernest Augustus (1629–1698) in 1658. In 1692 the electorate of Hanover was formed from the duchy of Brunswick-Luneburg, and Ernest Augustus became the first elector of Hanover. The first son born to Sophia (1630–1714) and Ernest Augustus (1629–1698) was George Lewis and he came to England's throne in 1714 as King George I, succeeding Queen Anne (1665–1714).

Frederick, the Winter King of Bohemia and Elizabeth's husband, died on November 19, 1632. Her first-born son had died in a freak accident in 1629. Meanwhile, in England, things were not going well for Elizabeth's family. When her father died in 1625, Elizabeth's youngest brother came to the English throne as King Charles I (1600–1649). However, Charles infuriated parliament and many citizens of England, and Civil War broke out. The monarchy was crushed, the King was beheaded in 1649, and Oliver Cromwell (1599–1658) became the nation's general and "lord protector." The monarchy was not restored in England until 1660. King Charles II (1630–1685), a son of Charles I, was formally crowned in Westminster Abbey on April 23, 1661.

Early in the reign of King Charles II, Elizabeth, the Winter Queen, returned to England. She died in England on February 13, 1662, and was buried at Westminster Abbey beside her favorite brother, Prince Henry (1594–1612).

Elizabeth's favorite child was Prince Rupert (1619–1682), and it was to him that she bequeathed most of her jewelry. She had little else to bequeath to anyone and substantial unpaid debt back in Continental Europe.

6. *Prince Charles, Duke of York and Albany, later Prince of Wales (1600–1649)*

Prince Charles came to the English throne as King Charles I in 1625. For his biographical sketch, see the chapter entitled King Charles I.

King Charles I

Charles acceded to the throne of England upon the death of his father, King James I, on March 27, 1625. His coronation at Westminster Abbey occurred on February 2, 1626, and he was monarch of England until he was beheaded on January 30, 1649. He had only one wife, Henrietta (1609–1669). The royal couple had nine named children, six of whom survived beyond infancy. Two of the male children later ruled England as kings.

7. *King Charles I (1600–1649)*

Charles was the fourth child of King James VI of Scotland (1566–1625), later King James I of England. His mother was the Queen Consort, Queen Anne (1574–1619). He was born at Dunfermline abbey in Scotland, on November 19, 1600, a very weak and sickly baby. Hasty arrangements were made for his baptism, out of fear that he might die immediately. A second, more elaborate baptism was held on December 23, 1600, beneath a magnificent silk pall, which had been elaborately worked in gold and silver by the baby's paternal grandmother, Mary, Queen of Scots (1542–1587). The King bestowed the Scottish title, Duke of Albany, upon young Charles. (Other titles were also bestowed on the baby at this time, but they are overshadowed by the titles he later received in England; i.e., Duke of York, and, later, Prince of Wales.)

Charles was given to the care of guardians. This followed the custom established for the royal couple's elder children (and was, indeed, the customary practice in Scotland at the time for young members of the royal family). In view of young Charles' sickly condition, the precaution of employing guardians was deemed particularly appropriate. The guardians were Alexander Seton, Lord Fyvie (–1622), and his wife. Alexander Seton was later made Earl of Dunfermline. The Setons were nominally Protestants, but held Roman Catholic sympathies, and King James hoped their religious influence would counter-balance the Presbyterianism of Scotland. (Some sources mention the possibility that King James hoped that this nod in favor of Catholicism might buy him some good will in England with the Roman Catholics there, because England was the kingdom, which James hoped to rule when Queen Elizabeth I [1533–1603] died.)

Soon after King James left Scotland to accept the crown of England in 1603, he was joined there by his wife and consort, Queen Anne, and by his eldest two children, Prince Henry (1594–1612) and Princess Elizabeth (1596–1662). Prince Charles was left behind in Scotland. At two and one half years of age he could still neither talk nor walk and was subject to fevers. He simply was not up to the rigors of a trip to England, a difficult journey in those days, even for royalty. In England, King James ruled as King James I, while retaining his Scottish title of King James VI. The King was concerned about his young son in Scotland and arranged to have a physician, Dr. Henry Atkins (1558–1635), attend to Prince Charles' health needs. Atkins' examinations confirmed that the Prince suffered from numerous medical difficulties, but by July 17, 1604, the doctor permitted Charles to leave Scotland to join his family in England.

Lord and Lady Fyvie accompanied Prince Charles on his journey to England, but they then returned to Scotland. Robert Carey (–1639) and his wife were appointed to care for Prince Charles in England. The Prince's health was still tenuous and he had difficulty walking. As the years passed his general stamina improved, but Charles was a nervous, undersized child with a stammer that he never lost. As an adult he was considered quite short for a Stuart, standing five feet four inches. In 1605 the young Prince was given the English title Duke of York.

In 1612 Charles' elder brother, Prince Henry, died. Then, in 1613 his only surviving sibling, Princess Elizabeth, married and sailed for Continental Europe with her new husband, Frederick V (1596–1632), Elector of the Palatinate, in Germany. Prince Charles had become heir apparent to the throne and, in recognition of that status, he was titled Prince of Wales on November 3, 1616.

During the period that Prince Charles was heir apparent he became involved in a convoluted effort to marry into the Spanish royal family. He even visited Europe in disguise, the object of his pursuit being Princess Maria, Infanta of Spain (–1646). That marriage effort failed, but King James desired to obtain a good marriage for his heir, Charles. Late in 1624, shortly before the King's death, both King James and Prince Charles ratified a marriage agreement under which Charles would marry Princess Henrietta (1609–1669) of France. She was a daughter of the former French King, Henry IV (1553–1610), and sister of the present French monarch, King Louis XIII (1601–1643).

Charles and Henrietta were married by proxy, and then the very Catholic Henrietta came to England where she and James were wed in person. The marriage got off to a bad start. Neither Charles nor Henrietta thought the other to be very good looking, and the 15-year-old Henrietta was very slow to perform her conjugal duties with any enthusiasm. At least two factors served to turn this cold marriage into a warm and fruitful one (they had nine named children). One of the turning points in the marital relationship was the introduction of Lady Carlisle as a member of the Queen's bedchamber. It was intended that Lady Carlisle would instruct the young Queen in the arts of love, and it appears that she was most successful in that enterprise. The other turning point was the death of George Villiers (1592–1628), Duke of Buckingham. Buckingham had been an intimate of Charles' father, King James I, and was very influential with Charles as well. Buckingham was murdered by John Felton (–1628) in August 1628. The departure of Buckingham led Charles to use his 18-year-old wife as a confidant and helped to bring life to the marriage.

By this time King James had died, and Charles had come to the thrones of both England and Scotland as King Charles I. His English coronation was at Westminster Abbey on February 2, 1626. Charles was crowned alone. His Catholic Queen Consort chose not to participate in the Protestant coronation ceremony.

King Charles I inherited a war in progress with Spain and soon added an unsuccessful war against France, but his most severe problems were domestic, rather than foreign. The new King soon won the hatred of England's parliament and managed to antagonize his father's friends in Scotland by attacking Scottish Presbyterianism. Charles was a studious man, but he understood books far better than people. He managed to let small problems grow beyond hope of resolution and allowed civil war to erupt.

On the religious front, King Charles vigorously pushed the views that he held to be right and proper. What King Charles wanted for the Church of England was a form of religion, which was the Episcopal Church, modeled on Arminian principles. These Arminian principles had grown from the writings of a Dutch theologian, Jacobus Arminius (1560–1609), who held that predestination (a core belief of the Presbyterians) was a flawed theological doctrine. Arminian theology carried two practical advantages over predestination: (1) for those allegedly predestined to condemnation, Arminianism offered some bait to attract improved behavior and (2) for those allegedly already guaranteed salvation, Arminianism took the guarantee away and made it contingent on behavior here on Earth. The man who did much to introduce Arminianism in the Church and England and aggressively promote it, even across the border into Presbyterian Scotland, was William Laud (1573–1645). He was honored for his efforts by progressive promotions to Archbishop of Canterbury.

The impact of the Arminian slant on churches in England was great during the early years of the reign of King Charles I. Many of these churches had been allowed to fall into disrepair since the days when Roman Catholicism had been the kingdom's official church. Most individual church structures had become rather drab. Now, under an Episcopal Church with an Arminian tilt, churches had become important, for it was there that prayers were said and sacraments given and received. Much of the business of salvation was the business of the local church.

Churches that had fallen into disrepair were made well — discreet pictorial representations of matters religious reappeared, and stained glass windows were reinstalled. These changes are vividly depicted in Mark Kishlansky's 1996 work entitled *A Monarchy Transformed: Britain 1603–1714*. Kishlansky specifically tells us that, "Since the weekly service now carried greater meaning, it had to be conducted with greater solemnity. The clergy were ordered to wear the surplice and to cover the communion table with a decorative cloth. The table itself might be removed from the centre aisle to the east end, to avoid its casual use. In any event, it should be railed so that children would not sit on it or dogs abuse it." And who, the King and Bishop Laud may have asked themselves, could object to such improvements?

It seems that many did. To the Puritans, and perhaps to others in England, these moves seemed too close to a return to Roman Catholicism. Indeed, to some observers, the changes seemed to be mere preambles to the reintroduction of the Roman Church as the Church of England. Didn't the King's own wife attend Roman Catholic Masses in her private chapel, attended by Catholic priests? These fears were not entirely fanciful. Catholicism did make some headway in England during this period. A number of Roman Catholic priests were ordained, and Queen Henrietta urged that English Catholics be permitted to pursue their faith. Emigration of Puritans from England to Massachusetts Bay Colony increased, and the Puritans who stayed in England were not happy about the direction that the Church of England was taking.

King Charles I and Bishop Laud visited Scotland to try to introduce religious reforms in that kingdom and they promoted use of a common prayer book (written in England by Laud and his fellow travelers). The Scots received these suggestions with scorn and a bit later their army would return the perceived insult by attempting to impose Presbyterianism upon England.

Charles' relations with the English parliament (and later with armies that parliament raised to fight him) hold much of the remaining story of King Charles' life. His relations with parliament had not been particularly good even when he was still Prince Charles. After his accession to the throne, these relations went downhill repeatedly. These developments occurred in an atmosphere of great religious and civil tension.

On the religious side (even before Bishop Laud and King Charles began their maneuvers), there was great concern in Protestant England about the fate of the Protestant faith, which was currently under military attack in Continental Europe in the Thirty Years' War. From the perspective of an English member of the Protestant Church of England, a question at the time that Charles came to the English throne in 1625 was whether the Reformation flame lit by Martin Luther (1483–1546), just a century earlier, would now be snuffed out by Roman Catholic military might.

On the civil side, educated Englishmen had come to believe that they had inherited certain rights (by the Magna Carta in A. D. 1215, and even earlier) and that these rights were being attacked and questioned by the crown. First there had been the blather about "Divine Right of Kings" from Charles' father, King

James I. Now the new monarch, King Charles I, was claiming new and expanded interpretations for "royal prerogative."

King Charles made it an early practice to isolate himself with his favorite advisor, Buckingham. He deviated from this and engaged in dialogue with parliament only to secure money (primarily to wage war) and to protect Buckingham from parliament's wrath. Martial law was declared with soldiers billeted in thousands of civilian cottages. To obtain money, the King demanded forced loans, which many Englishmen refused to pay. Among those thrown into prison for refusing loans to the King were five men, known as the five knights. When they were denied *habeas corpus*, parliament was outraged and responded in 1628 with a "Petition of Right." The King's ambiguous reply further aggravated the tension, and parliament fought back by withholding a much-needed grant of money. Only then did the King permit the "Petition of Right" to become law. Many of the rights in question are fundamental and represent landmarks in England's efforts to develop civil rights.

However, the King's conduct soon led many to believe that his assent to the "Petition of Right" had been a sham. Early in 1629, parliament reconvened and, although parliament had many grievances, they concentrated their vigorous attack on the King on two fronts: (1) religion, and (2) the form of customs duties called "tonnage & poundage." A single Remonstrance, or resolution, was prepared which declared as a public enemy (1) anyone who furthered Popery (Roman Catholicism) or Arminianism, and (2) anyone who collected tonnage and poundage, helped collect it, *or even paid it*! In 1629 King Charles dissolved parliament. He announced that he was in no hurry to reconvene that body, and thus began the eleven years of "personal rule."

The main problem that the King faced with personal rule was that, with no parliament to call upon for money, it was hard to maintain the royal treasury. Two solutions to this dilemma, which King Charles seized upon, were the sale of monopolies and imposition of "ship money" taxes. Under long-standing laws of England, the upkeep of the kingdom's fleet was to be paid for by all counties, since the fleet protected the entire kingdom. Over time an anomaly had developed whereby only maritime counties were required to pay "ship money." In 1635 King Charles levied ship money taxes on all of England. These ship money taxes became very unpopular. By the year 1639 only 20 percent of the ship money taxes that were assessed were collected.

In 1639 and 1640, troops under orders from King Charles fought wars against Scottish forces. King Charles and Bishop Laud had pushed their ideas of religious reforms too vigorously in Scotland, and the citizens of that kingdom were infuriated. When the Scots formally defied a royal order, King Charles decided to meet the insubordination with armed force, lest the attitude of defiance spread from Scotland to England and Ireland. However, Scotland possessed a large military force, seasoned by action on the European Continent in the Thirty Years' War. King Charles soon recognized the competence and ferocity of this Scottish army compared to his own undisciplined rabble. After eleven years of personal rule,

King Charles called parliament into session to provide funds with which to fight the Scottish forces. The English parliament, understandably, wished first to discuss and obtain redress of its grievances before voting money for war. In less than one month the King abruptly and unwisely dissolved this parliament, which is known to history as the "Short Parliament." King Charles then foolishly took up arms against the Scots again. The outcome was disastrous for King Charles. Scottish troops took control of northeastern England and remained there as a conquering army. Adding insult to injury, they demanded that they be paid 40,000 pounds per month to maintain their army in England, and although that sum was reduced by some haggling, King Charles had no funds at all for any payments. Thus Charles was again forced to call parliament into session. Called the "Long Parliament," this fiery session would last throughout the remainder of King Charles' life.

Parliament passed a bill of attainder against the King's chief adviser, Thomas Wentworth, Earl of Strafford (1593–1641), finding him guilty of treason and ordering his execution. To protect itself from dissolution by the King, this Long Parliament passed an act forbidding its dissolution without its own consent and a triennial act, which provided for triennial parliaments. The Long Parliament also abolished the Star Chamber, outlawed prerogative taxation, declared ship money illegal and granted the King tonnage and poundage, but only for two months.

There was broad support in both houses of the Long Parliament for these harsh measures, but when parliamentary leaders proposed to go much further in the Grand Remonstrance, there was dissent that divided the kingdom. The Grand Remonstrance passed parliament by a mere eleven votes. Among other features, the Grand Remonstrance denied the King the right to appoint ministers or bishops and took away royal control of the military. The English Civil War resulted.

King Charles found more support in the kingdom than might be suspected from the high-handed conduct of his reign, and he was able to assemble military forces of some strength. On August 22, 1642, King Charles I raised his royal standard at Nottingham, and the Civil War began. Against him were troops under the control of the Englishmen, Thomas Fairfax, Baron Fairfax of Cameron (1612–1671), and Oliver Cromwell (1599–1658), aided at times by fierce Scottish troops. King Charles' royalist forces ("the Cavaliers") were defeated.

The King was imprisoned for a time, but low ranking soldiers who had fought the Civil War believed that there could be only one acceptable end. The King must die.

Charles I was executed by beheading on January 30, 1649, at Whitehall Palace in London. Many, if not most, of the civil rights which the English parliaments had fought to obtain from King Charles I are now recognized by English speaking peoples on both sides of the Atlantic Ocean as fundamental, even inalienable, human rights. However, the death of King Charles I did not bring them to England; far from it.

With the death of King Charles I, the monarchy ended in England and Oliver Cromwell ruled as dictator. For a time after Cromwell's death in 1658, successors attempted to maintain his form of rule, but the kingdom, which had suffered the horrors of Civil War, failed to achieve meaningful redress of grievances. The monarchy was not restored to England until May 29, 1660, when the eldest son of King Charles I came to the throne as King Charles II (1630–1685).

8. *Queen Henrietta (1609–1669)*

Henrietta was born in Paris, France, on November 26, 1609. She was the youngest daughter of the French King, Henry IV (1553–1610) and his second wife, Marie de Medicis (1573–1642). Marie had not yet been crowned as Queen Consort when Henrietta was born, but she was crowned on May 13, 1610, and Henrietta attended her mother's coronation as a baby in the arms of her nurse. On the day following the coronation, May 14, 1610, King Henry IV was stabbed to death by an assassin. Marie de Medicis ruled France as regent for about seven years, until the male heir to the French throne (the dauphin), Louis XIII (1601–1643), was old enough to rule.

Henrietta was baptized at the time of her birth and again, publicly, on June 15, 1614. Her mother saw to it that her youngest daughter was raised as a very strict Roman Catholic, with equally strong notions of royal prerogatives. Her tutor was Monsieur de Brevis and she received extra religious instruction from the distinguished Carmelite nun Mere Magdeleine of Saint Joseph.

Marie de Medicis' goal was that all of her daughters should marry into royal families and become queen consorts. Toward that end she selected England's heir apparent, Henry, Prince of Wales (1594–1612), as the potential mate for Henrietta. After Prince Henry died in 1612, there were some clumsy maneuvers to negotiate a marriage treaty for Henrietta with England's Prince Charles (1600–1649), who was then next in line for the English throne. However, these negotiations were handled without finesse and they were discontinued. About this time, England's King, James I (1566–1625), had decided that Prince Charles should wed into the Spanish royal family. Prince Charles visited Europe in disguise, the object of his pursuit being Princess Maria, Infanta of Spain (–1646). By coincidence, it was on this European trip that Charles first saw his future bride, Princess Henrietta of France, but she made no impression upon him. There are at least two probable reasons for this lack of interest: (1) At that point Charles was on his way toward Spain, so his thoughts were still concentrated on the Infanta as his likely bride. (2) Princess Henrietta was then only 13 years old and had not yet blossomed into young womanhood. Charles' marriage negotiations in Spain failed, but England's King James viewed that effort as just one prong in his ambitious, but unsuccessful, efforts to secure help from Catholic Europe on behalf of his daughter, Princess Elizabeth (1596–1662). Elizabeth had recently been deposed as Queen Consort of Bohemia by Catholic military forces during the Thirty Years' War.

King James also desired to obtain a good marriage for his heir, Charles, and, late in 1624, shortly before King James' death, both the King and Prince Charles ratified a marriage agreement under which Charles would marry Princess Henrietta (1609–1669) of France. Romance and personal preferences mattered little when the high stakes game of royal marriage was played. Henrietta merely acquiesced to the wishes of her elder brother, Louis XIII, and Charles and Henrietta were married by proxy in France. Then the very Catholic Henrietta came to England where she and James were wed in person at Canterbury on June 13, 1625.

By this time King James had died, and Charles had come to the thrones of both England and Scotland as King Charles I. His English coronation was at Westminster Abbey on February 2, 1626. Charles was crowned alone. His Catholic Queen Consort chose not to participate in the Protestant coronation ceremony. Although there was no coronation for Henrietta, she was the Queen Consort of King Charles I. The marriage got off to a bad start. Neither Charles nor Henrietta thought the other to be very good looking, and the 15-year-old Henrietta was very slow to perform her conjugal duties with any enthusiasm.

At least two factors served to turn this cold marriage into a warm and fruitful one. (Petronelle Cook's *Queen Consorts of England: The Power Behind the Throne* tells us that Henrietta would produce nine children by Charles "even though she had a slightly deformed spine which in turn had affected her pelvis and made every birth a long torture for her.")

The first turning point involved George Villiers, Duke of Buckingham (1592–1628). In an effort to introduce some passion in the royal conjugal bed, Buckingham had a chat with Jeanne, Madame de St. George, one of the ladies of the bedchamber, whom Henrietta had brought with her from France. He suggested to this French lady that she persuade Henrietta to be more forthcoming in bed. Madame de St. George brusquely told Buckingham that she never interfered in such matters. As a result, Henrietta's entire retinue was fired, and the persistent Buckingham introduced the voluptuous and seductive wife of James Hay, Earl of Carlisle (–1636), Lucy Hay, Countess of Carlisle (1599–1660), as a member of the Queen's bedchamber. It was intended that she would instruct young Henrietta in the arts of love, and it appears that she was most successful in that enterprise. Soon after the countess joined Henrietta, it was reported that "she has already brought her to paint and in time will lead her into more debaucheries."

The other turning point in the marriage relationship also involved the Duke of Buckingham. He had been an intimate of Charles' father, King James I, and was also very influential with King Charles. When Buckingham was murdered by John Felton (–1628) in August 1628, his departure led the King to use his 18-year-old wife as a confidant and helped to bring life to the marriage.

In time, the gawky 13-year-old Henrietta, who had failed to prompt a glimmer in Prince Charles' eye on first sight, grew into a beautiful young lady, and King Charles fell very much in love with her. Once King Charles began to bring his Queen Consort into his deepest confidence, she fell in love with her husband. On account of their mutual love, Henrietta was able to exert considerable influence over the King. In Norah Lofts' work entitled *Queens of England*, Henrietta's influence is captured with these words: "Charles had many bad advisers, but the worst was the wife whom he adored."

Both King James I and Prince Charles had been anxious that the marriage negotiations for Henrietta succeed. Because of this, they had agreed to concessions in the marriage treaty concerning treatment of Catholics in England and Henrietta's own right to practice her Roman Catholic faith in Protestant England. Since Charles had pledged to the English parliament that no such concessions would be made, they were attached as a secret clause of the marriage treaty.

Early in her marriage Queen Henrietta not only practiced her Roman Catholic religion and regularly attended masses sung by Roman Catholic priests, but she also mocked the Protestant Anglican faith, the official Church of England. Initially, Henrietta took her elder sons to mass with her, but by the time the King and Queen were producing additional children on a regular basis, Queen Henrietta had become more reasonable and she allowed her children to be raised in the faith of the Protestant Church of England.

Queen Henrietta thought that her husband's notions about new and expanded interpretations for "royal prerogative" were entirely reasonable and she even agreed with her father-in-law's blather about "Divine Right of Kings." She knew nothing about the civil rights that Englishmen had inherited from the Magna Carta in A. D. 1215, and even earlier. When King Charles initially came under verbal attack from parliament, a marriage of the eldest daughter of the King and Queen, Princess Mary (1631–1660), to William II, (1626–1650), who later became Prince of Orange, was arranged, at least in part, because Queen Henrietta thought that the marriage might result in military aid to King Charles. Henrietta could see no side but her husband's and she did what she could to aid him. She appealed for help from the Pope and from her brother, the French King, Louis XIII. She took some of the English crown jewels and all of the jewels given to her by Charles to Holland, to pawn them to raise funds to purchase military arms for the royalists. Henrietta also hoped that, during her visit to Continental Europe, she could persuade Denmark and the family of her son-in-law, William II, to provide aid to King Charles.

Queen Henrietta returned to England while the Civil War was in progress, and although her ship carried no fighting men, it was loaded with munitions, which she had acquired to aid the royalist army. The day after she landed in England, parliamentary forces commanded by Captain William Batten (–1667) attempted to prevent the munitions from reaching the royalists. Shots fired in attempts to destroy the munitions ship came very close to hitting Queen Henrietta. Later, while in the Yorkshire area, awaiting a reunion with her husband, Henrietta received troubling pieces of news. She learned that in France her brother, Louis XIII, had died. France was now being governed by the regent, Anne of Austria, the consort of the former French King, and mother of the new heir, Louis XIV (1638–1715). News from London was also disconcerting. Henrietta was told that her Roman Catholic priests there were being persecuted and her personal chapel had been pillaged.

In England Queen Henrietta actually took to the field of battle. Fortunately, her nephew-in-law, Prince Rupert (1619–1682), arrived to escort the Queen from harm's way. Rupert was a son of Elizabeth (1596–1662), the sister of King Charles I, who had been deposed as Queen Consort of Bohemia during the Thirty Years' War. (Both Prince Rupert and his brother, Prince Maurice [1620–1654] provided valuable military aid to King Charles I during the English Civil War.)

While Queen Henrietta was in England during these adventures, she gave birth to the royal couple's ninth, and last, child, Princess Henrietta (1644–1670). This birth took place at Exeter, a royalist stronghold. Soon afterward, parliamentary forces led by Thomas Fairfax, Baron Fairfax of Cameron (1612–1671), began to threaten the area. King Charles became concerned for his wife's safety and, although she had not yet recovered from the childbirth, Henrietta was escorted to Falmouth, and then sailed to her native France accompanied by her bodyguard, Henry Jermyn (–1684), never to see her husband again.

Henrietta was well received by the French regent, her sister-in-law, Anne of Austria. Meanwhile, all but two of Henrietta's children were in England, and in danger. The two presumably safe children were her eldest daughter, Princess Mary, the Princess Royal (who had married William II, later Prince of Orange, and was living on the Continent with him), and her youngest child, the baby Henrietta, who was in France with Queen Henrietta. Henrietta again appealed to the Pope for military aid for King Charles. She also appealed to the French cardinal, Jules Mazarin (1602–1661), who was then prime minister of France, and controlled French foreign policies. Queen Henrietta's appeals fell on deaf ears.

Henrietta's former bodyguard, Henry Jermyn, had now become her personal secretary and a close personal relationship developed between the two. Some sources hint that they became lovers, others that they were secretly married. In any event, the relationship alienated Queen Henrietta from many of her children for some time. (After the Restoration, Jermyn returned to England, and in 1660 he was made Earl of St. Albans.) The maternal bond was too strong to remain ruptured indefinitely. Her son, Prince Charles (1630–1685), later wrote "...never any children had so good a mother," and the other son, who would later come to England's throne as King James II (1633–1701), declared her to excel in "all the good qualities of a good wife, a good mother and a good Christian."

By 1646, Henrietta's son, Prince Charles, had escaped from England, but Prince James had been captured by parliamentary military forces, as had most of Henrietta's younger children.

During the period that King Charles I was in captivity and then executed, which was followed by dictatorial rule of England by Oliver Cromwell (1599–1658) and his successors, Henrietta remained in exile. The monarchy was restored to England on May 29, 1660, when the eldest son of King Charles I and Queen Henrietta came to the throne as King Charles II (1630–1685). Henrietta, now the Queen mother, returned to England after the Restoration and received a parliamentary grant of 30,000 pounds per year as compensation for her dower lands, which had been taken. King Charles II also granted his mother 30,000 additional pounds per annum as a pension.

Henrietta commuted a bit between England and France until 1665, when she decided that England's climate was ill suited to her health. She then returned to France and settled in her chateau at Colombes, near Paris, where she died on August 31, 1669. Henrietta was buried in the French royal basilica of St. Denis, but her tomb was despoiled during the French Revolution.

Throughout this biographical sketch, the subject of the sketch has been referred to as Henrietta. Many, if not most, sources prefer to style her name as Henrietta Maria. One source tells us that although these are the names used today, during her lifetime and shortly thereafter she was referred to as Queen Mary.

9. *Prince Charles, Prince of Wales (1630–1685)*

Prince Charles came to the English throne as King Charles II when the monarchy was restored. For his biographical sketch, see the chapter entitled King Charles II.

10. *Princess Mary, Princess Royal (1631–1660)*

Mary was born at St. James' Palace in England on November 4, 1631, and baptized immediately, apparently because there was some doubt about her health and her ability to survive. The baptism was performed by William Laud (1573–1645), then Bishop of London and an ally of King Charles. This first daughter of King Charles I (1600–1649) and Queen Henrietta (1609–1669) was named for her maternal grandmother, Marie de Medicis (1573–1642).

Mary was brought up under the guidance of a governess, the Countess of Roxburgh, wife of Robert Ker, Earl of Roxburgh (–1650). Together with some of her siblings, Mary spent her early years mostly at St. James, but also out at Richmond or at Hampton Court. The Catholic Queen, Henrietta, attempted to have Mary exposed to Catholicism by introducing a young lady, who was secretly a Roman Catholic, into Princess Mary's company. King Charles firmly resisted all overtures intended to win Princess Mary and her soul for the Church of Rome, and he prevailed.

Princess Mary made her first public appearance in 1640 at the baptism of her youngest brother, Prince Henry (1640–1660). Young Mary served as her infant brother's only godmother.

Mary had been a child only briefly when inquiries started arriving about the possibility of securing her hand in marriage. It was bruited about that a son of King Philip IV (1605–1665) of Spain might make a good husband. However, Princess Mary would have none of it. By this time she had reached some conclusions regarding religion and knew that she did not wish to become a Roman Catholic. Since the

Spanish royal family was thoroughly Catholic, that possible match was quickly dismissed. Another possibility that was proposed very early in the game, but later came into play when actual decisions were being made, was William II (1626–1650), the son of Frederick Henry (1584–1647), Prince of Orange and stadtholder of several Dutch states. The mother of this potential mate was Amalia van Solms (1602–1675), Princess of Orange. This Amalia had been a lady-in-waiting to a sister of King Charles I, Elizabeth (1596–1662), who briefly was Queen of Bohemia. Amalia had become a close friend to Elizabeth and this Elizabeth would become very much involved in events later in Princess Mary's life. The first proposal that Princess Mary wed William II (1626–1650) was rejected by King Charles.

We need shed no tears concerning these failures to obtain a mate for Princess Mary, because all of the failed attempts occurred before she was ten years old. When King Charles initially came under verbal attack from parliament, later supported by military action in the Civil War, new consideration was given to a marriage of Princess Mary to William II, (1626–1650), son of the Prince of Orange. This marriage was successfully arranged, at least in part, because Queen Henrietta thought that the marriage might result in military aid to King Charles. During February 1641, the King announced to parliament that a marriage treaty had been brought to conclusion for Princess Mary to wed William II. This marriage treaty stipulated that Mary would remain in England until she was twelve years old, but later events caused a change in that plan.

This brings us to the introduction of the term "princess royal" in our vocabulary dealing with the English royal family. This title is bestowed on some (but by no means all) first-born daughters of the King of England. The practice began with King Charles I and therefore Princess Mary (1631–1660) was England's first Princess Royal. Geoffrey Wakeford's 1973 work entitled *The Princesses Royal* explains the decision to create this title with these words: "Charles I or his advisers devised the status of Princess Royal to distinguish his daughter Mary Stuart from the 'ordinary' foreign princesses who were not necessarily of the blood royal and some of whom were sadly tainted with morganatic blood." The gap between the pedigrees of the bride and groom was indeed wide. Since the titles of the father of the groom, Frederick Henry (1584–1647), were not hereditary, the rank of the groom was a dubious matter. The gap was so wide that it was narrowed when the groom was temporarily promoted to *ambassador* of the United Dutch States! When Mary finally arrived in Holland, her new father-in-law behaved with deference toward her, even though he himself held the titles of Prince of Orange and stadtholder of several Dutch states. Also, King Charles later bestowed titles upon his son-in-law to elevate his status. In 1645 the King made Mary's husband admiral of England, and in 1646 he became a member of the order of the garter, the oldest and highest of English orders.

We have gotten ahead of ourselves here, for we have not yet gotten Princess Mary wed. No hurry, to be sure, for she was not yet ten years old when she first met her husband-to-be (and he was then only 15). They were wed in England, at Whitehall, on May 2, 1641. The marriage treaty contained a number of financial conditions, which the Dutch were required to meet, and the subject of religion was also addressed. The marriage treaty provided that Mary and her household staff were to be allowed to freely exercise their religion, that of the Anglican Church of England. Although the Dutch Reformed Church is also a Protestant denomination, there were material differences between the two faiths, and the King desired his daughter to be free to practice hers.

Meanwhile, because of religion, the Catholic mother of the bride, Queen Henrietta, absented herself from the marriage ceremony itself. She and her own mother, Marie de Medicis, privately viewed the Protestant wedding ceremony from the confines of a small gallery or closet.

No parties or festivities were held to celebrate this wedding. King Charles I had already fought two wars against Scottish armies, and those armies were presently occupying northeastern England. Meanwhile, tensions were fast building between king and parliament and Civil War would begin in England in little more than a year. The kingdom was not in a festive mood. The bride and groom exchanged some formal courtesies and gifts, as tokens of mutual esteem, and then the new groom received a 120-gun salute and left for Holland.

Although the marriage treaty had specified that Princess Mary was to remain in England until she was 12 years old, the political and military situations in England had deteriorated greatly since that treaty was signed. King Charles and Queen Henrietta decided that it would be well for the Queen to visit the European Continent to raise aid for King Charles. As a ruse, Princess Mary was taken to Holland at this time, February 1642 (prior to her 12th birthday). A squadron of 15 Dutch ships came to England to escort their royal passengers to Holland.

The sea crossing was a rough one, and the royal party disembarked at their first opportunity and proceeded by land toward The Hague. Before reaching the city, at its outskirts, the royal English party was met by Princess Mary's aunt, Elizabeth (1596–1662), the deposed Queen of Bohemia.

In November 1643, a second wedding ceremony was held for Princess Mary and her groom, at The Hague. There was little ceremony to this affair. It was merely held to confirm that Mary had now reached the age of 12 stipulated in the marriage treaty. Even after this ceremony, Mary was not fully installed in her conjugal position as the bride of William until February 1644.

Mary's father-in-law, Frederick Henry (1584–1647), Prince of Orange and stadtholder of several Dutch states, died on March 14, 1647. The time of his death was 5:00 P.M., but representatives of the Dutch states met that same evening to promptly show their esteem for Mary's husband, William II, and they declared him successor to his father as stadtholder and leader of the armies. One by one, the remaining titles held by William's father accrued to Mary's husband and he became Prince of Orange.

Mary's mother-in-law, Amalia van Solms, was now the dowager Princess of Orange and she regarded her daughter in law with noticeable jealousy, a jealousy further aggravated when the term "princess royal" was uttered in her presence. Efforts were made at times to keep the two separated, to minimize friction. Mary had a good deal of contact with her English relatives. Her mother, of course, accompanied her on her initial trip to Holland and spent additional time with her over the years. Her aunt Elizabeth (1596–1662), the deposed Queen of Bohemia, also spent time with Mary and became rather a mother figure to her. When they were able to escape from England, both of the brothers who would later rule England as kings, Charles (1630–1685) and James (1633–1701), visited Mary, now Princess of Orange.

Princess Mary and her husband had only one child, but he would prove to be a very important person in English history, when he came to England's throne as King William III (1650–1702). After a miscarriage when Mary was 15, she did not conceive again until she carried the future English King.

Mary was near the end of her pregnancy with William at the time of her husband's death due to smallpox. Eight days later, William (1650–1702) was born on his mother's 19th birthday, November 4, 1650. The baby's cradle was swathed in black, in mourning for the recently departed William II. Since the office of stadtholder and title Prince of Orange were not hereditary, the baby did not succeed to these titles immediately upon birth. Even the baby's name was an issue. The mother, Princess Mary, wanted the child to be named Charles in honor of her father, King Charles I (1600–1649), who recently had been beheaded. But the paternal grandmother, Amalia van Solms, insisted that the child be named William, and the grandmother's wish prevailed. It was probably the better choice. The baby's great-grandfather had been William I, Prince of Orange (1533–1584), the founder of the Dutch Republic and its first stadtholder. Also, of course, the baby's father, William II, Prince of Orange (1626–1650), had William as his given name. Mary lost at the naming game and she only got half of the legal guardianship of her only child. One-half was the most that she could coax from the Dutch court that heard the dispute in 1651. When Mary attained her full majority (in her mid–20's), in accordance with the terms of her husband's will, Mary was acknowledged by the parliament of Orange as the sole regent for her son.

In general, the Dutch disliked this daughter of the deposed English King and their sympathies were with Oliver Cromwell (1599–1658). When Mary attempted to assert a number of her rights, she encountered resistance from the Dutch but, through her French mother, she enlisted the aid of the French. At one point a French war boat was involved against the Dutch, on Mary's behalf.

While she was a young widow in Holland, Mary had many suitors, one of whom was George Villiers, second Duke of Buckingham (1628–1687), son of the famous first Duke of Buckingham, George Villiers (1592–1628).

When monarchy was restored in England in 1660, Mary's son William became fifth in line of succession to the English throne, and Holland finally warmed to Mary and her son and provided them with royal honors.

In September 1660 Mary sailed for England, and upon her arrival there, she took immediate offense to the fact that her brother James (1533–1701) had married Mary's former maid of honor, Anne Hyde (1637–1671). Less than three months later Mary was seriously ill. Her mother tried to persuade her to accept the last rites of the Roman Catholic Church, but Mary declined. Instead she accepted her mother's second offer: that she be seen by Queen Henrietta's personal physician. This was a bad bargain, because the chosen doctor was a bleeder, and his blood-letting no doubt contributed to Mary's death on December 24, 1660. Since medical science did not yet exist, the smallpox with which Mary was infected would likely have taken her life in any event.

11. *Prince James, Duke of York and Albany (1633–1701)*

Prince James came to the English throne upon the death of his brother, King Charles II, on February 6, 1685 and was titled King James II. For his biographical sketch, see the chapter entitled King James II.

12. *Princess Elizabeth (1635–1650)*

Elizabeth was born at St. James' Palace in England on December 28, 1635. This daughter of King Charles I (1600–1649) and Queen Henrietta (1609–1669) was baptized the following Sunday by William Laud (1573–1645), then Archbishop of Canterbury and an ally of King Charles. She was named for her aunt Elizabeth (1596–1662), the deposed Queen of Bohemia and a sister of her father.

When the young Princess was just a few weeks old, she was placed in the care of a governess, the Countess of Roxburgh, wife of Robert Ker, Earl of Roxburgh (–1650). That lady had also been in charge of her elder sister, Princess Mary (1631–1660). Elizabeth was installed first at St. James' with her own train of attendants, including three "watchers" (i.e., nurses), a dresser and several grooms. However, a serious outbreak of plague occurred not long after Elizabeth's birth, and she and the other royal children at St. James' were removed to Richmond to minimize the danger of contagion. By an order of council, certain persons were barred from entering within the district where the royal nursery had been established, for fear they might be plague carriers. These undesirables were defined as "vagrants, lodgers and beggars."

When Elizabeth was not yet two years old, her maternal grandmother, Marie de Medicis (1573–1642), began suggesting that her marriage should be arranged. Toward that end the grandmother proposed that Princess Elizabeth might marry William II (1626–1650), the son of Frederick Henry (1584–1647), Prince of Orange and stadtholder of several Dutch states. King Charles accurately pointed out that William was far below Elizabeth's rank and the King dismissed the possibility of this marriage. (Later, when he was desperate for funds and allies to assist him in the Civil War, it was this same William II whom the King gladly accepted as a mate for his eldest daughter, Mary, the Princess Royal.)

As a result of the impending Civil War in England in 1642, both King Charles I and Queen Henrietta were forced to leave two of the royal children, Princess Elizabeth and her younger brother, Prince Henry, Duke of Gloucester (1640–1660), in the custody of parliament. Although parliament made no attempt to victimize the Princess and her brother, difficulties arose concerning the supply of funds for the maintenance of the two royal children. When the Countess of Roxburgh petitioned the House of Commons for additional funds, the speaker, William Lenthall (1591–1662), investigated and determined that parliament should provide more funds. The House of Commons agreed, but with an important proviso: a committee was first required to investigate, "to inform themselves what papists and other persons disaffected to Parliament are attendants or servants to the children at St. James' and to report to the House which of these should, in their opinion, be removed from office." The committee was also instructed to determine "what disaffected ministers were preaching to the children" and to appoint replacements; also "to see defaced and superstitious relics at the Chapel of St. James'." Upon receipt of the investigating committee's report, the House of Commons ordered that certain staff members be removed and that "none should be permitted to continue in attendance upon his majesty's royal children except those who were willing to subscribe to the solemn 'league & covenant.'"

Word of these events reached young Princess Elizabeth and displeased her. She wrote to the House of Lords appealing for better treatment. The House of Lords was very interested in the letter and discussed it at length. They focused not on the royal children and their treatment by the House of Commons, but that commons had dared to take such matters in its own hands without approval from the House of Lords. "Never," according to one source, "had a child of eight occasioned such a commotion among the elected to the nation!"

Accordingly, the imperious House of Lords conducted its own investigation and determined that changes were required in the staff, including a new governess for Elizabeth, changes in those appointed as chaplains to the royal children and "In future the household should listen to family prayers twice a day, the gates of the Palace must be locked at sun-down, and all members of the Court were required to subscribe to an oath: 'I promise, in the presence of the Almighty God, that I will not hinder the education of any of the King's children in the true protestant religion, piety or holiness of life....'" The multi-volume *Dictionary of National Biography*, published in London in 1909, captures the matter with these words: "Elizabeth ventured an appeal from the commons to the lords.... Her appeal was partially successful, the change was less sweeping than had been originally contemplated; but, to balance this act of complaisance, the poor children had to listen twice on Sunday to the dreary oratory of Stephen Marshall and his kind, besides being catechised in true puritan fashion."

Among the changes resulting from these parliamentary adventures was a new governess, the Countess of Dorset (–1645), who held impeccable Anglican credentials. Lady Southcote was made lady of the bedchamber to Princess Elizabeth.

In the summer of 1644, Princess Elizabeth and Prince Henry were removed from St. James' and placed in the residence of Sir John Danvers (–1655), at Chelsea. This was a precaution against plague. The plague menace was very real, and on account of it, the royal children were shifted from time to time among Whitehall, St. James' and Chelsea.

During these years Princess Elizabeth was very studious, and one of her tutors was Mrs. Basua Makin. The Princess studied languages and theology. We know that she could read and write Hebrew, Greek and Latin when she was about eight years old, and it is likely that she was also well versed in French and Italian. Although Princess Elizabeth was being raised in isolation from much of the world, the news leaked out that the young Princess was "learned" and scholars dedicated several erudite works in her honor.

Upon the death of the Countess of Dorset in 1645, Algernon Percy, Earl of Northumberland (1602–1668), was appointed guardian of Princess Elizabeth and Prince Henry. The Earl was able to secure a bit more freedom for Elizabeth, and she was now permitted to send an occasional letter, not to her father or mother, but at least to her elder sister, Mary, in Holland. Since Mary was in frequent contact with Queen Henrietta, the mother of both Elizabeth and Mary, young Elizabeth's news reached her mother through Mary.

In 1646, during the English Civil War, a son of the King's, James, Duke of York and Albany (1633–1701), was taken prisoner by parliamentary forces. General Thomas Fairfax (1612–1671) ordered that Prince James be placed in the custody of Earl of Northumberland. Thus Elizabeth and Henry were reunited with an elder brother. This brother was one of two who would later come to rule England after the monarchy was restored. The children were taken to St. James', and when the King learned that his children were located so near to him, he applied for permission to visit them. General Thomas Fairfax agreed to the meeting, and the King met with the children for two days. Princess Elizabeth was about 12 years old when this reunion with her father took place. Elizabeth, without any prompting, thanked General Fairfax for his kindness in having brought about the meeting and graciously added that she hoped that, some day, it would be within her power to return his favor. General Fairfax was touched and he stooped to kiss Elizabeth's hand.

Elizabeth and her brother were permitted additional meetings with their father while the King was a captive. Young Elizabeth continued to charm her enemies and was dubbed "Little Temperance," on account of her sweet temper and strict self-control, by parliamentarians, including Oliver Cromwell (1599–1658). During these meetings the King gave a number of instructions to young Elizabeth. She was forbidden to marry without his consent, or should he be unable to give consent, she must secure the blessing of her brother to any marriage proposal. She must be faithful to the Anglican Church of England, but on all matters other than religion, Princess Elizabeth was instructed to obey her Roman Catholic mother.

In 1648 Prince James made a daring escape from the custody of the Earl of

Northumberland, disguised as a woman. James arrived in Holland where he was established in the household of his sister Mary, Princess of Orange. Legend has it that young Princess Elizabeth played a key role in this escape by Prince James when she organized a game of hide and seek as a ruse, on the pretext of amusing young Prince Henry. The Earl of Northumberland was not blamed for this escape, and a few months later he succeeded in having the care of Princess Elizabeth and Prince Henry transferred to his sister, Dorothy, Countess of Leicester.

Princess Elizabeth and Prince Henry learned that their father had been tried and convicted and would soon be executed. They were permitted a final visit with their father on January 29, 1649. At that final meeting the King tried to console his young children. He gave Elizabeth his Bible and told her that it had been his constant companion and a comfort through his sorrows and he hoped that it would be thus for her also. He told the little princess, "Sweetheart, you will forget this." Elizabeth's reply proved to be more accurate when she told her father, "I shall never forget it whilst I live." Elizabeth wrote some recollections of this last visit in a journal that she kept. In it she said that her father stated that he was dying an honorable death for the good of the "laws and liberties of this land" and "for maintaining the true Protestant religion." Elizabeth went on to relate that her father pressed her to guard against popery (Roman Catholicism) and to forgive the King's enemies, but never trust them. (Where quotation marks are used concerning words spoken at the January 29, 1649 meeting, the exact words are an amalgam from several [very similar] sources. The exact words can never be known for no scribe was present to record them.)

King Charles I was executed by beheading on January 30, 1649. Parliament's plan for the children was to degrade them of all princely honors and place them with a family of trusted "Roundheads" (an anti-royalist element of the Civil War era), then maintain them in anonymity until their identity was lost, and then forcibly marry them as civilians. The plan to install them with a Roundhead family soon faltered. Following King Charles' execution, Scotland declared the King's eldest son, Charles, Prince of Wales (1630–1685), to be King of Scotland, with the title King Charles II. In August 1650, parliament learned that Scotland's new King had landed in that kingdom. Oliver Cromwell had barely begun his dictatorial reign and here was a threat to overturn it immediately with restoration of the monarchy. General panic ensued, and one result of that panic was the removal of Princess Elizabeth and Prince Henry to the Isle of Wight. Anthony Mildmay and his wife were given custody of the two children.

The party landed on the Isle of Wight on August 13, and Princess Elizabeth died less than one month later, on September 8, 1650. The Princess knew that she was being kept in the same place (Carisbrooke Castle, Isle of Wight) where her father had been held in captivity. Her general melancholy was aggravated by this connection.

Several sources attribute the cause Princess Elizabeth's death to chills brought on by being caught in a sudden rainstorm while playing a game of bowls with her brother, Henry. While the rainstorm was no doubt the proximate cause of

Elizabeth's early death (she had not yet celebrated her 15th birthday), she was probably already infected with tuberculosis or rickets, and thus in a weakened condition.

The Isle of Wight lies in the English Channel, just a few miles south of England. Its principal municipality is Newport, and it was there, at St. Thomas Church, that Princess Elizabeth was buried. Two centuries later, England's Queen Victoria (1819–1901) had a handsome monument erected in her memory, "a token of respect for her virtues and sympathy for her misfortunes."

13. *Prince Henry, Duke of Gloucester (1640–1660)*

Henry was born at Oatlands, near Weybridge in Surrey, England, on July 8, 1640. This son of King Charles I (1600–1649) and Queen Henrietta (1609–1669) was baptized on July 22, 1640. His title as Duke of Gloucester dates from about the time of his birth. Much later in 1659, Henry was reconfirmed as Duke of Gloucester by his brother, Charles (1630–1685), who was still in exile from England. The dukedom of Gloucester has always been reserved for royalty, although an earldom of Gloucester had previously been bestowed outside the royal family.

As a result of the impending Civil War in England in 1642, both King Charles I and Queen Henrietta were forced to leave two of the royal children, Prince Henry and his elder sister, Princess Elizabeth (1635–1650), in the custody of parliament. Although parliament made no attempt to victimize the children, difficulties arose concerning the supply of funds for their maintenance. The Countess of Roxburgh had custody of them when she petitioned the House of Commons for additional funds. The speaker of commons, William Lenthall (1591–1662), investigated and determined that parliament should provide more funds. The House of Commons agreed, but with an important proviso: a committee was first required to investigate "to inform themselves what papists and other persons disaffected to Parliament are attendants or servants to the children at St. James' and to report to the House which of these should, in their opinion, be removed from office." The committee was also instructed to determine "what disaffected ministers were preaching to the children" and to appoint replacements, also "to see defaced and superstitious relics at the Chapel of St. James'." Upon receipt of the investigating committee's report, the House of Commons ordered that certain staff members be removed and that "none should be permitted to continue in attendance upon his majesty's royal children except those who were willing to subscribe to the solemn 'league & covenant.'"

When the House of Lords learned that commons had taken these steps without involving them, the imperious upper house conducted its own investigation and determined that different changes in the royal household were appropriate. The multi-volume *Dictionary of National Biography*, published in London in 1909, captures the matter with these words: "…the change was less sweeping than had been originally contemplated; but, to balance this act of complaisance, the poor children had to listen twice on Sunday to the dreary oratory of Stephen Marshall and his kind, besides being catechised in true puritan fashion." Among the changes resulting from these parliamentary adventures was a new governess, the Countess of Dorset (–1645), who held impeccable Anglican credentials.

In the summer of 1644, Prince Henry and Princess Elizabeth were removed from St. James' and placed in the residence of Sir John Danvers (–1655), at Chelsea. This was a precaution against plague. The plague menace was very real, and on account of it, the royal children were shifted from time to time among Whitehall, St. James' and Chelsea. Upon the death of the countess of Dorset in 1645, Algernon Percy, Earl of Northumberland (1602–1668), was appointed guardian of the two young royal children.

In 1646, during the English Civil War, the King's son, James (1633–1701), was taken prisoner by parliamentary forces. General Thomas Fairfax (1612–1671) ordered that Prince James be placed in the custody of the Earl of Northumberland. Thus Henry and Elizabeth were reunited with an elder brother. This brother was one of two who would later come to rule England after the monarchy was restored. The children were taken to St. James', and when the King learned that his children were located so near to him, he applied for permission to visit them. General Thomas Fairfax agreed to the meeting, and the King met with the children for two days. Henry, Elizabeth and James were permitted additional meetings with their father while the King was a captive.

During these meetings the King instructed his children to be faithful to the Anglican Church of England, but on all matters other than religion, they were to obey their Roman Catholic mother.

In 1648 Prince James made a daring escape from the custody of the Earl of Northumberland, disguised as a woman. James arrived in Holland where he was established in the household of his sister Mary (1631–1660), Princess of Orange. Legend has it that young Princess Elizabeth played a key role in this escape when she organized a game of hide and seek as a ruse, on the pretext of amusing young Prince Henry. The Earl of Northumberland was not blamed for this escape and a few months later he succeeded in having the care of Prince Henry and Princess Elizabeth transferred to his sister, Dorothy, Countess of Leicester. Prince Henry was provided with an Anglican tutor, who had royalist sympathies, Robert Lovell.

Prince Henry and Princess Elizabeth learned that their father had been tried and convicted and would soon be executed. They were permitted a final visit with their father on January 29, 1649. At that final meeting the King tried to console his young children.

King Charles feared that, after his death, the parliamentary forces might try to use young Prince Henry as a puppet king. During this last meeting, the King took Prince Henry upon his knee and admonished him, "Sweetheart, now they will cut off thy father's head. Heed, my child, what I say; they will cut off my head, and perhaps make thee a king. But, mark what I say. You must not be a king so long as your brothers Charles and James doth live ... therefore, I charge you not be made a king by them." Prince Henry solemnly answered that "I will be torn in pieces first." (Although quotation marks are employed here, the exact words are an amalgam from several [very similar] sources. The exact words can never be known for no scribe was present to record them.)

Elizabeth wrote some recollections of this last visit in a journal that she kept. In it she said that her father stated that he was dying an honorable death for the good of the "laws and liberties of this land" and "for maintaining the true Protestant religion." Elizabeth went on to relate that her father pressed her to guard against popery (Roman Catholicism) and to forgive the King's enemies, but never trust them.

King Charles I was executed by beheading on January 30, 1649. Parliament's plan for the children was to degrade them of all princely honors and place them with a family of trusted "Roundheads" (an anti-royalist element of the Civil War era), then maintain them in anonymity until their identity was lost and then forcibly marry them as civilians. The plan to install them with a Roundhead family soon faltered. Following King Charles' execution, Scotland declared the King's eldest son, Charles, Prince of Wales (1630–1685), to be King of Scotland, with the title King Charles II. In August 1650, parliament learned that Scotland's new King had landed in that kingdom. Oliver Cromwell had barely begun his dictatorial reign and here was a threat to overturn it immediately with restoration of the monarchy. General panic ensued, and one result of that panic was the removal of Prince Henry and Princess Elizabeth to the Isle of Wight. Anthony Mildmay and his wife were given custody of the two children. The party landed on the Isle of Wight on August 13, 1650, and Princess Elizabeth died less than one month later. The ten-year-old Prince Henry was now alone.

In 1653 Prince Henry was permitted by parliament to leave England. He traveled to Holland, where he was received with enthusiasm by several family members, including his eldest sister, Mary, Princess of Orange. On Easter Sunday 1653, Henry was inducted into the order of the garter, the oldest and highest of English orders.

Henry then went to Paris for a reunion with his mother. Henrietta had promised her husband, King Charles I, that she would not attempt to convert any of their children to her Roman Catholic faith. When her eldest son Charles proposed to take Prince Henry to Germany with him, Henrietta objected. Charles agreed that Henry could be left in France, provided Henrietta made no attempt to convert him to Catholicism. Henrietta was unable to live up to these commitments because of her fervor to save Prince Henry's soul in the true church. However, Henrietta did not immediately send away Prince Henry's Anglican tutor, Robert Lovell. Prince Henry joined his brother James in the army and, when he returned to Paris, he was a spoiled, insufferable 14-year-old boy. Henry's conduct gave Henrietta the excuse that she needed to discharge Robert Lovell, the mild-mannered Anglican tutor. After doing so, she dispatched Henry to Pontoise, France, 18 miles northwest of Paris. There, it was intended that Walter Montague, the Roman Catholic abbot of Pontoise, would convert Prince Henry to Catholicism. Since Montague was himself an English royalist and a convert to Catholicism, Henrietta had reason to hope for favorable results.

However, Prince Henry resisted these overtures, and his mother personally joined in the evangelical effort. Nothing but hard feelings came of it. Prince Henry resented the attempt to convert him, and when his older brother, Charles, learned of it, he was furious. When Henry told his mother that he was firmly committed to the Protestant faith, she disowned him, and Henry was told to "Be sure that (your mother) sees your face no more!" Henry departed defiantly to a church service of the Anglican Church of England. When he returned from this worship service to his mother's palace, we are told, in Carola Oman's 1936 work entitled *Henrietta Maria*, that he "found, much to his dismay, that the sheets had been stripped from his bed, his horses were being turned out of their stables, and, by her majesty's commands, no dinner had been prepared for him."

Following this confrontation, Prince Henry spent some time with his sister, Mary, in Holland and with his brother, Charles, in Germany. Since Charles had already been crowned King of Scotland, the rulers of England clearly regarded him as a threat to restoration of the monarchy in England and they monitored his European travels with great interest. The Dutch states informed Mary, Princess of Orange, that a visit by the King of Scotland would be contrary to a treaty made with England in 1653, and, therefore, the King was not welcome. Nevertheless, both Charles and Henry spent some time in Dutch states. The English press reported that King Charles of Scotland had traveled with his siblings, Henry and Mary, from Cologne to Frankfort. A report in *Mercurius Publicus* stated that, although the party was purportedly traveling incognito, their identity was widely known, "...and, therefore, in every prince's country they passed through, they had the civility of a compliment by their chief officers...."

The multi-volume *Dictionary of National Biography* tells us that in December, 1656, Henry became a colonel of "the Old English regiment of foot in the Spanish army" and that he served with the Spanish army fighting side by side with his brother James.

In 1659 Henry was made Earl of Cambridge and was reconfirmed as Duke of Gloucester by his brother, the King of Scotland. When the monarchy was restored in England in 1660, Prince Henry accompanied King Charles II, to England. On May 31, 1660, Henry took a seat in the House of Lords. Soon afterward he was made high steward of Gloucester and ranger of Hyde Park. It was generally agreed that there was difficulty in finding an appropriate position for Prince Henry to fill.

The matter was resolved by Prince Henry's death prior to the English coronation of Charles II. Near the beginning of September 1660, Prince Henry became ill from the smallpox, which was then prevalent in London. He died on September 13, 1660, never having married. The Prince's death cast a shadow over a family reunion, which was held after the restoration. The Queen mother, Henrietta, celebrated the reunion at a banquet held at Dover, England, with her four surviving children: the new English King, Charles II, the Princess Royal, Mary of Orange,

Prince James, Duke of York and Albany, and the youngest child, Princess Henrietta (1644–1670).

Prince Henry, Duke of Gloucester, was buried at Westminster Abbey in the same vault as Mary, Queen of Scots (1542–1587).

14. *Princess Henrietta (1644–1670)*

Henrietta was born at Exeter, England, on June 16, 1644, during the English Civil War. She was the last child born to King Charles I (1600–1649) and Queen Henrietta (1609–1669). Princess Henrietta was baptized on July 21, 1644, in the Anglican Church of England at Exeter Cathedral. Her name was entered in the baptismal record as simply Henrietta. Later, when she had been taken to France by her mother and was being raised there as a Roman Catholic, at her confirmation she was given the confirmation name Anne. Thus many sources render her name as Henrietta Anne. To her family she was known by the diminutive Minette. Alison Plowden's *The Stuart Princesses* reports that the name Henrietta honored the baby's mother, while Anne was given in honor of the Queen Regent of France, Anne of Austria (1601–1666). Because he was fighting to defend his crown in the English Civil War, King Charles I was not present at either Henrietta's birth or baptism. On account of the Civil War, Queen Henrietta fled England for France when the baby was less than one month old. The Queen left the baby in England in the care of Anne Villiers, Countess of Dalkeith, a Protestant. Queen Henrietta was a fervent Roman Catholic, but the baby was in Anglican England ruled by her staunchly Anglican husband, King Charles I. The elder Henrietta would soon take steps in France to correct Princess Henrietta's religious affiliation.

King Charles had opportunities to visit his youngest child, Princess Henrietta, while she was in Exeter and on a visit during September 1644, he established a household for his baby daughter, arranged revenues for her support, and appointed Thomas Fuller (1608–1661) as her chaplain. Fuller was a member of the Protestant Church of England.

During the English Civil War, when parliamentary forces captured Exeter, Lady Dalkeith took her young charge to reside at Oatlands, near Weybridge, in Surrey, England. There Lady Dalkeith was forced to expend her own funds for the upkeep and safety of the baby Princess. Lady Dalkeith appealed for funds to maintain the Princess. Her appeals went to the leader of the parliamentary army, General Thomas Fairfax (1612–1671), and to the speakers of both houses of parliament. In reply, she was told to dismiss the Princess' household and make arrangements to transfer the infant to St. James' Palace to live with her royal siblings, Princess Elizabeth (1635–1650) and Prince Henry (1640–1660). However, Lady Dalkeith was determined to maintain custody of young Henrietta until she could turn the child over to one of the parents. Accordingly, she planned and executed an escape to France to reunite the baby with her mother. Bryan Bevan provides details in his

1979 work entitled *Charles II's Minette*: "She dared not confide the secret to members of the Princess's household except for two trusted servants named Lambert and Dyke…. Lady Dalkeith disguised herself as a beggar woman in a shabby cloak; at the same time she artfully concealed her graceful figure by putting a hump of rags on one shoulder."

Upon their safe arrival in France, Queen Henrietta joyfully vowed to have Princess Henrietta raised in the Roman Catholic faith. It seems clear that this was contrary to the instructions given to the Queen by King Charles I, but she bruited about some words that she was fully authorized to make these decisions until her children were in their early teens. Even when her eldest son, Charles, Prince of Wales (1630–1685), pointed out that a conversion of a member of the English royal family to Catholicism would do irreparable harm in England, Queen Henrietta turned a deaf ear. She was far more interested in the safety of her daughter's immortal soul in the true church than in any civil inconvenience that might arise in England. Father Cyprien de Gamaches was appointed as Princess Henrietta's Roman Catholic mentor. Lady Dalkeith, who was in France as Henrietta's governess, attended the religious instruction with her young charge, and Father de Gamaches even attempted to convert that Anglican lady to Catholicism. He failed in that effort, and after the death of her husband in 1651, Lady Dalkeith returned to England.

In France, Princess Henrietta and her mother initially lived in splendor as a result of the generosity of the French regent, Anne of Austria. However, the English Queen, Henrietta, was anxious to provide financial aid to her husband, King Charles I, for the English Civil War and she sold jewelry to acquire funds for that purpose. Also, a 1648 revolutionary movement, called the War of the Fronde, sapped French royal funds, and the English Queen and her daughter were forced to live on a reduced allowance until that war was over.

When Princess Henrietta was about six years old, her eldest brother, Prince Charles (1630–1685), came to Paris. There he lived with his mother and the young Princess. It was during this period that Charles (later King Charles II) came to be very fond of his Minette. Some sources say that she was the favorite sister or favorite sibling of King Charles II.

In 1654 Princess Henrietta made her first public appearances. In February she attended a ball given by Cardinal Jules Mazarin (1602–1661) and in March she participated in a ballet. Henrietta was now almost ten years old and the French regent, Anne of Austria, expressed the hope that her son might marry Henrietta. Both of Anne's sons were cousins of Henrietta. The son whom Anne had in mind was Louis XIV (1638–1715), soon to be King of France. As it turned out, Henrietta later married Anne's other son, Philip (1640–1701), a terrible choice.

Princess Henrietta, of course, became fluent in French, but she never gained much mastery of the English language. She developed literary and artistic tastes. Her special delights were poetry and music. As a young musician she played both the harpsichord and guitar. Henrietta also sang and danced with grace.

By 1660 the monarchy had been restored in England under Minette's eldest brother, King Charles II, and the Princess and her mother visited England in the fall of that year for a family reunion. All surviving family members attended. In addition to Princess Henrietta, her mother, and the English King, the reunion at Dover, England, was attended by Prince James, Duke of York and Albany (1633–1701), and the Princess Royal, Mary (1631–1660), who had become Princess of Orange. The gathering had a somber tone because of the recent death of Henrietta's brother, the 20-year-old Duke of Gloucester, Prince Henry (1640–1660).

Henrietta was married in late March 1661, to Philip, Duke of Orleans (1640–1701), by Daniel de Cosnac, the Catholic Bishop of Valence. Henrietta thus became the duchess of Orleans. The bride and groom were of the same religious faith, but had little else in common, and a disastrous marriage resulted. Some sources put the blame on the bride: "Her days were passed in an unceasing whirl of dissipation. For her husband she felt neither affection nor respect." Other sources convict the groom as the guilty party with words like these: "He was an effeminate homosexual and neglected his young wife for his male favorites." It appears pretty clear from the records that neither Henrietta nor Philip was free of blame. Henrietta was an adulteress. Philip held petty grudges, which interfered with important diplomatic relations between France and England. In spite of his interference, the King of France and Henrietta accomplished a major diplomatic success with the 1670 treaty of Dover. Some sources even attribute Henrietta's death to poisoning by friends or agents of Philip. It is clear that Henrietta thought that she had been poisoned as she was dying, but she likely was in error. The sad marriage produced four births: Marie Louise (1662–1689), who in 1679 married King Charles II (1661–1700) of Spain; Philip Charles, Duke of Valois (1664–1666); a daughter who died at birth on July 9, 1665; Anne Marie (1669–1728) who in 1684 married King Victor Amadeus II (1666–1732) of Savoy. (This husband also ruled, for a time, both Sicily and Sardinia.)

Marie Louise had no children, but Anne Marie did. Had it not been for England's Act of Settlement in 1701, Anne Marie's descendants would have entered the English line of succession to the throne early in the 19th century. However, these descendants were Roman Catholics and the 1701 act removed their eligibility for that reason.

Henrietta was a patroness of the arts and literature. Among the Frenchmen whom she supported were the playwright Pierre Corneille (1606–1684), the actor and playwright Jean B. Poquelin (1622–1673), whose pseudonym was Molière, and the dramatic poet Jean B. Racine (1639–1699).

The French King, Louis XIV, confided in Henrietta on a number of occasions. She often became privy to secret information that had been kept from the King's only brother, her husband. This infuriated the husband. In 1670 the French King wanted Henrietta to go to England to negotiate on his behalf with her brother, England's King Charles II. The etiquette in vogue at that time in France held that a lady required her husband's permission to travel abroad, even on a mission for the French King. Henrietta's husband was reluctant to grant that permission and, when he did so, he imposed time constraints, which were unreasonable in that era before the invention of airplanes.

Henrietta made the trip to England (and ignored her husband's time limits) and succeeded in her mission. At least two factors contributed to her success in negotiating the 1670 treaty of Dover: (1) She was a favorite of her brother, the English King. (2) She knew her brother well and was aware of his testosterone-driven appetite for pretty women. Henrietta brought with her to England her maid of honor, Louise Renee de Keroualle (1649–1734). This alluring young woman was then about 21 years old and she produced the desired affect on the King of England. At the conclusion of this English visit, Henrietta exchanged gifts with King Charles II. When asked which of Henrietta's jewels he wanted, the King replied that he wanted only her finest jewel, Louise Renee de Keroualle. Even the worldly Henrietta was embarrassed by this request. She answered that she was forced to decline because she was responsible to the girl's parents and had promised to bring Louise safely back to France. Some sources contend that at this juncture Henrietta made a counter offer, i.e., that Louise could be sent to live in England if the Queen Consort to King Charles II were to select Louise to be a maid of honor. It turned out that Louise was indeed sent back to England just a few weeks later, shortly after Henrietta's death. In England, Louise became a maid of honor to the Queen Consort, Queen Catherine (1638–1705). While serving in that capacity she also was a mistress of King Charles II.

The strategic planning by the French King and Henrietta was amply rewarded in the 1670 treaty of Dover, which the English King signed about one week after Henrietta's arrival in England. That treaty pledged that England and France would jointly attack the Dutch and that neither kingdom would make a separate peace treaty with the Dutch. The plan behind these words was that France would annex Holland and then England would be given some territory. There was also a second (secret) portion of the treaty of Dover concerning Catholicism. On behalf of herself and the French King, Henrietta had tried to persuade her brother, King Charles II, to restore Catholicism to England. In that, she failed, but she succeeded in securing her brother's agreement to a remarkable secret portion of the treaty. In that secret portion of the treaty, King Charles II announced his personal conversion to the Roman Catholic faith and the French King promised to provide Charles with an army to fight in England if disaffection arose from the 1670 treaty of Dover. (King Charles II later lied to parliament when he told the members that there were no secret clauses to this treaty.) King Louis XIV of France was so anxious to sign the treaty that he waited at Calais, a seaport in northern France, and, when the treaty was ferried across to him, he signed it immediately.

Henrietta then returned to France where she was warmly received by the French King, but faced a husband who was very jealous of his wife's triumph on the international diplomatic scene. She arrived in Paris on June 20, 1670, and ten days later she was dead. The physician on the scene attributed her death, at St. Cloud, France, on June 30, 1670, to natural causes, and he was probably correct. However Henrietta, herself, stated that she had been poisoned just before she died and several writers have bruited that about as a fact. Sources that attribute her death to poison state that this murder was done by friends or agents of Henrietta's husband. Although the question has not been completely resolved, there is circumstantial evidence that she was not poisoned; i.e., the fact that other people drank the same beverage that allegedly contained poison with no ill effects. (Their names are known and they reported their experiences about the time of Henrietta's death.)

In her last moments, Henrietta urged that her brother, the English King, not be told that she had been poisoned, lest he retaliate against France. It would appear that Louise de Keroualle was sent from France to England as a gesture to keep the goodwill of the English King toward France after his favorite sister's death under mysterious circumstances.

Henrietta received the last rites of the Catholic Church from Father Feuillet, an austere and fearless man of the cloth. Father Feuillet told Henrietta that she had lived a frivolous and self-indulgent life, that she had never known the true Christian faith, and that she must make a general confession. This she did with courage and dignity, despite the pain she was suffering.

KING CHARLES II

The monarchy was restored in England on May 29, 1660, and the eldest son of the former King, King Charles I, came to the English throne as King Charles II. He was crowned in Westminster Abbey on April 23, 1661, and he ruled England until his death on February 6, 1685. King Charles II had only one wife, Catherine of Braganza (1638–1705). The King had an active sex life, which produced numerous illegitimate children, but the royal union failed to produce any legitimate children. For this reason, when King Charles II died, he was succeeded on the English throne by his eldest brother, who ruled England as King James II.

15. *King Charles II (1630–1685)*

Charles was born at St. James' palace on May 29, 1630. This son of King Charles I (1600–1649) and Queen Henrietta (1609–1669) was the second royal child to be named Charles. The earlier Charles was the first child born to King Charles I and Queen Henrietta. That baby died at birth on May 13, 1629. When the next Charles was born on May 29, 1630, he became the eldest son of the King and thus eligible for the title Prince of Wales. Charles received that title, but because of difficulties associated with the prelude to the English Civil War, he was never officially created Prince of Wales; he was merely declared to be Prince of Wales.

When he was about five weeks old, Charles was baptized according to the rite of the Anglican Church of England by William Laud (1573–1645), then Bishop of London.

An early tutor was Brian Duppa (1588–1662). John Earle (–1665) succeeded

Duppa as tutor to the Prince of Wales. Both men were Anglicans and later became bishops of the Church of England.

The English Civil War erupted before Prince Charles reached his teen years. Charles and his brother, Prince James (1633–1701), accompanied their father at the battle of Edgehill, and Charles was at his father's side through some of the Civil War. Toward the end of that conflict he escaped to Continental Europe where he lived in France, Holland, and Germany.

The royalist side was defeated in the Civil War and King Charles I was beheaded on January 30, 1649. With the death of King Charles I the monarchy ended in England and Oliver Cromwell (1599–1658) ruled as dictator. For a time after Cromwell's death in 1658, successors attempted to maintain his form of rule, but the kingdom, which had suffered the horrors of civil war, failed to achieve meaningful redress of grievances. In 1650 Charles, Prince of Wales (now *de jure* King of England and Scotland), landed in Scotland and raised an army of 10,000 men. In 1651 he was crowned King of Scotland. Charles and his army marched south to England, but were defeated there at the battle of Worcester by Oliver Cromwell and his force, which was almost twice the size of Charles'.

After the battle of Worcester, George Monck, later Duke of Albemarle (1608–1760), was left in Scotland by Cromwell as commander-in-chief of the army there, and he later assumed broader military responsibilities. Following the death of Oliver Cromwell in 1658, England became weary of constitutional experiments and many longed for the return of the monarchy. General Monk led negotiations with Charles toward that end. There had been many changes in England since the death of King Charles I. For the monarchy to be restored, Charles was required by Monck to stipulate that not all royalist supporters could be restored to their former lands and money; that there would be a general amnesty, save for specific renegades; that arrears would be paid to the English army; that "tender consciences" in religion would be respected. The required stipulations were made by Charles in April 1660, while in exile in Holland, in the Declaration of Breda.

The return of Charles to England was greeted by enthusiastic crowds, from the time he landed at Dover, through his return to London on his 30th birthday, May 29, 1660. In London, he was warmly received by all. Winston Churchill tells us in his *A History of the English-Speaking Peoples* that even "the Presbyterian divines … [were] presenting the Bible amid their fervent salutations."

The crown was officially restored in England on May 29, 1660, and King Charles II was crowned King of England at Westminster Abbey on April 23, 1661.

As England's King under the restored monarchy, Charles II found it necessary to become an artful politician and appease various factions to preserve the monarchy. In many ways Charles skillfully accomplished the required Machiavellian gamesmanship. In light of this, it seems difficult to understand the King's reckless disregard of public opinion concerning two subjects: religion and marital fidelity. Regarding religion, the King flirted rather openly with Roman Catholicism, which he well knew was unpopular in England. With respect to marital fidelity, King Charles II had little or none.

While it had been agreed that there would be a general amnesty, there were scapegoats. Surprisingly, it was King Charles II who favored some moderation at this point, but inflamed Englishmen sought revenge for wrongs done by Cromwell and his successors. Nine men were executed for treason, and Cromwell and others were disinterred and their corpses were abused. The large standing army was dispersed and Charles promised (again) that nobody would suffer because of their religious beliefs. The King was not unusually tolerant concerning religion; he was indifferent. Throughout his reign King Charles II remained far more flexible than his parliaments concerning religious matters. In 1661 an act was passed which attempted to restrict municipal offices to royalist Anglicans, and in 1662 the Act of Uniformity prescribed liturgical conformity via common (Anglican only) prayer books. The English parliament continued, throughout Charles' reign, to impose one sect, the Anglican sect, as the Church of England.

In 1662 King Charles II married Princess Catherine (1638–1705), a Roman Catholic and a daughter of the Portuguese King, John IV (1604–1656). Catherine brought with her the rather enormous dowry of two million Portuguese gold crowns (then worth several hundred thousand English pounds), the important trading ports of Tangier in northern Africa and Bombay in India, as well as lucrative trading privileges in South America. In return, King Charles agreed to provide an army to help Portugal fight Spain. Catherine vowed to get rid of Charles' mistresses. In this she failed. King Charles II never had any legitimate children, but he produced numerous illegitimate children. No complete listing of them exists at this time and, even while the King lived, there was uncertainly about the paternity of children who were, or might have been, his. George Villiers, Second Duke of Buckingham (1628–1687), a member of the King's cabal, upon hearing someone refer to King Charles as "father of his people," remarked, "Well, a good many of them."

Sources knowledgeable on this esoteric subject put the number of illegitimate children at 14 or 15, or "13 acknowledged," born to seven women. Most of these women were mistresses to the King, but some were merely objects of his ever-wandering ardor. The acknowledged children and their mothers are listed — in order by given name, because of multiple surnames and titles — in the following table. (An additional child known as James La Cloche [1647–1668] is mentioned, as a natural son of King Charles II, by the multi-volume *Dictionary of National Biography* published in London in 1909. That source says James' mother is unknown, but *The Sex Lives of the Kings & Queens of England* by Nigel Cawthorne implies that the mother was Margaret de Carteret.)

Barbara Villiers, Duchess of Cleveland and Countess of Castlemaine (1641–1709):
    Anne Palmer, Countess of Sussex (1661–1722)
    Charles Fitzroy, Duke of Southampton and Cleveland (1662–1730)
    Charlotte Fitzroy, Countess of Lichfield (1664–1718)
    George Fitzroy, Duke of Northumberland (1665–1716)
    Henry Fitzroy, Duke of Grafton (1663–1690)

Catherine Pegge, Lady Green (–1668):
  Catherine (1658–)
  Charles Fitzcharles, Earl of Plymouth (1657–1680)

Elizabeth Killigrew, Lady Shannon (–):
  Charlotte Fitzroy, Countess of Yarmouth (1650–1684)

Louise Renee de Keroualle, Duchess of Portsmouth and Aubigny (1649–1734):
  Charles Lennox, Duke of Richmond (1672–1723)

Lucy Walter (–1658):
  James Scott, Duke of Monmouth and Buccleuch (1649–1685)

Mary ("Moll") Davis (–1669):
  Mary Tudor, Countess of Derwentwater (1673–1726)

Nell Gwyn (1650–1687):
  Charles Beauclerk, Duke of St. Albans (1670–1726)
  James Beauclerk (1671–), died age eight or nine

The list is rather appalling, but King Charles was charming and his ribald conduct was accepted by many English people. However, Puritans and puritanical-thinking people were aghast. When the Great Plague arrived in 1665, to be followed by the Great Fire of London in 1666, those disasters were interpreted as God's punishment of the sinful and licentious behavior of the King and members of his court.

Among the illegitimate children there was one who was very important in English history and in the life of King Charles II. He was James Scott, Duke of Monmouth and Buccleuch (1649–1685). During the anti–Catholic hysteria late in Charles' reign, Monmouth was vigorously proposed as the rightful heir to the throne. This was because Charles' brother, the Duke of York and Albany (1633–1701), next in the line of succession, was a professed Roman Catholic. Had England not recently been through one disastrous civil war, there might have been armed conflict over this issue.

In 1662 King Charles II sold Dunkirk (now Dunkerque) in northern France to King Louis XIV (1638–1715).

In North America, King Charles II granted a charter to Connecticut in 1662. In 1663 he granted Carolina (extending from the colony of Virginia to Florida) to eight Englishmen, and in 1664 he forcefully took New Netherland from the Dutch and awarded it to his brother Prince James, Duke of York and Albany. The Duke's proprietorship was renamed New York. England now controlled essentially all of America's Atlantic Ocean seacoast north of Georgia.

In the 1670 treaty of Dover, King Charles II and France's King Louis XIV pledged that England and France would jointly attack the Dutch, and that neither kingdom would make a separate peace treaty with the Dutch. The plan behind these words was that France would annex Holland and then England would be given some territory. There was also a remarkable second (secret) portion of the treaty of Dover concerning Catholicism. In that secret portion of the treaty, King

Charles II announced his personal conversion to the Roman Catholic faith, and the French King promised to provide Charles with an army to fight in England if disaffection arose from the 1670 treaty of Dover. (King Charles II later lied to parliament when he told the members that there were no secret clauses to this treaty.) King Louis XIV of France was so anxious to sign the treaty that he waited at Calais, a seaport in northern France, and when the treaty was ferried across to him, he signed it immediately.

In 1673, the King's eldest brother, Prince James, married Mary (1658–1718), a Roman Catholic, and by that time, James had declared his own conversion to Catholicism. Since James was next in the line of succession to the English throne and the present monarch had no legitimate children, James' Catholicism was a serious issue in Anglican England. The kingdom became gripped in an infamous anti–Catholic hysteria, which in some ways lingered on until 1829, when Roman Catholics were allowed to participate fully in English public and political civil life.

On account of the strong anti–Catholic sentiment, the King asked his Catholic brother to leave England to allow time for tempers to cool. Prince James complied. In England, King Charles II fought courageously (and effectively) to preserve the established line of succession. The King had few strong personal opinions, but on this question of succession he felt so strongly that he endured great personal risk to preserve it and refused to consider a modification under which his Protestant illegitimate son, the Duke of Monmouth and Buccleuch, would succeed him. (The King's position prevailed and, when he died, his Catholic brother, James, came to the throne as King James II [1633–1701]. However, because of his religion, the reign of King James II was brief.)

Anthony A. Cooper, Earl of Shaftesbury (1621–1683), held a remarkably harsh conversation with the King, in the presence of a number of awestruck notables, in which he demanded that Monmouth be named as royal successor. The King declined: "Let there be no delusion. I will not yield nor will I be bullied. Men usually become more timid as they become older; it is the opposite with me and, for what may remain of my life, I am determined that nothing shall tarnish my reputation. I have law and reason and right-thinking men on my side. I have the church (and here he pointed to Anglican bishops) and nothing will ever separate us."

As a product of his efforts to protect the established line of succession, King Charles II elected to rule with no parliament at times, and this exacerbated the problem of limited funds in the royal treasury. The King looked to France for funds and, in the process, England was made something of a tool of the foreign policy of King Louis XIV of France.

Prince James returned to England in 1682. There was genuine fear in some quarters that if Catholic James succeeded Charles as King, the choice would be between being Papist or being executed. The hare-brained Rye House Plot of 1683 was a product of this line of reasoning. In that failed plot the royal brothers, King Charles and Prince James, were to be intercepted at the Rye House on their return from Newmarket, England. The plot failed and its leaders were executed for treason.

On his deathbed, Charles was received in the Roman Catholic Church by

Father John Huddleston (1608–1698), who administered the last rites of the church to him in secrecy. The King died on February 6, 1685, and was buried according to the rites of the Anglican Church at Westminster Abbey.

During his life, King Charles II was a patron of the arts and sciences and he is listed among the official founders of the Royal Society, one of the world's most prestigious scientific societies. King Charles also understood the importance and implications of supremacy on the high seas and he supported a strong English navy.

Winston Churchill cautions in his work on the history of English-speaking peoples: "To represent him as a mere voluptuary is to underrate both his character and his intellect.... [Of] the twenty-five years of baffling politics through which he maintained himself on the throne, ... the last five years of his reign are those most honourable to his memory."

16. *Queen Catherine (1638–1705)*

Catherine was born on November 25, 1638, at Vila Vicosa, a ducal palace about 300 miles from Lisbon, Portugal. At that time, Portugal was ruled by Spain. Portugal successfully revolted, and in 1640 Catherine's father, the Duke of Braganza, came to the Portuguese throne as King John IV (1604–1656). Catherine's mother was Luisa de Gusmao, a daughter of the Duke of Medina-Sidonia.

She was baptized on December 12, 1638, by Father Antonio de Brito e Sousa, and named for the Roman Catholic saint whose feast day is on her birthday, November 25, i.e., Saint Catherine of Alexandria.

King John's primary concern for his newly independent kingdom of Portugal was securing foreign recognition and alliances to ward off inevitable hostile moves by Spain. The House of Braganza was rich in gold and silver, and these riches were put to use in Portugal's foreign relations. When Catherine was about eight years old, her father considered using her as a bride to help secure foreign support. Possibilities considered at this time were John of Austria, illegitimate son of King Philip IV of Spain (1605–1665), and the Duke of Beaufort, a grandson of Henry IV. France's Louis XIV (1638–1715) was suggested as a potential husband for Catherine by the French first minister, Cardinal Jules Mazarin (1602–1661). A treaty toward that end was signed on September 7, 1655. However, when Portuguese representatives visited France to ratify the treaty, the French were hostile. Later moves to strike an alliance between Portugal and France through a marriage of Princess Catherine to Louis XIV got nowhere, and France actually signed a treaty with Spain, instead. During the English Civil War it had been proposed that one of the princesses of the House of Braganza would be a suitable bride for Prince Charles, Prince of Wales (1630–1685), who was then heir-apparent to the English throne. The possibility of a marriage to the future King Charles II (1630–1685) then stalled on account of both the English Civil War and the Catholicism of the members of the House of Braganza.

After the monarchy was restored in England in 1660, the idea of marriage between Catherine and Charles was pursued again. During July 1661, a marriage contract between Princess Catherine and King Charles II was signed. (That treaty provided that Catherine would be permitted to practice her own Catholic religion, and this treaty provision was later respected by the King despite strenuous opposition to Catholicism in England.) The following April, Catherine sailed for England and arrived there at Portsmouth on May 24, 1662. Princess Catherine had not yet learned much, if any, of the English language and she was not even fluent in French, a language known to many royal Europeans. She came from Portugal with an entourage of ladies who were both Portuguese and Catholic and thus provided some buffer to her strange new surroundings. Her new husband happily began to teach his new Queen the English language.

Catherine brought with her the rather enormous dowry of two million Portuguese gold crowns (then worth several hundred thousand English pounds), the important trading ports of Tangier in northern Africa and Bombay in India, as well as lucrative trading privileges in South America. In return, King Charles agreed to provide an army to help Portugal fight Spain. England soon gave up Tangier to the Moors, but the island of Bombay gave English merchants a west-coast station in India and helped lead to English dominion over the colony of India.

Catherine and King Charles II were wed on May 31, 1662. Two ceremonies were held, both at Portsmouth. The first was secret and under the auspices of the Roman Catholic Church. The second ceremony was according to the rites of the Anglican Church of England and it was in public.

The King and Catherine rested for a few days at Portsmouth and then traveled to Hampton court palace, which would be the royal residence. There the new Queen was confronted by culture shock. In contrast to the high moral and religious atmosphere at the Portuguese court, English court life featured ribald conduct. Indeed, Catherine soon learned that her new husband would continue to frolic with his several mistresses. Catherine vowed to get rid of Charles' mistresses. In this she failed.

Not long after the royal couple had settled at Hampton court, King Charles suggested to Queen Catherine that she appoint one of his mistresses to her household staff. That mistress was Barbara Villiers, Countess of Castlemaine, and later Duchess of Cleveland (1641–1709). There was a distressing scene at court when King Charles, with uncharacteristic insensitivity, forced Queen Catherine to meet Barbara Villiers and accept her as a member of her bedchamber staff. The lecherous King was so anxious to accomplish this ludicrous arrangement that his conduct is described by a contemporary observer as like that of a "wild boar." The King and Queen soon argued about Barbara (in Spanish, the only language in which they could then communicate with each other). The churlish Charles threatened to dismiss most of Catherine's Portuguese staff and send them back to Portugal. A few weeks later, the King did exactly that when he sent most Portuguese members of the Queen's retinue back home. Portuguese members of the Queen's household who were allowed to remain included the priests from her chapel and the Countess of

Penalva. Queen Catherine was now homesick in England, lonely and estranged from her new husband. She swallowed her pride and acknowledged Barbara Villiers as a member of her court. The ungrateful mistress then proceeded to treat Catherine with contempt.

Queen Catherine sought refuge from the bawdy conduct of her husband and members of his court in her private chapel. However, King Charles was unusually attractive to women, and among the women who fell in love with him was his wife, Queen Catherine. She eventually accepted the situation and retained her dignity in spite of the mistresses. She became a most accommodating wife and earned the respect and affection of both King Charles and his dissolute court. Surprisingly, the King actually fell in love with his wife. One contemporary remarked that "Catherine is now a mistress, the passion her spouse has for her is so great." The Queen had begun to participate in a few harmless court frivolities, such as balls and masquerades, and the King warmed to this departure from piety and sanctimony.

However, Catherine failed in her primary duty: the production of one or more legitimate heirs to the English throne. She became pregnant several times, but always miscarried. It was urged upon the King, who was busily fathering illegitimate children, that he secure an annulment of his marriage. Charles would hear none of it. This type of suggestion was heard again later, more vigorously, when Prince James (1633–1701), the King's brother and heir-apparent to the throne, announced his conversion to the dread Roman Catholic faith. For her part, Queen Catherine displayed remarkable kindness toward the King's illegitimate children. Her favorite among them was James Scott, Duke of Monmouth and Buccleuch (1649–1685).

When Queen Catherine had reached the age of 33 and was still childless, she retired from Whitehall to remove herself from the King's present mistress, Louise Renee de Keroualle (1649–1734), later Duchess of Portsmouth and Aubigny. Catherine lived for a time at Somerset House, and her private chapel there became popular with English Roman Catholics. Protests were heard in Protestant England. The Queen's religious devotions allowed time for an occasional evening game of cards and attending the concerts, which were held at her court.

In 1678 a "Popish Plot" purported to reveal a Roman Catholic plot to assassinate King Charles so his Catholic brother, James, would take the throne. The plot was a fabrication, but its tone reflected the anti–Catholic hysteria in England at that time. A number of alleged "Popish" conspirators, including five Jesuit priests, were tried and executed. In Portugal there was great concern over this turn of events, but the English official who was resident in Lisbon assured the Portuguese crown that Charles' support, loyalty, and affection for Catherine had not wavered for a single moment.

During October 1683, Catherine's brother, King Alfonso VI (1643–1683), died. Queen Catherine spent a period in prayer and mourning following her brother's death.

Two decades earlier, King Charles II had forcefully taken New Netherland, in

North America, from the Dutch and awarded it to his brother, Prince James, Duke of York and Albany. The Duke's proprietorship was renamed New York. Now, on November 1, 1683, a county in New York, Queens County, was named for Queen Catherine. Manuel Andrade e Sousa tells us, in his 1994 biography entitled *Catherine of Braganza: Princess of Portugal: Wife to Charles II,* that King Charles chose the county's name to honor his Queen Consort.

In early February 1685, King Charles went to his deathbed. Queen Catherine asked her husband to forgive her if she had ever offended him. The King exclaimed, "Alas! Poor woman! She beg my pardon! I beg hers with all my heart." Before his death on February 6, 1685, the King received the last rites of the Roman Catholic Church in secrecy. Catherine, now England's dowager Queen, went into a period of prayer and mourning.

Following the death of King Charles II, the King's brother briefly came to the English throne as King James II (1633–1701). On account of his Roman Catholic faith, he was soon forced to leave England, and the throne passed to King William III (1650–1702) and Queen Mary II (1662–1694), who ruled as joint sovereigns. Catherine did not return to Portugal immediately. Instead, she remained in England for some seven years. In 1685 the King's illegitimate son, James Scott, Duke of Monmouth and Buccleuch, made an unsuccessful bid to seize the throne. Catherine appealed that his life be spared, but the request was denied and Monmouth was executed.

While King James II still ruled England, Catherine contacted her brother, King Pedro II (1648–1706), asking his permission to return to Portugal. However, King Pedro had several reasons for disliking the idea, probably foremost among them was preservation of good relations between Portugal and England. The Portuguese King initially declined Catherine's request, and when he later accepted, Catherine happened to be too ill to take advantage of the offer.

Because of this, Catherine still resided in England when her Catholic brother-in-law, King James II, was deposed, and the very Protestant King William III and Queen Mary II took the throne. Queen Mary was hostile toward Catherine, as was her sister, Princess Anne (1665–1714). Catherine resolved to leave England, but there were obstacles. William and Mary turned a deaf ear to her request for a ship to transport her, and the Portuguese King was reluctant to send one of his ships to England because it might hurt diplomatic relations. On the other hand, the Portuguese King could not officially request the new Protestant English monarchs to transport Catherine because he had not yet officially recognized them. Even the French King, Louis XIV, was reluctant to grant hospitality in France to Catherine because he treasured her Roman Catholic presence in England.

In 1692 Dowager Queen Catherine finally succeeded in securing transportation to take her to Continental Europe, and she received permission from the French King to land at Dieppe, in northern France. Her departure carriage was greeted enthusiastically by crowds in London, and in France the King invited her to a reception at his court in Versailles. Catherine declined that invitation, but she was touched by this gesture and by the affection shown to her by people of both London and France.

In late 1692 Catherine arrived in Portugal where great officials of church and state greeted her warmly. Triumphal arches were even erected in her honor. At Lumiar, Portugal's King Pedro II welcomed his sister home. Back in Portugal, Catherine continued the custom she had acquired in England of frequently changing residences. For this, and for the style of dress favored by Catherine and the ladies of her court, she was considered highly eccentric. However, these eccentric fashion notions soon provided employment to a number of French tailors who came to Portugal to cater to the dress trend among Portuguese ladies.

On May 28, 1704, King Pedro II appointed his sister, Catherine, as regent of Portugal, while he went to the Spanish border to fight against Spain. Later that year, King Pedro returned to the capital, but he was weary from defeats his army had suffered at the Spanish border and his health soon began to fail. On January 3, 1705, King Pedro re-appointed his sister as regent of Portugal. In that capacity, Catherine displayed ability in recruiting troops and planning their military maneuvers.

On December 31, 1705, Catherine of Braganza, still regent of Portugal, died at Bemposta Palace. In accordance with her request, Catherine was buried alongside her brother, Teodosio, who died at the tender age of 17. Their burial vaults are behind the main alter of Jeronimos monastery in Belem.

KING JAMES II

James acceded to the throne of England upon the death of his brother, King Charles II, on February 6, 1685. His coronation at Westminster Abbey occurred on April 23, 1685, and he ruled England as King James II until December 11, 1688, when he first attempted to leave the kingdom. James had two wives. They were Anne Hyde (1637–1671) and Mary of Modena (1658–1718). Since Anne Hyde died before James came to the throne, she was never Queen Consort of England, although two of Anne's daughters, Mary (1662–1694) and Anne (1665–1714), came to the throne as monarchs of England. James' marriage to Anne Hyde produced eight named children, but the only two to survive infancy were Mary and Anne. James' union with Mary of Modena was also blessed with fecundity, producing six named children, but only two children of this second marriage survived infancy.

17. *King James II (1633–1701)*

James was born at St. James' palace on October 14, 1633, a son of King Charles I (1600–1649) and Queen Henrietta (1609–1669). About the time of his baptism, he was made Duke of York. The Scottish dukedom of Albany was also given to James, although this honor may have been delayed until 1660. Prince James later became next in the line of succession to the English throne, but he was not the eldest son of a king and, therefore, he was never made Prince of Wales.

James accompanied his brother, Prince Charles (1630–1685), and his father on early adventures in the English Civil War and he was with them at the battle of Edgehill. When Oxford fell to parliamentary forces, Prince James was surrendered to them and he was given as a captive to the Earl of Northumberland (1602–1668). However, in 1648 Prince James managed to escape and flee to Holland.

In Holland, Prince James lived for a time with his sister, Mary (1631–1660), who was then married to Prince William II (1626–1650) of Orange. In Continental Europe, James gained practical military experience when he volunteered for service in French and, later, Spanish armies. He is remembered for those days as a brave soldier and good commander.

While still in exile in Continental Europe, James fell in love with Anne Hyde (1637–1671). She was one of his sister Mary's maids of honor and a daughter of Edward Hyde, later Earl of Clarendon (1609–1674), a very influential English statesman. When Hyde learned that his daughter was pregnant by Prince James, he was furious and he threw a temper tantrum of memorable proportions. James' brother, who had very recently acceded to the throne as King Charles II, ordered James to marry Anne. This was done in a public ceremony at Worcester House on September 3, 1660. For purposes of giving legitimacy to the first child to be born of this marriage, both James and Anne stated that there had been a formal declaration giving the date of November 24, 1659, as the date that their marriage had been contracted. Both James' mother, Henrietta (1609–1669), and his eldest sister, Mary (1631–1660), took haughty offense that a member of the royal family would marry so far beneath his station.

On October 22, 1660, James' wife delivered the child who had caused the Earl of Clarendon's fury. It was a boy, who was named Charles and given the title Duke of Cambridge. He died on May 5, 1661.

In all, Anne, Duchess of York and Albany, delivered eight children to James before she died. The causes of Anne's death were both cancer and complications from the birth of her last child. Two of the children of James and Anne would soon rule England as monarchs. They were Queen Mary II (1662–1694) and Queen Anne (1665–1714). The complete roster of the named children of James and Anne, in order of birth, follows:

> Prince Charles, Duke of Cambridge (1660–1661)
> Princess Mary (1662–1694)
> Prince James, Duke of Cambridge (1663–1667)
> Princess Anne (1665–1714)
> Prince Charles, Duke of Kendal (1666–1667)
> Prince Edgar, Duke of Cambridge (1667–1671)
> Princess Henrietta (1669–1669)
> Princess Catherine, or Katherine (1671–1671)

James' sexual appetite, like that of his brother, Charles, was vigorous. His ribaldry produced numerous children by two wives and several illegitimate children from affairs with mistresses or other women. An exact census of the illegitimate children does not exist. Apparently many of James' lovers were rather plain, because Charles jokingly remarked to his brother that the women must have been suggested as a penance by James' confessor.

The following table lists some illegitimate children under two known mothers (in order by given name because of multiple surnames and titles):

Arabella Churchill (1648–1730):
    Arabella
    Henrietta Fitzjames, Lady Waldegrave (1667–1730)
    Henry Fitzjames, Duke of Albemarle (1673–1702)
    James Fitzjames, Duke of Berwick (1670–1734)

Catharine Sedley, Countess of Dorchester (1657–1717):
    Catherine (or Katherine), Lady Darnley, Duchess of Buckinghamshire (1679–1743)
    James Darnley (1684–)

In North America, King Charles II forcefully took New Netherland from the Dutch in 1664 and awarded it to his brother, Prince James, Duke of York and Albany. James' enormous proprietorship was renamed New York, and Prince James was awarded more power over his domain than any other English proprietor.

In 1660 James had been named Lord High Admiral. This was no mere figurehead position. Prince James personally commanded the fleet when the English defeated the Dutch at the battle of Lowestoft in 1665, and he was in the thick of combat against the Dutch at the battle of Sole Bay.

In 1673 James married for the second time. His new wife was Mary of Modena (1658–1718), an Italian Catholic, then but 15 years old. By this time, it was becoming widely known that Prince James, himself, had converted to the Roman Catholic religion. The conversion of James to Catholicism, and his subsequent refusal to convert back to the Anglican faith, had enormous political implications at that time and produced results that controlled England's royal line of succession for centuries.

Unlike many of the other women of James II, Mary was a beauty. With her, the King demonstrated his fecundity once more and the royal couple produced six named children:

> Princess Catherine (1675–1675)
> Princess Isabel (1676–1681)
> Prince Charles, Duke of Cambridge (1677–1677)
> Princess Charlotte (1682–1682)
> Prince James Francis Edward, Prince of Wales (1688–1766)
> Princess Louisa (1692–1712)

The person next in the line of succession to the throne in Protestant England was James, a Roman Catholic with a devout Catholic wife. James was not a mere passive concerning his Catholicism. Rather, he held the fire and zeal of a typical convert. Protestant England was wary, and the response was vigorous. In 1673 a Test Act was passed which forbade Catholics to hold many government positions. As a result, James was forced to resign as Lord High Admiral. In 1678 a "Popish Plot" purported to reveal a scheme by Jesuits in England to assassinate King Charles II and thereby secure the succession of the Catholic James II. The "Popish Plot" was nothing but lies, but the lies were widely believed. A number of alleged "Popish" conspirators, including five Jesuit priests, were tried and executed. An Exclusion Crisis from 1679 to 1681 followed, during which parliament attempted to dictate the line of succession and direct that line away from the Catholic James.

On account of the strong anti–Catholic sentiment, the King asked his Catholic brother to leave England to allow time for tempers to cool. Prince James complied. In England, King Charles II fought courageously (and effectively) to preserve the established line of succession. The King had few strong personal opinions, but, on this question of succession, he felt so strongly that he endured great personal risk to preserve it and refused to consider a modification under which his Protestant illegitimate son, the Duke of Monmouth and Buccleuch, would succeed him.

For his part, James also demonstrated that he was willing to risk the crown for the sake of his faith. An offer was made to James that he convert to the Anglican Church of England to secure himself in the English line of succession. James refused to abandon his cherished Roman Catholic faith.

By 1680, James had returned to the island of Great Britain and was restored to office as Lord High Commissioner of Scotland. There, Prince James watched, apparently unmoved, as Convenanters (Presbyterians) were brutally tortured and executed. He was less pleased to learn of the hanging and quartering in Scotland of priests of his own Roman Catholic faith, but these deaths he would soon avenge. Back in London, James was restored to the admiralty.

James issued declarations to comfort a wary kingdom and attempted to dispel notions that he was vindictive. Many Englishmen were suspicious and believed, that once James came to the throne, their choice would be "the Mass or the stake." The hare-brained Rye House plot of 1683 was a product of this line of reasoning. In that failed plot, the royal brothers, King Charles and Prince James, were to be intercepted at the Rye House on their return from Newmarket, England. The plot failed, and its leaders were executed for treason.

On February 6, 1685, King Charles II died, and his eldest brother, James, acceded to the throne of England. Parliament voted James a generous annual allowance. King James II began to attend Roman Catholic Masses in his chapel. Anglican clergymen who learned of this were alarmed, but it took some time for the news to spread through the country. On April 22, 1685, James was crowned, under rite of the Roman Catholic Church, at his chapel at Whitehall. His Anglican coronation occurred on the following day at Westminster Abbey, with no communion.

In May 1685, King James II assured parliament that he would protect the Anglican Church, but he promptly proceeded to break that promise with great vigor.

It is certain that King James II wanted Roman Catholics to be free to practice their religion in England, and it is quite possible that the new King wanted more; i.e., the return of Catholicism as the official Church of England. King James did not rule very long. His reign was cut short in a bloodless coup initiated to protect Protestant England from Roman Catholicism. A listing of the significant events during James' short reign contains a string of events triggered by the Catholic-Protestant tension of the day.

King James II decided upon toleration as a first step toward a more profound goal, and he extended the protection of the crown to Nonconformist Protestants, as well as Catholics, in England.

In Holland, there lived an illegitimate son of King Charles II, James Scott, Duke of Monmouth and Buccleuch (1649–1685). Because he was Protestant and James was not, Monmouth had been proposed as successor to King Charles II while the King still lived. Now, fugitives from the ill-fated Rye House plot urged Monmouth to seize England and the crown. In 1685 Monmouth made an unsuccessful bid to seize the throne. James did not yet have a large army to resist Monmouth, but he did have some troops and, more importantly, the support of parliament. Monmouth was defeated, and he was executed. With Monmouth defeated and parliament still loyal, King James II was at the height of his powers. He soon squandered the good will.

The King had given commissions to several Catholic officers during the Monmouth emergency, and he told parliament that he now had no intention to dismiss these Catholics. This was a violation of the Test Act of 1673, which restricted public offices to Anglicans, and, therefore, James' plan was illegal.

James wanted, and got, a large and well-equipped standing army, as well as a loyal navy. The new King looked to France for a role model, where he saw King Louis XIV (1638–1715) ruling with a heavy hand and a sharpened sword. James warmly approved of the Catholic French King's persecution of Protestant Huguenots.

King James II dismissed parliament. It would never meet again while he was King. The Catholic King arranged a test case to try the validity of the Test Act under circumstances where royal dispensing power had been used to contravene the act. Since the King had packed the court with men who favored his ideas, he was not surprised when a pro–Catholic verdict was reached. The King responded to the verdict by granting more dispensations to Catholics and by admitting Roman Catholic peers to the Privy Council.

In 1686 King James II established an Ecclesiastical Commission consisting of seven members, with sweeping disciplinary powers. In the King's mind, the purpose of this body was to prevent Anglican clergymen from preaching against Catholicism.

The King's standing army had grown to impressive proportions. He camped the army near London, where it would be noticeable, and took steps to make himself popular with all ranks by frequently visiting officers and men. James allowed Mass to be celebrated in the army camp. For this purpose, a wooden chapel on wheels was placed in the center of the camp between cavalry and infantry.

King James II frequently pondered what the royal line of succession would be upon his death. He did not yet have a male heir and he knew that his first legitimate female child, Princess Mary (1662–1694), and her husband, the Dutch Prince William of Orange (1650–1702), were unshakably Protestant. James suggested to his next eldest daughter, Princess Anne (1665–1714), that he would support her for the line of succession and the crown if she would convert to Catholicism. Anne and her close associates were appalled, and the offer was firmly refused.

King James II continued his Catholic provocation. He attempted to install a Catholic as president of one of the colleges of Oxford University and received Count Ferdinand d'Adda as a papal nuncio. The King worked vigorously to prepare Catholics to sit in parliament and placed Catholics in municipal corporations. The composition of the judiciary was changed to contain perhaps a majority of non–Anglicans. Even the Pope and other Vatican officials cautioned James that his zeal might be excessive. He hardened his heart and strengthened his army.

The conduct of King James in the short time that he had reigned had disheartened a wide swath of his citizens. Whigs and Tories were now united against him. From peasant to well-to-do, Englishmen were threatened in "all they cared for in this world or the next."

Among the leaders who emerged during this period to begin to scheme against the King was Thomas Osborne, Earl of Danby (1632–1712). Danby had arranged the 1677 marriage of Princess Mary to the Dutch Prince of Orange, William III. Now Danby and his fellow travelers considered inviting William to come to England and take the throne for Protestantism by force.

In 1688 King James II issued a pro–Catholic second Declaration of Indulgence and ordered that it be read in all churches. Seven Anglican Bishops refused to comply. A trial was ordered, and the Bishops, who refused bail, were committed to the Tower of London. On June 10, 1688, while the trial of the Bishops was still pending, the Roman Catholic Queen Consort gave birth to Prince James Francis Edward. England, weary from a recent civil war and its horrible aftermath, may well have been content to wait for King James II to die. With him would die the Catholic threat, because his two eldest children, Princess Mary (1662–1694) and Princess Anne (1665–1714), were both resolutely Protestant. Now, however, a legitimate male offspring had been born to the King. Baby Prince James became next in the line of succession to the throne. The legitimate heir to the throne was now a Catholic son, born to a Catholic King and a Catholic mother. In Anglican England, this would never do. Rumors were circulated, with vigor, that the birth of this child was a sham; that a baby had been smuggled in to validate the lie. The truth is that there was no sham and there was no lie. The Catholic baby, James Francis Edward, had merely been born at a very inconvenient moment in England's history. Though he was clearly next in the established line of succession, there was no possibility that England would allow him to take the throne.

The trial of the seven imprisoned Anglican Bishops helped to form a center around which fury against the King and his religion swirled. In late June 1688, all seven Bishops were tried and found not guilty. Widespread joy greeted the verdict, even among the King's army.

Revolutionary leaders met and composed a letter inviting William of Orange to invade England. During the last few months of his reign, King James II made a large number of dramatic concessions, abandoning previous positions to preserve his reign. This was too little, too late.

William of Orange sailed toward England with a force of some 14,000 regular Dutch troops. In addition to those, William had with him French Huguenot volunteers, Swedes, Danes, Prussians, English, and Scottish. In all, his forces numbered more than 21,000 men. When William landed, his allies were already in place, and as he moved toward London, city after city in England revolted against the King. In spite of his large standing army, King James II found resistance to William's force impractical. He sent his Queen Consort and their newest baby, Prince James, to escape from England. One day later, the King made his own escape, pausing to fling the kingdom's great seal into the Thames River, to promote anarchy in England. King James boarded a ship, but missed favorable tides and was recognized and captured before he could leave England. After his forced return, there were a few days of suspense before James was allowed (or forced) to leave. This time he left England forever.

The English parliament ruled on January 28, 1689 that King James II had abdicated his crown. The throne passed to King William III (1650–1702) and Queen Mary II (1662–1694), who ruled as joint sovereigns. However, James remained *de facto* King of Catholic Ireland. In July 1690, a large army of mostly French troops who were loyal to James met defeat at the battle of the Boyne, in Ireland, by a force of roughly equal in size to the one commanded by King William III.

On June 28, 1692, James' last child was born to Mary, his Queen Consort in exile. Princess Louisa (1692–1712) was born in France and was baptized with great pomp in the chapel of St. Louis at St. Germain. The French King Louis XIV attended her baptism as her sponsor. The youngest Princess would be a source of joy to the exiled King James in his final years.

James spent the remainder of his life in France planning schemes to regain the English crown, but none of them amounted to anything. During the final two or three years of his life, James devoted much of his time to religious prayer and contemplation.

On August 24, 1701, James was attending Mass when he suffered a stroke. He died shortly afterward, on September 6, 1701, at St.-Germain-en-Laye. Initially, the body of King James II was taken to the Church of the English Benedictines, on the Rue St.-Jacques, in Paris. There his coffin remained, unburied, and merely resided in one of the side chapels. During the French Revolution, the King's coffin was despoiled. It was not until 1813 that the corpse of King James II was taken to rest at the parish church of St.-Germain-en-Laye.

18. *Anne Hyde (1637–1671)*

Anne was born in England, at Windsor Park, on March 12, 1637. Her father was Edward Hyde, later Earl of Clarendon (1609–1674), a very influential English statesman. Anne's mother was Hyde's second wife, Frances Aylesbury (1617–1667), a daughter of Sir Thomas Aylesbury. Anne was the eldest child of this marriage and the eldest child of Edward Hyde, since his first marriage, to Anne Ayliffe, had produced no children.

In 1649, as the English Civil War was ending, Edward Hyde became a royalist in exile in Continental Europe. He took his wife, Frances Aylesbury Hyde, their daughter, Anne, and some other Hyde children to live in the Dutch States. Edward Hyde then performed diplomatic work in Spain. While in the Dutch States, Edward Hyde's family took up residence in Breda, in what today is the Netherlands. Also living in the Dutch States at that time was the Princess Royal of England, Princess Mary (1631–1660). Mary was the eldest sister of England's Prince James (1633–1701), and she was the wife of William II (1626–1650), an important personage in the Dutch States. When one of Princess Mary's maids of honor died of smallpox, she decided upon Anne Hyde as a replacement. This was done, and in 1654, Anne joined the staff of Princess Mary as a maid of honor.

Although Anne Hyde was not a great beauty, and even rather plain, this was not necessarily an obstacle to randy young men. Among the men who viewed Anne with interest was Henry Jermyn (1636–1708), Sir Spencer Compton.

The mother of both Princess Mary and Prince James was Henrietta (1609–1669). Henrietta was living in Paris, France, when Princess Mary and her entourage paid a visit in 1656. During that visit, Anne Hyde chanced to meet Prince James. They flirted, and James was taken with Anne's cheerful, yet forceful, personality.

Back at Breda, Prince James and Anne Hyde became well acquainted. In fact, Anne became pregnant with James' child.

When the monarchy was restored in England in 1660, Prince James returned to England. Edward Hyde also returned then to assist England's new King, Charles II (1630–1685). Once established in England, Hyde sent for his wife and daughter, Anne, to join him. Hyde was thinking of marriage prospects for his daughter, Anne, and had one possibility in mind. However, soon after Anne and her mother arrived in England, Edward Hyde learned that his daughter, Anne, was pregnant by Prince James. Edward Hyde was furious.

The elder Hyde's fury led to a temper tantrum of memorable proportions. He even proposed that parliament should send his daughter to the Tower of London for execution. Even years later, he wrote about this tantrum, with no hint of regret. Edward Hyde told his wife that Anne was to be confined to her room and that she was not welcome to eat meals with the family. However, Frances Hyde helped her daughter visit her lover, Prince James, during the period that Anne was confined to her room.

Edward Hyde was a very important English statesman when these events unfolded, and the new King, Charles II, had no desire to offend him. King Charles ordered his brother, James, to marry Anne. This was done in a ceremony at Worcester House on September 3, 1660. For purposes of giving legitimacy to the first child to be born of this marriage, both James and Anne stated that there had been a formal declaration, at Breda, giving the date of November 24, 1659, as the date that their marriage had been contracted.

Both James' mother, Henrietta (1609–1669), and his eldest sister, Mary (1631–1660), took haughty offense that a member of the royal family would marry so far beneath his station. Mary declared that she would never accept, as a sister-in-law, a former maid of honor who had once "stood as a servant behind her chair." History tells us that when she was dying, Mary expressed regret for her harsh remarks. Anne also eventually won over her mother-in-law. No doubt Henrietta was appalled at the adulterous conduct of her two sons, Charles and James, and took pity on Anne Hyde, the innocent victim of her husband's infidelities. On January 1, 1661, Henrietta consented to see Anne and, on that occasion, Henrietta said that she had always liked Anne. As the years progressed, and Anne produced numerous legitimate births, Henrietta surely approved because, during this period, her two sons, King Charles II and Prince James, were fathering numerous illegitimate children.

On October 22, 1660, James' wife delivered the child who had caused the Earl of Clarendon's fury. It was a boy, who was named Charles and given the title Duke of Cambridge. He died on May 5, 1661. King Charles II, perhaps in an effort to ease family tensions, made Edward Hyde baron Hyde in 1660, and viscount Cornbury and Earl of Clarendon in 1661.

Prince James insisted that, unless Anne were officially acknowledged as his wife, he would leave the kingdom and spend the rest of his life abroad. However, some friends of Prince James had offered to claim Anne's child as their own (or at least publicly declare that she had been intimate with them before the birth). King Charles II took pity on Anne and the marriage, and the friends were obliged to withdraw their accusations. King Charles II paved the way to acceptance of the awkward marriage by complimenting Anne's father, Edward Hyde. Charles told Hyde that his "daughter was a woman of great wit and excellent parts; she would take good advice from her father and exert her beneficial influence over her husband." The King of England was pleased with the marriage. Who could fail to agree?

While Prince James may have insisted that Anne be publicly acknowledged as his wife, he made little attempt to hide his infidelities. Moreover, James humiliated his wife by picking plain women. We know that many of James' lovers were rather plain, because Charles jokingly remarked to his brother that the women must have been suggested as a penance by James' confessor.

With his wife, Anne, James had eight children before Anne died of complications from the birth of her last child, while she had cancer. Two of these children of James and Anne would soon rule England as monarchs. They were Queen Mary II (1662–1694) and Queen Anne (1665–1714). The complete roster of the named children of James and Anne, in order of birth, follows:

Prince Charles, Duke of Cambridge (1660–1661)
Princess Mary (1662–1694)
Prince James, Duke of Cambridge (1663–1667)
Princess Anne (1665–1714)
Prince Charles, Duke of Kendal (1666–1667)
Prince Edgar, Duke of Cambridge (1667–1671)
Princess Henrietta (1669–1669)
Princess Catherine, or Katherine (1671–1671)

With his mistresses and other women, Prince James was busily siring a crop of illegitimate children. An exact census of these children does not exist. Arabella Churchill (1648–1730) produced four or five of his children, and Catharine Sedley, Countess of Dorchester (1657–1717), had at least two children by James. James' wife was naive enough to complain to King Charles II about his brother's adulterous behavior. The ribald Charles, who had a good sense of humor, was amused.

Anne studied with interest the journals her husband had meticulously kept while serving with the military in Continental Europe. She had a bit of artistic and literary talent of her own and was a patron of the artist, Sir Peter Lely (1618–1680). Anne's quick intelligence enabled her to make friends easily and even turned some early enemies into friends.

Anne's husband, the Duke of York and Albany, enjoyed his wife's company and admired her wit. He was not reluctant to take advice from her. Among Anne's faults were a tendency to overeat and perhaps splurge a bit on jewelry, but her overall influence on the household budget was favorable. Anne's daughter, Princess Anne (1665–1714), learned to delight in eating tasty treats with her mother, and some contend that this early exposure to overeating contributed to the later gluttony of England's Queen Anne.

During the late summer of 1665, Prince James and his wife traveled to the northern portion of England. The trip was partially motivated by political considerations, but the Great Plague was then resident in London, and a desire to avoid it surely was a factor. On this trip, Prince James treated his wife with great public deference and insisted that others do the same.

It was also during this trip that it was first noticed that Henry Sidney (1641–1704) displayed evidence of romantic interest in Anne. This surely delighted her. Never a beauty, Anne had become quite overweight, and to capture the designs of the handsome 24-year-old Sidney was a feat of note. In his 1934 work entitled *King James the Second*, F. M. G. Higham comments: "But no woman, least of all a plain one, could resist a flirtation with so beautiful a creature and, if he were also rather stupid, that made it none the worse for one whose brains enabled her to command the situation." Better yet, her husband's jealousy was aroused, and Prince James arranged to have Sidney dismissed from Anne's household, where he had been master of the horse. Although there was some malicious gossip, there is absolutely no reason to believe that Anne was unfaithful to her husband on this or any other occasion during their marriage.

Not long after this Henry Sidney intrigue, Prince James publicly took a mistress, Lady Margaret Denham (–1667), and insisted that his wife allow Lady Denham to be a lady of her bedchamber. Anne, of course, objected, but her views were ignored and Margaret Denham was installed in the royal household. This arrangement was of very short duration. Lady Denham died under mysterious circumstances in January 1667. Some suspected that Anne had poisoned her husband's newest mistress. This suggestion lacks credibility, particularly because a far more plausible explanation exists. If Lady Margaret Denham were poisoned (and this is not certain), it is likely that her husband administered the lethal dose. That husband was Sir John Denham (1615–1669), a poet, who suffered insanity for a short period as a result of Margaret's infidelity with Prince James. During his period of insanity, Sir John Denham visited the court of Prince James and engaged in wild and sacrilegious talk. On that occasion Sir Denham claimed to represent the Holy Ghost of Christianity's Trinity.

In 1667 Anne's father, Edward Hyde, was dismissed from his position of power in England. Anne and her husband became melancholy and, about this time, one observer reported that Anne had discontinued receiving communion from the Anglican Church of England.

Both Anne and her husband, Prince James, became interested in theological studies. James, no doubt, came to those studies earlier than did Anne, but she pored over theological tracts with vigor.

In 1670 Anne became a secret convert to the Roman Catholic Church. Although it is certain that this happened (Anne wrote a letter, in which she confirmed it), sources containing biographical information dealing with Anne Hyde present conflicting views about the motivation for this religious conversion. We know that her husband, James, was about to profess and, subsequently, very vigorously defend his own conversion to the Roman Catholic faith. Some sources contend that Anne converted to please James. Others indicate that, after her conversion, Anne influenced James toward Catholicism. Whatever Anne's motives, it now seems apparent that James would have become a Catholic no matter what his first wife did.

Anne's decision to embrace Catholicism was not popular with her family. Her father wrote a detailed letter to her from his exile, which defended the Anglican Church of England that his daughter was abandoning. Edward Hyde told his daughter that the Anglican faith was "the best-constituted church and the most free from error in Christendom. You will bring irreparable dishonour on your father and your husband, and ruin to your children." In addition to these judgments, Anne's father offered the very practical advice that Anne keep her new religion secret to avoid harm to her children.

Anne died on March 31, 1671, at St. James' Palace, having first received the last rites of the Roman Catholic Church. Both cancer and complications from the birth of her last child contributed to her death. Anne Hyde, Duchess of York and Albany, was buried at Westminster Abbey on April 5, 1671.

Many works dealing with English history refer to Anne Hyde as the duchess of York. Rarely is she called the duchess of York and Albany, although her husband,

Prince James, was Duke of both York and Albany. Chronology explains the apparent discrepancy. The English title Duke of York was given to Prince James about the time of his baptism, so from the time that the marriage of Anne Hyde to Prince James was acknowledged, references to her as duchess of York became accurate. However, the Scottish dukedom of Albany was not awarded to James until 1660. Therefore, Anne was only duchess of York and Albany from 1660 until her death in 1671.

19. *Queen Mary of Modena (1658–1718)*

Mary Beatrice d'Este, Princess of Modena, was born on October 5, 1658. Her father was Alfonso d'Este, Alfonso IV, Duke of Modena (1634–1662). Since 1452, Modena had been an independent duchy in Italy. Although ill with tuberculosis during the last years of his life, Mary's father ruled his duchy until his death in 1662. Mary's mother was Laura Martinozzi, who became Duchess of Modena when she married Alfonso d'Este. The seat of government for the duchy of Modena was the quiet university town named Modena, in northern Italy, and it was there that our Mary was born.

Mary's father had been in failing health during the months preceding his death, and he died when Princess Mary was just four years old. Thus it fell to Mary's mother to set the regimen for Mary and other children of the household, and a demanding program it was. Mary's mother was a stern taskmaster concerning both educational drills and observances of fasts required by the family's Roman Catholic faith. However, summers were generally spent at a delightful country palace in Sassuolo, ten miles southwest of the capital at Modena. Years later Mary recalled with fondness the summers she had spent at Sassuolo.

But Mary's childhood years were destined to be few. By the time she was 14 years old, Mary had expressed a desire to become a nun. It was explained to her that she could provide far greater service to the Roman Catholic Church by marrying the recently widowed Prince James (1633–1701) of England. He was next in the line of succession to the English throne. Perhaps, with Mary's assistance, James could bring the Catholic Church back as the Church of England! Mary was not impressed. She had never even heard of England and certainly had no desire to marry a man who had been born earlier than her own father.

On behalf of England, Henry Mordaunt, Earl of Peterborough (–1697), was in Modena negotiating for Mary's hand. In desperation, Mary suggested to Mordaunt that perhaps one of her aunts would make a more suitable bride for England's Prince James. Poor Mary had powerful forces allied against her. Mary's mother was a niece of Cardinal Jules Mazarin (1602–1661), who had recently been the powerful first minister of France. The French King, Louis XIV (1638–1715), wanted all the Catholic friends he could find to plant in Protestant England. Even the Pope wrote a personal letter to young Mary, urging her to marry Prince James of England.

Princess Mary of Modena was married by proxy at Modena, in a Catholic ceremony, to England's Prince James. The ceremony was performed on September 30, 1673, just five days before Mary's 15th birthday. England's representative was Henry Mordaunt, Earl of Peterborough, but he excused himself from those aspects of the Roman Catholic marriage ceremony that offended his Anglican sensibilities.

During the early stages of Mary's journey to England, she delighted in visiting important shrines and convents of the Roman Catholic Church. In France, King Louis XIV treated Mary as a very honored guest of state. Meanwhile, in Protestant England, bigots were at work trying to abort the marriage of their heir-apparent to this Catholic woman. On November 5, the annual Guy Fawkes (1570–1606) day celebrations brought forth a special outpouring of anti–Catholic passion. The entourage was warned that if Mary were to arrive in England on November 5, "she would certainly be martyred." Among the uneducated English country folk, a rumor was spread that Mary of Modena was the Pope's eldest daughter.

These rumors and passions were symptoms of a fundamental underlying tension in Protestant England against the Roman Catholic Church. While King Charles II (1630–1685) ruled England, the dynamics of the tension existed in one context. Later, when Charles died and King James II took the throne, the tension increased, but stress fractures were avoided until the Catholic King James II and his Catholic wife, Mary of Modena, produced a Catholic son, who became heir-apparent to the throne. That son was Prince James Francis Edward, Prince of Wales (1688–1766).

But we have gotten ahead of our story. Mary has not even left Continental Europe to meet and wed her new husband. Princess Mary of Modena embarked for England from Calais, in northern France, on December 1, 1673, and arrived at Dover, England on November 21, 1673.

Perhaps a word or two about the calendars in use in Europe at this juncture in history would be useful here. Since 1582, the Gregorian calendar had been in use in Continental Europe. That calendar had been a departure from the previous Julian calendar. The Gregorian calendar lopped off some ten days from the prior Julian calendar, to more closely align the years with actual movements of the earth about the sun. But the new calendar had been adopted under the authority of the Roman Catholic Pope Gregory XIII (1502–1585) and, worse yet, it had been named for that Pope. In 1673, Protestant England had not yet adopted this new calendar.

Prince James was a widower and had been involved with many lovers, but most of these women were rather plain — so much so that King Charles II had jokingly remarked to his brother that the women must have been suggested as a penance by James' confessor. James' new bride was a beauty and he was taken with her at first sight. Mary's first impression of her new husband was much the opposite.

Prince James and Mary were wed in a Protestant ceremony at Dover, England, on November 21, 1673. Mary of Modena was now Duchess of York and Albany. Her husband had been made Duke of York about the time of his baptism; however, the Scottish dukedom of Albany was not awarded to Prince James until 1660. Many works dealing with English history omit the Scottish title, Albany, for Mary's title, after her marriage, but prior to her coronation as England's Queen Consort. These works merely refer to Mary as the Duchess of York during that period.

At court, Prince James introduced his new wife to her stepdaughters, Princess Mary (1662–1694) and Princess Anne (1665–1714), as their new "playmate." He was not very wide of the mark in that assessment. Mary of Modena was far closer in age to both of James' daughters than she was to her new husband. It was not long before the three girls, all teenagers, formed a friendship.

The young Italian girl found England interesting, yet disquieting. During her first winter in England she delighted in pelting her husband with snowballs. Mary was puzzled that her two stepdaughters, Mary and Anne, both children of two Catholic parents, were not only Protestant, but very determined in their religious views. Mary of Modena had been so sheltered as a child that she didn't really know what a Protestant was.

Although Prince James was rather stuffy, he was quite handsome, and Mary eventually changed her first impression of him. Although she never fully adjusted to his continuing infidelities, it is fair to say that young Mary of Modena fell in love with her husband. The royal couple produced six named children:

> Princess Catherine (1675–1675)
> Princess Isabel (1676–1681)
> Prince Charles, Duke of Cambridge (1677–1677)
> Princess Charlotte (1682–1682)
> Prince James Francis Edward, Prince of Wales (1688–1766)
> Princess Louisa (1692–1712)

The person next in the line of succession to the throne in Protestant England was Mary's husband, Prince James, a Roman Catholic with a devout Catholic wife. James was not a mere passive concerning his Catholicism. Rather, he held the fire and zeal of a typical convert. Protestant England was wary, and the response was vigorous. In 1673 a Test Act was passed which forbade Catholics to hold many government positions. In 1678 a "Popish Plot" purported to reveal a scheme by Jesuits in England to assassinate King Charles II and thereby secure the succession of the Catholic James II. The "Popish Plot" was nothing but lies, but the lies were widely believed. A number of alleged "Popish" conspirators, including the secretary to Mary of Modena, Edward Coleman (–1678), and five Jesuit priests, were tried and executed. An Exclusion Crisis from 1679 to 1681 followed, during which parliament attempted to dictate the line of succession and direct that line away from the Catholic Prince James.

Because of the strong anti–Catholic sentiment, the King asked his Catholic brother to leave England to allow time for tempers to cool. Prince James complied and he took his wife, Mary, with him. In England, King Charles II fought courageously (and effectively) to preserve the established line of succession.

James issued declarations to comfort a wary kingdom and attempted to dispel notions that he was vindictive. Many Englishmen were very suspicious and believed that, once James came to the throne with his Catholic wife, Mary, their choice would be "the Mass or the stake." The hare-brained Rye House plot of 1683 was a product of this line of reasoning. In that failed plot, the royal brothers, King Charles and Prince James, were to be intercepted at the Rye House on their return from Newmarket, England. The plot failed, and its leaders were executed for treason.

On February 6, 1685, King Charles II died, and his eldest brother, James, acceded to the throne of England as King James II. The Anglican coronation was a gorgeous ceremony at Westminster Abbey. There, on April 23, 1685, James was crowned King of England, and Mary was crowned as his Queen Consort. The ceremonial words were Protestant, and the Catholic James refused to recite them. However, the Catholic Queen Consort, Mary, openly responded during the coronation ceremony.

A new Roman Catholic chapel was opened at Whitehall on Christmas Day, 1686. Grand new apartments were also erected at Whitehall for the new Queen Consort.

James had not been particularly modest about his Roman Catholic faith when he had been heir-apparent to the English throne. Now that he was King, he became vigorous in asserting important places for Catholics in England. King James II decided upon toleration as a first step toward a more profound goal, and he extended the protection of the crown to Nonconformist Protestants, as well as Catholics, in England.

The King had given commissions to several Catholic officers during an emergency, and he told parliament that he now had no intention to dismiss these Catholics. This was a violation of the Test Act of 1673, which restricted public offices to Anglicans, and therefore James' plan was illegal.

The Catholic King granted still more dispensations to Catholics, and he admitted Roman Catholic peers to the Privy Council. In 1686 King James II established an Ecclesiastical Commission with sweeping disciplinary powers. In the King's mind, the purpose of this body was to prevent Anglican clergymen from preaching against Catholicism.

The King's standing army had grown to impressive proportions. He camped the army near London where it would be noticeable, and allowed Mass to be celebrated in the army camp. For this purpose, a wooden chapel on wheels was placed in the center of the camp.

King James II continued his Catholic provocation. He attempted to install a Catholic as president of one of the colleges of Oxford University and received Count Ferdinand d'Adda as a papal nuncio. The King worked vigorously to prepare Catholics to sit in parliament and placed Catholics in municipal corporations. The composition of the judiciary was changed to contain perhaps a majority of non–Anglicans. Even the Pope and other Vatican officials cautioned James that his zeal might be excessive. He hardened his heart and strengthened his army.

The conduct of King James, in the short time that he had reigned, had disheartened a wide swath of his citizens. Whigs and Tories were now united against him. From peasant to well-to-do, Englishmen were threatened in "all they cared for in this world or the next."

In 1688 King James II issued a pro–Catholic second Declaration of Indulgence and ordered that it be read in all churches. Seven Anglican Bishops refused to comply. A trial was ordered, and the Bishops, who refused bail, were committed to the Tower of London. On June 10, 1688, while the trial of the Bishops was still pending, Mary of Modena, the Roman Catholic Queen Consort, gave birth to Prince James Francis Edward.

England, weary from a recent civil war and its horrible aftermath, may have been content to wait for King James II to die. With him would die the Catholic threat, because his two eldest children, Princess Mary (1662–1694) and Princess Anne (1665–1714), were both resolutely Protestant. However, now a legitimate male offspring had been born to the King and his Catholic wife. Baby Prince James became next in the line of succession to the throne. The legitimate heir to the throne was now a Catholic son, born to a Catholic King and a Catholic mother. In Anglican England, this would never do. Rumors were circulated, with vigor, that the birth of this child was a sham; that a baby had been smuggled in to validate the lie. The fact is that there was no sham and there was no lie. The Catholic baby, James Francis Edward, had merely been born at a very inconvenient moment in England's history. Though he was clearly next in the established line of succession, there was no possibility that England would allow him to take the throne.

The baby boy, whose birth would trigger a turning point in English history and its royal line of succession, was at first sickly. It was suggested that since all of Mary's previous children had died young, perhaps her breast milk was unhealthy. This reasoning was first tested by taking the baby from Mary's breast and feeding him a revolting gruel mixture. When young James' health continued to fail, a wet-nurse was summoned, and she breast-fed the infant back to health. No good deed goes long unpunished, and it was soon being bruited about that the wet nurse was the "real" mother of James Francis Edward.

Queen Mary of Modena made the eminently sensible suggestion to her husband that the birth of James Frances Edward should be celebrated by granting a general amnesty to all who were imprisoned in James' kingdom for religious offenses. King James II imperiously brushed that suggestion away.

English revolutionary leaders met and composed a letter inviting William of Orange (1650–1702) to invade England. During the last few months of his reign, King James II made a large number of dramatic concessions, abandoning previous positions, in order to preserve his reign. This was too little, too late.

In spite of his large standing army, the King found resistance to William's force impractical. He sent Mary and their newest baby, Prince James, to escape from England, and King James soon also left England, forever. Mary, her husband and her youngest child, James, Prince of Wales, took up residence in France, where they were very popular and treated with great courtesy.

The last child born to Mary and James was Princess Louisa, who was born in France on June 28, 1692.

Mary of Modena lived 17 years after the death of her husband in 1701, and there was much drama during those years because her son was alive and well and considered by many to be the rightful King of England. Those who supported the claims of the Prince of Wales to England's throne were known as Jacobites. To them, Prince James Francis Edward, Prince of Wales (1688–1766), was England's King James III. Since Protestant England successfully fought off that Catholic threat, history more accurately refers to James as "the Old Pretender."

The ultimate failure of Prince James to ascend to the throne of England followed a number of attempts and failures, most of which had an impact on the domestic tranquility of Mary of Modena, while she lived her final days in France. In addition to the emotional trauma of these events, they had a significant economic impact on Mary, when hordes of Jacobites arrived in France in need of financial aid. When King Louis XIV died in 1715, Mary's situation worsened. The new French regent was less supportive of Mary of Modena, and the growing hordes of Jacobite exiles in France reduced Mary to virtual penury.

Mary of Modena died at St.-Germain-en-Laye, France on May 7, 1718. She was buried at the nearby Roman Catholic Chaillot convent, where she had spent many happy hours.

20. *Princess Mary (1662–1694)*

Princess Mary came to the English throne as Queen Mary II in 1689, and ruled England as joint sovereign with her Husband, King William III (1650–1702). For Mary's biographical sketch, see the chapter entitled William and Mary.

21. *Princess Anne (1665–1714)*

A Declaration of Rights was given statutory form in December 1689, and, because of the provisions contained in this statute concerning succession to the throne of England, Anne acceded to the throne of England in 1702, upon the death of King William III. For Anne's biographical sketch, see the chapter entitled Queen Anne.

22. *Prince James Francis Edward, Prince of Wales (1688–1766)*

The first son of King James II (1633–1701) to be named James was born July 12, 1663. He was Prince James, Duke of Cambridge (1663–1667). His mother was Anne Hyde (1637–1671), and he died in infancy.

Queen Mary of Modena (1658–1718) was the second wife of King James II, and she was the mother of the second son of King James II named James. He was born at St. James' palace on June 10, 1688, and his birth triggered immediate political trauma for England, because he was a Roman Catholic and, as a male heir, the existing royal line of succession moved him above both of his Protestant sisters, Princess Mary (1662–1694) and Princess Anne (1665–1714).

The birth of Prince James brought to an immediate head a fundamental religious tension that had been brewing in England since the time of King Henry VIII (1491–1547). It was not a question of separation of church and state. The Church of England had been recognized as the established religion of the kingdom for centuries. Rather, the dispute centered on whether that established religion should be the Roman Catholic Church or Protestantism's Anglican denomination. Contention over this fundamental issue had been sublimated with varying degrees of success from the time of King Henry VIII until the birth of Prince James Francis Edward (1688–1766).

Rumors were circulated, with vigor, that the birth of this child was a sham, that a baby had been smuggled in to validate the lie. The fact is that there was no sham and there was no lie. The Catholic baby, James Francis Edward, had merely been born at a very inconvenient moment in England's history. Though he was clearly next in the established line of succession, there was no possibility that England would allow him to take the throne. The baby was hastily baptized as a Catholic, within 24 hours of his birth, by Ferdinand d'Adda, the papal nuncio, who was resident in London. King James II gave his new baby son the title Prince of Wales. That title is not hereditary, but it is reserved for the male heir to the throne of England. At his public baptism on October 15, 1688, James Francis Edward was described as "H. R. H., the Prince of Wales."

The baby boy, whose birth would trigger a turning point in English history and its royal line of succession, was at first sickly. It was suggested that since all of Mary's previous children had died young, perhaps her breast milk was unhealthy. This reasoning was first tested by taking the baby from Mary's breast and feeding him a revolting gruel mixture. When young James' health continued to fail, a wet-nurse, Mrs. Frances Smith, was summoned, and she breast-fed the infant back to health. It was soon being bruited about that Mrs. Smith was the "real" mother of James Francis Edward.

English revolutionary leaders met and composed a letter inviting William of Orange (1650–1702) to invade England. In spite of his large standing army, the King found resistance to William's force impractical. He sent his wife, Queen Mary of Modena, and their newest baby, Prince James, to escape from England. King James also soon left England, forever. In his place, there came to the throne of England King William III (1650–1702), who ruled as joint sovereign with his wife, Queen Mary II (1662–1694).

Queen Mary of Modena, King James II, and their youngest child, James, Prince of Wales, took up residence in France, where they were very popular and treated with great courtesy.

Mary of Modena lived 17 years after the death of her husband in 1701, and there was much drama during those years because her son was alive and well and considered by many to be the rightful King of England. Those who supported the claims of the Prince of Wales to England's throne were known as "Jacobites." That term derived from the Latin version of the name for "James," which is *Jacobus*. To the Jacobites, Prince James Francis Edward, Prince of Wales (1688–1766), was England's King James III.

This biographical sketch centers on the role of Prince James (1688–1766) as it relates to the throne of England, but the thrones of England and Scotland had been united since the time that Scotland's King James VI (1566–1625) acceded to the throne of England in 1603. That earlier James' name was thenceforth styled King James I of England and King James VI of Scotland. Thus the Jacobites claimed Scotland as well as England, and the most dramatic military activity on behalf of the Jacobite movement centered in Scotland during the life of Prince James.

The French King, Louis XIV (1638–1715), was a Roman Catholic and a vigorous proponent of the notion that Catholicism should be the Church of England. The French King proposed that upon the eventual death of King William III of England, Prince James should replace him as King James III of England. Both King James II and Queen Mary of Modena rejected that idea and indicated that it was inappropriate for the son to take the throne as long as his father, King James II, was alive. However, in 1701, when King James II died, the French King, Louis XIV, lost little time in proclaiming Prince James as King of England.

Perhaps the following table will help the reader follow the flurry of activities, actions and reactions during the period when the Jacobite movement still hoped that Prince James (1688–1766) would attain the throne of England:

1688	Birth of Prince James Francis Edward, Prince of Wales (1688–1766).
1689	A declaration of Rights is given statutory form by the English parliament. It provides for the accession to the throne of England of King William (1650–1702), jointly with Queen Mary II (1662–1694), and later for that of Queen Anne (1665–1714).
1694	Death of Queen Mary II, joint sovereign of England. King William III continues as England's monarch.
1696	Jacobite plot to assassinate King William III fails.
1700	Death of Prince William (1689–1700), the only surviving child of the Protestant Princess Anne (1665–1714), who later ruled England as Queen Anne.
1701	Settlement Act of 1701 sets aside the claims of numerous Roman Catholics to the throne of England in favor of Sophia, Electress of Hanover (1630–1714), a Protestant granddaughter of King James I (1566–1625).
1701	Death of England's King James II (1633–1701) in France.

1701	King Louis XIV of France proclaims Prince James as King of England.
1701	Parliament passes a bill of attainder against Prince James.
1702	Death of England's King William III leaving no legitimate children.
1702	Queen Anne takes the throne of England.
1705	King Louis XIV of France hears reports that Scotland will support the Jacobite cause and begins fitting an expedition, but it is doomed by false starts and bad weather.
1708	Prince James attempts an invasion of Scotland, but is driven away by the British fleet before landing.
1713	Prince James is expelled from France because of terms of the treaty of Utrecht, but he is welcomed in Lorraine.
1714	Prince James refuses suggestions that he renounce Catholicism and convert to the Anglican Church of England in the hope that he would thus become heir to the throne after Queen Anne.
1714	Death of Sophia, Electress of Hanover, seven weeks before the death of England's Queen Anne.
1714	Death of Queen Anne, leaving no surviving children.
1714	King George I (1660–1727) accedes to throne of England.
1715	The French King, Louis XIV, dies on September 1.
1715	John Erskine, Earl of Mar (1675–1732), leads Jacobite uprising in Scotland. That coup meets defeat, but news reaches Continental Europe of success and Prince James again lands in Scotland intent on seizing the throne, this time from King George I.
1716	Prince James' Scottish invasion fails, and James flees to France, never to return to the British Isles.
1717	Prince James takes up residence in Italy.
1718–1719	Cardinal Julio Alberoni (1664–1752), prime minister of Spain, encourages forces loyal to Prince James. Nothing comes of it.

Had Prince James Francis Edward been allowed to take the English throne upon the death of his father, King James II, he would have ruled England for 64 years, longer than any English monarch, including, by a few months, Queen Victoria (1819–1901).

But we have not seen the last of the Jacobites. On May 28, 1719, Prince James (1688–1766) married (by proxy, while he was in Madrid, Spain) Maria Clementina Sobieski (1702–1735). Maria was a granddaughter of the former King of Poland, John III Sobieski (1629–1696). The marriage of Prince James and Maria Sobieski was not a harmonious union, but it did produce two children:

Charles Edward Louis John Casimir Silvester Maria Stuart (1720–1788)
Henry Benedict Thomas Edward Maria Clement Francis Xavier Stuart (1725–1807)

The surnames Stuart at the end of the lengthy names of Charles and Henry may seem strangely out of place. After all, the royal House of Stuart had ruled Scotland from 1371 to 1689, and also acquired the thrones of England and Ireland, starting in 1603. Even when King James II (1633–1701) was forced from the throne, royal Stuart blood was represented on the throne in the persons of Queen Mary II (1662–1694) and Queen Anne (1665–1714). Until that chain began to break, with the birth of Prince James (1688–1766), it had been rather redundant to tack the surname Stuart on the names of the members of the royal family. But the Stuart surname is inserted here intentionally. To Jacobites, it gave validity to their claims to the English throne.

The never-say-die Jacobites gave "titles" to both of these children: Charles III to the first, and Henry IX to the second. However, Henry became a Catholic priest and advanced to be a cardinal. For whatever practical purposes survived in the Jacobite movement, "Charles III" was to be the champion. History knows him as the "Young Pretender," while his father, Prince James (1688–1766), is dubbed the "Old Pretender." The Jacobite movement's last gasps were heard in 1745, and 1746, when the "Young Pretender" and his forces invaded England and were defeated.

The subject of our sketch, Prince James (1688–1766), lost interest in becoming King of England when he was still a relatively young man. In 1727 he was given a papal pension. Although Prince James gave some financial assistance to his elder son's 1745–1746 military efforts in England, his active days on the royal stage ended several years earlier.

Prince James Francis Edward died on January 1, 1766, in Rome, in the Papal States. He was buried there at St. Peter's basilica.

23. *Princess Louisa (1692–1712)*

Princess Louisa was born at St.-Germain-en-Laye, near Paris, France, on June 28, 1692. This daughter of King James II (1633–1701) and Queen Mary of Modena (1658–1718) was born while the royal couple were in exile in France, and she was the last child born to them. Since questions of validity had plagued King James II and Queen Mary of Modena about the birth of their previous child, Prince James Francis Edward, Prince of Wales (1688–1766), no effort was spared to provide appropriate witnesses for Princess Louisa's birth.

In attendance to view the birth were the chancellor of France, the president of the parliament of Paris, the archbishop of Paris and the wife of the Danish ambassador to France. In addition there were many, if not all, French princesses of royal blood, as well as some noble English ladies at the court at St.-Germain-en-Laye. One would think this list adequate to attest to the historical fact of the birth, on this day, at this location, to Queen Mary of Modena, but Mary and James had been burned before by false allegations of a fraudulent birth. In addition to those who attended the birth, King James II had extended invitations to a cast of hundreds in Great Britain. Early in 1692, he had announced the expectation that a child would be born to his wife and he invited his eldest daughter, England's Queen Mary II (1662–1694), to be present to attest to the birth. James also extended the same invitation to all the peers and peeresses of Great Britain and promised that the King of France, Louis XIV (1638–1715), would grant safe conduct for the voyage, and return, to all who chose to come. By the time that the birth was imminent, tensions developed between France and Great Britain to thwart the feasibility of visitors from Great Britain, but the gesture had been made, and a sweeping gesture it was.

King James II had hoped for a boy, but received his new daughter with a tender caress and expressed joy to Mary of Modena: "See what heaven has sent us to be our comforter in the land of exile."

Louisa was baptized with great pomp in the Roman Catholic chapel of St. Louis at St.-Germain-en-Laye. The French King, Louis XIV, returned from the siege of Mons in time to attend her baptism as godfather. The French King's sister-in-law, Elisabeth Charlotte, Duchess of Orleans (1652–1722), was Louisa's godmother. The French ladies present at the ceremony were astonished to see the tiny baby dressed in robes of state, complete with shoes and stockings, for the baptism. The exiled Queen Mary of Modena was much admired at the French court, and her fashion ideas for the baptism of her child were considered worthy of emulation.

The baby's full given name was Louisa Maria Theresa. The names Louisa and Maria were bestowed during the baptism, while the given name, Theresa, was added later, presumably at her Catholic confirmation ceremony.

Louisa was only four years younger than her brother, Prince James Francis Edward, Prince of Wales (1688–1766), and they were raised together in France. The surname of both of these children was, of course, Stuart, although that surname is often omitted. After all, the royal House of Stuart had ruled Scotland from 1371 to 1689, and also acquired the thrones of England and Ireland, starting in 1603. Even when King James II (1633–1701) was forced from the throne, royal Stuart blood was represented on the throne in the persons of Queen Mary II (1662–1694), and Queen Anne (1665–1714). Until that chain began to break with the birth of Prince James (1688–1766), it had been rather redundant to tack the surname Stuart onto the names of the members of the royal family.

Louisa learned at an early age the significance of her surname and the meaning of the term "Jacobite." In Louisa's mind, Jacobite families had sacrificed their lands and their livings for the sake of her father's crown. Princess Louisa personally paid from her own funds for the education of several daughters of Jacobites, who were living in France. Although much of the drama of the Jacobite movement may be viewed as attempts to secure justice for Catholic members of the English royal family, as far as Louisa was concerned, the issues were larger than religious differences, and the beneficiaries of Louisa's educational stipends included Protestant, as well as Catholic, girls.

Louisa's governess is referred to in some accounts as the Countess of Middleton, in others as Lady Middleton. Her tutor was a learned Roman Catholic priest, Father Constable, who instructed his young charge in Latin and history as well as religious topics.

Contemporary accounts describe young Louisa as an engaging, high-spirited child. James Drummond, Earl of Perth (1648–1716), a Jacobite in France, who was well acquainted with both Princess Louisa and her brother, Prince James, praised the affability that seemed to come naturally to Louisa.

In June 1701, both Queen Mary of Modena and her ill husband, King James II, returned to St.-Germain. They had been away tending to the illness of the exiled King, but they returned to celebrate the June birthdays of both of their children, Prince James and Princess Louisa. It was the thirteenth birthday of Prince James on the tenth of June, and the ninth birthday of Princess Louisa on June 28. *Fêtes*, or "celebrations," were held on both of these birthdays for the Prince and Princess and for the children of Jacobite exiles. Two months later, King James II suffered a stroke, and he died two weeks after that stroke. Fortunately he was still of sound mind when his two exiled children paid their final visits to him. After embracing and blessing Louisa he said to her, "Adieu, my dear child. Serve your Creator in the days of your youth. Consider virtue as the greatest ornament of your sex. Follow close the great pattern of it, your mother, who has been, no less than myself, over-clouded with calumny; but time, the mother of truth, will, I hope, at last make her virtues shine as bright as the sun." (To avoid any possibility of misunderstanding, let the record show that although King James II was guilty of adultery on many occasions, there never was any hint that his wife, Queen Mary of Modena, was untrue. The "calumny" to which James referred to here no doubt involved the anti–Catholic hysteria and related anti–Mary of Modena hysteria, earlier, in England.)

Upon the death, in 1701, of England's King James II, in absentia in France, the French King, Louis XIV, proclaimed Princess Louisa's brother, Prince James (1688–1766), as King of England. Louisa and her brother, James, were taken to Passy. There the two royal children were cared for by Antoine Nompar de Caumont, Duke of Lauzun (1633–1723), and his duchess of Lauzun. The Countess of Middleton continued at Passy as governess to Princess Louisa. Louisa made her first holy communion in 1704.

Princess Louisa had inherited her mother's beauty. Louisa's godmother, the Duchess of Orleans, referred to that beauty and said that the girl's eyes were even more beautiful than those of her mother. In July 1705, the 13-year-old English Princess was a highly honored guest at a ball held at Marli. She was given an armchair of honor at the upper end of a long, spacious saloon, second in rank only to the three armchairs occupied by the King of France, Louisa's mother, the widowed Queen Consort of England, and Louisa's brother, who, at least in the mind of the

French King, was now England's King James III, in absentia. Thus Princess Louisa was seated above the French princesses, who were only entitled to folding chairs. When Princess Louisa and her brother, James, danced together, King Louis XIV paid them the respect of standing throughout their dance. He did this two or three more times, until Mary of Modena graciously thanked him, but asked that the 67-year-old King stand no more.

Louisa enjoyed dancing and also took pleasure in the opera. She was a very popular personage at the French court. The possibility of a marriage between Princess Louisa and the youngest grandson of the French King, Louis XIV, was a topic of conversation. That grandson was Charles Ferdinand de Bourbon, Duke of Berry (1685–1714). Peggy Miller's 1971 work, entitled *James,* refers to the Duke of Berry as "...certainly an eligible young man, being Louis' youngest grandson and the one he seemed to prefer. He was reasonably good-looking, amiable, well-behaved and, although not religious, he was more so than the other grandchildren of the King." One source indicates that the potential for romance never bloomed here because Princess Louisa wanted to remain with her mother as long as the mother lived. Another source indicates that, as the grandson of the aging King of France, the Duke of Berry needed a bride with a clearer hold on one of Europe's royal houses. In any event, the two went their separate ways and both died young.

Sweden's King Charles XII (1682–1718), who had been that kingdom's monarch since 1697, was also suggested as a potential mate for Princess Louisa. However, he was not a Roman Catholic, and Louisa's mother had other concerns about that potential match, and it was dropped.

For whatever reasons, Princess Louisa never married, nor did she have any children.

When Prince James and Princess Louisa were children, the Prince was rather sickly, while the Princess had a more rugged constitution. In April 1712, both James and Louisa contracted smallpox. Ironically, James recovered and went on to live another 54 years, but Louisa was felled by the dread disease and died at St.-Germain-en-Laye, near Paris, France. The date of her death is given by some very reputable authorities as April 8, but other equally reputable sources place the date as April 18. Presumably the discrepancy arises from our old nemesis, the Julian versus Gregorian calendar. If so, according to the calendar now in use throughout all of Europe and the entire English-speaking world, Princess Louisa died on April 18, 1712.

Princess Louisa's body was taken to the taken to the Church of the English Benedictines, on the Rue St.-Jacques in Paris, to be placed next to the remains of her father, King James II.

WILLIAM AND MARY

On February 13, 1689, King William III and his wife, Queen Mary II, were proclaimed joint monarchs of England. Their coronation was at Westminster Abbey on April 11, 1689. William and Mary ruled as joint sovereigns until the death of Queen Mary II on December 28, 1694. After Mary's death, William ruled alone until his death on March 8, 1702. The royal couple had no children.

24. *King William III (1650–1702)*

William was born in The Hague, Holland, on November 4, 1650. His mother was England's Princess Royal, Princess Mary (1631–1660), and his father was William II (1626–1650), Prince of Orange and stadtholder of several Dutch states. William III was born eight days after his father's death, on his mother's nineteenth birthday.

The baby's cradle was swathed in black, in mourning for the recently departed William II. Since the office of stadtholder and the title Prince of Orange were not hereditary, the baby did not succeed to these titles immediately upon birth. Even the baby's name was an issue. The mother, Princess Mary, wanted the child to be named Charles in honor of her father, England's King Charles I (1600–1649), who recently had been beheaded. But, the paternal grandmother, Amalia van Solms (1602–1675), insisted that the child be named William, and the grandmother's wish prevailed. It was probably the better choice. The baby's great-grandfather had been William I, Prince of Orange (1533–1584), the founder of the Dutch Republic and its first stadtholder. Also, of course, the baby's father, William II, Prince of Orange (1626–1650), had William as his given name. Mary lost at the naming game, and she only got half of the legal guardianship of her only child. One-half was the most that she could coax from the Dutch court that heard the dispute in 1651. When Mary attained her full majority (in her mid–20s), in accordance with the terms of her husband's will, Mary was acknowledged by the parliament of Orange as the sole regent for her son.

In 1650, when William III was born in the Dutch Republic, the monarchy had been banished in England with the execution of King Charles I, and Oliver Cromwell (1599–1658) was ruling England as a dictator. Cromwell was relatively popular with the Dutch, and William's mother, the imperious Princess Mary, the Princess Royal, did little to ingratiate herself with the Dutch people.

While affection for young William was not automatic, the rigid Dutch made certain that written instructions, in minute detail, were prepared to guide his secular and religious training. By 1654, Constantijn Huygens (1596–1687) had compiled these written instructions, 412 paragraphs in length. Reverend Cornelius Trigland was appointed as the boy's chaplain, Abraham Ranguineau was chosen to supervise William's secular instruction, and Mrs. Walburg Howard van Kerckhoven was his governess. A program of physical education was also on the menu, although care was taken in this area because of the poor stamina of the frail, asthmatic William.

William later studied at Leiden University, the oldest university in the United Provinces and one of the most distinguished in Europe.

William was the only child of William II (1626–1650), Prince of Orange, but the titles Prince of Orange and stadtholder were not an hereditary right, and our William acquired his titles a bit at a time. He was made Prince of Orange in 1650. In 1660 William's mother died, and guardianship was left to his paternal uncle, Frederick William, Elector of Brandenburg (1640–1688). In 1666 or 1667, William was made a ward of the Dutch states by the States-General and, in 1668, he was given the title first noble of Zeeland.

In 1672 French forces successfully invaded the Netherlands. Johan de Witt (1625–1672), Pensionary of Holland, was wounded, and his leadership was discredited. Prince William of Orange was elected captain-general and admiral and, although there had been an earlier decree (the Perpetual Edict of 1667) that the offices of stadtholder and captain-general (which formerly had been held simultaneously by the Princes of Orange) should never again be held by the same person, the wisdom of that policy was reassessed, and William III, Prince of Orange, was made stadtholder of various Dutch states in stages, starting in 1672 when he was named stadtholder of Holland, Zeeland, Utrecht and Westerwolde. In 1675 Gelderland and Overijssel were added to the list of states of which William III was stadtholder.

In England, Thomas Osborne, Earl of Danby (1632–1712), had been busy on the diplomatic front. He arranged a peace between England and Holland, and also was responsible for arranging the marriage of the Dutch Prince William of Orange, William III, to Princess Mary (1662–1694), the eldest daughter of England's Prince James (1633–1701). At that time, King Charles II (1630–1685) was England's King, but he had no legitimate children. His eldest brother, Prince James, was next in the established line of succession. Thus Princess Mary was a worthy bride from the Dutch perspective.

Princess Mary was a first cousin of the Prince of Orange. He had met her in 1670 on his first visit to England. On November 4, 1677, Prince William III of Orange and Princess Mary of England were married at St. James' Palace in England. Although Mary had little enthusiasm for the prospect of living the rest of her years in the Netherlands, it was there that the royal couple went to live. They brought with them one Elizabeth Villiers (–1733) to serve as a maid of honor to Mary and as a mistress to William of Orange. The less said about this arrangement the better, for it is a difficult one to understand. William's sexual interests apparently were bisexual. The marriage of William and Mary produced no children, but the couple did have some sexual activity. Mary was rumored to have suffered two miscarriages while living in Holland.

The dramatic political events surrounding the English royal family are central to our biographical sketch of William III of Orange. In 1685 England's King Charles II died, and his eldest brother, James, came to the throne as King James II (1633–1701). James was a Roman Catholic and his Queen Consort was also a practicing Catholic. England was not only Protestant in name, but thoroughly Protestant in temperament. Because of that religious attitude, some rather extreme measures had been tried to prevent the accession of James to the throne, but they failed. Protestant England was comforted by the fact that none of the children born to James' second (Catholic) wife had survived infancy. England, weary from a recent civil war and its horrible aftermath, may well have been content to wait for King James II to die. With him would die the Catholic threat, because his two eldest children (both from his first marriage), Princess Mary (1662–1694) and Princess Anne (1665–1714), were both resolutely Protestant.

This patient and reasonable plan was foiled on June 10, 1688, when the Roman Catholic Queen Consort gave birth to Prince James Francis Edward (1688–1766). Now a legitimate male offspring had been born to the King. Baby Prince James became next in the line of succession to the throne. The legitimate heir to the throne was now a Catholic son, born to a Catholic King and a Catholic mother. In Anglican England, this would never do. Rumors were circulated, with vigor, that the birth of this child was a sham, that a baby had been smuggled in to validate the lie. The truth is that there was no sham and there was no lie. The Catholic baby, James Francis Edward, had merely been born at a very inconvenient moment in England's history. Though he was clearly next in the established line of succession, there was no possibility that England would allow him to take the throne.

Revolutionary leaders met and composed a letter inviting Prince William III of Orange to invade England.

Since French troops were menacing both Dutch and German states when these events in England unfolded, it was not clear that the Dutch States-General would grant William permission to leave to fight in England. However, the permission was received, and William of Orange sailed toward England with a force of some

14,000 regular Dutch troops. In addition to those, William had with him French Huguenot volunteers—Swedes, Danes, Prussians, English and Scottish. In all, his forces numbered more than 21,000 men. When William landed, his allies were already in place, and as he moved toward London, city after city in England revolted against King James II. In spite of his large standing army, the King found resistance to William's force impractical. He sent his Queen Consort and their newest baby, Prince James, to escape from England, and King James II soon made his own escape.

The English parliament met on January 28, 1689, and declared that King James II had abdicated his throne when he fled from England. This opened the door for a new monarch and it was obvious whom England wanted for its new monarch: Princess Mary (1662–1694), the Protestant eldest daughter of the recently deposed King James II. William of Orange rejected that notion and further rejected accepting England's crown by right of conquest. A suggestion was made that William might have a role rather like that of a consort. William demurred, stating that he was not prepared "to become his wife's gentleman-usher." William demanded and received nothing less than joint monarchy with his wife, Mary. The conquering hero's demands were accepted and, on February 13, 1689, William and Mary were proclaimed as joint sovereigns of England, to rule as King William III and Queen Mary II. Before their joint coronation, King James II began an attempt to regain his kingdom. James' initial efforts were in Ireland, where his Roman Catholic support was strong. On April 11, 1689, King William III and Queen Mary II were crowned at Westminster Abbey.

On July 1, 1690, King William's forces defeated King James II's Irish forces and William later subjugated Scotland as well. In achieving victory in Scotland, William's troops committed a brutal atrocity. It was the massacre of the men, women and children of the MacDonald clan in February 1692. *The Oxford Illustrated History of the British Monarchy* by John Cannon and Ralph Griffiths, published in 1998, cites two features that made the massacre all the more odious: (1) it was based on a legal technicality concerning a deadline, and (2) "the soldiers who shot and bayoneted their victims had been quartered upon them and had lived with them on terms of friendship for eleven days." The extent of personal guilt attributable to King William III is in doubt, but Cannon and Griffiths assure us that the King "showed no great zeal in punishing the guilty."

Since there was no separation of church and state in England, William and Mary were the leaders of the Anglican Church of England. William took no interest in church affairs and left those matters in the hands of Queen Mary II. King William III elevated his Dutch friends to English positions of political and military importance, and William often left the kingdom to pursue the matter of greatest interest to him, the struggle to contain the aggressions of the French King, Louis XIV (1638–1715).

It has been observed, with some accuracy, that England's King William III cared less for Great Britain than for the European continent. Personal affection and whim accounted for some of this, but much of the attention toward the

European continent was forced upon King William III by the French King, Louis XIV, and his insatiable appetite for conquest.

In 1689, in an attempt to contain French ambitions, King William III brought England into the league of Augsburg, which thereafter was known as the Grand Alliance. If William had possessed an ounce or two of charisma, the English people might have found reasons to excuse his disinterest in England and its domestic affairs, but William was anything but charismatic. He had been raised in the forbidding doctrines of the Calvinist religion and he was cold. He was not cruel, being far too pragmatic to waste time on minor revenges. William's lack of social graces was notorious. At meals, he was silent, surly, and indifferent to women. He grumbled about the defects of London.

However, the military and diplomatic accomplishments of King William III were great. Whatever skill he lacked as a military tactician, he more than made up for in the diplomatic arena, and although William did not live to see the final results, much of his work against the French King Louis XIV was effective. The treaty of Ryswick in 1697 formally ended the Grand Alliance. In that treaty, the French King surrendered much of the territory that he had captured.

In 1694 King William lost his wife, Queen Mary II, to smallpox. He had treated her rather shabbily during much of their life, but his grief at losing her was very real. After Mary's death, William carried a lock of her hair with him at all times.

From 1696 to 1699, England pursued a policy of weakening its military strength, and King William was so depressed by England's isolationist tilt that he seriously considered abdicating his throne and returning to Holland.

In 1700 Prince William, Duke of Gloucester (1689–1700), died. He was the only surviving child of Princess Anne (1665–1714). In response, parliament passed, in 1701, an Act of Settlement, to protect the Protestant line of succession to the English throne, and *en passant*, to express some unhappiness with King William III. The act specified that the House of Hanover (known to be thoroughly Protestant) would be next in the line of succession after the death of Princess (later Queen) Anne. The act also specified that no foreign-born monarch could wage Continental wars without consent and that the foreigners were not to sit in parliament nor on the Privy Council.

On February 21, 1702, the horse, on which King William III was riding, stumbled in a mole hole and the King was thrown to the ground. The King broke his collarbone, which should not have been a fatal wound, but he was not a particularly good patient, and bad luck played a role as well. King William III died on March 8, 1702. He had been invited to England to save the kingdom from Catholicism and he had succeeded in that. The marriage of William and Mary had produced no children. Queen Mary II died first. Then, upon the death of King William III, his Protestant sister-in-law acceded to the throne as Queen Anne (1665–1714).

Gratitude is rarely a commodity with a lengthy life span, but in the case of King William III, it was appallingly short. The funeral of King William III was held at midnight and was private to the point of obscurity. The Privy Council ordered a monument for the King's burial place in Westminster Abbey, but it was never erected.

The English author Daniel Defoe (–1731) was among those who were shocked at the ingratitude of the English people toward their King. Defoe was an admirer of King William III, and he wrote a stinging satire against the English people entitled *The Consolidator*. It was published in 1705.

25. *Queen Mary II (1662–1694)*

Princess Mary was born on April 30, 1662, at St. James' Palace. Her father was England's Prince James (1633–1701), who later ruled England as King James II. Mary's mother was Anne Hyde (1637–1671), the first wife of Prince James. Mary was the second child born to James and Anne, and since the first-born, Prince Charles, Duke of Cambridge (1660–1661), died in infancy, Mary was the first child of Prince James' to live beyond infancy. That fact would soon be very important in the turbulent English royal line of succession.

Mary's father's family had held the English throne for several generations, but Mary's mother, Anne Hyde, needs a word or two of introduction. Anne Hyde's father was Edward Hyde, later Earl of Clarendon (1609–1674), a very influential English statesman. Anne's mother was Hyde's second wife, Frances Aylesbury (1617–1667), a daughter of Sir Thomas Aylesbury. Anne Hyde was the eldest child of this marriage and the eldest child of Edward Hyde, since his first marriage, to Anne Ayliffe, had produced no children.

When the monarchy was restored in England in 1660, Prince James returned to England. Edward Hyde also returned then to assist England's new King, Charles II (1630–1685). Once established in England, Hyde sent for his wife and daughter, Anne, to join him. Hyde was thinking of marriage prospects for his daughter, Anne, and had one possibility in mind. However, soon after Anne and her mother arrived in England, Edward Hyde learned that his daughter, Anne, was pregnant by Prince James. Edward Hyde was furious. King Charles II took steps to calm Edward Hyde's fury, and among the steps he took was ordering Prince James to marry Anne Hyde. This was done, but had the first child born of that marriage survived, there would have been doubts about its legitimacy.

When Princess Mary was born in 1662, there were no doubts about her legitimacy, but the bad feelings surrounding the marriage of Prince James and Anne Hyde were recent enough to sour the atmosphere.

E. Thornton Cook describes Mary's early life in a work entitled *Royal Marys: Princess Mary & Her Predecessors*: "Mary's nursery was in her grandfather Lord Clarendon's house at Twickenham but she was often at St. James' and Hampton Court. She can never have lacked for playmates, for both brothers and sisters came in quick succession to share her establishment and Lady Francis Villiers, under whose care the royal children lived, had six daughters of her own." Two Anglican chaplains were provided as tutors to Princess Mary and Princess Anne. These tutors were Dr. Edward Lake (1641–1704) and Dr. Doughtie.

Princess Mary was destined to face a large amount of death before she had even become a teenager. All of her legitimate siblings, except Princess Anne (1665–1714), died by 1671, and in March 1671, before her ninth birthday, Princess Mary's mother died. Her father soon remarried, to a 15-year-old Italian beauty, Mary of Modena (1658–1718). When Prince James introduced his new wife to Princess Mary and Princess Anne as "their new playmate," he was not wide of the mark. Mary of Modena was far closer in age to both of James' daughters than she was to her new husband. It was not long before the three girls were all teenagers, and together they formed a friendship.

Since the stepmother of the two royal princesses, Princess Mary and Princess Anne, was a Roman Catholic, and since it was becoming rather well known that their father, Prince James, had also converted to that faith, England's reigning monarch, King Charles II, felt obliged to assure the kingdom concerning the religious faith practiced by the two royal princesses. Dr. Lake and Dr. Doughtie had been doing their duty. They had given the two royal princesses meticulous instruction in the dogma of the Anglican Church of England, and had led them in daily prayers and in devotions on appropriate saints' days. King Charles II wanted a vigorous Anglican to lead the debate with Prince James, the Catholic father of Princess Mary and Princess Anne, concerning the faith in which they would be confirmed. This was necessary because Prince James was no mere nominal Catholic. He had all the fire and enthusiasm for his new faith of a typical convert, but no faith other than the Anglican Church of England would do for the confirmation of Princesses Mary and Anne. To combat the father's Roman Catholic influence, King Charles II appointed Henry Compton (1632–1713), the Anglican Bishop of London, as spiritual mentor to Princess Mary and Princess Anne to buttress their Anglican faith.

Thoughts began to wander toward a potential mate for Princess Mary. Since King Charles II showed little prospect of producing a legitimate heir, his eldest brother, James, was next in line for the English throne, and after James came his eldest daughter, Princess Mary. Romance and personal preferences mattered little when the high stakes game of royal marriage was played. Early consideration was given to William III, Prince of Orange (1650–1702), who was captain-general and admiral of Dutch forces and stadtholder of several Dutch states. Another possibility considered worthy of Princess Mary's hand in marriage was the dauphin, or heir apparent to the throne of France. However, the Dutch states were at war with France, so an overture to either party might anger the other.

It fell to England's Thomas Osborne, Earl of Danby (1632–1712), to attend to some important diplomatic efforts. Danby arranged both a peace between England and Holland and, also, the marriage of the Dutch Prince William III of Orange to England's Princess Mary. If royal English brides were given a vote in such matters, the marriage negotiations would surely have aborted. Prince William was in poor health, rude, ill tempered, and not at all handsome. Although Princess Mary was not a beauty, her appearance was statuesque, perhaps even pretty, and far superior to that of the Dutch William. Mary was five feet eleven inches tall; William was just a shade above five feet six. Princess Mary hated the thought of leaving England to live in Holland, but that is what she would have to do if the match were carried to conclusion.

England's King Charles II made the marriage decision on behalf of England, and instructed his brother, Prince James, to tell the bride-to-be. Prince James obeyed and Princess Mary wept, but the wedding was held. Prince William III of Orange and Princess Mary were first cousins. They had little else in common. On November 4, 1677, Prince William and Princess Mary were married at St. James' Palace in England. Although Mary had no enthusiasm for the prospect of living the rest of her years in the Netherlands, it was there that the royal couple went to live. They brought with them one Elizabeth Villiers (–1733) to serve as a maid of honor to Mary and as a mistress to Prince William of Orange. The less said about this arrangement the better, for it is a difficult one to understand. William's sexual interests apparently were bisexual. The marriage of William and Mary produced no children, but the couple did have some sexual activity. Mary was rumored to have suffered two miscarriages while living in Holland.

Although Princess Mary was not delighted by the prospect of spending her remaining life in Holland, by the time she had been greeted by a tremendous reception in The Hague, Mary was at least full of curiosity to see these Dutch people, about whom she had heard much, but knew very little. For their part, the Dutch people were anxious to see and meet Mary. The grand reception that was held for the bride and groom was the sort of affair that William normally detested. When the coaches, which carried William and Mary, reached the bridge at the entrance to The Hague, a 31-gun salute was fired in their honor. In their 1973 work entitled *William & Mary*, Barbara Van der Zee and Henri Van der Zee provide a colorful word picture: Twenty-four young girls, "all dressed in white, surrounded the coach, scattering sweet herbs and singing songs of praise as the Prince and Princess of Orange drove slowly into town. The streets were lined with cheering crowds and decorated with garlands and arches loaded with oranges."

Mary made an excellent impression on her new countrymen. One contemporary account described her as "beautiful, young and good and praised by everyone," and the "regal bearing of the young girl" was also noted. Mary was then just a girl of 15 years.

In Holland, Mary's husband was a militant leader of Protestant forces allied against the Catholic King, Louis XIV (1638–1715), of France. William had married Princess Mary as a political expedient, and he found his child bride to be rather boring. William much preferred the company of Elizabeth Villiers (–1733), and Mary was often left alone, rather like a lonely only child. She read, painted, and made an occasional excursion on a barge.

While William may have found the company of young Mary to be boring, she found her husband to be a tyrant, intent on teaching her the proper behavior he expected of an ideal wife. However, matters improved as time went on. Mary took an interest in gardening and became an avid collector of blue and white china.

William and Mary became devotedly attached to each other, and Mary adapted well to life in Holland.

Word reached Holland that a male heir to the throne of England had allegedly been born to Mary's Roman Catholic father, King James II, and Mary's stepmother. At least initially, Mary accepted as fact the widely spread rumor that the birth of Prince James Francis Edward (1688–1766) was a sham, that a baby had been smuggled in to cover the lie. The truth is that there was no sham and there was no lie. The Catholic baby, James Francis Edward, had merely been born at a very inconvenient moment in England's history. Though he was clearly next in the established line of succession, there was no possibility that England would allow him to take the throne.

In England, revolutionary leaders met and composed a letter inviting Prince William III of Orange to invade England. He accepted that invitation, routed the forces of King James II and forced King James to flee from England. The English parliament met on January 28, 1689, and declared that King James II had abdicated his throne when he fled from England. This opened the door for a new monarch, and it was obvious whom England wanted for its new monarch: Princess Mary (1662–1694), the Protestant eldest daughter of the recently deposed King James II. William of Orange rejected that notion and further rejected accepting England's crown by right of conquest. A suggestion was made that William might have a role rather like that of a consort. William demurred, stating that he was not prepared "to become his wife's gentleman-usher." William demanded and received nothing less than joint monarchy with his wife, Mary.

Mary was summoned to come to England from Holland and she did so. In England Mary supported her husband's position concerning the English throne. Although William had often treated his wife in a highhanded fashion, in his own way he adored her. For her part, Mary loved her husband. The conquering hero's demands were accepted by England's leaders, and on February 13, 1689, William and Mary were proclaimed as joint sovereigns of England, to rule as King William III and Queen Mary II. Their joint coronation was held at Westminster Abbey, two months later, on April 11, 1689.

Since there was no separation of church and state in England, William and Mary became the leaders on the Anglican Church of England. William took no interest in church affairs and left those matters in the hands of Queen Mary II. Mary took an active interest in the church and insisted that the Church of England preach more frequently against vice and debauchery. Queen Mary II made it her business to upgrade morals along a broad swath. She insisted that laws against drunkenness be enforced and Sundays be kept free of music and other disruptions in the Sabbath tone of the day.

Elizabeth Hamilton tells us in her 1972 work entitled *William's Mary,* "The Queen saw to it that her own household was not immune. The officers of the Guards were told that it was 'Her Royal Pleasure that they strictly enjoin all the soldiers under them to refrain from swearing and drunkenness.' She was also known to 'mulct' those who failed to attend church services.... A number of societies were formed as a result of the Queen's lead, which helped put right many abuses, and gave help to the poor and the sick."

While Queen Mary II enjoyed her active role as head of the Church of England, she disliked responsibilities associated with affairs of state and engaged in those activities only when her husband was absent from the kingdom on his military missions.

Queen Mary II also enjoyed directing architectural works and laying out related formal gardens in the Dutch style. Queen Mary II was largely responsible for the construction of the ornamental water known as the Serpentine, in Kensington Gardens.

A surprising feature in the life of Queen Mary II after she had returned to England was her "homesickness" for Holland. Mary had a premonition that this would become a problem for her on the eve of her departure for England. There were reasons aplenty why Mary may have failed to find happiness in England. Perhaps, in her own mind, she had usurped the crown that rightfully belonged to her father. That is merely a speculation, but it is known that she quarreled with her nearest English blood relative, her sister, Princess Anne, and that the circumstances of Mary's death prevented a proper reconciliation between the sisters. Also Mary was childless, in an age when a childless woman was something less that a complete woman, and as a childless Queen, Mary had failed in her duty to pass the royal baton to the next generation.

Near the end of her life, Queen Mary II found a cause worthy of her support, a new institution of higher learning in England's North American colony of Virginia. A clergyman of the Church of England, James Blair (1656–1743), interested Queen Mary in founding such a college in Virginia, halfway between the northern and southern plantations. The idea captured the fancy of the queen immediately, and she even managed to nudge a bit of enthusiasm for the idea from her grumpy husband, King William III. The institution was founded under a royal charter, based on plans designed by the renowned Christopher Wren (1632–1723), and opened in 1693 as the College of William & Mary. It was the second institution of higher learning to be founded in North America. This fine college is still alive and well today in Williamsburg, Virginia, with an undergraduate enrollment of some 5,500 students.

William and Mary generally preferred to keep their royal court at rural Kensington, Palace, away from the foul air of crowded London.

In December 1694, Queen Mary II fell ill with smallpox. Her sister, Princess Anne, was pregnant, but offered to visit the Queen on her deathbed to perhaps smooth the rough edges that had developed in their relationship. Both King and Queen sent their thanks to Princess Anne, but stated that the Queen was too ill and suggested that the visit be postponed. Queen Mary died of her smallpox affliction on December 28, 1694, at Kensington Palace.

King William III had treated his wife rather shabbily during much of their life, but his grief at losing her was very real. After Mary's death, William carried a lock of her hair with him at all times.

A magnificent funeral for Queen Mary II was held at Westminster Abbey and attended by the members of both houses of parliament. The Queen's body was laid to rest at Westminster Abbey.

After the death of the childless Queen Mary II, her husband remained on the English throne until his own death in 1702. By then, parliament had assured a consistently Protestant line of succession to the English throne. In 1701, an Act of Settlement had been passed, which specified that the House of Hanover (known to be thoroughly Protestant) would be next in the line of succession, after the death of Princess (later Queen) Anne (1665–1714) and her heirs.

QUEEN ANNE

A Declaration of Rights was given statutory form in December 1689, and because of the provisions contained in that statute concerning succession to the throne of England, Anne acceded to that throne on March 8, 1702, upon the death of King William III. Her coronation at Westminster Abbey occurred on April 23, 1702, and she ruled England until her death on August 1, 1714. Anne had only one husband, George (1653–1708), a Prince of Denmark and Norway. The royal couple had five named children. There were more than a dozen additional pregnancies, but they resulted in either miscarriages or stillbirths. Indeed, only one of the five named children, Prince William, Duke of Gloucester (1689–1700), survived infancy, and even he died 14 years before his mother.

26. *Queen Anne (1665–1714)*

Princess Anne was born on February 6, 1665, at St. James' Palace. Her father was England's Prince James (1633–1701), who later ruled England as King James II. Mary's mother was Anne Hyde (1637–1671), the first wife of Prince James. Princess Anne was the fourth child born to James and Anne, and she was named for her mother. Soon after her birth, Princess Anne was baptized according to the rites of the Anglican Church of England. Her godfather was Gilbert Sheldon (1598–1677), who was then Archbishop of Canterbury. Two godmothers were provided: Anne's elder sister, the three-year-old Princess Mary (1662–1694), and Anne

Scott, Duchess of Monmouth and Buccleuch. England's reigning King, Charles II (1630–1685), wanted the Anglican nature of this ceremony stressed, because there had been Roman Catholic fears troubling Anglican England.

Anne's father's family had held the English throne for several generations, but Princess Anne's mother, Anne Hyde, needs a word or two of introduction. Anne Hyde's father was Edward Hyde, later Earl of Clarendon (1609–1674), a very influential English statesman. Anne's mother was Hyde's second wife, Frances Aylesbury (1617–1667), a daughter of Sir Thomas Aylesbury. Anne Hyde was the eldest child of this marriage and the eldest child of Edward Hyde, since his first marriage, to Anne Ayliffe, had produced no children.

When the monarchy was restored in England in 1660, Prince James returned to England. Edward Hyde also returned then to assist England's new King, Charles II. Once established in England, Hyde sent for his wife and daughter, Anne, to join him. Hyde was thinking of marriage prospects for his daughter, Anne, and had one possibility in mind. However, soon after Anne and her mother arrived in England, Edward Hyde learned that his daughter, Anne, was pregnant by Prince James. Edward Hyde was furious. King Charles II took steps to calm Edward Hyde's fury, and among the steps he took was ordering Prince James to marry Anne Hyde. This was done, but had the first child born of that marriage survived, there would have been doubts about its legitimacy.

E. Thornton Cook describes the early life of Princess Anne and her elder sister, Princess Mary, in a work entitled *Royal Marys: Princess Mary & Her Predecessors*: "Mary's nursery was in her grandfather Lord Clarendon's house at Twickenham but she was often at St. James' and Hampton Court. She can never have lacked for playmates, for both brothers and sisters came in quick succession to share her establishment and Lady Francis Villiers, under whose care the royal children lived, had six daughters of her own." Two Anglican chaplains were provided as tutors to Princess Mary and Princess Anne. These tutors were Dr. Edward Lake (1641–1704) and Dr. Doughtie.

Princess Anne was a rather sickly child, and plagues had been in sporadic attendance in London for centuries. The Great Plague of 1665 had been particularly brutal. In 1668 Princess Anne was sent to live in France for a time, with her grandmother, the dowager Queen Henrietta (1609–1669). While in France, the child's grandmother died, and not long after Princess Anne's 1670 return to England, her mother died.

About the time that Princess Anne returned from France to England, she first met Sarah Jennings (1660–1744). Anne was then about five years old and Sarah was about ten. Over the years a very close relationship developed between Anne and Sarah, and because of Sarah's influence over Anne, the relationship came to have political and military consequences.

In 1673, Princess Anne's father remarried to a 15-year-old Italian beauty, Mary of Modena (1658–1718). When Prince James introduced his new wife to Princess Anne and Princess Mary as "their new playmate," he was not wide of the mark. Mary of Modena was far closer in age to both of James' daughters than she was to her new husband. It was not long before the three girls were all teenagers, and together they formed a friendship.

Since the stepmother of the two royal princesses, Princess Anne and Princess Mary, was a Roman Catholic, and since it was becoming rather well known that their father, Prince James, had also converted to that faith, England's reigning monarch, King Charles II, felt obliged to assure the kingdom concerning the religious faith practiced by the two royal princesses. Dr. Lake and Dr. Doughtie had been doing their duty. They had given the two royal princesses meticulous instruction in the dogma of the Anglican Church of England, and had led them in daily prayers and in devotions on appropriate saints' days. However, King Charles II wanted a vigorous Anglican to lead the debate with Prince James, the Catholic father of Princess Mary and Princess Anne, concerning the faith in which they would be confirmed. This was necessary because Prince James was no mere nominal Catholic. He had all the fire and enthusiasm for his new faith of a typical convert, but no faith other than the Anglican Church of England would do for the confirmation of Princesses Anne and Mary. To combat the father's Roman Catholic influence, King Charles II appointed Henry Compton (1632–1713), the Anglican Bishop of London, as spiritual mentor to Princess Mary and Princess Anne to buttress their Anglican faith.

In 1677 Anne's sister, Princess Mary, married William III, Prince of Orange (1650–1702), who was captain-general and admiral of Dutch forces and stadtholder of several Dutch states. Marriage of Anne's close friend, Sarah Jennings, came soon afterward, either in late 1677 or early 1678. Sarah's husband was John Churchill (1650–1722), who later was made Duke of Marlborough. The people involved in these two marriages were important in the life of our Princess Anne and would play central roles in the civil and military history of England.

By 1680, Princess Anne had reached her fifteenth birthday, and thoughts in England began to touch on marriage possibilities for her. In December 1680, the German Prince, George Lewis (1660–1727), paid a visit to England, and marriage rumors linking Anne with that George were noted. Nothing came of this, and in 1681 Prince George (1653–1708) of Denmark and Norway paid a visit to England as a preliminary to marriage to Princess Anne. That marriage took place on July 28, 1683, in England at St. James' Palace.

At this point it seems appropriate to comment on the marriage of Princess Anne and Prince George. It was a happy marriage, indeed, with a very active sex life. Assessments of both Prince George and Princess (later Queen) Anne are rather denigrating. Apparently, neither George nor Anne was terribly bright, or well educated, but they were devoted to each other and did their utmost to produce an heir. That word picture seems clear enough, if a bit unflattering, but then we must complicate matters by adding a few words about Mrs. Sarah Churchill (nee Sarah Jennings). It is certain that Sarah and Anne were devoted friends and it appears fairly certain that they were also lesbian lovers—this in the midst of a harmonious marriage between George and Anne.

There is no doubt that the intense, and rather masculine-minded, Sarah

Churchill managed to dominate Anne, and by the time that Anne was Queen of England, that domination produced results in the political and military affairs of England and on the battlefields of Continental Europe.

Following the marriage of Princess Anne to George, the game of royal musical chairs moved swiftly in England. In 1685, King Charles II died and was succeeded on the throne by his eldest brother, Anne's father, James, who ruled England as King James II. However, the rule of James II was brief, on account of his Catholic religion and the unpopularity of that faith in Anglican England.

England, weary from a recent civil war and its horrible aftermath, may well have been content to wait for King James II to die. With him would die the Catholic threat, because his two eldest children (both from his first marriage), Princess Mary (1662–1694) and Princess Anne (1665–1714), were both resolutely Protestant.

This patient and reasonable plan was foiled on June 10, 1688, when the Roman Catholic Queen Consort gave birth to Prince James Francis Edward (1688–1766). Now a legitimate male offspring had been born to the King. Baby Prince James became next in the line of succession to the throne. The legitimate heir to the throne was now a Catholic son, born to a Catholic King and a Catholic mother. In Anglican England, this would never do. Rumors were circulated, with vigor, that the birth of this child was a sham, that a baby had been smuggled in to validate the lie. The truth is that there was no sham and there was no lie. The Catholic baby, James Francis Edward, had merely been born at a very inconvenient moment in England's history. Though he was clearly next in the established line of succession, there was no possibility that England would allow him to take the throne.

Revolutionary leaders in England summoned Princess Anne's brother-in-law, William III, Prince of Orange (1650–1702). William's forces quickly assumed control of England. King James II fled and William and his wife, Mary, were awarded the throne as joint sovereigns, titled King William III and Queen Mary II.

Our Princess Anne had been on the periphery of these events, although her agreement was sought and secured when she renounced her own right to the English throne until both her sister Mary, and King William III died.

Animosity was not long in developing between Princess Anne and the joint monarchs, William and Mary. King William III developed rudeness to something on an art form, and Anne bristled. To appreciate Anne's vexation, we must remember that her life was largely within a closed circle consisting of a husband whom she adored, and Sarah Churchill, with whom she was infatuated. Princess Anne's tight circle also included Sarah's husband, John Churchill.

King William was happy to share his low opinion of Princess Anne's husband with anyone he could get to listen to him, and King William surrounded himself with Dutch favorites. In 1692 the King imprisoned Sarah's husband, John Churchill, in the Tower of London. In defiance of the King and Queen, Princess Anne continued her close relationship with Sarah Churchill. When Princess Anne was obliged to leave court for her conduct, she took Sarah Churchill with her. In 1694 Queen Mary II died, and King William III took steps to mend his rift with Princess

Anne, who was now heiress-apparent to the throne. King William III and Princess Anne shared a strong desire to have Anne's son, Prince William, Duke of Gloucester (1689–1700), eventually accede to the throne and, thereby, thwart any attempt by a Jacobite to rule England. Anne and her husband were given St. James' Palace for their London residence, and King William even showed favor toward John and Sarah Churchill.

In April 1697, while Sarah Churchill was serving as a lady of the bedchamber to Princess Anne, a vacancy in the household staff developed on account of the illness of Ellen Bust (–1697). Ms. Bust was a bedchamber woman, a rank clearly inferior to that of Sarah Churchill's. To fill the vacancy, Sarah recommended one of her relatives, Abigail Hill (–1734), who was then unmarried but, in 1707, married Samuel Masham (–1758). In time, Abigail would replace Sarah as Anne's intimate.

Events in the English royal musical chairs continued to move briskly, with increasingly direct impact on Princess Anne. The royal couple had five named children:

> Princess Mary (1685–1687)
> Princess Anne Sophia (1686–1687)
> Prince William, Duke of Gloucester (1689–1700)
> Princess Mary (1690–1690)
> Prince George (1692–1692)

There were more than a dozen additional pregnancies, but they resulted in either miscarriages or stillbirths. In 1700 the last of the named children, Prince William, Duke of Gloucester, died. Although Anne was only 35 years old, her health was very poor for her age, and there was now no realistic hope that she would produce an heir. In 1701, to insure Protestant succession to the throne, parliament passed the Settlement Act. This act provided that Sophia, Electress of Hanover (1630–1714), a Protestant, would be next in the line of succession after the death of Princess (later Queen) Anne.

In 1702 King William III died, and Anne succeeded to the throne of England on March 8, 1702. She was crowned at Westminster Abbey on April 23, 1702.

Queen Anne captured the heart of her kingdom. She was a high-church Anglican and took great personal interest in church affairs. This was certainly appropriate, for she now headed both church and state in England. In 1704 she granted a portion of her crown revenues to supplement the pitifully poor stipends of clergymen in the poorest parishes. That gift was known as "Queen Anne's Bounty."

The reign of Queen Anne was relatively brief, but on the whole it represented England's first manifestation as a world power. The earlier years of her reign were particularly glorious. Repeated military conquests were achieved by England and her Continental allies over the powerful French King, Louis XIV (1638–1715). That the victories were achieved at all was great; that the military leader who led England and her allies to those victories was the Queen's bosom friend, made them glorious. He was, of course, John Churchill, Duke of Marlborough (1650–1722).

During the reign of Queen Anne, England won a series of important battles on the European continent, including the battles of Blenheim, Ramillies, and Oudenarde. The Queen rewarded Marlborough for Blenheim with the gift of the royal manor at Woodstock, where the Queen had constructed Blenheim Palace for the Duke and Duchess of Marlborough.

In 1707 a civil union of England with Scotland was achieved, when Scottish representation in the parliament of England began, and the name Great Britain was officially born for the two countries, united in one kingdom. (The Presbyterian Church remained the official Church of Scotland.)

Throughout much of Queen Anne's adult life, a close circle had surrounded and, to some extent, controlled her. The circle consisted of Anne's husband George, but more dominant personalities in the circle were Anne's lover, Sarah, and Sarah's husband, John. If one were to add to that list the name Sidney Godolphin, Earl of Godolphin (1645–1712), it would be rather accurate to describe it as the smallest and most effective ruling clique that England had known.

The death of Queen Anne's beloved husband George, Duke of Cumberland and Earl of Kendal, occurred in 1708. Any clique built on the shifting sands of romantic ardor is subject to change and, in this case, another significant change came when Abigail Hill Masham came to replace Sarah Jennings Churchill in the affections of Queen Anne. The shift occurred in stages, but was essentially complete by 1710, and in that year Sidney Godolphin was dismissed by the Queen as England's ranking statesman and replaced with Robert Harley, Earl of Oxford (1661–1724). Harley owed his new position to the influence of his cousin, Abigail Hill Masham.

In 1713, the agreements known collectively as the treaty of Utrecht were finally signed among England, various of her allies, France and Spain. Both France and Spain agreed to renounce attempts to unify the crowns of their two kingdoms. The French also agreed to accept Protestant succession on the throne of England. Further, France agreed to demolish its fortifications of Dunkirk, and to cede to England certain specified territories in North America and the West Indies; i.e., Hudson Bay, Newfoundland, Nova Scotia, and St. Christopher. Spain agreed that England would hold Gibraltar and Minorca, and in Spanish South America, England was given the sole right to import slaves into the New World for a period of 30 years.

By 1714, the health of Queen Anne had become poor, and it was evident that she would not live much longer. In the summer of 1714, Queen Anne became ill and she commenced to suffer a series of strokes. However, the person who was next in line to the English throne, Sophia, Electress of Hanover (1630–1714), died on June 8, 1714, well before Queen Anne died on August 1, 1714.

Queen Anne was buried at Westminster Abbey. Protestant control of the throne of England was assured when England reached all the way to Hanover, in Germany, and took a son of the recently deceased Sophia (1630–1714) of Hanover to succeed Queen Anne on England's throne. He was George Lewis, Elector of Hanover (1660–1727).

27. *George, Duke of Cumberland and Earl of Kendal (1653–1708)*

George, the husband of England's Queen Anne, was born in Copenhagen in April 1653 (various April dates are shown in different sources) as the third son of the King of Denmark and Norway, Frederick III (1609–1670). George's mother was Sophia Amelia of Brunswick-Luneburg (1628–1685). Throughout Prince George's life, Denmark controlled Norway. He is referred to rather consistently as Prince George of Denmark, but a more complete version would be Prince George of Denmark and Norway.

Prince George was one of eight legitimate children, and his father had at least one illegitimate child as well. George was the sixth legitimate child born to the King and was his last legitimate son.

Young George's governor from 1661 to 1665 was Otto Grote.

George was brought up as a strict Lutheran. Although this is a Protestant denomination, there are significant differences between the Lutheran Church and the Anglican Church of England. George's religion was the compelling reason that he rejected efforts in 1674 to place him on the Polish throne. George had an aversion to the Roman Catholicism of Poland. When George later came to England as husband to Princess (later Queen) Anne (1665–1714), his Lutheran religion did not mesh with the Anglican Church of England. George kept his personal chapel in England in the Lutheran way, even after his wife became Queen of England. He also voted in favor of the Occasional Conformity Bill of 1702, which was desirable to George on a personal level. That bill did not pass.

In Denmark and Norway, George was a Prince of the kingdom. He also was invested with the Danish Order of the Elephant. (Plentiful titles awaited him in England, but one has the feeling that many of these were showered upon him in an attempt to hide the fact that, although he was the Queen's husband, he had no meaningful official position.) Prince George received naval training and saw some naval duty under arms.

It was decided in England that it would be wise to marry Princess Anne to a Protestant, and this was accomplished by arranging her marriage to George, the Protestant Prince of Denmark and Norway. The ceremony was performed in England in the Chapel Royal at St. James' Palace on July 28, 1683. George was not a particularly remarkable man, but the gratuitous insults heaped upon him by historians, and even several English monarchs, seem deplorable. George was a devoted husband to Anne and their mutual love was strong. George and Anne produced five named children, and there were more than a dozen additional pregnancies, which resulted in either miscarriages or stillbirths.

That George did his part to maintain the English royal line of succession in this manner certainly says something in his favor. Moreover, George and Anne maintained their strong mutual love steadfastly until George's death in 1708. George certainly deserves credit for his part in maintaining this marital union, not only because Anne aged very rapidly and became increasingly unattractive as the years went by, but because his love was apparently unaffected by Anne's relationship with Sarah Churchill (1660–1744). It is certain that Sarah and Anne were intimate friends, and it appears fairly certain that they were also lesbian lovers.

In spite of George's unwavering love and support of his wife, at least three English monarchs have seen fit to publicly insult him. King Charles II (1630–1685) declared that "I've tried him drunk and tried him sober and there was nothing in him either way." King William III (1650–1702) also had mostly ill to say about Anne's husband, but perhaps we can discount this a bit since the Dutchman's lack of social graces was notorious. At meals he was silent, surly and indifferent to women. He grumbled about the defects of London. However, even England's Queen Victoria (1819–1901) joined in the abuse heaped upon Queen Anne's mild mannered and kind husband when she referred to him as "the very stupid and insignificant husband of Queen Anne."

If the *Guinness Book of Records* had a category for "English consort most maligned by monarchs of England," surely Prince George of Denmark and Norway would rank high on the list.

Following the marriage of Princess Anne to George, the game of royal musical chairs moved swiftly in England. In 1685 King Charles II died, and was succeeded on the throne by his eldest brother, Anne's father, James, who ruled England as King James II (1633–1701). However, the rule of James II was brief on account of his Catholic religion and the unpopularity of that faith in Anglican England. Revolutionary leaders in England summoned Princess Anne's brother-in-law, William III, Prince of Orange (1650–1702). George supported his father-in-law, King James II, briefly, but deserted him at Andover in 1688 and went over to the side of William of Orange. (George was rewarded for this shift in loyalty when William and Mary came to the throne; i.e., he was rewarded with an act of naturalization and elevation to the peerage.) William's forces quickly assumed control of England. King James II fled, and William and his wife Mary were awarded the throne as joint sovereigns titled King William III (1650–1702) and Queen Mary II (1662–1694).

George's wife Princess Anne had been on the periphery of these events, although her agreement was sought and secured when she renounced her own right to the English throne until both her sister Mary and King William III died. Mary died in 1694, and William ruled England alone until his death on March 8, 1702. It was on that date that Princess Anne acceded to the throne of England, with her title styled Queen Anne. The new Queen proposed that her devoted husband be made King Consort of England. She even attempted to have the Dutch accept him as a stadtholder in the Netherlands as well, replacing the dead William III in that position. The Dutch quickly rejected this notion, but, in England, the Queen's idea was rejected more tactfully. After all, Anne was now Queen of England and could insist on the title King Consort for her husband. However, enough leading Englishmen with tact were found to dissuade Queen Anne from this proposed title for her husband. Her coronation at Westminster Abbey occurred on April 23, 1702.

At her coronation, the Queen's husband "paid her homage," the first occasion on which the husband of a reigning English sovereign had done so. The first and only repetition of this unusual gesture occurred in 1953 at the coronation of Queen Elizabeth II (1926–). At her coronation, Elizabeth's husband Philip, Duke of Edinburgh (1921–), also "paid homage" to his wife, the Queen.

In Winston S. Churchill's *A History of the English-Speaking Peoples*, the author provides this assessment of the early years of Queen Anne's reign; i.e., the years during which England scored major victories on the European Continent, resulting in major increases in power and some increases in possessions: "The Age of Anne is rightly regarded as the greatest manifestation of the power of England which had till then been known…. The intimate, long-developed friendships of the Cockpit circle now found their expression in the smallest and most efficient executive which has ever ruled England. Sarah managed the Queen, Marlborough managed the war, and Godolphin managed the Parliament." "Sarah" being Sarah Jennings Churchill, Duchess of Marlborough (1660–1744), "Marlborough" being John Churchill, Duke of Marlborough (1650–1722), and "Godolphin" being Sidney Godolphin, Earl of Godolphin (1645–1712). Godolphin's title was Lord High Treasurer, but in reality he was England's prime statesman.

Concerning our subject George, the Queen's husband, there is no direct reference to him in Churchill's assessment of the effectiveness of this tight ruling clique, but that omission is an error in both the strictly technical sense and, more importantly, the shared emotional bonds which built the clique into the effective body that it was.

First, we will discuss the error of omission from a technical standpoint. When Queen Anne's desire that her husband be named King Consort was rebuffed, the Queen insisted that her husband be granted certain prestigious titles, and this was done. Among George's titles was "generalissimo of all the forces," and as such he technically was the superior military officer over the Duke of Marlborough. This is not to say that George deserves much credit for England's marvelous victories in battle in Continental Europe. That credit belongs to Marlborough.

"Generalissimo…" was only one of many titles bestowed upon Queen Anne's husband. Others included his titles of nobility as Duke of Cumberland and Earl of Kendal, as well as the lesser noble title, Baron of Wokingham (or Ockingham). In addition, George was named Constable of Windsor Castle, Lord High Admiral, Lord Warden of the Cinque Ports (a maritime confederation in Kent and Sussex), and Captain General of the Honourable Artillery Company. George was also invested as a Knight of the Garter, England's oldest and highest order of knights. He was also named "chief mourner" for the funerals of two English kings: King Charles II and King William III. He was sworn in as a privy councilor in 1685 and again in 1689, the second time under the joint sovereigns William and Mary. Our George was even Chief High Commissioner of Greenwich Hospital. From a technical standpoint, Queen Anne's husband was not deficient in titles.

After reading about George in several dozen historical works, one is inclined to gather that his titles were ceremonial with no real clout to them. Although that is probably an accurate assessment for most of George's titles most of the time, we must infer that he also had some real power, because he was attacked by the Whigs during the period 1704–1708 for the way he managed his duties as Lord High Admiral. *The Admiralty* by N. A. M. Rodger, published in 1979, indicates that George (referred to here and by many other sources as "Prince George of Denmark") served as England's Lord High Admiral from May 20, 1702 until his death in 1708.

But, getting back to the clout that Queen Anne's husband did or did not have in the tight clique that so effectively ruled England, note Winston Churchill's reference to the importance of "the intimate, long-developed friendships of the Cockpit circle." Surely, it was here that George, with his mild and easy-going temperament, played a key role in keeping these intimate relationships harmonious, and that this harmony aided England's "smallest and most efficient" clique to earn that praise. That the praise comes from Winston Churchill (1874–1965), one of England's greatest statesmen and historian of note, only adds its luster. (In addition to Winston Churchill's many other distinctions, he, like the subject of this biographical sketch, was "Lord Warden of the Cinque Ports.")

On the domestic scene, the marriage of Anne and George produced five named children:

> Princess Mary (1685–1687)
> Princess Anne Sophia (1686–1687)
> Prince William, Duke of Gloucester (1689–1700)
> Princess Mary (1690–1690)
> Prince George (1692–1692)

There were more than a dozen additional pregnancies, but they resulted in either miscarriages or stillbirths. In 1700 the last of the named children, Prince William, Duke of Gloucester, died. Although Anne was then only 35 years old, her health was very poor for her age, and there was now no realistic hope that she would produce an heir. The great tragedy of the harmonious marriage of Queen Anne and George is that no royal heir was produced to succeed Anne. This personal tragedy would result in a practical problem for England as well, since the heir to the throne when Queen Anne died in 1714 was her half-brother, James Francis Edward (1688–1766); but, James Francis Edward was a Catholic, and England wanted no Catholic on its throne. The kingdom closed ranks against James Francis Edward and all other Catholic contenders for the crown and reached all the way to Hanover, in Germany, for a successor to Queen Anne.

With respect to George's conduct as a father, most sources give the mild mannered Dane high marks. However, Norah Lofts' *Queens of England* has nothing good to say about George as a parent: "One of her children lived past early infancy; he was abnormal, with a hydrocephalic head and weak legs. He had a poor sense of balance, and knew it, so he welcomed help on stairs. His father beat him for accepting help." Among the sources that rate George as a very good father with a keen interest in Prince William, Duke of Gloucester, is *Brewer's British Royalty*, by David Williamson, published in 1996.

George died at Kensington Palace on October 28, 1708, of a severe asthmatic malady. His death preceded Queen Anne's by six years. In accordance with a stipulation in an unsigned will of Queen Anne, the Queen and her Consort are buried adjacent to each other at Westminster Abbey.

28. *Prince William, Duke of Gloucester (1689–1700)*

Prince William was born on July 24, 1689, at Hampton Court Palace. His mother was Princess Anne (1665–1714), who would later come to England's throne as Queen Anne. William's father was Princess Anne's husband, George (1653–1708), who, just a few weeks earlier, had been made Duke of Cumberland and Earl of Kendal. Since William's father was a son of the former King of Denmark and Norway, Frederick III (1609–1670), baby William was a product of Scandinavian royalty as well as English royalty.

The marriage of Anne and George produced numerous pregnancies, but only five named children survived childbirth, and Prince William was the only child of the union to live beyond infancy. He was a delicate child and had an unusually large head (some sources attribute the head formation to a hydrocephalic condition; i.e., "water on the brain.") However, for a time there was hope that William would survive to accede to the throne of England.

On July 27, 1689, Prince William was baptized as William Henry by Henry Compton (1632–1713), the Anglican Bishop of London. The baby's principal godfather was England's King William III (1650–1702), and Prince William was named for him. His godmother was the marchioness of Halifax. A second godfather for the baptismal ceremony was King Christian V (1646–1699) of Denmark and Norway, an uncle on the baby's father's side. Christian V was the ruling monarch of Denmark and Norway at the time of the baptism and was represented at the ceremony by a proxy, Charles Sackville, Earl of Dorset (1638–1706).

King William III bestowed the title Duke of Gloucester on baby William on the day of his baptism, July 27, 1689.

Princess Anne wanted to raise her children away from the polluted air of London. This matter was particularly important to her because, when Prince William was less than two months old, according to Edward Gregg's work entitled *Queen Anne*: "in September, 1689 Gloucester 'was seized with convulsive fits, every day they expect his death, no one of the doctors thinks he can live.'"

In an attempt to save the baby's life, a series of wet nurses were summoned to suckle the infant. The women who tried to fulfill this capacity and failed were (listed in the order of their attempts) Mrs. Shermon, Mrs. Wanley, and Mrs. Ogle.

When hope was nearly abandoned, a final wet nurse was tried. She was Mrs. Pack (–1694), a Quaker from Kingston Wick. Very soon after the Prince began to suckle at Mrs. Pack's breasts, improvement was obvious and within a few days the baby had completely recovered his health. Mrs. Pack was a hero and remained with the Prince until he was weaned, after which she was, for a time, dry nurse to Prince William.

Although Gloucester had bounced back, Princess Anne was still concerned about staying away from the polluted air of London. She rented accommodations for Prince William first at Kensington gravel pits, and later at Campden House, further west and still outside central London.

By 1690, the Welshman Jenkin Lewis was assigned as personal servant and page to the Duke of Gloucester. Lewis also became the favorite companion of the Prince, and he encouraged Prince William's early interest in military toys and even a bit of military history. In 1693 Reverend Samuel Pratt (–1723) was appointed tutor to the Prince. Pratt was a Cambridge scholar and he made no secret of his low opinion of the education Jenkin Lewis had been providing.

From 1690 to 1693, Princess Anne had three pregnancies, which ended in the immediate deaths of the children. These traumatic events, coupled with Prince William's precarious health, put psychological stress on Princess Anne. Prince William's tenuous hold on life was a constant source of worry to his mother, and by 1694 Princess Anne had become morbid.

Princess Anne had a profoundly harmonious relationship with her husband, but she also carried on an intimate (probably lesbian) relationship with Sarah Jennings Churchill, Duchess of Marlborough (1660–1744). England's ruling King, William III, maintained a hostile attitude toward Sarah Churchill and her husband, John Churchill, Duke of Marlborough (1650–1722). That hostility came to extend to Princess Anne and to Anne's husband George, Duke of Cumberland and Earl of Kendal. During the period of this clash of personalities, King William was ruling England as joint sovereign with his wife, Queen Mary II (1662–1694).

Despite King William's hostility toward Princess Anne and her intimate associates, King William and Queen Mary took a great interest in their nephew, the Duke of Gloucester. They frequently invited him to visit them at their royal residences. Princess Anne was not enthusiastic about these visits, because of the friction between the King and the Princess, but she generally agreed to the visits that were suggested. It was the right thing to do and, on a more practical level, the visits usually resulted in generous gifts to the Duke from the King and Queen.

Between March and May 1695, Prince William was repeatedly ill with fever, and Princess Anne visited him frequently at Campden House.

In 1695 or 1696, Prince William was invested as a knight of the garter, England's oldest and highest order of knights. The ceremony was attended by the whole court, except the King, who was fighting a military battle in the Spanish Netherlands. However, it was King William III who decided that Gloucester should receive the garter, and the King had the occasion celebrated at a dinner and ball at his expense.

When Prince William was just eight years old, he was given his own household at St. James' Palace. His household staff consisted of about 100 people. To maintain it, parliament granted him an annual allowance of 50,000 pounds, but King William III sought fit to reduce that to 15, 000 pounds per annum. Prince William's mother, Princess Anne, let it be known that she considered that stipend inadequate.

King William III appointed his nephew Prince William as nominal commander of King William's Dutch regiment of foot guards.

In December 1694, Queen Mary II had died, and King William had begun to rule England alone. He decided that it was time to mend some fences. Toward that end, in 1697 or 1698, the King suggested that John Churchill, Duke of Marlborough, be made governor of Prince William, Duke of Gloucester, and of Gloucester's household staff. Also, Bishop Gilbert Burnet (1643–1715) was appointed to replace Reverend Samuel Pratt as Prince William's head tutor, although Reverend Pratt was retained as sub-tutor and almoner. Bishop Burnet provided young William with a rather comprehensive course of study, lasting some three hours each day, and it was bruited about that Gloucester was an excellent student. This may have been entirely true, or perhaps partially phrased to please the vanity of the student, who was, after all, a Prince of England.

On July 24, 1700, Prince William's eleventh birthday was celebrated at Windsor Castle with a banquet and a ball. The dancing left the frail Prince exhausted. On the following day he complained of a headache, nausea, and a sore throat. He soon became feverish. The profession of medicine did not become very much of a science until the 20th century. Certainly in 1700 it offered few tools to cope with serious medical problems. The usual treatments of that day, bloodletting and blistering, were tried, in a vain attempt to save the Prince's life. He suffered several days more before dying at Windsor Castle on July 30, 1700.

The body of Prince William, Duke of Gloucester, was interred at Westminster Abbey in the chapel of England's King Henry VII (1457–1509).

Although Princess Anne, who was next in England's line of succession to the throne, was only 35 years old when Prince William died, her health was very poor for her age, and there was now no realistic hope that she would produce an heir. Indeed, the great tragedy of the harmonious marriage of Queen Anne and George is that no royal heir was produced to succeed Anne. This personal misfortune would result in a practical problem for England as well, since the heir to the throne when Queen Anne died in 1714 was her half-brother, James Francis Edward (1688–1766); but James Francis Edward was a Catholic, and England wanted no Catholic on its throne.

Howard Nenner's 1995 work entitled *The Right to Be King: The Succession to the Crown of England: 1603–1714* makes an interesting point concerning King William III's reaction to the death of Prince William, Duke of Gloucester. Nenner discusses King William's efforts to clarify royal succession matters before the deaths of the key players, and he contrasts those efforts with the earlier, potentially disastrous, "do nothing" approach of Queen Elizabeth I (1533–1603) as she neared the end of her life. In Nenner's words, "When William met with his fifth parliament in February 1701, the matter of the Protestant succession was at the head of his legislative agenda. One hundred years after Queen Elizabeth had categorically refused to allow parliament anything to do with the transfer of the crown, William instructed the Lords and Commons that the loss of the Duke of Gloucester had 'made it absolutely necessary that there should be a further provision for the succession in the Protestant line.' It was a popular move, William being applauded in the press as a King who 'had rather have a successor declar'd, than confusion should make havock (sic) of the state,' something 'which the best of his predecessors cou'd never endure to think of.' To do nothing would encourage the kingdom's enemies. It would be 'a tacit indication that the nation is prepared to receive a prince that shall be nameless,' and an open invitation to Louis XIV to supply a successor as it had been feared Philip might attempt to do after Elizabeth.... Following the Duke's death in July, he met with Sophia at Loo in September 1700, and later that year he summoned a parliament to meet with him in February."

A more complete description of the individuals mentioned in the quote from Nenner would be: King Louis XIV (1638–1715) of France, and Sophia (1630–1714) Electress of Hanover. The "Philip" whom Nenner mentions might have been either King Philip II (1527–1598) of Spain or his son, King Philip III (1578–1621) of Spain, since both of them had pondered attempting to succeed Queen Elizabeth I on England's throne.

In any event, King William got what he wanted in terms of both Protestant succession to the throne and specificity concerning the official line of succession after the death of both himself and Princess (later Queen) Anne. The plan was spelled out in the 1701 Act of Settlement. It declared Sophia (1630–1714) Electress of Hanover, in Germany, next in the line of succession after William and Anne. The 1689 prohibition against Roman Catholics acceding to the throne of England was preserved. Sophia died on June 8, 1714, before the death of England's Queen Anne. In keeping with the Act of Settlement, England reached all the way to Hanover in Germany, and took a son of the recently deceased Sophia of Hanover to succeed Queen Anne on England's throne. He was George Lewis, Elector of Hanover (1660–1727).

Some of the comments about Prince William that have come down to us over three centuries should be regarded as anecdotal, since many of them are not readily substantiated. If any of these anecdotes contain errors, most would be rather harmless, because Prince William's early death removed him from the English royal line of succession before he was old enough to have formed character traits worthy of serious evaluation. However, it must be admitted that Prince William represented, during his brief life, one focal point in the bitter struggle still in progress between those who favored and those who opposed the concept that England's former Roman Catholic King James II (1733–1701) or his Catholic heirs should be monarchs of England; i.e., the Jacobites. Thus, there is some possibility that, among the anecdotal trivia concerning Prince William (1689–1700), a few of the comments may have been inspired by those with axes to grind in the Jacobite controversy.

KING GEORGE I

George acceded to the throne of England upon the death of Queen Anne on August 1, 1714. His coronation at Westminster Abbey occurred on October 20, 1714, and he ruled England as King George I until his death on June 22, 1727. George married only once, to Sophia Dorothea (1666–1726), and they had two children before their marriage was terminated in December 1694. Both of those legitimate children survived infancy.

29. *King George I (1660–1727)*

George Lewis was born on May 28, 1660 at Osnabruck Castle, at Leineschloss in Hanover, Germany. His birth date is given in many sources on English history and biography as June 7, 1660. The difference is due to the use of the Gregorian calendar, which had been in use since 1582 in Continental Europe. That calendar had been a departure from the previous Julian calendar. The Gregorian calendar lopped off some ten days from the prior Julian calendar, to more closely align the years with actual movements of the earth about the sun. But the new calendar had been adopted under the authority of the Roman Catholic Pope Gregory XIII (1502–1585) and, worse yet, it had been named for that pope. In 1660 Protestant England had not yet adopted this new calendar.

George's father was Ernest Augustus (1629–1698) of Brunswick-Luneburg. Ernest Augustus advanced in power and prestige in Germany, becoming Prince-Bishop of Osnabruck in 1661 and Duke of Brunswick-Luneburg in 1679. The duchy of Brunswick-Luneburg managed to obtain control of Hanover in 1692, and Ernest Augustus became the first elector of Hanover in that year. He formally ruled

Hanover as elector until his death in 1698, although his son George took over many of his duties when his father became disabled. In 1698, when the elector died, his eldest son George Lewis formally succeeded him as elector of Hanover.

The mother of George Lewis was Sophia (1630–1714) who, in 1701, was the Dowager Electress of Hanover. The year 1701 is important for it was then that parliament passed the Settlement Act to insure Protestant succession to the English throne. This act provided that Sophia, Electress of Hanover (1630–1714), a Protestant, would be next in the line of succession after the death of Princess (later Queen) Anne (1665–1714). However, Sophia, Dowager Electress of Hanover, died on June 8, 1714, before Queen Anne died on August 1, 1714. It was through George Lewis' mother Sophia, that George had a drop or two of English royal blood in him to justify his right to hold the throne of England. George's mother, Sophia (1630–1714), was a daughter of Princess Elizabeth (1596–1662), who herself was a daughter of King James I (1566–1625). In reality, it was not the bloodlines that were key to George becoming King of England. It was his Protestant religion. The leaders of England had deliberately stacked the deck so that no Roman Catholic could become monarch of England.

But we have failed to tag a few bases here. We have taken George from his birth and announced that he is King of England. Fifty-four years intervened between the two events.

The childhood of George's mother had been an unhappy one and she took pains to insure that her children enjoyed a happy home environment.

As early as the age of 15 George Lewis became active in military affairs. The military activities were directed primarily at the goal, which was in fact achieved, of enlarging the power and status of his father's realm. He showed himself to be courageous in battle. Campaigns in which he participated included the Dutch campaign and support of the Holy Roman Empire in its Turkish wars.

By 1680, England's Princess Anne had reached her 15th birthday, and thoughts began to touch on marriage possibilities for her. In December 1680, George Lewis (1660–1727) paid a visit to England, and marriage rumors linking Anne with that George were noted. Nothing came of this.

As it turned out, George's father selected his bride for him. Romance and personal preferences mattered little when the high stakes game of royal marriage was played, but the marriage that George's father arranged became a disaster. The bride was Sophia Dorothea (1666–1726) of Celle.

The bride was the only surviving daughter of George William (1624–1705), Duke of Brunswick-Luneburg-Celle. She was beautiful and a first cousin of George's. The bride's mother was Eleonore Desmiers d'Olbreuse (1639–1722). George and Sophia were wed on November 22, 1682. Sophia Dorothea had turned 16 just two months earlier, in September, 1682, and only last-minute diplomacy by George's mother, Sophia (1630–1714), averted a marriage contract that Sophia Dorothea was contemplating signing on her 16th birthday with a different suitor.

The marriage of George and Sophia Dorothea produced two children before it crumbled under the weight of adultery, animosity and a murder. The children were:

> George August (1683–1760), later King George II of England
> Sophia Dorothea (1687–1757), later Queen Consort of Prussia

The marriage was forced on both bride and groom by their parents, but many marriages of important European royal couples have survived and prospered under similar handicaps.

At least two prominent adulteries contributed to the ultimate dissolution of the marriage of George and Sophia Dorothea. On George's side, we know that he fell in love with one of his mother's ladies in waiting, Ehrengard Melusina von der Schulenburg (1667–1743), whom King George I later made duchess of Kendal in England. There is no doubt that George Lewis and Ehrengard von der Schulenburg maintained a lasting affair while George was still married. On Sophia Dorothea's side, we know that she formed a romantic attachment to a handsome Swedish military officer, who was a mercenary employed by Hanover. He was Count Philip von Konigsmarck (1665–1694). Sources consulted differ on whether or not Sophia and von Konigsmarck actually committed adultery. What was not in doubt was that von Konigsmarck, while in the employment of the duchy of Hanover, had paid grievous insult to his employer by his romantic dalliance with George's wife. While George was pondering the appropriate punishment for Count von Konigsmarck, Sophia simplified George's deliberations by declaring that she no longer intended to cohabit with him, her husband. Sophia was fed up with Hanover and expressed a desire to move to Celle to live with her parents. George was fed up with Sophia and rather liked her suggested method of removing herself from his scene. But Sophia Dorothea's father was in no mood to facilitate another of his daughter's tantrums. He ordered her to return to Hanover.

George Lewis was away in Berlin and his mother, the Electress, was also away at her summer residence. George Lewis had by now had enough from Sophia Dorothea and her purported lover. He authorized Clara Elizabeth Meisenbuch, Countess von Platen (1648–1700), to administer appropriate justice to von Konigsmarck, probably intending that he would be ordered to leave Hanover. However, Countess Platen, for reasons of her own, found it expedient to have von Konigsmarck murdered. This was done by four armed men on her orders in July 1694. Later that year, in December, George Lewis convened a special tribunal of jurists and Lutheran Church officials and obtained a dissolution of his marriage on the grounds of his wife's refusal to cohabit with her husband.

The right to remarry was reserved to George alone, and Sophia Dorothea was condemned to life imprisonment in the castle of Ahlden. Harsh terms, indeed, but not quite as bad as they seem on the surface. Her imprisonment was in strict but comfortable seclusion. In 1700, on the pretext that the French army might capture Sophia Dorothea, her mother, Eleonore, persuaded her father, George William, to transfer his daughter to the fortified castle at Celle.

George Lewis developed an animosity toward his only legitimate son, George August (1683–1760), later King George II of England. The cold relationship between them would sour court life in England when George I later came to its throne. Some sources attribute George Lewis' ill will toward his son to knowledge that his son adored his mother, whom George Lewis now hated.

In 1692 George's father became the first elector of Hanover, but he died in 1698. On January 9, 1699, Emperor Leopold I (1640–1705) of the Holy Roman Empire named George as successor to his father as elector of Hanover. As Hanover's new elector, George supported the European countries that were allied against the French King, Louis XIV (1638–1715). Hanover absorbed other German territories and, by 1705, Hanover's population was about 400,000. The elector of Hanover's status in Germany was elevated by the marriage, in 1706, of his only legitimate daughter, Sophia Dorothea (1687–1757), to Frederick William (1688–1740), crown Prince of Prussia, who, in 1713, came to rule Prussia as King Frederick William I (1688–1740).

In 1700, in England, the last of the named children of Princess Anne died. Although Anne was only 35 years old, her health was very poor for her age and there was now no realistic hope that she would produce an heir. In 1701, to insure continued Protestant succession to the throne, parliament passed the Settlement Act. This act provided that Sophia, Electress of Hanover (1630–1714), a Protestant, would be next in the line of succession after the death of Princess (later Queen) Anne. In 1702 King William III died, and Anne succeeded to the throne of England on March 8, 1702. She was crowned at Westminster Abbey on April 23, 1702.

By this time, George, the Elector of Hanover, was well aware of the parliamentary maneuvers and acts that had been passed in England concerning succession to the English throne after the deaths of England's King William III (1650–1702) and Queen Anne (1665–1714), but his interest in these English statutes was diminished by the fact that they involved his mother, rather than himself, in the English line of succession. (This is undoubtedly an incomplete explanation concerning George's lack of interest at this stage, because he continued, after he came to the throne of England, to show more interest in Hanover and Germany, than in England.)

On June 8, 1714, Sophia, Dowager Electress of Hanover (1630–1714), died. England had designated her to succeed Queen Anne, but that reward was now left to her eldest son, George Lewis, Elector of Hanover (1660–1727), when Queen Anne died on August 1, 1714.

As mentioned in the discussion leading up to the end of George's marriage, our George, Elector of Hanover, was an adulterer. His father had introduced him to an active sex life. The father had many mistresses and even shared at least one with his son, George, briefly.

About the time that George arrived in England in September 1714, to begin ruling England as King George I, two of his German mistresses found their way to England, as well. They were Baroness Sophia Charlotte von Kielmannsegge (1675–1725), later made countess of Darlington, and Ehrengard Melusina von der

Schulenburg (1667–1743), subsequently ennobled as duchess of Kendal. Some sources indicate that Baroness von Kielmannsegge is mistakenly identified as a mistress of George I, but she was actually his illegitimate half-sister. In fact she was both. One of the mistresses of George's father, Ernest Augustus (1629–1698), was Clara von Meisenbuch (1648–1700), later countess von Platen. Clara had some children fathered by Ernest Augustus, and one of them, Baroness Sophia Charlotte von Kielmannsegge, became a mistress of George I. (To complicate this incestuous family tree, George took as a mistress a daughter-in-law of Clara von Meisenbuch [1648–1700], later countess von Platen. That relationship ended when George left Hanover. George refrained from bringing this particular mistress to England with him, because she was a Roman Catholic and George feared that her religion might be offensive in England.) It is clear that King George I had several illegitimate children during his life, but he deliberately refrained from officially acknowledging any of them as his own. His reluctance to acknowledge his illegitimate children can be traced to adamant instructions George's father had given to him as a young man. A number of sources either state or imply that George had three illegitimate daughters and one illegitimate son. Nigel Cawthorne's 1994 work entitled *The Sex Lives of the Kings & Queens of England* indicates that Ehrengard Melusina von der Schulenburg (1667–1743) was the mother of three of George's illegitimate children. Ragnhild Hatton's 1978 biography entitled *George I: Elector & King* supplies some specifics concerning George's alleged illegitimate children:

Unacknowledged son, born 1676; name unknown.

Anna Louise Sophie von der Schulenburg (1692–1773). Christened as a child of Friedrich Achaz von der Schulenburg (1647–1701) and his wife Margarathe Gertrud von der Schulenburg (1659–1697), but natural daughter of George I and Ehrengard Melusina von der Schulenburg.

Petronella Melusina von der Schulenburg (1693–1778). Christened as a child of Friedrich Achaz von der Schulenburg (1647–1701) and his wife Margarathe Gertrud von der Schulenburg (1659–1697), but natural daughter of George I and Ehrengard Melusina von der Schulenburg.

Margarathe Gertrud von Oeynhausen (1701–1726). Registered as a child of Rabe Christoph von Oeynhausen and his wife Sophie Juliane von Oeynhausen. Actually, she was a natural child of George I and Ehrengard Melusina von der Schulenburg. Elsewhere in that same work, Ragnhild Hatton describes her as George's youngest daughter and a constant companion to her father from childhood onward. Hatton also mentions that her death, early in her twenties, caused the King great grief.

George I acceded to the throne of England on August 1, 1714, upon the death of Queen Anne, and he was crowned at Westminster Abbey on October 20, 1714. The coronation ceremony was conducted in Latin, in deference to the new King's limited knowledge of the English language.

Scotland also recognized King George as its King.

Winston Churchill's *A History of the English-Speaking Peoples* captures in just a few words the disdain that King George I had for his new kingdom: "This fortunate German Prince, who could not speak English, viewed his new realms without enthusiasm. In accepting the throne … he was conferring, as it seemed to him, a favour upon his new subjects. He was meeting the convenience of English politicians. In return he expected that British power and wealth would be made serviceable to his domains in Hanover and to his larger interests on the European scene. His royal duties would entail exile from home in an island he had only once previously visited and which he did not like."

Churchill's words may seem overly harsh, but actually they pretty much hit the mark. The only limited argument that might be advanced to parry Churchill's words would be to add mention that George did learn a little bit of English and was fluent in French, a language then rather well known in Europe among high statesmen and monarchs. Even if King George I were alive today to read these comments by Churchill, King George I, himself, might agree with much of it.

In 1714, the clause in the 1701 Act of Settlement, which forbade the King of England to go abroad without parliamentary approval, was repealed. King George I waited to take advantage of this freedom until the Jacobite uprising of 1716 was crushed. After that he frequently visited Hanover, and some of his absences were lengthy.

King George I realized that he had come to the throne of England to protect the Protestant line of succession. Although he was not a particularly religious person, King George I took it as a point of honor to maintain his Protestant religion himself and that his descendants must do the same.

The new King's lack of interest in England gave the kingdom's statesmen considerable freedom to act upon their own wishes. Other points in George's favor include his willingness to put aside a personal animosity toward Robert Walpole, Earl of Oxford (1676–1745), who became one of England's great prime ministers. Also, the greatest disaster in England during the reign of King George I was the bursting of the notorious financial bubble of the South Sea Company. Neither King George I nor Robert Walpole was tainted by the scandal associated with this affair, although the King's mistresses managed to profit before the speculative bubble burst.

While the nobility and politicians of England may have enjoyed having a King who cared little about the kingdom and pretty much let them have their way with it, that opinion was not shared by the common folk of England. An estimated five out of six persons were "Jacobites," meaning that, in spite of his Roman Catholicism, these common folk would have preferred to see Prince James Francis Edward (1688–1766) on their throne, rather than the disinterested King George I. During the early years of the reign of King George I, there were some bona fide attempts by the Jacobites to return to power, but they were all resisted and in the end nothing came of them. In 1717 the Triple Alliance of Britain, France, and the Dutch Republic even forced Prince James Francis Edward to leave France.

King George I was the first English monarch of the House of Hanover, later styled Windsor on account of anti–German hysteria associated with World War I. King George and his successors put to rest, once and for all, the rather impudent notion that the English monarch ruled by "Divine Right."

In 1714, Hanover, in Germany, coveted the seaports of Bremen and Verden, which were then controlled by Sweden's King Charles XII (1682–1718). Denmark and Norway, then ruled by King Frederick IV (1671–1730), also wanted to seize these ports. Since England's King George I was still the elector of Hanover, opinion in that German duchy held that their elector should use his newly acquired power as King of England to acquire these seaports for Hanover. England's Act of Settlement forbade such direct use of England's naval power. However, an English fleet was dispatched "to protect British trade," but the commanding English admiral was instructed to use his discretion in collaborating with the Danes. Hanover obtained Bremen in 1715 and Verden in 1719.

During the closing years of the life of King George I, he maintained hostility toward his son, George, Prince of Wales (1683–1760), and toward his son's vivacious wife, Caroline (1683–1737).

King George I frequently visited his German dominions, where the happiest years of his life had been spent. During the early phase of the final visit of King George I to Hanover, he became ill and died on June 22, 1727, in the same room in Osnabruck Castle in which he had been born. He was buried at Leineschloss Church at Hanover, but because of damage to that church during World War II, in 1957, the sarcophagus of King George I was moved to a mausoleum on the grounds of Herrenhausen, Germany.

By 1727 sanity had broken out in England. There were no plots or conspiracies. The person next in the official line of succession to the English throne, King George II (1683–1760), acceded to his father's throne without incident on June 22, 1727.

30. *Sophia Dorothea (1666–1726)*

Sophia Dorothea was born during September 1666, at Celle in Germany. She would marry George Lewis (1660–1727), who later ruled England as King George I (1660–1727), but their marriage was dissolved before George became England's King, and Sophia Dorothea never even visited England. She is not styled as a former Queen Consort of England, although she was alive while King George I ruled, and George I never had any other wife than Sophia Dorothea. Several sources on the history of England and its royal family indicate that it is an open question whether or not she can be considered a Queen of England. The explanation for that uncertainty will become clearer, as the life of Sophia Dorothea unfolds. For now let us say that it is very likely, if not certain, that her son, England's King George II (1683–1760), would have brought her to England and recognized her as

Queen mother, if she had managed to live longer than King George I, but she died before George I did.

The exact date of Sophia Dorothea's birth varies among sources, and the confusion cannot be attributed to the old Gregorian calendar versus Julian calendar dispute, since only five days separates the two most widely mentioned birth dates, September 10 and September 15, 1666. (Although the dates do not agree, they are of some importance since they are both in mid–September, 1666, which clearly places Sophia Dorothea's birth well beyond nine months from the mid–November, 1665, "marriage of conscience" of her parents.)

Sophia Dorothea's father was George William (1624–1705), Duke of Brunswick-Luneburg-Celle, in Germany. He was of royal birth, having been born to the ruling Duke of Calenberg, George (1582–1641). Her mother was Eleonore Desmiers d' Olbreuse (1639–1722), a French Huguenot lady of a noble, but untitled, family. Technically Sophia Dorothea was initially considered to be illegitimate, because her father merely entered into a "marriage of conscience" with her mother in mid–November, 1665. At that time Eleonore's rank was so inferior that she was simply referred to as Frau van Harburg. In 1675, or 1676, the couple entered into a legal marriage; Sophia Dorothea then became more definitely legitimate, and Eleonore Desmiers d' Olbreuse was made duchess of Celle.

The questionable legitimacy of Sophia Dorothea's birth would later bring difficulty to the task of finding a royal husband to accept her as his bride.

Sophia Dorothea enjoyed comfort and luxury as a child growing up, perhaps enhanced by the fact that she was the only child of her parents' marriage to survive childbirth.

Sophia Dorothea's father arranged to have the French King, Louis XIV (1638–1715), issue a certificate that recognized Sophia Dorothea as a citizen of France. The Duke of Celle arranged for this document to be issued to protect his daughter in the event of his death. The document has one rather remarkable phrase, where it mentions that Sophia Dorothea is a Protestant. This from the French King who was instrumental in an attempted counter reformation to return Roman Catholicism to all of Christendom.

Ruth Jordan's *Sophia Dorothea*, published in 1971, provides a glimpse of Sophia Dorothea's early life at the court at Celle: "She was brought up after the fashion of the day, trained in all the accomplishments expected of a young lady of rank. She could sing, dance, embroider and make pretty conversation. She spoke German and French ... had a lively mind and a quick wit, and more than a touch of French vivacity. She had an instinctive flair for clothes and elegance, which was encouraged and guided by her mother."

By the age of twelve, Sophia Dorothea had acquired a reputation of being "highly flighty." When love letters were found in her possession, she was ordered to sleep with her parents in their bedroom.

Sophia Dorothea's father and her uncle, Ernest Augustus (1629–1698), who were brothers, decided that Sophia Dorothea should marry her cousin, George Lewis (1660–1727), the eldest son of Ernest Augustus. Romance and personal preferences mattered little when the high stakes game of royal marriage was played, but this particular arranged marriage became a disaster.

While George Lewis may not have been overjoyed with the bride that had been provided to him, he made it his business to insure that the financial arrangements were to his advantage. A dowry was given to George. It provided that his young wife would be completely dependent upon her husband. On the death of her parents, all of their revenues and possessions would henceforth become the property of George Lewis.

George and Sophia were wed on November 22, 1682. Sophia Dorothea had turned 16 just two months earlier, in September, 1682, and only last-minute diplomacy by George's mother, Sophia (1630–1714), averted a marriage contract that Sophia Dorothea was contemplating signing on her 16th birthday with a different suitor.

Clearly, the bride Sophia was a beauty. George Lewis had several brothers and not all of them were old enough to appreciate the attractions of the opposite sex, but those brothers who were congratulated George on his good fortune to land such a beauty as his bride. Even George's father thought his new daughter-in-law was most attractive, and apparently his interest in her was obvious to the point of embarrassment.

Sophia Dorothea's mother-in-law, Sophia (1630–1714), went out of her way to make the bride feel welcome and comfortable in her new surroundings.

The marriage of George and Sophia Dorothea produced two children before it crumbled under the weight of adultery, animosity, and a murder. The children were:

> George August (1683–1760), later King George II of England
> Sophia Dorothea (1687–1757), later Queen Consort of Prussia

The marriage was forced on both bride and groom by their parents, but many marriages of important European royal couples have survived and prospered under similar handicaps.

At least two prominent adulteries contributed to the ultimate dissolution of the marriage of Sophia Dorothea and George. On George's side, we know that he fell in love with one of his mother's ladies in waiting, Ehrengard Melusina von der Schulenburg (1667–1743), whom he later (as King George I) made duchess of Kendal in England. There is no doubt that George Lewis and Ehrengard von der Schulenburg maintained a lasting affair while George was still married to Sophia Dorothea.

In addition to the adultery of her husband, Sophia Dorothea found that George had become cool and distant when he was around her, and he was often away on military ventures. One of her husband's brothers, Carl Philipp (1669–1690), introduced Sophia Dorothea to one of his friends. This friend was a handsome, dashing, and debonair military officer, who was a mercenary employed by Hanover. He was Count Philip von Konigsmarck (1665–1694). Konigsmarck was just one year older than Sophia Dorothea and, in comparison to her lackluster husband, he was irresistible. She formed a romantic attachment to him and the resulting affair lasted five or six years. The affair became less and less of a secret as time went by, and the lovers were warned to put an end to it by friends and relatives. They ignored those warnings. Sources consulted differ on whether or not Sophia and von Konigsmarck actually committed adultery, although letters found hidden in the lining of curtains in Sophia Dorothea's quarters suggest that adultery was, in fact, committed. What was not in doubt was that von Konigsmarck, while in the employment of the duchy of Hanover, had paid grievous insult to his employer by his romantic dalliance with George's wife. While George was pondering the appropriate punishment for Count von Konigsmarck, Sophia simplified George's deliberations by declaring that she no longer intended to cohabit with him, her husband. Sophia was fed up with Hanover and expressed a desire to move to Celle to live with her parents. George was fed up with Sophia and rather liked her suggested method of removing herself from his scene. But Sophia Dorothea's father was in no mood to facilitate another of his daughter's tantrums. Shortly after her arrival at Celle, Sophia Dorothea's father ordered her to return to Hanover.

George Lewis was away in Berlin and his mother, the Electress, was also away at her summer residence. George Lewis had by now had enough from Sophia Dorothea and her purported lover. Konigsmarck was never seen again, and there is some uncertainty concerning what actually happened to him. However, among the various explanations encountered, two sources provide sketches that seem credible. According to those two sketches, George Lewis authorized Clara Elizabeth Meisenbuch, Countess von Platen (1648–1700), to administer appropriate justice to von Konigsmarck while he, himself, was away in Berlin. He probably intended that Konigsmarck would merely be ordered to leave Hanover. However, Countess von Platen, for reasons of her own, found it expedient to have von Konigsmarck murdered. This was done by four armed men on orders from Countess von Platen in July 1694. The two sources drawn on in reaching this particular version were John Van der Kiste's *The Georgian Princesses*, published in 2000, and David Hilliam's *Kings, Queens, Bones & Bastards: Who's Who in the English Monarchy from Egbert to Elizabeth II*, also published in 2000.

The fathers of Sophia Dorothea and George agreed that the marriage must be terminated and that the safe grounds of the wife's refusal to cohabit with her husband should be used, rather than stronger allegations. Later that year, in December 1694, a special tribunal of jurists and Lutheran Church officials was convened, and they granted George Lewis a dissolution of his marriage on the grounds of his wife's refusal to continue to cohabit with her husband.

The right to remarry was reserved to George alone, and Sophia Dorothea was condemned to life imprisonment in the castle of Ahlden. She was even forbidden to see either of her children. Harsh terms, indeed, and her father even refused to visit her. Her imprisonment was in strict, but comfortable, seclusion. About this time she was given the title duchess of Ahlden, so she is referred to in some works as Sophia Dorothea, Duchess of Ahlden (1666–1726). She had access to adequate income to enable her to live in the style appropriate to her rank. Sophia Dorothea was even allowed to venture outside once each day, although sources consulted differ on whether this was for an eight-mile walk or for a ride in a coach. In 1700, on the pretext that the French army might capture Sophia Dorothea, her mother, Eleonore, persuaded her father, George William, to transfer his daughter to the fortified castle at Celle, where her confinement continued.

On January 9, 1699, Emperor Leopold I (1640–1705) of the Holy Roman Empire named George Lewis as successor to his father, as elector of Hanover. In 1714 George acceded to the throne of England. This unusual turn of events was prompted by England's strong desire to have only Protestants on its throne. After the last possible successor to Princess (later Queen) Anne (1665–1714) died, a Settlement Act was passed in England which provided that Sophia, Electress of Hanover (1630–1714), a Protestant, would be next in the line of succession after the death of Anne (1665–1714). However, Sophia, Dowager, Electress of Hanover, died on June 8, 1714, before Queen Anne died on August 1, 1714, and thus it was George, Elector of Hanover, who succeeded Queen Anne to England's throne as King George I.

While all these important events were taking place on the world's stage, our Sophia Dorothea lived in captivity in the castles at Ahlden and Celle.

Sophia Dorothea attempted to obtain release from England's Queen Anne, on the grounds that her imprisonment was unfitting for the mother of a future King of Great Britain. This appeal was unsuccessful. Late in her life, Sophia Dorothea fell prey to two embezzlers. They were Count Christian de Bar (1684–1765) and Count Ludemann. Sophia Dorothea's daughter, the Queen Consort of Prussia, suspected the fraud and alerted her mother to it. Sophia Dorothea was willing to believe that Ludemann was betraying her, but could not believe this of Bar, until Bar stumbled when he took additional funds from her on the pretext of using it in Amsterdam to secure aid toward Sophia Dorothea's release. When Bar's perfidy was revealed to her, she allowed court proceedings against him, but his disloyalty broke what little spirit remained in her. She died on November 2, 1726, but even death did not end the indignities toward her.

Sophia Dorothea's body was placed in a lead vault awaiting instructions from King George I about funeral arrangements. None came. Eventually, an envoy from King George I arrived with instructions to bury Sophia Dorothea in the castle garden. However, an adjacent river had flooded, making the castle garden a swamp. When informed of this, King George I merely issued instructions to have her buried with her parents, in the ducal vault at Celle, which was done.

King George I allowed his hatred of his former wife, Sophia Dorothea, to extend to their son, George August (1683–1760), later King George II of England, and the King forbade his son to make any public demonstration of grief about his mother's death. The *London Gazette* even reported her death as if it were of no consequence. However, the power of King George I did not extend to Prussia, where the couple's other legitimate child was reigning as Queen Consort of Prussia. She was Sophia Dorothea (1687–1757), wife of King Frederick William I (1688–1740) of Prussia, and the Prussian court went into mourning upon the death of the elder Sophia Dorothea.

31. *Prince George, Prince of Wales (1683–1760)*

Prince George came to the English throne as King George II in 1727. For his biographical sketch, see the chapter entitled King George II.

32. *Princess Sophia Dorothea (1687–1757)*

Sophia Dorothea was born in Hanover, Germany on March 26, 1687, and her life was so thoroughly associated with Germany that little mention is made of her as a Princess of England. She did in fact become a Princess of England in 1714, when her father came to England's throne as King George I (1660–1727). Princess Sophia Dorothea might even have been designated as the Princess Royal of England, because she qualified for that status. It was her engagement to the Crown Prince of Prussia, Frederick William (1688–1740) that removed her as a candidate for the title Princess Royal. (Her husband was next in the line of succession to Prussia's throne, which would soon make Princess Sophia Dorothea the Queen Consort of Prussia. According to the informal rules surrounding the use of the title "princess royal," her more lofty title as Queen of Prussia was deemed to be sufficient honor.)

But, before leaving the subject of Sophia Dorothea's formal status in England and dwelling on her life in Germany, we should note that there was never a period when she was next to her brother, George (1683–1760), in the line of succession to the English throne. That was because the English throne passes following the rule of primogeniture, along the male line of the family. When Sophia Dorothea's father came to England's throne in 1714, her brother George had already sired one legitimate son, Frederick (1707–1751). Under primogeniture along the male side, Frederick became next in the line of succession (after his father) from birth.

Sophia Dorothea's father was George Lewis (1660–1727). In 1687, when Sophia Dorothea was born, George Lewis' father, Ernest Augustus (1629–1698), of Brunswick-Luneburg, had not yet been made the first elector of Hanover, which took place in 1692. Late in his life, Ernest Augustus became rather disabled, so George Lewis began to perform many of his duties as elector. On January 9, 1699, Emperor Leopold I (1640–1705) of the Holy Roman Empire named George Lewis as successor to his father, as elector of Hanover. In 1714, upon the death of England's Queen Anne (1665–1714), Sophia Dorothea's father became King of England with his name styled King George I. Thenceforth, until his death, Sophia Dorothea's father ruled both Great Britain and Hanover in Germany.

Sophia Dorothea's mother was also named Sophia Dorothea (1666–1726), and some sources say that our Sophia Dorothea was named for her mother. That mother was the daughter of George William (1624–1705), Duke of Brunswick-Luneburg-Celle, in Germany. He was of royal birth, having been born to the ruling Duke of Calenberg, George (1582–1641). However, the younger Sophia Dorothea's grandmother was Eleonore Desmiers d' Olbreuse (1639–1722), a French Huguenot lady of a noble, but untitled, family. Technically, the elder Sophia Dorothea (1666–1726) was initially considered to be illegitimate because her father merely entered into a "marriage of conscience" with her mother in mid–November, 1665. At that time, Eleonore's rank was so inferior that she was simply referred to as Frau van Harburg. In 1675, or 1676, the couple entered into a legal marriage. The elder Sophia Dorothea then became more definitely legitimate, and Eleonore Desmiers d'Olbreuse (1639–1722) was made duchess of Celle.

The younger Sophia Dorothea's parents were forced into their marriage by their parents, and initially there seemed some hope for that marriage. In 1683 Sophia Dorothea's only legitimate sibling, George August (1683–1760), was born. This is the George who succeeded his father on England's throne as King George II. By 1686, the elder Sophia Dorothea had become indifferent to her husband, George Lewis. Our Sophia Dorothea was born as the couple's second and final child in 1687, and then the marriage fell apart under the weight of adulteries by both of Sophia Dorothea's parents. In December 1694, when Sophia Dorothea was just seven years old, George Lewis convened a special tribunal of jurists and Lutheran Church officials and obtained a dissolution of his marriage, on the grounds of his wife's refusal to cohabit with her husband. Some thought had been given to obtaining the dissolution based on harsher charges against the wife, but this course was chosen, at least in part, to protect the legitimacy of Sophia Dorothea and her brother, George August.

The right to remarry was reserved to George alone, and his former wife was condemned to life imprisonment in the castle of Ahlden. She was also forbidden to see her children ever again.

From this point forward, Sophia Dorothea was brought up by a governess, overseen by her paternal grandmother, Sophia (1630–1714), Electress of Hanover. Young Sophia Dorothea was a gentle-mannered girl, with brown hair and blue eyes. A tribute to young Sophia Dorothea recorded by the political and philosophical writer John Toland (–1722) has survived. That commentary mentioned her lively personality and stated, "In minding her discourse to others, and by what she was pleased to say to myself, she appears to have a more than ordinary share of good sense and wit. The whole town and court commend the easiness of her manners, and the evenness of her disposition; but above all her other qualities, they highly extol her good humour, which is the most invaluable endowment of either sex, and the foundation of most other virtues."

Young Sophia Dorothea's grandmother, the Electress of Hanover, had a great many visitors at her court, and the child Sophia asked her grandmother why no visits were paid by the child's mother, Sophia Dorothea, who now bore the title Duchess of Ahlden. Young Sophia Dorothea also peppered her grandmother with other questions about her mother, many of which must have been difficult for the grandmother to effectively dissemble.

Somehow young Sophia Dorothea was able to enter into a secret correspondence with her mother, which continued until the mother's death in 1726.

A number of attractive marriage matches were considered for Sophia Dorothea and it was deemed, by those who had the power to deem such things, that Sophia Dorothea would wed Frederick William (1688–1740), Crown Prince of Prussia. The Dowager Electress of Hanover (1630–1714) had some reservations. She had noted that, on his visits to Hanover, this aggressive young Prussian had often bullied his cousin, George August (1683–1760), Sophia Dorothea's brother. The dowager electress hoped that, as the boy became a man, this bullying tendency would abate. Sadly, this did not happen.

A vast collection of clothing was ordered from France for Sophia Dorothea's wedding. The French King, Louis XIV (1638–1715), said that he wished all German princesses had such extravagant trousseaux, because it was good for trade.

Our Sophia Dorothea (1687–1757) was wed by proxy to her first cousin, the Crown Prince of Prussia. The proxy marriage took place at Hanover on November 14, 1706. The couple were married again in person, at Berlin, on November 28, 1706. The royal couple made their home in Berlin in the Crown Prince's court. Although the marriage was an unhappy one, the couple remained married until Sophia Dorothea's husband died in 1740. Sophia Dorothea never married a second time.

At first, the Prussian Crown Prince was very much in love with his beautiful cousin. However, he was a year older than his wife, had a wandering eye for other women, and boorish manners. The marriage, which on the surface had seemed splendid, became a failure. In addition to his adulterous activities, Frederick William was incredibly parsimonious and had atrocious manners.

The Crown Prince's father, King Frederick I of Prussia (1657–1713), died in 1713, and Sophia Dorothea's husband came to the Prussian throne as King Frederick William I.

It may seem, from the comments that follow, that the author is ignoring the faults of Sophia Dorothea (1687–1757), merely because she is the subject of this sketch, and heaping unfair abuse upon her husband, the King of Prussia. No doubt Sophia Dorothea had some faults, but none of them could begin to match the crude barbarity of her stingy, boorish husband, the King of Prussia. This King of Prussia was not just churlish toward his wife; indeed, he saved some of his more malicious shots for his son, Frederick (1712–1786), who nevertheless followed his father to Prussia's throne and ruled as King Frederick II, also called Frederick the Great (1712–1786).

While Sophia Dorothea's husband was committing adulteries and otherwise abusing her, she was bearing him a large number of children, many of whom survived infancy. The first-born child, Frederick Louis, arrived in November 1707, but the cannons fired to celebrate his christening threw the baby into a severe fit, from which he never fully recovered. He lived only a few weeks. The children who survived infancy are listed in the following table, in order of their birth:

Princess Wilhelmina, Margravine of Bayreuth (1709–1758)
Prince Adolphus Frederick (1710–1771), later king of Sweden
Prince Frederick (1712–1786), later King Frederick II, Frederick the Great of Prussia
Princess Frederica Louise, Margravine of Ansbach (1714–1784)
Princess Phillipine Charlotte, Duchess of Brunswick-Bevan (1716–1801)
Princess Sophia Dorothea, Margravine of Brandenburg-Schwedt (1719–1765)
Princess Louise Ulrica (1720–1782), Queen Consort of Sweden via marriage to
  King Adolphus
Prince August William (1722–1758)
Princess Amelia (1723–1787)
Prince Henry Louis (1726–1802)
Prince Ferdinand (1730–1813)

Sophia Dorothea insisted in raising her children in the French manner, rather than according to German customs. She and her husband, the King, argued endlessly about this. Sophia Dorothea is known to have succeeded, at least with her eldest son and her eldest daughter, in passing on aesthetic tastes, artistic leanings, and love of opera and ballet.

Sources consulted offer remarkably differing opinions on Sophia Dorothea's capability as a mother. David Williamson's *Brewer's British Royalty*, published in 1996, quotes from the memoirs of her eldest daughter, Wilhelmina, Margravine of Bayreuth (1709–1758): "My mother never loved any of her children. She cared for them only as they served her ambitious purposes." However, John van der Kiste's *The Georgian Princesses*, published in 2000, indicates that when Sophia Dorothea died, her eldest son, King Frederick the Great of Prussia, was heart-broken. Although she had become somewhat peevish and tedious late in life, Frederick the Great only remembered the times when she had protected him from his father's rages; in hindsight, she seemed a glamorous and enlightened mother.

John van der Kiste's *The Georgian Princesses* provides the following description of Sophia Dorothea as she approached and entered middle age: "Tall and well-built, with the passing years she became more matronly and, as her contemporaries discreetly noted, her waist 'rapidly increased in amplitude.' Armchairs were enlarged in order to support her weight; 'her demeanor,' it was said was 'noble and majestic.'"

Sophia Dorothea entered into a complicated intrigue with her father, England's King George I, to marry two of her children to two of the children of King George II. Sophia Dorothea and King George I actually reached an agreement, without bothering to involve certain key players. Those from whom advice and consent was neither requested nor received included the parents of the two potential mates in England and her own husband, the King of Prussia. The intended match-making failed. Presumably one reason that the arrangement failed to gain support was the fact that Sophia Dorothea's brother, Prince George, Prince of Wales (1683–1760), had no use for his only sister. Lord John Hervey (1696–1743) said of

George's attitude about his sister: "He had the contempt she deserved and a hatred she did not deserve."

Late in the life of our Sophia Dorothea's mother, i.e., the Sophia Dorothea still imprisoned in a German castle, the elder Sophia Dorothea fell prey to two embezzlers. They were Count Christian de Bar (1684–1765) and Count Ludemann. Sophia Dorothea of Prussia alerted her mother to the problem. The alerted mother took appropriate action against Ludemann, but couldn't bring herself to believe Bar was betraying her. Only when Bar went too far by taking additional funds from her on the pretext of using it in Amsterdam to secure aid toward Sophia Dorothea's release, would the mother act against him, and doing so broke what little spirit she had left.

When the mother of the Queen Consort of Prussia died in 1726, the Prussian court went into mourning. In England, where King George I still held his grudge, mourning was prohibited and little mention of the death was made in The *London Gazette*.

Our Sophia Dorothea survived the death of her husband for about 17 years and was dowager Queen during the reign of her son, Frederick the Great. She died at Monbijou Palace in the Berlin area on June 28, 1757, and was buried at Potsdam.

KING GEORGE II

George acceded to the throne of England as King George II upon the death of his father, King George I, on June 22, 1727. His coronation at Westminster Abbey occurred on October 11, 1727, and he ruled England until his death on October 25, 1760. He had one wife, Caroline of Ansbach (1683–1737). The royal couple had eight named children, seven of whom survived beyond infancy. An additional child, a son, was stillborn in 1716.

33. *King George II (1683–1760)*

The man who would later come to England's throne as King George II was born in Germany on October 30, 1683, and named George August. At that time there was no reason to believe that he would ever become a member of England's royal family, and certainly not its king.

His father was George Lewis (1660–1727), the eldest son of Ernest Augustus (1629–1698) and Sophia (1630–1714). Ernest Augustus then was Duke of Brunswick-Luneburg, in Germany. The duchy of Brunswick-Luneburg managed to obtain control of Hanover in 1692, and Ernest Augustus became the first elector of Hanover in that year. This royal title, "elector of Hanover," subsequently passed from Ernest Augustus to George Lewis, and then to the subject of this biographical sketch, George August. Sophia (1630–1714) was a daughter of England's Princess Elizabeth (1596–1662), who herself was a daughter of England's King James I (1566–1625).

The mother of George August (1683–1760) was Sophia Dorothea (1666–1726), a daughter of George William (1624–1705), Duke of Brunswick-Luneburg-Celle, in Germany. He was of royal birth, having been born to the ruling Duke of Calenberg, George (1582–1641). However, George August's maternal grandmother was Eleonore Desmiers d'Olbreuse (1639–1722), a French Huguenot lady of a noble, but untitled, family. Technically, Sophia Dorothea (1666–1726) was initially considered to be illegitimate, because George William merely entered into a "marriage of conscience" with Eleonore in mid–November, 1665. At that time, Eleonore's rank was so inferior that she was simply referred to as Frau van Harburg. In 1675, or 1676, the couple entered into a legal marriage. Sophia Dorothea (1666–1726) then became more definitely legitimate, and Eleonore Desmiers d'Olbreuse (1639–1722) was made duchess of Celle.

George August lost his mother, Sophia Dorothea (1666–1726), at the age of eleven, not to death, but as a result of the dissolution of the marriage of his parents in December 1694, and the subsequent imprisonment of his mother in German castles, where she was denied the right to see her children.

After the dissolution of the marriage, the legal guardians of the two children of that marriage were the elector and electress of Hanover; i.e., the paternal grandparents. George August and his sister, Sophia Dorothea (1687–1757), were brought up with loving care by their grandmother, Sophia (1630–1714), Electress of Hanover. Their father, George Lewis (later to be England's King George I), took no interest in the raising of his two children. The mistress of the robes to the electress, Frau Katherine van Harling (1624–1702), was in charge of the care of the children. The electress was careful to engage English tutors for her grandchildren and great-grandchildren, on account of England's 1701 Settlement Act. That act provided Sophia, Electress of Hanover (1630–1714), a Protestant, would be next in the line of succession to the English throne after the death of Princess (later Queen) Anne (1665–1714). The English tutors had little impact on George August, since he was about 18 years old when England passed the Settlement Act.

Young George August displayed exuberance and garrulity in his youth and had an excellent memory for dates, genealogy, and all matters of a military nature, particularly the army. The political and philosophical writer John Toland (–1722) noted that the young George August had 'a winning countenance, speaks gracefully for his Years, a great Master of History, a generous Disposition and virtuous inclinations.' George August would soon shed those virtuous inclinations, at least those concerning sexual relations.

He was said to be methodically minded but lacking intellectual curiosity. As one result, he had no interest in literature or art. His passion was the army.

His education was typical of that given German Princes of his day, and included instruction in the classics, French, Italian and English. However, throughout his long 77-year life, George August never lost his heavy, guttural German accent when speaking English.

The Electress Sophia had another grandson, the Crown Prince of Prussia, Frederick William (1688–1740). Sophia intended to educate George August and Frederick William together, but an experiment toward that end worked badly. Although Frederick William was about five years younger than George August, he was larger and stronger, and he preferred to settle arguments with his fists rather than with words. The education experiment ended when Frederick William was sent back to Berlin after giving George a bloody nose.

In 1705, following passage in England of the Settlement Act, Sophia (1630–1714), now Dowager Electress of Hanover, and her descendants, including George August, were naturalized by an act of the English parliament. Also in 1705, on September 1, George married Caroline of Ansbach (1683–1737), a daughter of John Frederick, Margrave of Brandenburg-Ansbach (–1686), and his second wife, Eleanor, Margravine of Brandenburg-Ansbach (–1696). Eleanor was a daughter of the Duke of Saxe-Eisenach.

The marriage of George and Caroline was remarkable from a number of standpoints. Caroline was much more intellectual than her husband, and when George and Caroline became King and Queen Consort of England, it was Caroline with whom the politicians found they needed to curry favor. George loved his beautiful and buxom wife dearly. He found her very physically attractive until her death. Nevertheless, George had numerous affairs with numerous women, some of them his mistresses, but he did so not because he preferred them to his wife, but because he felt it his royal duty to have mistresses. Nigel Cawthorne's *The Sex Lives of the Kings & Queens of England* quotes Lord John Hervey (1696–1743): "Though he is incapable of being attached to any woman but his wife, he seemed to look upon his mistresses as a necessary appurtenance of his grandeur as a Prince rather than an addition to his pleasure." A bit more will be told about George's unusual sex life. A point worth making here is that Caroline almost never objected to her husband's adulteries. Many of these strange relationships might seem to be products of folklore, but they are not. King George II is one of the better-known English monarchs, partially because two critics, both gifted with the ability to draft deft and acid criticism, were at hand to record many facts about this King. These critics were Lord John Hervey (1696–1743) and Horace Walpole (1678–1757). Another remarkable feature of the marriage of George and Caroline was their intense dislike of their eldest son, Frederick, Prince of Wales (1707–1751). A complete roster of their children, who survived infancy, is presented in the following table:

> Prince Frederick, Prince of Wales (1707–1751)
> Princess Anne, Princess Royal (1709–1759)
> Princess Amelia (1711–1786)
> Princess Caroline (1713–1757)
> Prince William, Duke of Cumberland (1721–1765)
> Princess Mary (1723–1772)
> Princess Louisa (1724–1751)

In 1714 George August's father acceded to the throne of England as King George I, upon the death of Queen Anne. George August came to England and was made Prince of Wales during 1714. The father and son hated each other, and the son anxiously awaited his father's death so that he could free his mother from captivity in Germany. That plan aborted when Sophia Dorothea (1666–1726) died on November 2, 1726, a few months before King George I died on June 22, 1727.

For the first three years of his father's reign, Prince George, Prince of Wales (1683–1760) attended cabinet and privy council meetings and acted as interpreter for his German-speaking father. However, in 1717, a serious rift between the King and the Prince of Wales occurred. The proximate cause was a dispute concerning the godparents to be chosen for Prince George William (1717–1718). The rift was reminiscent of the alleged sham when Prince James Francis Edward, Prince of Wales (1688–1766), was born.

The rift grew out of proportion, and the Prince and Princess of Wales moved their court from St. James' Palace to Leicester House, where the Prince and his vivacious Princess surrounded themselves with a raffish set of men and women with lively minds. The Prince and Princess of Wales made Leicester House their chief residence until King George I died.

The first of England's six King Georges died on June 22, 1727, and the Prince of Wales acceded to the throne of England as King George II on that day. The coronation of the new King and his Queen Consort took place at Westminster Abbey on October 11, 1727. The new King was 44 years old.

King George II ran his court along strict lines of formality and insisted on rigid punctuality and etiquette. He was a courteous and courtly man, and his ministers appreciated those qualities. However, the King had a hasty temper, which might blow on odd occasions. The King's eldest son, whom we know was anything but an admirer of his father, described him as "an obstinate, self-indulgent, miserly martinet."

David Williamson's *Kings & Queens of Britain* tells us that, "...although she (Caroline) remained more German than English in outlook and temperament all her life, she was to play a greater role in affairs of state than any Queen Consort since the Middle Ages." Robert Walpole, Earl of Orford (1676–1745), cemented his position in the nation's power structure through Queen Caroline. He was England's powerful prime minister from the beginning of George II's reign until 1742. This early decision to allow Walpole to continue as prime minister freed George from major political problems for the first 15 years of his reign. George was content to allow Caroline and Walpole run things, and the Queen acted as his regent during George's frequent absences on visits to Hanover. The King spent much of his free time in the company of his mistresses, hunting stags (deer), and playing cards.

King George II was a man of limited intellectual ability and his lack of application enhanced that handicap. He often bragged about his contempt for books and letters and claimed that he had hated such material since infancy. Although he remained madly in love with his wife until her death in 1737, he often nagged Queen Caroline about her fondness for reading. On at least one occasion, he told her that she spent her time more like a schoolmistress than a queen.

When Caroline was on her deathbed, she begged her husband to remarry.

Why she would care is a bit puzzling, since she had been nothing but tolerant throughout their marriage about George's many mistresses. Before she died, the King averred that he would not remarry, explaining that he would, instead, have mistresses. He was true to his word.

The King's mistresses, before and after his wife's death, are too numerous to attempt to list. Indeed, it is unlikely that George himself could have listed all his paramours. One of them is worthy of mention, since the 1909 edition of England's *Dictionary of National Biography* mentions her as a possible mother of an illegitimate son of George's. She was Amelia Sophia, Baroness von Walmoden (1704–1765). After Queen Caroline's death, the King brought her to England and made her countess of Yarmouth. John Louis von Walmoden (1736–1811) was the child who might have been fathered by King George II. The *Dictionary of National Biography* tells us, "He rose to the rank of field-marshal in the Hanoverian army, which he commanded...." (George II was simultaneously King of England and ruler ["elector"] of Hanover in Germany until his death.)

Other sources are silent on this subject, and George himself followed the Hanoverian custom of refusing to acknowledge paternity of any illegitimate children.

Having spent a good deal of time introducing George and discussing the first half of his life, it is now appropriate to mention the impact of King George II on Great Britain and its emerging prominence as a world power.

An English naval captain named Robert Jenkins (–1738) claimed to have had an ear chopped off while engaging in slave trading on the high seas. The ear was allegedly lost to a Spanish sword in 1731. In any event, Captain Jenkins showed up in the House of Commons with an ear in a bottle and claimed that it was the ear that had been chopped off by the brutal Spaniards. There had been much tension between England and Spain about England's rights to engage in trade with its American colonies in general, and the slave trade in particular. This dramatic tale of Captain Jenkins' offended British honor sufficiently to trigger war with Spain in October 1739. It was initially called the War of Jenkins' Ear, but was soon subsumed in the War of the Austrian Succession.

Prompted by this dramatic, albeit possibly fraudulent, ear in a bottle, England entered a course which would lead to significant world power before the end of the reign of King George II. Military glory had always been George's desire and, although he was aloof to many of the details of government, he kept himself well informed about the status of England's military power, and even knew the names of the regimental colonels of his army.

The move toward becoming a world power got off to a bad start. Admiral Edward Vernon (1684–1757) was dispatched with a squadron to the West Indies, but he failed in 1741 to take the strongly fortified Cartagena from Spain. At that time, Cartagena was second only to Mexico City in importance to Spain in the Western Hemisphere.

In 1743 King George II became the last British monarch to take to the field of battle when, sword in hand, at the age of 60, he led his troops and achieved a victory over French forces during the War of the Austrian Succession. The King's victory occurred on June 27, 1743, in the battle of Dettingen.

In 1745 a Jacobite invasion of Britain, led by Charles Edward Stuart (1720–1788), was crushed by King George's son, Prince William, Duke of Cumberland (1721–1765). After this, the Jacobite claim of the Stuart line to the throne of England was no longer a serious issue.

The Continental war ended in 1748 with the treaty of Aix-la-Chapelle, and in 1751 the King's eldest and hated son, Frederick, Prince of Wales, died.

In 1755 the French were expelled from Nova Scotia, and in 1756 the Seven Years' War began. Although King George II did not care for William Pitt, Earl of Chatham (1708–1778), the King reluctantly asked him to form a government. Pitt's leadership proved to be most effective. The French were so preoccupied in fighting the Seven Years' War on the European Continent that they were unable to effectively defend their overseas possessions. William Pitt took full advantage of this on behalf of King George II, and the power of Great Britain ranged around the world. In 1757 Lieutenant-Colonel Robert Clive (1725–1774) recaptured Calcutta in India and, that same year, forces under Clive took the French Bengal portion of India, giving Britain control of most of India.

The French preoccupation with European military engagements left their North American possessions exposed, and England took advantage of the situation. General Jeffrey Amherst (1717–1797) was made commander-in-chief in America and sent with an expeditionary force to wrest Canada from France. Soon after capturing the all-important fortress of Louisbourg, at the entrance to the Gulf of St. Lawrence, in 1758, the fortress of Quebec also fell to British forces. England now controlled much of Canada.

In 1759 a series of victories by England destroyed French power in the East Indies and Guadeloupe. The British royal navy was now supreme at sea. The strange, unpopular German King had become very popular in England. Under King George II, the population had grown, imports and exports had greatly increased and prosperity reigned alongside the King. While it would be inappropriate to give King George II all the credit for shrewd statesmanship in advancing England as a world power, it must be admitted that he readily accepted advice from those with able judgment.

In the United States, we tend to think of the American Revolution as the result of problems that the American colonists had with King George III (1738–1820) and his associates in London. That is, of course, true, but the problems that finally culminated in the American Revolution, and the birth of the United States of America, were prominent during the reign of King George II, and even earlier.

By law, the English crown had supremacy over the American colonies. Each of these colonies had a legislature of its own, but under King George II, England took steps to unify colonial administration and control the colonists' western settlements and Indian relations. The American colonists were then mostly of English ancestry, but they considered themselves English freeholders and greatly resented the royal encroachment of establishing a central "board of trade and plantations."

While the English position was not entirely selfish (there was, after all, the menace of French imperialism on the frontiers of the American colonies), selfishness in London caused most of the problem.

King George II died on October 25, 1760, near the height of his popularity in England, at Kensington Palace. The cause of death was a massive heart attack. The King was buried at Westminster Abbey.

Under the law of primogeniture, which had governed the succession to the English throne since the era of the Norman Conquest, the throne passed, not to the eldest surviving son of King George II, but to the eldest son of the King's first-born son. That first-born son was Prince Frederick, Prince of Wales (1707–1751). When King George II died, the throne passed to Frederick's eldest surviving son, George, who had already been named Prince of Wales. He came to England's throne as King George III.

In *The Oxford Illustrated History of the British Monarchy*, published in 1998, John Cannon and Ralph Griffiths provide assessments of King George II, quoted, in large part, from two of his contemporaries, Horace Walpole and John Hervey. "Horace Walpole, who started off by disliking George II intensely, finished by according him a grudging respect, paying tribute to his moderation and lack of rancour. His faults—fussiness, pomposity, irritability—were largely on the surface: beneath was common sense and judgement. He did not seek to undermine the constitutional settlement which had brought his family to the throne and, though there were sharp and persistent quarrels with ministers, they were legitimate disagreements about the extent and use of the royal prerogatives.... Among those who knew him well, there was a good deal of unanimity of opinion. He had a clear but unsubtle mind, a fierce but forgiving temper. His painful honesty was at the bottom of his appalling rudeness: he never learned to dissemble, and deviousness was not among his failings.... The King's predilection for Hanover, where his authority was unquestioned, had not been allowed to influence his conduct in Britain. He was nearly thirty-one when he first landed in England and he remained all his life something of an observer of its strange ways."

34. *Queen Caroline (1683–1737)*

Caroline was born on March 1, 1683, in Ansbach, the capital of the small German state of Brandenburg-Ansbach. Her father was John Frederick (–1686), the Margrave of Brandenburg-Ansbach from 1667 until his death in 1686. At that time, the term *margrave* signified the ruler or military governor of a border province in Germany. Caroline's mother was the second wife of John Frederick. Her name was Eleanor Erdmuthe Louise (–1696), and as the daughter of the Duke of Saxe-Eisenach, Eleanor had been titled Princess Eleanor. Upon her marriage to John Frederick, she became Margravine of Brandenburg-Ansbach.

Caroline was christened Wilhelmina Caroline, but was always known by her second name, and in sources dealing with the history of England and biographies of English royalty, she is usually referred to as Caroline of Ansbach.

Two years later, a brother was born to Caroline's parents.

When Caroline's father died from smallpox in 1686, he was succeeded as margrave of Brandenburg-Ansbach by one of his sons from his first marriage. Caroline's mother soon realized that the new margrave had no interest in either her or her children, and she took the two children to live with her in her former German home, in Eisenach. In 1692 Caroline's mother remarried to John George IV (1668–1694), Elector of Saxony. The marriage was a disaster for Caroline and her mother. Fortunately, Frederick III (1657–1713), then elector of Brandenburg (later King Frederick I of Prussia), had promised that he would look after Caroline if anything disastrous happened to her mother. This became necessary, and Caroline moved to Berlin where she was brought up by her guardians, the elector and electress of Brandenburg.

The electress of Brandenburg was Sophia Charlotte (1688–1705), a daughter of Sophia (1630–1714), Electress of Hanover, who was the link between the English throne and the House of Hanover in Germany. Caroline (1683–1737) thus became acquainted with members of the Hanover family at any early age.

As Caroline entered her late teenage years, marriage possibilities were considered for her. One early possibility was Duke Frederick II of Saxe Gotha, whose daughter, Augusta of Saxe Gotha (1719–1772), would later become a daughter-in-law of Caroline's in England. Nothing came of this possible match for Caroline, nor did a grandiose scheme to marry her to the future Holy Roman Emperor Charles VI (1685–1740) get far, because Caroline could not accept his Catholicism. Some sources use the phrasing "staunch Protestantism" here, but, at least in later life, Caroline was more of an agnostic or atheist than a staunch Protestant. This never became much of an issue. As long as Caroline kept away from Roman Catholicism, England was prepared to accept her, whatever her religious views from time to time.

Sophia (1630–1714), Electress of Hanover, selected Caroline as a suitable bride for her grandson, George August (1683–1760), and the two Germans, Caroline and George August, were married at Herrenhausen, Germany on September 1, 1705.

Although Caroline would remain, throughout her life, more German than English in her manners and outlook, she did begin to study the English language in anticipation of someday becoming a member of the English royal family. She eventually became fluent in English, but preferred French to English as the language for her writing.

The newlyweds were but eight months apart in age and they were well suited to each other. George fell madly in love with his wife from the start and he continued to adore her until her death. (Years later, in England, Caroline and George had to be interrupted from an afternoon session in the conjugal bed to receive the news that King George I [1660–1727] was dead and that they were the new King and Queen Consort of England.)

Caroline was blonde, beautiful, and very intelligent, and George, a man of lesser intellectual prowess, was generally content to let his wife make decisions. To make this work, Caroline often skillfully dissembled, to allow George to think her ideas were his own.

Caroline's arrival near the center of England's royal stage was appropriate from a religious standpoint. She had refrained from pursuit of at least one earlier good marriage prospect since it conflicted with her anti–Catholic religious views. Since her father-in-law (King George I) was selected as England's monarch primarily because he wasn't Catholic, the pieces now fit nicely.

Caroline of Ansbach was described by Antonia Fraser in her *The Lives of the Kings & Queens of England* as "an extremely intelligent and lively woman ... large, blonde, blatantly sensual and earthy. A tremendous flirt, Caroline knew precisely what she was doing in charming men to advance her own political influence."

Caroline and George's marriage was not only happy but also blessed with fecundity. Four of their eight named children were born in Hanover, Germany, before King George I was crowned King of England and Caroline and her husband also moved to England. Since King George I had no Queen Consort (his former wife was imprisoned in a German castle), Caroline, who was now Princess of Wales, became the first lady of the land. Also because the King had no Consort, the only feasible royal court was the court of the Prince and Princess of Wales, George and Caroline.

The marriage of George and Caroline was remarkable from a number of standpoints. Caroline was much more intellectual than her husband. Later, when George and Caroline became King and Queen Consort of England, it was Caroline with whom the politicians found they needed to curry favor. George loved his beautiful and buxom wife dearly and found her very physically attractive until her death. Nevertheless, George had numerous affairs with numerous women, some of them his mistresses, but he did so not because he preferred them to his wife, but because he felt it his royal duty to have mistresses. Nigel Cawthorne's *The Sex Lives of the Kings & Queens of England* quotes Lord John Hervey (1696–1743): "Though he is incapable of being attached to any woman but his wife, he seemed to look upon his mistresses as a necessary appurtenance of his grandeur as a Prince rather than an addition to his pleasure." Caroline almost never objected to her husband's adulteries. This strange relationship might seem to be the product of folklore, but it is not. King George II is one of the better-known English monarchs, partially because two critics, both gifted with the ability to draft deft and acid criticism, were at hand to record many facts about this King. These critics were Lord John Hervey (1696–1743) and Horace Walpole (1678–1757). Another remarkable feature of the marriage of George and Caroline was their intense dislike of their eldest son, Frederick, Prince of Wales (1707–1751). A complete roster of the children of Caroline and George who survived infancy is presented in the following table:

Prince Frederick, Prince of Wales (1707–1751)
Princess Anne, Princess Royal (1709–1759)
Princess Amelia (1711–1786)

Princess Caroline (1713–1757)
Prince William, Duke of Cumberland (1721–1765)
Princess Mary (1723–1772)
Princess Louisa (1724–1751)

A stillborn son was born to Caroline in November 1716. Princess Caroline and her German retinue attributed this misfortune to English doctors, who insisted on using instruments during the childbirth. That practice was contrary to the natural childbirth methods then in vogue in Germany. Caroline henceforth insisted on having a German midwife in attendance when bearing her children.

English aristocrats had very little contact with their own children, so they were genuinely startled to see Caroline spanking her royal children in public when they misbehaved. However, Caroline was anything but a stereotypical mother. Her interests were intellectual and included politics, philosophy and religion. Caroline's husband loved her but not her intellectual pursuits, so she found a private room in which to retire to pursue her studies and conduct private discussions with prominent intellectuals, such as Gottfried Wilhelm von Leibniz (1646–1716).

In 1717 a serious rift between the King and the Prince of Wales occurred. The proximate cause was a dispute concerning the godparents to be chosen for Prince George William (1717–1718). The rift was reminiscent of the alleged sham when Prince James Francis Edward, Prince of Wales (1688–1766) was born. The rift grew out of proportion, and the Prince and Princess of Wales moved their court from St. James' Palace to Leicester House, where the Prince and his vivacious Princess surrounded themselves with a raffish set of men and women with lively minds. The Prince and Princess of Wales made Leicester House their chief residence until King George I died.

King George I had allowed Robert Walpole, Earl of Orford (1676–1745), to serve as prime minister from 1715 to 1717. When King George I died, George and Caroline acceded to the throne as King and Queen Consort immediately and they were crowned at Westminster Abbey on October 11, 1727. Caroline became the first of England's many German Queen Consorts. She would wield more power over English affairs of state than any queen consort since the Middle Ages.

By this time, Robert Walpole had built a powerful partnership between Caroline and himself, which lasted until Caroline's death. Caroline particularly approved of Walpole's reluctance to involve England in the incessant wars on the European continent. Caroline felt that England offered far better prospects for her children's inheritance than did Hanover, in Germany. Although the new King had been poised to remove Walpole from influence, Caroline persuaded him to leave Walpole at the center of power. This worked to the advantage of King George II also, and, for the first 15 years of his reign, George was content to allow Caroline and Walpole to run things, and the Queen acted as his regent during George's frequent absences on visits to Hanover. The King spent much of his free time in the company of his mistresses, hunting stags and playing cards.

Walpole and Queen Caroline met in private with some frequency to discuss important pending political business and reach decisions. Then, on account of her husband's conceit, Caroline adopted a strategy which was recorded by the court chronicler, Lord John Hervey: "She always at first gave in to all his notions ... and made him imagine any change she wrought in them to be an afterthought of his own." Petronelle Cook's *Queen Consorts of England: The Power Behind the Throne*, published in 1993, assures us that Caroline's "method worked like a charm."

Queen Caroline knew that her husband was madly in love with her, but she also knew that there was nothing she could do to end his extramarital affairs. While she could not avoid them, she could and did use them to her advantage. She wisely limited her husband's mistresses to those less beautiful than herself, a fairly easy task for the beautiful and vivacious Caroline. Then she attempted to manage her husband through his mistresses. This strategy generally was successful, and worked particularly well with the King's long-time mistress, Henrietta Howard (1681–1767), later Countess of Suffolk.

Queen Caroline's patience toward her husband's sex life was remarkable, but there was at least one occasion when the King tried to go too far and the Queen communicated her strong displeasure to him. The King was on one of his many trips to Hanover, Germany (his reigns as ruler of Hanover and King of England were simultaneous), and there he became involved in a sexual relationship with Amelia Sophia, Baroness von Walmoden (1704–1765). King George proposed, in a communication to Caroline, that he bring Amelia back to England with him. Caroline's great patience broke on this occasion and she let her husband know that she was greatly displeased.

Biographers of Queen Caroline speak well of her and fault her only perhaps as a somewhat cool mother to her children, and rather more severely for her intense hatred of her eldest son, Prince Frederick. She also had little affection for her younger son, Prince William.

However, Queen Caroline was certainly fond of her daughters and became upset when Princess Anne (1709–1759), her eldest daughter, the Princess Royal, expressed a desire to marry the Dutch William IV, Prince of Orange (1711–1751). The Queen found it difficult to accept him as a match for Princess Anne, because of his physical deformity. John van der Kiste's work entitled *King George II & Queen Caroline*, published in 1997, provides a description of him indicating that he was almost a dwarf, possibly because of curvature of the spine or a tubercular condition. However, suitable royal mates were in short supply because England insisted that the search be limited to European Protestants. Accordingly, the Queen gave her consent and the couple were married on March 14, 1734.

After Queen Caroline passed her 50th birthday, her physical health declined greatly. Fortunately, her intellectual faculties remained sharp, and it was with intellectual pursuits that she found her greatest pleasure. By 1737 she could no longer disguise the fact that she was probably fatally ill.

Caroline died in the latter part of 1737 at St. James' Palace. The date given for her death differs among various reputable sources; some show November 20, others November 25, and still others cite December 1. This is certainly unfortunate, because Queen Caroline was anything but an insignificant person in England's history. Presumably the cause of the variation is the difference between the Julian calendar and the Gregorian calendar. Since 1582, the Gregorian calendar had been in use in Continental Europe. That calendar had been a departure from the previous Julian calendar. The Gregorian calendar lopped off some ten days (eleven days after 1700) from the prior Julian calendar, to more closely align the years with actual movements of the earth about the sun. But the new calendar had been adopted under the authority of the Roman Catholic Pope Gregory XIII (1502–1585) and, worse yet, it had been named for that pope. In 1737 Protestant England had not yet adopted this new calendar, although that would finally be done in September 1752, aligning the dates used in England and her American colonies with those in use elsewhere in Christendom.

Under this explanation for the death date, we would say that Queen Caroline died on November 20, 1737 (Julian calendar), but that date became December 1, 1737 under the Gregorian calendar, when it was adopted in 1752. These pieces fit nicely if we just ignore the "25 November/ 1 December" death date given in David Williamson's *Kings & Queens of Britain*, published in 1992.

King George II took up residence on a cot at the foot of Queen Caroline's bed as she was dying. The Queen asked him to promise that he would remarry. He refused, saying that he would have mistresses, instead. Princess Amelia (1711–1786) and Princess Caroline (1713–1757) were also beside their mother when she died. Although Queen Caroline had expressed some interest in the theology of England's official church, the Anglican Church, and earlier attended church services regularly, by the time she faced death, she apparently had lost her faith. She allowed the Archbishop of Canterbury, John Potter (–1747), to pray at her deathbed, but apparently refused to take the church's sacrament, for Bishop Potter evaded questions on this subject after leaving the Queen's side.

She was buried at Westminster Abbey, but Queen Caroline's story does not end yet. When her husband, the King, later died in 1760, he left explicit instructions that he was to be buried touching his wife's corpse; i.e., that sides of her coffin and his were to be removed and the remains pressed adjacent to each other. This unusual request was obeyed. The remains of Caroline and George were buried in one huge stone sarcophagus, in the vault of the chapel of King Henry VII (1457–1509). About a century after the funeral of King George II, the planks, which had been removed from the two coffins, were found resting against a nearby wall.

35. *Prince Frederick, Prince of Wales (1707–1751)*

This eldest son of King George II (1683–1760) and his Queen Consort, Queen Caroline (1683–1737), was born in his grandfather's palace in Hanover, Germany, in early 1707. The precise date of his birth seems to be a mystery.

In *The King Who Never Was: The Story of Frederick, Prince of Wales* by Michael De-la-Noy, published in 1996, the author provides the results of his frustrated attempts to pin down the precise birth date. Footnote 1 to the first chapter of that work states, "There has been considerable confusion and conflict of opinion over the date of Prince Frederick's birth. There seems, for example, not to be not a scrap of evidence for 6 January, the date given in the *Dictionary of National Biography* and followed by a modern American researcher into Frederick's achievements as a patron of the arts, Kimberly Rorschach ... Nor for 20 January ... Nor yet for 31 January...." De-la-Noy goes on to discuss some evidence supporting perhaps a February 4 date and then wrestles with the difference between the Gregorian calendar, then in use where Frederick was born, versus the Julian calendar, then still in use in England and its American colonies.

Frederick eventually would become heir apparent to the throne of England, but that was far from clear at the time of his birth. Queen Anne (1665–1714) was still reigning in England. The only child of Anne's to survive infancy had died in 1700. Because the English parliament thought it unlikely that Anne would bear additional children, and because of the anti–Catholic mood in England, in 1701 parliament passed the Settlement Act to insure Protestant succession to the English throne. That act provided that Sophia, Electress of Hanover (1630–1714), a Protestant (Frederick's paternal great-grandmother), would be next in the line of succession to England's throne after the death of Princess (later Queen) Anne. However, Sophia of Hanover died before Queen Anne's death, which put Frederick's paternal grandfather, George Lewis, Elector of Hanover (1660–1727), next in line for the English throne. He took that throne in 1714, and upon his death in 1727 his only son took the throne as King George II.

Frederick Louis (whose baptismal name was the German version, Friedrich Ludwig) was born in relative secrecy in the presence of only one doctor and a midwife. The secrecy was ordered by George Lewis (1660–1727) who then ruled Hanover. The baby's great-grandmother, Sophia, Electress of Hanover, wisely pointed out that the absence of official witnesses to the baby's birth could lead to later allegations that the child was stillborn and replaced with some anonymous baby from a foundling hospital. That made no impression, and nearly a week went by before George Lewis even permitted an official announcement to be made of the birth of this important baby.

This secrecy may seem strange and puzzling, but it provides merely a glimpse of the strange and puzzling relationships and family hatreds that would surround Frederick all his life. Indeed, Frederick was perhaps the greatest victim of the venom that flowed through the Hanover family. Many authors have speculated on reasons behind this hatred and some of the explanations seem plausible, but the truth went to the graves long ago with the principal players. What is known to be factual is that both of Frederick's parents came to hate him when he was still quite young, and he eventually grew to enormously dislike his parents. (The other fact which is known, but hardly serves to explain this unfortunate arrangement of emotions, is that from the time that the future King George I caused his marriage to be dissolved, and his former wife to be imprisoned in German castles, the eldest male in this genealogical line either hated or strongly disliked his eldest son.)

When England's Queen Anne died in 1714 and Frederick's parents and grandfather moved to London to assume their places of importance in England, Frederick was left behind in Hanover. His education was left to ordinary teachers, but young Frederick was a bright enough lad to master the material and become well educated and fluent.

When Frederick was about eleven years old, his grandfather, now the King of England, invested him as a knight of the garter, the oldest and highest order of English knights. About the same time he was styled as Duke of Gloucester and over the years he would be flooded with various other titles of nobility. The title Prince of Wales was harder for him to obtain. That title is reserved for (male only) heirs apparent to the throne of England.

Young Frederick, isolated from his family, sowed wild oats in Hanover and freely fraternized with members of lower classes.

In 1727 King George I died, and Frederick's parents came to England's throne as King and Queen Consort.

Meanwhile, Frederick, still living in Hanover, Germany, had marriage possibilities on his mind and he gave early consideration to wedding his cousin, Princess Wilhelmina (1709–1758), the eldest daughter of Queen Sophia Dorothea (1687–1757) of Prussia. That possibility drew strong negative reactions from the kings of both Prussia and England.

Late in 1728, King George II finally sent emissaries to bring Frederick to London. Even when he arrived, he was given no official reception and had to hire a hackney carriage to take him to the palace. Prince Frederick had not seen his parents in 14 years. Little enthusiasm was afforded him at the reunion. The King was quite reluctant to create Frederick Prince of Wales, and did so in January 1729, only as a result of pressure he received from English government officials.

The allowance bestowed upon Prince Frederick was quite meager for a member of the royal family, and the plan was that he should have no household of his own. In spite of these handicaps, he made a good impression on London society.

A glimpse at a portion of the index to John Walters' 1972 biography entitled *The Royal Griffin: Frederick, Prince of Wales 1707–1751* provides a view from 30,000 feet of Prince Frederick's life during his early residence in England, after he had been created Prince of Wales:

> friendship with Lord Hervey
> loses his official seals for a night
> relationship with mother and sisters in early years of English domicile
> musical appreciation
> marriage plot with Lady Diana Spencer
> makes Miss La Tour his mistress
> gambling
> practical jokes and hoaxes

writes five-act comedy
rift with Hervey over Anne Vane
his royal barge
joy in the countryside
gardening at Kew
alliance with Dodington
complete alienation with parents
son by Anne Vane
baby by Anne Vane's maid

Lord Hervey was Lord John Hervey (1696–1743), Lady Diana Spencer was later Duchess of Bedford, and Dodington was George Bubb Dodington (1691–1762), later Baron Melcombe. "Kew" was a house with gardens near London, in the village of Kew. Prince Frederick made it his home in the early 1730s and it was his favorite residence for the rest of his life.

Prince Frederick by now had acquired a talent for scheming behind his father's back for political influence, but he realized that he would have to go through his father if he wished to be married. He did so, and a marriage was arranged to which Prince Frederick agreed. The bride to be was Augusta (1719–1772), the youngest daughter of the German Frederick II, Duke of Saxe Gotha. The wedding date is given by some sources as April 27 and by others as May 8, 1736. For this discrepancy there is an explanation; i.e., the difference between the Julian calendar and the Gregorian calendar. Since 1582, the Gregorian calendar had been in use in Continental Europe. That calendar had been a departure from the previous Julian calendar. The Gregorian calendar lopped off some ten days (eleven days after 1700) from the prior Julian calendar, to more closely align the years with actual movements of the earth about the sun. But the new calendar had been adopted under the authority of the Roman Catholic Pope Gregory XIII (1502–1585), and worse yet, it had been named for that pope. In 1736 Protestant England had not yet adopted this new calendar, although that would finally be done in September 1752, aligning the dates used in England and her American colonies with those in use elsewhere in Christendom.

The marriage produced nine named children, one of whom would later come to England's throne. A complete roster of the children of Frederick and Augusta is presented here:

Princess Augusta (1737–1813). Her daughter, Caroline (1768–1821), would wed King George IV (1762–1830)
Prince George (1738–1820), who came to England's throne as King George III.
Prince Edward Augustus, Duke of York and Albany (1739–1767)
Princess Elizabeth Caroline (1740–1759). This year of birth is Julian; Gregorian, it is 1741.
Prince William Henry, Duke of Gloucester (1743–1805). His son, William Frederick (1776–1834) married Princess Mary (1776–1857), a daughter of King George III.

Prince Henry Frederick, Duke of Cumberland (1745–1790)
Princess Louisa Anne (1749–1768)
Prince Frederick William (1750–1765)
Princess Caroline Matilda (1751–1775). Married King Christian VII (1749–1808) of
    Denmark and Norway. Until her 1772 divorce, she was Queen Consort of that
    kingdom.

Prince Frederick was a devoted father and husband, although, true to the
Hanoverian form, which dated back at least to his great-grandfather, he was
unable to be faithful to his wife. Horace Walpole (1678–1757) observed: "His
chief passion was women, but like the rest of his race, beauty was not a necessary
ingredient."

Prince Frederick was a man of culture, a patron of the arts and a sportsman.
Michael De-la-Noy's *The King Who Never Was: The Story of Frederick, Prince of
Wales* is particularly helpful in explaining Prince Frederick's popularity among the
English people in contrast to the grudging respect paid to his father, the King. "It
was no wonder Frederick found easy popularity by being pleasant to the English,
and pleasant about them. He was the first member of the royal family to play
cricket. He would drape his arm round someone's shoulder...."

Frederick died on March 20, 1751 (Julian calendar), which very soon became
March 31, 1751, when England finally adopted the Gregorian calendar in 1752.
King George II feigned sadness at the death, but the masses of London were genuinely grieved at the loss of the member of the royal family who had been closest
to them.

Under the law of primogeniture, which had governed the succession to the
English throne since the era of the Norman Conquest, when Prince Frederick's
father, King George II, died in 1760, the throne passed, not to the eldest surviving
son of King George II, but to the eldest son of the King's first-born son. That first-
born son was Prince Frederick, Prince of Wales, and his eldest son came to England's
throne in 1760 as King George III.

36. *Princess Anne, Princess Royal (1709–1759)*

This eldest daughter of King George II (1683–1760) and his Queen Consort,
Queen Caroline (1683–1737), was born at Herrenhausen in Germany, on November 2, 1709. She was their second child, a brother, Frederick, having been born in
1707.

Anne eventually would become Princess Royal of England, but that was far
from clear at the time of her birth. Queen Anne (1665–1714) was still reigning in
England. The only child of Queen Anne's to survive infancy had died in 1700.
Because the English parliament thought it unlikely that Queen Anne would bear
additional children, and because of the anti–Catholic mood in England, in 1701

parliament passed the Settlement Act to insure Protestant succession to the English throne. That act provided that Sophia, Electress of Hanover (1630–1714), a Protestant (Anne's paternal great-grandmother), would be next in the line of succession to England's throne after the death of Princess (later Queen) Anne. However, Sophia of Hanover died before Queen Anne's death, which put Anne's paternal grandfather, George Lewis, Elector of Hanover (1660–1727), next in line for the English throne.

However, Sophia, the Dowager Electress of Hanover, had the English throne very much on her mind at the time of our Anne's birth, and Veronica Baker-Smith tells us in her 1995 work entitled *A Life of Anne of Hanover, Princess Royal*, that Sophia saw to it that the baby girl was named in honor of the reigning Queen of England, Queen Anne (1665–1714). The compliment was part of an attempt to shore up the position of the German House of Hanover with England's Queen Anne. Sophia was still uncertain about Queen Anne's loyalty to her Roman Catholic father, England's former King James II (1633–1701). It was the Roman Catholic son of that King, Prince James Francis Edward (1688–1766), who had been Prince of Wales and, in the opinion of some, had a greater right to the throne of England that any of the German Hanovers.

When England's Queen Anne died in 1714, Princess Anne's parents and grandfather moved to London to assume their places of importance in England, and the princess accompanied them. Their journey took them first by coach to The Hague, where they spent three days sightseeing. By coincidence, Anne would later marry the man who, in 1747, would become the stadtholder, or ruler, of the Dutch States.

Anne's grandfather, King George I (1660–1727), disliked his son, Anne's father, and a great rift between the King and Anne's parents occurred in 1717. Prince George and Princess Caroline moved to Leicester House. The King kept his grandchildren, including Princess Anne, with him and forbade his son to even visit his children. (The children involved here are all those who had thus far been born, except Prince Frederick [1707–1751], who had been left behind in Germany when the rest of the family came to England.) Thus, Princess Anne was the eldest of the King's grandchildren being held in this odd captivity. Princess Caroline was allowed some access to her children, but the arrangement was a terrible one, particularly for the children. When Anne was about age nine she once burst out, "We have a good father and a good mother, and yet we are like charity children." As the eldest child on the scene, Anne tried to do what she could as an intermediary, and she used Charlotte Clayton (–1742), her mother's lady-in-waiting, to pass some messages between children and parents. The rift remained for about a year and a half.

In April 1720, Princess Anne came down with smallpox. Her life was in danger for a few days, but then she began her full recovery. A sad consequence of this bout with smallpox was a badly scarred complexion.

Veronica Baker-Smith provides a glimpse of Princess Anne's early education in her 1995 work entitled *A Life of Anne of Hanover, Princess Royal*. Baker-Smith mentions that Jane Martha, Countess of Portland (1672–1751), was appointed as royal governess to the children by King George I, and that she was an inspiring teacher for them. The governess remarked, "Princess Anne speaks, reads and writes German and French to Perfection, knows a great deal of History and Geography, speaks English very prettily and dances very well." The governess was speaking of Anne at age five; later Anne would add fluent Italian to her repertoire. Princess Anne also learned to play the harpsichord, and she was taught to sing by the great composer George F. Handel (1685–1759), a German by birth, who had come to England and would eventually become a naturalized citizen. Anne was a great fan of Handel's and defended him with vigor during debates associated with England's opera season.

The illness had a good side. It brought about the beginnings of some harmony between the King and his son and daughter-in-law.

In 1727 King George I died and Anne's parents came to England's throne as King and Queen Consort.

Anne and her sisters were much involved in the glittering coronation of her parents on October 11, 1727. Anne was no longer a mere Princess; she had become the "princess royal." She was only the second Princess in England's history to hold the Princess Royal designation. An explanation of the term "princess royal" as it relates to the English royal family is appropriate here. This title is bestowed on some (but by no means all) first-born daughters of the King of England. The practice began with King Charles I (1600–1649), and therefore Princess Mary (1631–1660) was England's first "princess royal." Geoffrey Wakeford's 1973 work entitled *The Princesses Royal* explains the decision to create this title with these words: "Charles I or his advisers devised the status of Princess Royal to distinguish his daughter Mary Stuart from the 'ordinary' foreign princesses who were not necessarily of the blood royal." By coincidence, England's first Princess Royal, Mary, was wed to a Dutch Prince of Orange and England's second Princess Royal, our Princess Anne, would also wed a Dutch prince of Orange.

Sad to say, our Princess Royal came to have rather exalted ideas of her status. She had been high-handed with her lady-in-waiting as a child and now enlarged her horizon to become rather a snob in general.

However, Princess Anne's interests were not confined to subjects with high snob appeal. She also joined with family members in card games, backgammon, and other games of chance. In the country, she enjoyed riding with her father when he went hunting stag.

John Van der Kiste's *The Georgian Princesses*, published in 2000, tells us, "When King Louis XV of France was seeking a bride, a betrothal with the Princess Royal of England seemed a good way of helping to reconcile the two countries which had so often been enemies. A marriage contract was drawn up, and matters were virtually regarded as settled until the French court insisted that the future Queen Anne of France should be received into the Roman Catholic Church. The House of Hanover could not afford to be compromised by such a Catholic connection, and no more was heard of the matter." The House of Hanover owed its position on the British throne to anti–Catholic hysteria in England.

By the time Princess Anne had reached her early twenties, the subject of finding a suitable mate for her became rather desperate. It was the custom to limit the search to royal Europeans. The problem of finding a suitable mate, who was interested in Anne, was not an easy one to solve. She was far from pretty. Princess Anne had residual scars on her complexion from her childhood bout with smallpox, a slightly bulbous pair of Hanoverian eyes, and the beginnings of a serious weight problem, which even gorgeous clothing could not conceal.

Moreover, from her father's standpoint, Princess Anne was a special princess, for she was the Princess Royal. It was the custom for English princesses to marry royalty, but the King had a problem in selecting a mate for Princess Anne. Most of the European fellow monarchs of King George II were Roman Catholics, and Anglican England wanted no Catholic in the royal family. However, a husband was found. A long version of his name and title was William Charles Henry, Prince William IV of Orange and Stadtholder of the United Provinces (1711–1751). The Prince had an even longer title with Nassau, Friesland, Groningen, and Guelderland, inserted at appropriate intervals, and he was also encumbered with physical deformity. John Van der Kiste's *King George II & Queen Caroline*, published in 1997, describes Prince William IV as "almost a dwarf," possibly because of curvature of the spine or a tubercular condition.

When this marital choice was presented to Princess Anne, she showed interest. Indeed, when Anne's mother, Queen Caroline, expressed doubts about the prospective bridegroom, because of his physical deformity, Princess Anne pressed her mother to allow the marriage plans to go forward, and they did. In preparation for a new life in the Netherlands, Princess Anne studied Dutch history and learned to paint in the style of the Flemish artist Anthony Van Dyke (1599–1641).

Princess Anne and William IV, Prince of Orange, were wed on March 14 (Julian calendar) or March 25 (Gregorian calendar), 1734. The ceremony was conducted in the Chapel Royal at St. James' Palace. David Williamson's work entitled *Brewer's British Royalty*, published in 1996, provides this description of the ceremony: "The bride was attired in 'virgin robes of silver tissue, having a train six yards long which was supported by ten Dukes' and Earls' daughters, all of whom were attired in robes of silver tissue.'"

Prince William IV and his bride, now the Princess of Orange, took up residence in Leeuwarden Palace in the Netherlands, but when Prince William joined the Holy Roman Emperor's army on the Rhine River, his homesick and pregnant wife returned to England. After much coaxing, Princess Anne reluctantly agreed to return to the Netherlands to await the birth of her child with her husband, but the pregnancy ended disastrously with no heir being born.

On February 23, 1743, a daughter was born to Anne and William. Her baptismal name was Wilhelmina Carolina, but she was known simply as Carolina (1743–1787). In March 1748, a son followed, and he inherited his father's title, Prince of Orange. He was William V (1748–1806), Prince of Orange.

On October 22, 1751, William IV, Prince of Orange, suffered increasingly poor health, due in part to his twisted backbone, which culminated in a massive stroke. He died at the age of 40.

The widowed Princess of Orange did not return to England, but remained in the Dutch States, where she pursued her intellectual and artistic interests. She was still arrogant and, with little charm, she had few friends. She died on January 12, 1759, of dropsy, at The Hague.

37. *Princess Amelia (1711–1786)*

This daughter of King George II (1683–1760) and his Queen Consort, Queen Caroline (1683–1737), was born at Herrenhausen in Germany, on June 10, 1711. Her baptismal name was Amelia Sophia Eleanor (or a German version of that: Amalie Sophie Eleonore), but she is referred to as Amelia in most works dealing with English history and England's royal family. Within the family, she was known as "Emily."

Amelia eventually would become a Princess of England, but that was not yet certain at the time of her birth. Queen Anne (1665–1714) was still reigning in England. The only child of Queen Anne's to survive infancy had died in 1700. Because the English parliament thought it unlikely that Anne would bear additional children, and because of the anti–Catholic mood in England, in 1701 parliament passed the Settlement Act to insure Protestant succession to the English throne. That act provided that Sophia, Electress of Hanover (1630–1714), a Protestant (Amelia's paternal great-grandmother), would be next in the line of succession to England's throne after the death of Princess (later Queen) Anne.

Sophia doted on her great-grandchildren and showered them with presents, some of which were handicrafts she made herself. Even their gruff paternal grandfather, George Lewis (1660–1727), Elector of Hanover, showed affection toward his grandchildren, which he had not bestowed upon his own children. Although Amelia was still too young to appreciate it, her early years in Hanover, Germany, were spent in luxurious palaces. Six hundred prize horses, the envy of much of Europe, were kept close at hand in the stables. Perhaps this early proximity to fine horses played a role in Amelia's later love of horses.

Sophia of Hanover died before Queen Anne of England did, which put our Amelia's paternal grandfather, George Lewis, next in the line of succession for the English throne.

When England's Queen Anne died in 1714, and our Amelia's parents and grandfather moved to London to assume their places of importance in England, Amelia, now an English Princess, accompanied them.

In England, young Princess Amelia spent a good deal of time in the company of Charlotte Clayton (–1742), her mother's lady-in-waiting.

Amelia's grandfather, King George I (1660–1727), disliked his son, Amelia's father, and a great rift between the King and Amelia's parents occurred in 1717.

Prince George and Princess Caroline moved to Leicester House. The King kept his grandchildren, including Princess Amelia, with him, and forbade his son to even visit his children. (The children involved here are all those who had thus far been born, except Prince Frederick [1707–1751], who had been left behind in Germany when the rest of the family came to England.) Princess Caroline was allowed some access to her children, but the arrangement was a terrible one, particularly for the children.

Jane Martha, Countess of Portland (1672–1751), was appointed as royal governess to the children by King George I, and she was an inspiring teacher for them.

During this period, it was remarked that Princess Amelia was charming. The blonde Princess Amelia was also much prettier than her elder sister, Princess Anne, the Princess Royal (1709–1759), whose complexion had been marred by a childhood smallpox infection. However, Amelia lacked robust health and frequently suffered from colds, bronchitis, and swollen neck glands. Smallpox, of course, could well kill her were she to contract it.

A rather astounding practical medical experiment was conceived by Amelia's intellectual mother, Caroline. It was three-quarters of a century before the English physician, Dr. Edward Jenner (1749–1823), developed a vaccination for smallpox, when Caroline conceived of her plan, and aggressively pursued it, to use such a vaccination to immunize her children. Princess Caroline got the basic idea from Lady Mary Wortley Montagu (1689–1762), and although she pursued it aggressively, she was also prudent. Her first step was to secure six condemned criminals from the London prison, Newgate, who had never contracted smallpox. On condition that their lives would be spared for participating in the experiment, the criminals underwent vaccination. The air was thick with criticism, at this stage, from both doctors and clergymen. This experiment was so successful that Princess Caroline had it repeated on six charity children. Once again, the experiment succeeded, so Caroline had two of her daughters, Amelia and Caroline, inoculated in April 1722.

Princess Amelia continued to suffer from delicate health as a teenager and was advised to use the waters at Bath, England, to improve her health. The extent of her visits to Bath as a teenager is not clear, but we know that Bath became one of her favorite haunts in later years, and that she indulged, there and elsewhere, in one of her favorite activities, high stakes card games.

Princess Amelia never married, but we need shed no tears for her, because Amelia was delighted with her life as a "spinster." There had been an effort to wed her to her first-cousin, Frederick, the Crown Prince of Prussia (1712–1786), who was heir to the Prussian throne. Frederick's mother was Sophia Dorothea (1687–1757), a daughter of King George I, and wife of King Frederick William (1688–1740) of Prussia. Sophia Dorothea nurtured a desire to see her eldest son wed to one of the Hanover ladies, who were now Princesses of England. Since Princess Amelia shared Prince Frederick's passion for horses, perhaps a marriage could be built upon that common interest. Prince Frederick was more than willing to marry Amelia, or anybody else, if doing so would remove him from the tyranny of his father, the King.

The Prussian Queen, Sophia Dorothea, and her father, King George I, were astoundingly brazen in pursuing the details of this marriage and a second with which it was to be paired. They never mentioned the matter to Princess Amelia, or even to her parents, the Prince and Princess of Wales. The marriage plot fell apart and nothing came of it.

Although Amelia never married, she did enjoy a period of sexual activity and was known, for a time, as the family flirt. She had brief affairs with Thomas Pelham-Holles, Duke of Newcastle (1693–1768), Charles Fitzroy, Duke of Grafton (1683–1757), and a "Lord Chamberlain."

In 1727 King George I died, and Amelia's parents came to England's throne as King and Queen Consort. Amelia and her sisters were much involved in the glittering coronation of her parents on October 11, 1727. John Van der Kiste's 1997 work entitled *King George II & Queen Caroline* tells us that Caroline's "...train-bearers were her daughters Anne, Caroline and Amelia, in purple robes of state, with circlets on their heads; their coronets were borne behind them by three peers...."

Ten years after that coronation, Queen Caroline was on her deathbed. Her husband, the King, was at her side, and Princess Amelia slept on a couch-bed in the corner of the room, while her mother awaited her final summons.

Amelia spent a great deal of time with her younger brother, Prince William, Duke of Cumberland (1721–1765). They shared a number of common interests, and she often served as his hostess when he entertained. During this period, when English aristocrats sent invitations to social functions, they understood that brother and sister were both to be invited.

Apparently Princess Amelia had only limited interest in political matters, but Englishmen who wished to manipulate her politically powerful brother toward their ends, often tried to work through Amelia to reach Cumberland. The Duke of Cumberland was very active in military campaigns, and during this period of their lives, brother and sister had grown so close that Princess Amelia fretted about his welfare, particularly when he was near the front lines of combat.

In 1752 Amelia was appointed ranger of Richmond Park. Amelia's concept was that the park should be reserved for members of the royal family and their guests. When the public insisted that they had a right of passage through the grounds, the imaginative Princess Amelia provided them access ... a few rickety old ladders were placed against the park walls and common folk were permitted to use them, at their own risk. A court case followed, which Amelia lost, and she resigned her position as park ranger. John Van der Kiste's *The Georgian Princesses*, published in 2000, states that Amelia declared "that the downfall of England commenced with the opening of Richmond Park."

Princess Amelia was also a frequent companion to her father after the Queen's death. On his own deathbed, on October 25, 1760, the King called to have Amelia brought to his side. Amelia then had become rather deaf, and upon her arrival she put her ear close to her father's face to hear what he wished to say. She remained there for some time until she realized that he was dead.

John Van der Kiste's *King George II & Queen Caroline* tells us that Amelia was "an active, extroverted young woman," who was fond of hunting, and that "she became increasingly eccentric and shocked fellow members of the congregation at Hampton Court church by arriving in riding clothes and carrying a dog under each arm." Rex Whitworth's 1992 biography of Amelia's brother, William, tells us that Amelia had tremendous reserves of energy. The title of that work is *William Augustus, Duke of Cumberland: A Life.*

Delightfully eccentric, Amelia was accustomed to taking snuff while she played high stakes card games at Bath, England. One evening, an elderly general in an adjacent seat took some snuff from Amelia's box. Amelia ordered her footman to throw the snuff box in the fire and fetch her a new box.

Princess Amelia apparently also shocked the wife of the new King, George III (1738–1820). In 1761 the new King had married Charlotte (1744–1818) of Mecklenburg-Strelitz, and the new Queen was very big on decorum and shocked by gaming. Whitworth's biography of the Duke of Cumberland relates, "She immediately set about improving standards. Cards were abolished and no courts were held on Sundays. Cumberland and Amelia were no doubt glad to escape from the monotony of St. James'."

Princess Amelia lived to be the last surviving child of King George II. She died at her house in London, on Cavendish Square, on October 31, 1786, and was buried in the chapel of King Henry VII (1457–1509) at Westminster Abbey.

The two great chroniclers of the reign of King George II, Horace Walpole (1678–1757) and Lord John Hervey (1696–1743), provide strikingly different assessments of Princess Amelia. Walpole's comments were quite favorable, even glowing. Hervey's comments, however, were so harsh and one-sided against Amelia that one wonders if there weren't some personal grudge between Lord Hervey and Princess Amelia.

38. *Princess Caroline (1713–1757)*

This daughter of King George II (1683–1760) and his Queen Consort, Queen Caroline (1683–1737), was born at Herrenhausen in Germany, on June 10, 1713. She was baptized two days later as Caroline Elizabeth.

Caroline eventually would become a Princess of England, but that was not yet certain at the time of her birth. Queen Anne (1665–1714) was still reigning in England. The only child of Queen Anne's to survive infancy had died in 1700. Because the English parliament thought it unlikely that Anne would bear additional children, and because of the anti–Catholic mood in England, in 1701 parliament passed the Settlement Act to insure Protestant succession to the English throne. That act provided that Sophia, Electress of Hanover (1630–1714), a Protestant

(Caroline's paternal great-grandmother), would be next in the line of succession to England's throne after the death of Princess (later Queen) Anne.

Sophia doted on her great-grandchildren and showered them with presents, some of which were handicrafts she made herself. Even their gruff paternal grandfather, George Lewis (1660–1727), Elector of Hanover, showed affection toward his grandchildren, which he had not bestowed upon his own children. Although Caroline was far too young to appreciate it, her early years in Hanover, Germany, were spent in luxurious palaces.

Sophia of Hanover died before Queen Anne of England did, which put Caroline's paternal grandfather, George Lewis, next in the line of succession for the English throne.

When England's Queen Anne died in 1714, Caroline's parents and grandfather moved to London to assume their places of importance in England. Two of Caroline's elder sisters accompanied their parents to London, but Caroline was not yet two years old, and she was not in good health when the family (apart from Frederick, who was left in Germany for a number of years) left for England. The German doctors felt that young Caroline's health was too fragile to make the then rather arduous trip from Hanover, Germany, to London, England.

This is the first reference we have seen linking Caroline with poor health. There will be many more, and the tone encountered in many of the references to her health by family members is annoyingly patronizing. Caroline's elder sister, Princess Amelia (1711–1786), had a rather sharp tongue for almost everyone on almost every subject, so perhaps her remarks on the subject of Caroline's health should be ignored, but others in the family also projected an air of long suffering on this subject.

The facts are that Princess Caroline *was* in poor health for much of her life, and that her poor health was likely a root cause of the depression from which she suffered near the end of her life. In addition, although she had never suffered the rigors of childbirth, she died at the rather tender age of forty-four.

Legend has it that there is a gravestone in a cemetery at Key West, Florida, on which the lady buried below proclaims to all the world: "See; I told you I was really sick!" Princess Caroline well deserved a similar memorial but never got it, not on stone, nor on the printed page.

Mention will be made of Princess Caroline's unusual fondness for John Hervey (1696–1743). Although the evidence is circumstantial, it would seem likely that Caroline's fondness for Hervey was built, at least in part, on the mutual foundation of poor health and less than sympathetic responses to their health maladies.

Caroline's grandfather, King George I (1660–1727), disliked his son, Caroline's father, and a great rift between the King and Caroline's parents occurred in 1717. Prince George and Princess Caroline moved to Leicester House. The King kept his grandchildren, including Princess Caroline, with him and forbade his son to even visit his children. The children involved here are all those who had thus far been born, except Prince Frederick (1707–1751), who was still living in Germany.

Princess Caroline's mother was allowed some access to her children, but the arrangement was a terrible one, particularly for the children.

Princess Anne, the Princess Royal (1709–1759), had contracted smallpox and her life had been in danger for a period of days. Since Princess Caroline lacked robust health (and frequently suffered from colds, bronchitis, and swollen neck glands), smallpox, of course, could well kill her. A rather astounding practical medical experiment was conceived by Caroline's intellectual mother. It was three-quarters of a century before the English physician, Dr. Edward Jenner (1749–1823), developed a vaccination for smallpox, when Caroline's mother arrived at her plan, and aggressively pursued it to vaccinate, and thus immunize, her children. The basic idea was given to her by Lady Mary Wortley Montagu (1689–1762), whose husband, Edward Wortley Montagu, had been ambassador to Constantinople. That couple had been in Constantinople together, and there they had observed the Turks successfully practice inoculation for smallpox. Being given a good idea is one thing, but aggressively pursuing it in the face of opposition from physicians and clergymen is something else again. But that is precisely what the future Queen Caroline (1683–1737) did for her children. Moreover, she was prudent, as well as aggressive. Her first step was to secure six condemned criminals from the London prison, Newgate, who had never contracted smallpox. On condition that their lives would be spared for participating in the experiment, the criminals underwent vaccination. This experiment was so successful that Princess Caroline had it repeated on six charity children. Once again the experiment succeeded, so Caroline had two of her daughters, Caroline and Amelia, inoculated in April 1722.

The daughters of George and Caroline were still technically in the custody of their grandfather, King George I (1660–1727), until his death, but an infant, Prince George William (1717–1718), had been born to George and Caroline on November 13, 1717, and died three months later. That death served to draw the three royal sisters closer together, and even the gruff King George I realized that his popularity would be at great risk if any of the children in his custody were to die. Accordingly, the King allowed their mother essentially unlimited access to her daughters. Although the royal girls were officially in the King's care, as a practical matter it was Mrs. Henrietta Howard (1681–1767), later Countess of Suffolk, who was really in charge of them. Jane Martha, Countess of Portland (1672–1751), was royal governess of the younger children, assisted by Lady Charlotte de Roucy, who was called the Princesses' "companion."

The three royal sisters were fond of their grandfather, the King, as he was of them. Occasionally they would stroll with the King through the gardens and observe construction of new paths and the cultivation of rare plants destined for transfer to Hampton Court.

John Van der Kiste has written two books brimming with useful information about relatively obscure members of the families of England's first four King Georges. Those works are *The Georgian Princesses*, published in 2000, and *King George II & Queen Caroline*, published in 1997.

In those works, Van der Kiste provides some comparisons among the three royal princesses, Anne (1709–1759), Amelia (1711–1786), and Caroline (1713–1757), during the period that they were officially in the custody of King George I (until his death in 1727). In those comparisons, Caroline was ranked as the prettiest of the girls, all three were said to adore their mother, but two of the three spoke about their father, at times, with lack of respect, picked up at the King's court. (King George I hated his only son.) However, "the sweet-natured Caroline" spoke no ill of her father.

English aristocrats had very little contact with their own children, so they were genuinely startled to see Queen Caroline spanking her royal children in public when they misbehaved.

In 1727 King George I died, and Caroline's parents came to England's throne as King and Queen Consort. Caroline and her sisters were much involved in the glittering coronation of her parents on October 11, 1727. Van der Kiste's *King George II & Queen Caroline* tells us that Caroline's "...train-bearers were her daughters Anne, Caroline and Amelia, in purple robes of state, with circlets on their heads; their coronets were borne behind them by three peers...."

At the coronation, the air was thick with music by the great composer George F. Handel (1685–1759), and King George II appointed Handel as music master to Princess Caroline and Princess Amelia.

From this point on, Princess Caroline's life followed a more subdued orbit than that of her sisters, and even different from her intellectual mother. Queen Caroline's interests were intellectual and included politics, philosophy and religion. The Queen's husband loved her, but not her intellectual pursuits, so she found a private room in which to retire to pursue her studies and conduct private discussions with prominent intellectuals such as Gottfried Wilhelm von Leibniz (1646–1716). The Queen also busied herself at court with more feminine activities, such as needlework, cards, and gossip. Princess Caroline was drawn to these stuffy pursuits and at some point she began to age prematurely.

Horace Walpole's *Memoirs of the Reign of King George the Second*, published in 1846, tell us that Princess Caroline was her mother's favorite child.

Like her elder sister, Amelia, Princess Caroline was a life-long spinster. But unlike Amelia, Princess Caroline was unable to find joy in the freedom of spinsterhood. There is little evidence that she tried to attract a mate. On the contrary, we have only her strange fondness for Lord John Hervey (1696–1743). One source calls this fondness "a romantic attachment," while another says it "bordered on semi-avuncular infatuation."

Having brought the Lord Hervey mystery into the open, let us comment on the facts that are known. It is known that Lord Hervey was sickly, and his status as a chronic invalid "and hypochondriac" was widely known at court. So well known at court that Queen Caroline asked Hervey's advice to relieve her pain as she waited for death to take her. Hervey suggested "snakeroot" for the Queen, and just a short time later, Princess Caroline, who, according to Van der Kiste, had been at her mother's side most of the day, was seized with pains, "...so Hervey produced another of his concoctions, which made her worse as well ... [The Queen] commiserating with Princess Caroline, still suffering from the effects of Hervey's pills, she comforted her with the certainty that 'we shall soon meet again in another place.'" (During the last hours of her life Queen Caroline commended the care of her several younger children to Princess Caroline.)

It may well strike the reader as backwards that the dying Queen would comfort her favorite daughter by predicting that she also would die soon, but that is what Queen Caroline meant, because she knew her despondent daughter well enough to realize that death was something she was looking forward to. It was the never-ending business of living that Princess Caroline found to be a chore.

But back to the mysterious affection of Princess Caroline for Lord Hervey: He was some 17 years older than the Princess. In 1720 he married Mary Lepell (1700–), and they had at least three sons. After Lord Hervey's death in 1743, Princess Caroline entered a very extended period of grief, and she made it her business to see that Lord Hervey's children were provided with adequate financial support.

What little zest for living Princess Caroline had was stifled by the death of her mother in 1737, and the death of Lord Hervey in 1743.

Since Princess Caroline's family had regarded her as a hypochondriac, Princess Amelia needed no explanation when she casually mentioned in a letter to her sister, Anne, in Holland, cited by Van der Kiste, that Caroline was better "though pray don't mention it to her for she only allows of not being worse."

Princess Caroline's later life was that of a recluse. She gave generously of her monies to charities, and surprisingly large amounts went to the jails of London. Between her charitable contributions and support of others, such as Lord Hervey's children, Princess Caroline gave away essentially all income that she received. She saw few people other than her father, sister Amelia, and brother Prince William, Duke of Cumberland (1721–1765).

In delicate health to the end of her days, Princess Caroline died on December 28, 1757, at St. James' Palace, and was buried in the chapel of King Henry VII (1457–1509) at Westminster Abbey.

39. *Prince William, Duke of Cumberland (1721–1765)*

This son of King George II (1683–1760) and his Queen Consort, Queen Caroline (1683–1737), was born at Leicester House in London. At the time of his birth the Julian calendar was still in use in England, so his birth date is recorded on the Julian scale as April 15, 1721. His birth date on the Gregorian calendar was April 26. Perhaps a word about the calendars in use in Europe at this juncture in history would be useful here. Since 1582, the Gregorian calendar had been in use in Continental Europe. That calendar had been a departure from the previous Julian calendar. The Gregorian calendar lopped off some ten days (eleven days after 1700) from the prior Julian calendar, to more closely align the years with actual movements of the earth about the sun. But the new calendar had been adopted under the authority of the Roman Catholic Pope Gregory XIII (1502–1585), and worse yet, it had been named for that Pope. In 1721 Protestant England had not yet adopted this new calendar. However, the Gregorian calendar was adopted for Great Britain and her American colonies during Prince William's lifetime (in September, 1752). Unless otherwise noted, dates mentioned in this biographical sketch will be Julian until 1752, and Gregorian thereafter.

When Prince William was born, King George I (1660–1727) was still alive and ruling. Thus, William's parents had not yet come to England's throne. At the time of his birth, his parents were Prince and Princess of Wales. Selection of the godparents for an earlier child born to the Prince and Princess of Wales had caused a great rift in 1717 between the parents and the King. Presumably the air was thick with tension when this subject was addressed for Prince William's baptism. Fortunately, both the King and William's parents were extremely reasonable on this occasion, and the King accepted the recommendations of the baby's father. The godparents recommended, and selected, were the King and Queen Consort of Prussia, King Frederick William I (1688–1740) and his Consort, Queen Sophia Dorothea (1687–1757). An additional godfather was Ernest Augustus, Duke of York and Albany (1674–1728), a younger brother of King George I. Baby William was christened as William Augustus on May 2, 1721. Most important to the baby's mother, Caroline, Princess of Wales, the King permitted her to take custody of this baby.

Apart from a stillbirth and a son who died when he was three months old, Prince William was the first of the many royal children of the House of Hanover (now called Windsor) to be born in England. All the earlier ones had been born in Germany. Rex Whitworth's biography of Prince William entitled *William Augustus, Duke of Cumberland: A Life*, published in 1992, calls William "the first truly British member of the Hanoverian royal dynasty."

The eclectic and brilliant Sir Andrew Fountaine (1676–1753) was selected to be the young William's early tutor. At the ages of four and five, a number of titles of nobility were heaped upon William, and in July 1726 he was made a Royal Duke, styled Duke of Cumberland.

Other tutors and instructors of the first rank were provided to Prince William. They included gentlemen named Phillips (classical grammar), Palairet (French), Smith (mathematics), Harding (English history and law), and Zollman (history, geography and German). Numerous men taught Prince William essentials of military science, ballistics and tactics. The mathematics tutor, Robert Smith (1689–1768), had come particularly well recommended. He was chosen by the peerless Sir Isaac Newton (1642–1727).

Cumberland was educated for the navy but permitted to follow his preference for the army.

In 1727 King George I died, and Cumberland's father came to the throne as King George II. Although both King George II and his Queen Consort disliked their eldest son, and would have much preferred that Prince William succeed his father to England's throne, such preferences were of no consequence. England's laws were quite specific on the line of succession. Because of the law of primogeniture, Prince William did not become next in line for the throne when his eldest brother, Frederick, Prince of Wales (1707–1751), died, nor even in 1760, when King George II died. Under the law of primogeniture, which had governed the succession to the English throne since the era of the Norman Conquest, the throne passed, not to the eldest surviving son of King George II, but to the eldest son of the King's first-born son. That first-born son was Frederick, Prince of Wales. So when King George II died, the throne passed to Frederick's eldest surviving son, George, who had already been named Prince of Wales. He came to England's throne as King George III (1738–1820).

King George II ruled Hanover in Germany, at the same time (precisely) that he was King of England. In 1739 he became concerned that Hanover was threatened by the French, and he began looking into schemes to protect Hanover. One possibility considered by the English King would involve marrying his son, the Duke of Cumberland, to Princess Louise of Denmark and Norway to improve relations with that Scandinavian kingdom. That marriage possibility remained active for about three years, but nothing came of it, and in fact, William never married.

Although Prince William never married, it is fairly clear from anecdotes dealing with his youth that he possessed the typical raging hormones of a young man, and that he bedded a number of young women. Details are in short supply here, because Prince William left few written notes (about anything), and the authors of material dealing with his youthful sexual adventures often had political axes to grind, which inhibited trustworthy disclosures. We know that Prince William had a fondness for actresses, and that he had a summer affair about 1744 with Anne Montagu, who was six years older than the prince. After the affair, Anne married Joseph Jekyll.

Cumberland saw considerable combat action. In 1742 he was made a major general, and the following year he served with his father, the King, in combat on the European continent. At the battle of Dettingen, the English troops were trapped by a larger French force, but succeeded in fighting their way to safety and scoring a victory.

Christopher Sinclair-Stevenson's 1980 work entitled *Blood Royal: The Illustrious House of Hanover* provides a glowing commentary on Cumberland at the battle of Dettingen: "George was elated. Not only had he taken a definite part in the action himself, but his son, the Duke of Cumberland, had distinguished himself. The latter's horse, too, had run away with him, but it had the good grace to go forwards in the direction of the enemy. Cumberland had also performed an act of self-sacrifice. His Royal Highness's generosity was no less conspicuous on this occasion than his courage, Having found a French officer in the field covered with gore, whose bravery he had noted in the action, he ordered him to the surgeons and had his wounds dressed before his own; this hero disregarded his own safety to show how much he honoured valour in a foe...."

He was promoted to lieutenant general following the battle of Dettingen. Since

Cumberland was severely wounded in the leg during the action at Dettingen, the commentary quoted should serve to offset some of the less favorable remarks directed at Cumberland for his military actions during and after the Jacobite rising of 1745–1746. The Dettingen leg wound healed rather imperfectly and continued to trouble him.

Prince William served as captain-general of the army from 1745 to 1757. He was in command at the battle of Fontenoy in 1745. His combat effectiveness in that engagement drew mixed reviews. Geoffrey Treasure tells us in his *Who's Who in Early Hanoverian Britain (1714–1789)* that Cumberland "distinguished himself" at Fontenoy. Other sources give him poor marks for combat effectiveness. In any event, England lost the battle, and suffered heavy casualties, as well.

Later in 1745, a Jacobite rising was launched from Scotland. England's King James II (1633–1701) and his heirs had not taken their expulsion from the English royal line of succession gracefully, and a case can certainly be made that right was on their side. What they were lacking was effective military might. From time to time, King James II, his heirs, and others acting on their behalf, took military steps to recapture the English throne for the Stuart family. These attempts, known as "Jacobite risings," all failed, and the final failure began late in the summer of 1745. By that time it was a grandson of King James II who entered the field of battle to claim the throne. His name was Charles Edward Stuart (1720–1788). The rising culminated in the battle of Culloden, Scotland, in 1746, when the Jacobite forces were completely routed by forces commanded by the Duke of Cumberland.

It was Cumberland's actions following the battle of Culloden, which many observers felt were brutal and sickening, and had earned him, fairly or not, the warm hatred of the Scots and the nickname 'Butcher Cumberland.' David Hilliam's *Monarchs, Murderers & Mistresses: A Book of Royal Days*, published in 2000, calls it a "sickening slaughter," and says, "Over two thousand men were killed in cold blood, and in the weeks that followed hundreds of fugitives were pursued without mercy. The harrowing of the glens almost annihilated the population of the Highlands." Rex Whitworth's biography of Cumberland, mentioned earlier, paints a more favorable picture: "...his name is thus linked to the image of a capricious sadist. Nothing could be more unfair.... Almost without exception, historians and other writers have concentrated on just six months of the Duke's life: the Battle of Culloden in April, 1746 and subsequent efforts to root out Jacobites and other supporters of Charles Edward, the Young Pretender, in Scotland...."

Prince William, Duke of Cumberland did not, of course, spend all his time engaged in military combat. He also had a life. He served as chancellor of St. Andrews University, and as chancellor at Dublin University. He was also ranger of Windsor Forest, Great Park and Cranborne Chase.

Prince William had a favorite sister, Princess Amelia (1711–1786), with whom he shared a number of common interests. They spent a good deal of time together, and Princess Amelia often served as Cumberland's hostess when he entertained. During this period, when English aristocrats sent invitations to social functions, they understood that brother and sister were both to be invited.

In 1757 Prince William took command of forces to protect Hanover in Germany, but the French forced Hanoverian troops to concede. Since King George II was the ruler (elector) of Hanover, he felt humiliated by this defeat, so, favorite son or not, the Duke of Cumberland was forced to resign all military command and retire to private life.

Cumberland loved to gamble, particularly on horse racing. He arranged improvements of the horse racing course at Ascot and its meeting schedule. To this day, the British royal family has a special enclosure at Ascot and there are very strict rules concerning those who may enter it.

Prince William became extremely stout during his middle age and he suffered a series of strokes. During the Prince's illness, in March 1765, the infamous Stamp Act had been passed to extract monies from the English colonists in North America and the West Indies. This was the first direct tax ever levied by parliament upon America. Prince William, who was now a very powerful politician, agreed to participate in some discussions about the Stamp Act, which was scheduled to become effective on November 1, 1765. Despite his failing health, Cumberland participated in those discussions during October 1765. The London politicians were genuinely puzzled by the growing uproar in North America, but no definitive solution was found during this October meeting, and Cumberland escaped further participation by attending the horse races at Newmarket. On October 28, he returned to London, where he died from a final stroke on October 31, 1765. Prince William, Duke of Cumberland, was buried at Westminster Abbey.

40. *Princess Mary (1723–1772)*

This penultimate daughter of King George II (1683–1760) and his Queen Consort, Queen Caroline (1683–1737), was born at Leicester House in London. At the time of her birth, the Julian calendar was still in use in England, so Mary's birth date is recorded on the Julian scale as February 22, 1723. Her birth date on the Gregorian calendar was March 5. Perhaps a word about the calendars in use in Europe at this juncture in history would be useful here. Since 1582, the Gregorian calendar had been in use in Continental Europe. That calendar had been a departure from the previous Julian calendar. The Gregorian calendar lopped off some ten days (eleven days after 1700) from the prior Julian calendar, to more closely align the years with actual movements of the earth about the sun. But the new calendar had been adopted under the authority of the Roman Catholic Pope Gregory XIII (1502–1585), and, worse yet, it had been named for that Pope. In 1723 Protestant England had not yet adopted this new calendar. However, the Gregorian calendar was adopted for Great Britain and her American colonies during Princess Mary's lifetime (in September 1752), and after her marriage she lived and died in Germany. Unless otherwise noted, dates mentioned in this biographical sketch will be Julian until Mary's proxy wedding in England, and Gregorian thereafter.

When Princess Mary was born, King George I (1660–1727) was still alive and ruling. Thus, Mary's parents had not yet come to England's throne. At the time of her birth, Mary's parents were Prince and Princess of Wales. They had their own court at Leicester House and the Prince and his vivacious Princess surrounded themselves with a raffish set of men and women with lively minds.

It was Mary's mother who guided her education, both when Caroline was Princess of Wales at Leicester House and, starting in 1727, as Queen Consort. Rex Whitworth's 1992 biography of Mary's elder brother, Prince William (1721–1765), entitled *William Augustus, Duke of Cumberland: A Life,* provides an interesting behind-the-scenes glimpse of the first class educational environment in which Princess Mary was immersed. "Caroline was a strong personality.... Blessed with an enquiring mind and encouraged to exercise it, widely read and allowed to think for herself, ... it was natural that Caroline, with her enthusiasm for the intellectual pleasures, should guide the education not only of her daughters, but of her beloved son William. The choice of Sir Andrew Fountaine (1676–1753) as tutor was very probably hers.... Caroline knew that education was something much broader than lessons in a schoolroom, however, and encouraged her children to learn the pleasures of stimulating company — which they could find within the walls of their own home. Chiefly thanks to her, Leicester House was a hub of intellectual activity, visited by philosophers and poets, scientists and theologians, scholars and artists of every kind; men like Sir Isaac Newton (1642–1727) ... and Jonathan Swift (1667–1745).... In summer, when the King's household moved to Hampton Court, the gaiety and gossip at Leicester House was similarly transferred to Richmond Lodge ... where additional delights such as hunting were shared by the children."

English aristocrats had very little contact with their own children, so they were genuinely startled to see Caroline spanking her royal children in public when they misbehaved. However, Caroline was anything but a stereotypical mother.

John Van der Kiste has written two books brimming with useful information about relatively obscure members of the families of England's first four King Georges. Those works are *The Georgian Princesses*, published in 2000, and *King George II & Queen Caroline*, published in 1997.

In Van der Kiste's *The Georgian Princesses*, we are told that in 1737, when Mary's mother was dying, she sent to have all of her children brought to her (except her eldest son, whom she could not abide) and asked that they not leave until she died. "To Caroline she commended the care of the younger children, entreating her ... to do what she could to support the meek and mild disposition of Princess Mary." The son who was excluded from the farewell gathering was Frederick, Prince of Wales (1707–1751). The Caroline reference pertains to Mary's sister, her elder by ten years, Princess Caroline (1713–1757).

David Williamson's *Brewer's British Royalty*, published in 1996, reports of young Princess Mary that, "According to a contemporary, she was 'a lover of reading, and far more solicitous to improve the mind than to adorn the body.'"

Given the meek and mild disposition of Princess Mary, and the fact that European royal marriages were usually arranged with little thought to romantic interest, we should not be surprised to learn, in E. Thornton Cook's *Royal Marys: Princess Mary & Her Predecessors*, that Princess Mary's marriage was arranged. "The King, impatient to be off to the Hanover he loved, made a brief announcement to the effect that the marriage of his fourth daughter to Prince Frederick of Hesse, son of the Landgrave, would take place a few days later...." Cook goes on to explain that the bride's father, King George II, being habitually parsimonious, had vetoed the proposal of an expensive wedding in England. Representatives of the Church of England objected to a proxy marriage, but the King felt it beneath his dignity, according to Cook, "to send his daughter to a man who when she arrived 'had it in his power to call her his wife or not.'" Representatives of the judiciary weighed in with legal opinions. They asked, "Did not the Act of Succession stipulate that the marriage of a member of the royal family performed in England must be according to the form of the Anglican Church? And that form, by virtue of the Act of Uniformity, was the service for Holy Matrimony in the Book of Common Prayer." The impatient (and parsimonious) King stated: "I will hear no more of your church nonsense, nor your law nonsense.... I will have my daughter married here...."

Parliament voted Princess Mary a "marriage portion," or dowry, of 40,000 pounds. And, so it was that the 17-year-old Princess Mary was married by proxy on May 8, 1740, in the evening, in the Chapel Royal at St. James' Palace. Princess Mary's elder brother, Prince William, Duke of Cumberland (1721–1765), stood in as proxy for the groom, Frederick, Hereditary Prince of Hesse-Cassel (1720–1785), the only surviving son and heir of William VIII, Landgrave of Hesse-Cassel (1682–1760) and his wife, Dorothea Wilhelmina of Saxe-Zeitz (1691–1743).

After the proxy marriage ceremony itself, there were further ceremonies to be endured. Since one of the speeches touched directly on the subject of the Protestant religion and its importance to England and its royal family, a subject which would soon loom large as a personal problem to Mary, this additional quotation from E. Thornton Cook's work is pertinent: "'May God grant,' added the loyal representative of the City of London, 'that your royal house may forever supply the great Protestant Families of Europe with such invaluable blessings as are now secured to His Serene Highness, the Prince of Hesse, by the going forth of this Royal Progeny who had been formed by Religion and Virtue on the illustrious pattern set by your majesty....'"

As we have now twice introduced a misuse of the name "Hesse," clarification of geographic terms provided in *Kings, Rulers & Statesmen*, compiled and edited by L. F. Wise and E. W. Egan, should be helpful: "Hesse emerged as a fief of the Holy Roman Empire in the 13th century," and it maintained that identity, ruled at all times by a person titled "landgrave" until the death of Philipp (1504–1567), Landgrave of Hesse. "After the death of Philipp, Hesse was divided into several successor states, of which the chief were Hesse-Cassel and Hesse-Darmstadt." Hesse-Cassel was ruled by a person titled "landgrave" from 1567 to 1803. "The Landgrave of Hesse-Cassel assumed the title of Elector in 1803, Wilhelm IX, becoming the Elector Wilhelm I." In 1815, while Elector Wilhelm I was still in power "Hesse-Cassel annexed to Kingdom of Westphalia." *Wilhelm*, of course, is the German version of "William."

The encyclopedic *Kings, Rulers & Statesmen* lists important information about the landgraves of Hesse-Cassel, during the time period that is of interest to us (using German renderings for names):

Period of rule		Birth-death years
1751–1760	Wilhelm VIII, Landgrave of Hesse-Cassel	1682–1760
1760–1785	Friedrich II, Landgrave of Hesse-Cassel	1720–1785
1785–1803	Wilhelm IX, Landgrave of Hesse-Cassel	1743–1821
1803–1807	Wilhelm I, Elector of Hesse-Cassel	1743–1821

After the proxy marriage in London, Mary set sail from Greenwich, England, and her route to Hesse-Cassel took her through Holland. She was married in person on June 28, 1740, in the city of Cassel, in Hesse-Cassel.

Brewer's British Royalty tells us that the groom was "tall and handsome." Those are the last favorable words about Mary's husband that will appear in this biographical sketch. The sources for this sketch are largely English and Protestant, which no doubt introduces a one sided view of things, but the fact that Mary's father-in-law took Mary and her children to live with him, when her marriage fell apart, implies that the English and Protestant view in this case is probably an accurate one.

Before discussing the rupture of the marriage, let us introduce the children of that marriage. They were all boys, and the eldest son, William, succeeded his father, Landgrave Frederick II (1720–1785) as landgrave of Hesse-Cassel, when his father died in 1785:

Prince William IX, Landgrave of Hesse-Cassel (1743–1821) who later became William I, Elector of Hesse-Cassel (1743–1821)
Prince Charles (1744–1836)
Prince Frederick (1747–1837)

During their marriage, Mary's husband bullied her mercilessly. In 18th century Germany, male chauvinism was not uncommon, and if Mary's shrewd mother had assessed her daughter as "meek and mild" while on her deathbed, that assessment was probably not far from the mark. Thus, when sources dealing with Mary's life tell us that her husband bullied her mercilessly, they are probably speaking the truth. That alone does not explain the breakdown of the marriage and the separation of Mary from her husband.

The short version of that story is that Mary's husband became a Roman Catholic, and the staunch Protestant, Mary, whose family owed their place in the English royal family to Protestantism, could not abide continuing to live with a husband of that religious faith. After all, Mary's family, for years, had lived in the shadow of the Jacobite threat of returning the Stuarts, and Catholicism, to rule England.

The longer version of the tale differs only in adding some details. That version is given in John Van der Kiste's *The Georgian Princesses*: "After the birth of the youngest of three sons ... Prince Frederick of Hesse-Cassel walked out on his wife and family. After a long silence, she received a letter from him to say that, prior to their marriage, he had been greatly attached to a well-born Catholic lady and had asked her to marry him, but she rejected him, as he was Protestant, and begged him to espouse the Catholic faith. Fearing the reaction of his subjects, he held out for a long time.... Shortly before the birth of his third son, he was informed that she was dying. On her deathbed, she asked him to become a Catholic 'that their Souls might be united in Heaven.' As he did not have the heart to refuse, he wrote to his wife. A furious King George II ordered his daughter to return to England, and never live with her husband again. She replied that 'it was Her Duty to remain in the situation in which it had pleased God to place Her; but that she would make her *own terms* for the sake of her sons, as they were brought up Protestant.'"

When invading French forces threatened their safety, Mary's father-in-law, the landgrave of Hesse-Cassel, took Mary and the children to live with him. They were all forced to flee the French, and by the end of 1757 Mary was in exile with her father-in-law in Hamburg, Germany. There she was subsidized by the British government.

Mary's eldest son, William, became the reigning count of Hanau. (Today's Hanau is a city in Hesse, Germany, with a population of some 80,000.) There was a period (from February 1, 1760 until October 13, 1764) when Mary acted as regent for the count of Hanau. *Brewer's British Royalty* states that, during her regency, "...she struck silver coins bearing her name, including a very handsome thaler and half-thaler with her portrait bust on the obverse and the arms of Hesse-Cassel and Great Britain on the reverse."

Mary died on January 14, 1772, at Hanau, Germany, and was buried at a Protestant church, the Reformed Church, there.

41. *Princess Louisa (1724–1751)*

Princess Louisa was a daughter of King George II (1683–1760) and his Queen Consort, Queen Caroline (1683–1737). She was born at Leicester House in London, in December 1724. John Van der Kiste's *King George II & Queen Caroline* tells us that, "When courtiers came to congratulate the father, who had particularly wanted another son, he said a little testily, 'No matter, 'tis but a daughter.'" But Princess Louisa was the last child that Queen Caroline would bear. The birth was difficult and the mother suffered a hernia, which added to her already poor health and contributed to her death just 13 years later.

At the time of Louisa's birth, the Julian calendar was still in use in England, so Louisa's birth date is recorded on the Julian scale as December 7, 1724. Her birth date on the Gregorian calendar was December 18. Perhaps a few words about the calendars in use in Europe at this juncture in history would be useful here. Since 1582, the Gregorian calendar had been in use in Continental Europe. That calendar had been a departure from the previous Julian calendar. The Gregorian calendar lopped off some ten days (eleven days after 1700) from the prior Julian calendar, to more closely align the years with actual movements of the earth about the sun. But the new calendar had been adopted under the authority of the Roman Catholic Pope Gregory XIII (1502–1585), and worse yet, it had been named for that Pope. In 1724 Protestant England had not yet adopted this new calendar. However, the Gregorian calendar was adopted for Great Britain and her American colonies in September 1752, shortly after Louisa's death in 1751. However, Princess Louisa was married in Continental Europe in 1743, where the Gregorian calendar was in use, and lived the remainder of her brief life in the kingdom of Denmark and Norway. Unless otherwise noted, dates mentioned in this biographical sketch will be Julian until Louisa's weddings (proxy and actual) and Gregorian thereafter.

When Princess Louisa was born, King George I (1660–1727) was still alive and ruling. Thus Louisa's parents had not yet come to England's throne. At the time of her birth, Louisa's parents were Prince and Princess of Wales. They had their own court at Leicester House, and the Prince and his vivacious Princess surrounded themselves with a raffish set of men and women with lively minds.

It was Louisa's mother who guided her education, both when Caroline was Princess of Wales at Leicester House and, starting in 1727, as Queen Consort. Rex Whitworth's 1992 biography of Louisa's elder brother, Prince William (1721–1765), entitled *William Augustus, Duke of Cumberland: A Life,* provides an interesting behind-the-scenes glimpse of the first class educational environment in which Princess Louisa was immersed. "Caroline was a strong personality.... Blessed with an enquiring mind and encouraged to exercise it, widely read and allowed to think for herself, ... it was natural that Caroline, with her enthusiasm for the intellectual pleasures, should guide the education not only of her daughters, but of her beloved son William. The choice of Sir Andrew Fountaine (1676–1753) as tutor was very probably hers.... Caroline knew that education was something much broader than lessons in a schoolroom, however, and encouraged her children to learn the pleasures of stimulating company — which they could find within the walls of their own home. Chiefly thanks to her, Leicester House was a hub of intellectual activity, visited by philosophers and poets, scientists and theologians, scholars and artists of every kind; men like Sir Isaac Newton (1642–1727) ... and Jonathan Swift (1667–1745).... In summer, when the King's household moved to Hampton Court, the gaiety and gossip at Leicester House was similarly transferred to Richmond Lodge ... where additional delights such as hunting were shared by the children."

In 1727 King George I died, and Louisa's parents came to the throne as King and Queen Consort of England.

Among the intellectuals who had contributed to the lively atmosphere at Leicester House was the poet and dramatist John Gay (1685–1732). It was Louisa's mother, rather than her father, who kept the intellectual fires burning in the royal household, and Louisa's father, soon after acceding to the throne, made clear his lack of respect for matters of the intellect when he offered John Gay a position as gentleman usher to Princess Louisa at an annual salary of 200 pounds. Gay took this for the insult to his talents that it was intended to be, and soon set to work on theatrical productions, which mocked political corruption.

English aristocrats had very little contact with their own children, so they were genuinely startled to see Caroline spanking her royal children in public when they misbehaved. However, Caroline was anything but a stereotypical mother.

In addition to his *King George II & Queen Caroline*, published in 1997, John Van der Kiste has written another book, brimming with useful information about relatively obscure members of the families of England's first four King Georges. That work is *The Georgian Princesses*, published in 2000.

In Van der Kiste's *The Georgian Princesses*, we are told that in 1737, when Louisa's mother was dying, she sent to have all of her children brought to her (except her eldest son, whom she could not abide) and asked that they not leave until she died. "To Caroline she commended the care of the younger children, entreating her not to let the 'vivacity' of Louisa 'draw her into any inconveniences....' She told Louisa, at thirteen the youngest, to 'remember I die by being giddy and obstinate, in having kept my disorder a secret.'" The son who was excluded from the farewell gathering was Frederick, Prince of Wales (1707–1751). The Caroline reference pertains to Louisa's sister, her elder by eleven years, Princess Caroline (1713–1757). Louisa was carefully brought up by her mother and, after her mother's death, by Princess Caroline.

Rex Whitworth's biography of Louisa's elder brother, William (1721–1765), entitled *William Augustus, Duke of Cumberland: A Life*, published in 1992, provides information on two topics of interest to us. (1) Whitworth quotes a description provided by a Baron von Bielfeld, one of the secretaries of the King of Prussia, about how dull English court life had become after the death of Queen Caroline: "Since the death of the Queen, the King has never kept a public table. H. M. dines and sups alone in his own apartment. The Prince and Princess of Wales neither lodge or come to court. The Duke of Cumberland and Princesses Amelia, Caroline and Louisa eat also in private and admit none whatever to their table or even to be spectators of it. This life of perpetual retirement renders the court to the last degree spiritless." (2) Whitworth also gives us some background on the reasons that King George II decided that his youngest, prettiest and most vivacious daughter, Princess Louisa, should be married off to the Crown Prince of Denmark. In 1739, when Louisa was 15 years old, "After twenty five years of peace, the country's defences (sic) had fallen into disrepair, and the standing army — such as it was, for the nation had objected to the cost of obtaining it during peacetime — was a shambles.... In October war was declared on Spain.... At home, anxious preparations were made to repel a possible Franco-Spanish invasion."

Whitworth states that it was in this atmosphere that, "Meanwhile, the King's attention had turned to Hanover, now under threat from France; he feared that Denmark too would fall to the sticky embraces of the French, and signed a deal agreeing to pay Denmark for 6,000 troops ... and the King began to seek other ways of securing Danish support. In the time-honoured fashion he decided that a dynastic match might be the solution, and started lengthy negotiations to marry his youngest daughter, Louisa, apparently the prettiest and liveliest, to the King of Denmark." Here Whitworth errs; he should have said either "crown prince of Denmark" or "future King of Denmark." It was Crown Prince Frederick (1723–1766) that King George II had in mind for his daughter, not his father, King Christian VI (1699–1746).

Whitworth gives us a hint that Louisa's marriage will be an unfortunate one for her, when he relates that "negotiations with the Danish royal family had been continuing for years, with George II proposing a double marriage: the Duke (of Cumberland) with Princess Louise of Denmark, and her brother, the Crown Prince with the Duke's youngest sister, Louisa."

However, Cumberland had no enthusiasm for marriage, or for the particular bride proposed. He saw combat on the horizon and wanted to be a part of it. Cumberland solved his dilemma by asking such a huge marriage settlement that parliament would not approve it. That scheme worked. "The King blamed Parliament, and the Danes, thereafter, proved less amenable to George's requests for troops to join the Pragmatic Army. Louisa's marriage, however, was arranged for the following autumn."

Louisa's marriage had now been arranged. She would be wed in a proxy ceremony in Germany. Louisa's father ruled Hanover, Germany, as elector, the entire time that he was King of England, so it was at Hanover that the proxy marriage took place, with Louisa's brother, Prince William, Duke of Cumberland, standing in as proxy for the groom. The groom was Crown Prince Frederick (1723–1766), son of King Christian VI (1699–1746) of Denmark *and Norway*. (Denmark controlled Norway from 1397 until 1814, but many sources take a shortcut and style the kingdom's name as merely "Denmark.") The groom's mother, the Queen Consort, was the former Princess Sophie Magdalene (1700–1770) of Brandenburg-Kulmbach.

The proxy marriage took place on November 10, 1743, followed by a marriage in person at Christiansborg Castle, in the kingdom of Denmark and Norway, on December 11, 1743.

John Van der Kiste's *King George II & Queen Caroline* indicates that there were initial signs that the marriage would be a happy one. "One lady at court was touched to see them, soon after their marriage, eating a bowl of cherries together; one holding the stalk between the lips while the other bit the fruit off."

Although Louisa was generally acknowledged to be the most attractive of her parents' daughters, her husband did not pay enough attention to her to keep her happy. In fact, in Geoffrey Wakeford's 1973 work entitled *The Princesses Royal*, we are told that Louisa's husband "plagued her with his mistresses." As the children began arriving, any gaiety within the marriage dwindled. In 1746 Louisa's father-in-law died, and her husband took the throne as King Frederick V (1723–1766) of Denmark and Norway. Louisa was his Queen Consort until her death. A list of the children born to Louisa and her husband is presented in the following table:

Prince Christian (1745–1747)
Princess Sophia Magdalene (1746–1813)
Princess Caroline (1747–1820)
Prince Christian VII (1749–1808), later King of Denmark and Norway
Princess Louisa (1750–1831)

During her final pregnancy, Queen Louisa underwent a painful operation for a rupture, and she died on December 19, 1751, in Christiansborg Castle. Queen Louisa was buried at Roskilde Cathedral.

Although Louisa's husband had paid little attention to her in life, he was genuinely upset by her death at the tender age of 27. King Frederick V remarried seven months after Louisa's death, and he had one child, a son named Frederick (1753–1805), by his second Queen Consort, Juliana Maria of Brunswick-Wolfenbuttel (1729–1796). In January 1766, King Frederick V died and was succeeded on the throne by his mentally retarded son, Christian VII (1749–1808).

That mentally retarded son married into England's royal family. England's King George III (1738–1820) permitted his youngest sister, Princess Caroline Matilda (1751–1775), to marry in 1766 King Christian VII (1749–1808), who was extremely retarded. Before the wedding, it was known in England that the groom-to-be was a tiresome, conceited little man, and Princess Caroline Matilda dreaded the marriage. It seems unlikely that King George III would have permitted the marriage if he had known the extent of Christian VII's mental retardation.

Perhaps a caveat is in order concerning comments here about Christian VII's mental retardation. Sources dealing with the history of England and its royal family provide a rather uniform impression that Christian VII was always mentally retarded, and later became insane. There is a contrary opinion, which is expressed in John Danstrup's *A History of Denmark*, published in Copenhagen in 1948: "He was an intelligent boy with insanity lurking within him." Assessing these things at a distance of two and one-half centuries is tenuous business.

When Juliana Maria's stepson, King Christian VII (1749–1808), was finally acknowledged to be insane, Juliana Maria and her son, Frederick (1753–1805), ruled Denmark and Norway as regents.

KING GEORGE III

George acceded to the throne of England as King George III upon the death of his grandfather, King George II, on October 25, 1760. His coronation at Westminster Abbey was held on September 22, 1761. The King died on January 29, 1820, but his rule of England ended a decade earlier because of his physical and mental disabilities. He had one wife, Charlotte (1744–1818). The royal couple had 15 named children, 13 of whom survived beyond infancy.

42. *King George III (1738–1820)*

Events in the life of King George III that deal with his treatment of his English colonists in America and England's loss of the American colonies in the American Revolution form a significant portion of this King's biography.

America's final English royal monarch was born on June 4, 1738, at Norfolk House, St. James' Square, London. His father was Frederick, Prince of Wales (1707–1751), and his mother was Augusta, Princess of Wales (1719–1772), a daughter of the German Frederick II, Duke of Saxe Gotha.

The baby was baptized by Thomas Secker (1693–1768), who was then Bishop of Oxford, and later, Archbishop of Canterbury. The baby Prince was baptized as George William Frederick. He was a grandson of the reigning king of England, King George II (1683–1760), and his father was heir-apparent to that throne.

George was a sickly infant and was suckled, not by his mother, but by a wet nurse named Mary Smith.

In 1760 Prince George would succeed his grandfather on the throne of England, because of the law of primogeniture. Under that law, which had governed the succession to the English throne since the era of the Norman Conquest, when King George II died in 1760, the throne passed not to the king's eldest surviving son, but to the eldest son of the King's first-born son. That first-born son was Frederick, Prince of Wales, who died before King George II's death.

Prince George was brought up with his younger brother, Prince Edward Augustus (1739–1767), and Lady Charlotte Finch (1725–1813) was initially given charge of the two boys as governess. They were placed in the hands of tutors about 1745. Annette Joelson's *England's Princes of Wales* tells us that, "They were taught Latin, music, mathematics, fencing, elocution, drawing and watercolor painting...."

Of the tutors, we know that the first was Reverend Francis Ayscough (1700–1763), but the boys' father, the Prince of Wales, was dissatisfied with him and substituted George Lewis Scott (1708–1780), a mathematics scholar. It was probably while Scott was his tutor that Prince George developed his life-long interest in astronomy.

Additional subjects to which young Prince George was exposed included French, German, and some elements of Greek. His instruction also included British and European history from ancient times to current events. He learned to play both the harpsichord and the flute. The harpsichord, now rather obsolete, would figure prominently on occasions later in King George's life; e.g., when his bride-to-be tried to learn how to play it, to please her fiancé, and less happily, near the end of his life, when the insane old King played the instrument and explained to the servants at hand that the harpsichord had been played by the King of England when he used to live here.

John Brooke's 1972 biography entitled *King George III* explains that George's education was wider "than he would have received had he been born the son of a country gentleman and attended Eton or Westminster. Its most serious deficiency was one which could hardly be overcome at that period: his lack of contact with boys of his own age (apart from his brother) and his utter ignorance, except from books or what his tutors told him, of life outside the school-room and the Court."

In April 1751, one month after his father's death, George was made Prince of Wales. Also in 1751, Simon Harcourt, Earl of Harcourt (1714–1777), was named governor of Prince George, the new heir-apparent to the throne. Thomas Hayter, Bishop of Norwich (1702–1762), also had some influence about this time on George's education, and Prince George's mother, Augusta, certainly also played a role in the character formation of the future King of England.

However, the main player in this game was, without question, John Stuart, Earl of Bute (1713–1792). In 1755 Lord Bute became Prince George's tutor, and Bute exerted an enormous influence on the development of young George's personality and character. Certainly the influence was greater than it should have been in a perfect world, but it is clear that the fault was Prince George's in becoming greatly dependent upon, and even idolizing, Bute. Lord Bute taught George to view the world with suspicion, full of plots to entangle or even dethrone him. A genuine anxiety plaguing George's mind was that his uncle, Prince William, Duke of Cumberland (1721–1765), might attempt to obtain, by force of arms, the throne which primogeniture was denying to him. On one occasion, Cumberland, a military man, drew his sword merely to amuse Prince George. The Prince feared the worst.

It seems appropriate, at this juncture, to dispel an ugly rumor about Bute. After Prince George's father died, leaving his widowed mother the dowager Princess of Wales, she formed a friendship with John Stuart, Earl of Bute. The evidence seems clear that Augusta and Bute were never lovers, although the air is thick with rumors that they were, and those of a Freudian persuasion have inferred much from the strong mentor relationship that Bute had over George.

The depravity of the time in which Prince George lived (both his father and the King, his grandfather, were sexually active outside the conjugal bed) influenced George strongly toward the moral high ground. These words are noted in various assessments of young Prince George: Solemn, priggish, censorious, mistrustful, suspicious, shy, dutiful and kindly, with a strong sense of his royal responsibility.

At the age of 18, when George attained his majority, he elected to maintain the policies of his father, and to remain close to many of his father's former advisors, including Charles Wyndham, Earl of Egremont (1710–1763), as well as Lord Bute.

Although Prince George was of strong moral character, he also was equipped with the strong Hanoverian sex drive. The 15-year-old Sarah Lennox (–1826) came into George's view just when his testosterone levels were peaking. Initially, Prince George panted and sighed about the 15-year-old beauty and felt that he must have her. Dutiful to a fault, even in sexual matters, George allowed himself to be persuaded by his mother and Bute that the Lennox girl was not a suitable candidate for him.

In sexual matters, one tends to want what one wants when one wants it, and delayed gratification is not terribly appealing. However, George agreed to wait for sex until he married, but he demanded that a bride be found soon!

To satisfy the two-fold need that the bride be both royal and Protestant, the list of potential mates was soon narrowed to German princesses.

Consideration had already been given to marrying George to a German Brunswick princess, but Prince George's mother objected on the grounds that her son was only 17. That particular marriage prospect was finally abandoned, although not until 1759.

King George II died on October 25, 1760, and his grandson, George, acceded to the throne on that date as King George III. A 22-year-old sovereign had replaced one aged 77. Since the new King was unmarried, it would be at least two decades before British politicians could look to the royal family for "royal opposition" to the King. The political environment that had prevailed since King George I (1660–1727) took the throne in 1714 had been drastically altered.

The kingdom that the young monarch inherited was a mighty one, possessing an empire upon which the sun never set. England was also enjoying a period of great prosperity when King George III took his throne.

Being King required George to make some political decisions and take some actions, but first things first. There was this unanswered sex need that required attention. George mentioned that, since he was limited to Protestants who were royal, he might review an almanack (sic) to try to find lists of German princesses. It was a sensible plan. In those days Germany was divided into so many principalities and duchies that it was often difficult to throw a snowball very far in any direction without hitting a new one.

Apparently, the list with which George was presented to choose his bride consisted exclusively of German princesses. George, influenced by his mother's recommendation, selected Princess Charlotte, even though "she was not in every particular as I could wish...."

This Charlotte was Charlotte Sophia, or Sophie Charlotte (sources consulted are in conflict on the form of her name) (1744–1818), a princess from the tiny German principality of Mecklenburg-Strelitz. She was a daughter of the former Prince of Mirow and Duke of Mecklenburg-Strelitz, Charles Louis Frederick (1708–1752), and his wife, Elisabeth Albertina of Saxe-Hildburghausen (1713–1761). Charlotte Sophia's brother came to rule as Duke Adolf Frederick IV of Mecklenburg-Strelitz (1738–1794).

David Graeme was sent to Germany to negotiate the marriage in a preliminary way. Charlotte's dying mother readily agreed to the proposal to marry her 17-year-old daughter to the King of England. Graeme pointed out that the marriage contract would require Charlotte to join the Anglican Church of England. Charlotte was a Lutheran, but her mother agreed that the marriage contract's provisions concerning the Anglican Church were not a problem.

The contract was written in Latin and specified that Charlotte must leave for England immediately, join the Anglican Church of England, and be married according to Anglican rites. Charlotte's mother could scarcely have dreamed of a finer match for her daughter. She signed the marriage contract for her daughter on her deathbed, and this was none too soon, because she then died on July 12, 1761.

Simon Harcourt, Earl of Harcourt (1714–1777), was dispatched to escort the bride-to-be to England from Mecklenburg-Strelitz, "if he can find it," said one wit of the day, because the tiny principality was about the size of an average English county. George and Charlotte did not meet until their wedding day. They were married by Thomas Secker (1693–1768), the Archbishop of Canterbury, on September 8, 1761, at St. James' Palace.

King George III and his new Queen Consort were crowned at Westminster Abbey on September 22, 1761.

George had asserted that his only important wish in his bride was that she provide a fruitful marriage. This desire for fecundity in the royal marriage was fulfilled, early, and often. The first-born child, the future King George IV, arrived in August 1762. King George III and his Queen Consort were faithful to one another (a rare arrangement for English monarchs of that era). They had 15 named children, 13 of whom survived beyond infancy. The two who failed to survive were Prince Octavius (1779–1783) and Prince Alfred (1780–1782).

David Williamson's work entitled *Brewer's British Royalty*, published in 1996, tells us that "George was a man of very simple habits and tastes, and he and Queen Charlotte adopted a lifestyle far more akin to that of the rising middle class than to that of the nobility and gentry."

King George III was the first British monarch since Queen Anne (1665–1714) to have been born in England. He was also the first of the Hanoverian kings of England to speak the English language without a thick German accent.

It appears, however, that George III had an utter inability to perform his role as King of England with any skill. He had developed a need to micro-manage everything, and the concept of the "big picture" never occurred to him. As one consequence, King George III had very little time for travel and, by the end of his life, he had been almost nowhere and seen almost nothing first-hand.

John Cannon and Ralph Griffiths tell us in *The Oxford Illustrated History of the British Monarchy*, published in 1998, that "the first six years of George's reign were an incomparable tragicomedy.... He was full of schemes for turning people out without much corresponding desire to invite others in...."

It must be stipulated that the new King did succeed in the first two objectives he announced after his accession to the crown:

1. To bring Lord Bute into the political administration and thereby inaugurate an era of virtue in the kingdom.
2. To bring an end to the war in which England was then involved, which would later be known as the Seven Years' War.

Bute initially held only a court appointment, but he became secretary of state in 1761. In 1762 he was named first lord of the treasury. He was the King's first, or "prime" minister until he resigned from the weight of the office in April 1763. The fault here was all the King's. George continued to rely on Bute as if he was still his boyhood mentor, and the King sought Bute's approval on a host of trivial matters. Bute was also the victim of scurrilous accusations about his relationship with the King's mother, and he was accused of continuing to influence the king (as a "minister behind the curtain") even after he left political office. The first accusation was a lie, and the second one was true only because the King continued to pester Bute for guidance.

The new King's second objective was also achieved on February 10, 1763, when the treaty of Paris was signed, ending the Seven Years' War. Henry Fox (1705–1774) deserves most of the credit for achieving this peace on terms that guaranteed British supremacy in both North America and India, but King George III also deserves a bit of credit. Unlike his great-grandfather, King George I, and his grandfather, King George II, King George III held no romantic notions about the importance of Hanover in Germany. Although King George III ruled it as elector of Hanover, he realized that the war served mainly the interests of Hanover and not Great Britain.

In 1764 King George III suffered his first attack of the illness that eventually led to his disabling insanity. Williamson's *Brewer's British Royalty* calls it "an illness now believed to have been porphyria, the 'royal malady' (though suspicion has also fallen on lead poisoning through the drinking vessels he used)." The type of porphyria to which Williamson refers is an inherited liver malfunction that can cause, among other symptoms, intermittent psychic changes with features of hysteria.

Among the events of George III's troubled reign were a series of government acts attempting to maintain strict control of the colonies in America. The colonists took umbrage, and the eventual result was the American Revolution. There is irony here. Had King George III and other English power figures bent far enough to keep the American colonies in England's hands, there would have been no Louisiana Purchase nor a Manifest Destiny taking the United States from "sea to shining sea." Thus the very shabby treatment of the English colonists in America by King George III gave rise to a nation that became a world power, powerful enough to rescue England and its European allies from defeat in World War I, and again in World War II.

From 1761 to 1763 England imposed limitations on colonial settlements west of the Allegheny Mountains. (In 1761 the order prohibited new settlements there; that was modified by the harsher Proclamation of 1763, which ordered colonists already settled in that region to remove themselves.) In 1765 the Stamp Act and Quartering Acts were passed, both of which imposed oppressive burdens on the American colonists. In case the colonists had failed to notice that they were subject to the whim and caprice of the King of England and his politicians, a Declaratory Act was passed in 1766 to tell them that they were. In 1767 Townshend duties were imposed on the American colonies. Named for their author, Charles Townshend (1725–1767), the duties were additional aggravated assault on England's presumably weak and un-united American colonies. John Cannon's *The Oxford Companion to British History*, published in 1997, notes of Townshend that "having lit the fuse for an American time-bomb, he died in September, 1767, of a fever at the age of 42."

Massachusetts was an early focal point in the escalating hostility between the colonies and the mother country. It was the Massachusetts assembly who had declared that there must be "No taxation without representation."

In March 1770, minor clashes between British troops and American colonists escalated into the Boston Massacre. The following month the Townshend duties were withdrawn *except on tea*. In 1773 the King and his cronies turned their attention from America to India and imposed a Regulating Act to extend government control of the East India Company, and parliament passed the Tea Act to reduce customs duties on tea imported into Britain, but retaining the higher duties on tea shipped to the American colonies. On December 16, 1773, infuriated Boston colonists boarded tea-bearing ships moored in Boston harbor, and dumped all of the tea (342 chests) into the harbor's water.

In September 1774 the King of England put his foot down. "The die is now cast. The colonies must either submit or triumph. I do not wish to come to severer measures, but we must not retreat." That same month, the American colonists, realizing that individually they were no match for the power of Great Britain, met in congress to unite. Twelve of the colonies were represented in that congress, now known as the first Continental congress. The colonial delegates agreed to certain provocative demands and action plans.

In April 1775 the American Revolution began, with armed conflict between British soldiers and armed colonists in Massachusetts, at both Concord and Lexington. About 60 years later, America's Ralph Waldo Emerson (1803–1882) wrote a stirring poem which gloriously recalled the heroism displayed by those colonists: "...Here once the embattled farmers stood, and fired the shot heard 'round the world.... Spirit, that made those heroes dare to die to leave their children free...." The American Revolution had begun.

In 1776 Virginia's Thomas Jefferson (1743–1826) drafted a Declaration of Independence of the American colonies from England. It was signed by representatives from 13 British colonies. The treason against his majesty was now official. A very difficult series of battles followed and it was not until the British surrender at Yorktown, Virginia, in 1781 that victory for America was assured. After surrendering, the British continued to fight here and there to improve their negotiating position at the peace conference, which would follow the Revolution.

Cannon and Griffiths tell us in *The Oxford Illustrated History of the British Monarchy* that King George III's loss in the American Revolution was no more than a speed bump, and "Britain shook off the defeat with remarkable ease." Most sources consulted, however, recognize the loss for the great blow to the King that it was, and David Williamson's 1992 *Kings & Queens of Britain* implies that the defeat was a major factor in triggering the King's second attack of porphyria in 1788 and 1789. His recovery from this episode was full and, in gratitude, King George and Queen Charlotte attended a service of thanksgiving at St. Paul's Cathedral.

It is clear that King George III was an oppressive force against the American colonists, and that he was joined in perpetrating that oppression by his ministers, parliament, and military personnel. However, there were notable Englishmen who voiced their opposition to this treatment of their American brethren. John Wilkes (1727–1797), Thomas Howard, Earl of Effingham (1746–1791), and William Pitt, Earl of Chatham (1708–1778), are among the Englishmen who supported the American colonists.

In 1812, while King George III was still eight years away from death, the British attacked our young nation again and forced the United States of America to fight and win a second war for independence, the War of 1812. We cannot assign any blame to King George III for this continued harassment, because he had been declared insane before the attacks began and he played no part in England's government after that.

While America's two wars for independence from England represent the matters of greatest interest on this side of the Atlantic, from the beginning of the reign of King George III until his death, there were other events of consequence across the ocean during this period.

Winston Churchill's *A History of the English-Speaking Peoples* tells of the important events in India during the reign of George III. England's East India Company had been formed purely for commercial reasons, and in 1700 "probably no more than fifteen hundred English people dwelt in India," and a hundred years later the figure had grown to many thousands. "Of India it has been well said that the British Empire was acquired in a fit of absence of mind."

Two of the brothers of King George III had married women whom the King felt were unsuitable, and he responded by securing passage in 1772 of the Royal Marriages Act. That act placed strict limitations on the rights of members of the royal family under age 25 to marry without the approval of the "sovereign in council." It also carried less restrictive limitations on the rights of royal family members aged 25 and older to marry. King George III was a prude, and the provisions of this act reflect that personality trait. However, sensitivity concerning marriage issues vis-à-vis members of the royal family did not end when King George III left the scene. As recently as 1936, King Edward VIII (1894–1972) abdicated his crown rather than give up the woman whom he loved. She was a divorced American lady. Since the King of England rules both church and state, his marital choices are limited.

The French Revolution gave the king further cause for concern. The reader will recall that, as a youth, George had been taught to view the world with suspicion, full of plots to entangle or even dethrone him. Now, just a few hundred miles to the east, in Paris, France, royal heads were being chopped off with great abandon. On May 15, 1798, while King George III was on prominent display at Hyde Park, a man standing near him was wounded by a musket-ball. It was assumed by many that the intended target was the King. That same evening the King insisted on attending the Drury Lane Theatre as planned. Williamson's *Kings & Queens of Britain* describes the events there: "…accompanied by the Queen and some of their daughters [and a] moment after he had entered the royal box a man in the pit fired at him but a person near the would-be assassin was able to deflect his aim so that the bullet missed the King and lodged in the roof of the box. George remained quite calm and turned to the Queen and Princesses who were just entering the box, saying 'Keep back, keep back; they are firing squibs for diversion, and perhaps there may be more.'" The audience responded with a spontaneous outburst of "God Save the King."

In 1801 an Act of Union between England and Ireland was passed. It was intended to pave the way for Catholic Emancipation, but King George III refused to support that. It was not until 1829, during the reign of King George IV (1762–1830), that Roman Catholics won the right to vote and participate fully in public life in Britain.

During the era of the Napoleonic Wars, England was periodically threatened by invasion.

In 1809 King George III began the 50th year of his reign and a Jubilee was held to celebrate it.

King George's youngest daughter, Princess Amelia (1783–1810), was just 27 years old when she died. The king's final recorded mental disturbance was apparently triggered by her death. One reliable witness reported that the king had begun to drift into insanity one day before Princess Amelia died. Christopher Hibbert's *George III: A Personal History*, published in 1998, tells us that the King, himself, knew that he was again losing his sanity and stated, "This one is occasioned by poor Amelia."

The Regency Act was invoked, and Prince George, Prince of Wales (1762–1830), took over the duties of the crown. The King lived his final years, essentially blind, deaf, and insane, at Windsor. He was unaware of Napoleon's defeat at Waterloo on June 18, 1815, and even the death of his wife, Queen Charlotte, on November 17, 1818, went unnoticed by him. King George III died on January 29, 1820, at Windsor Castle, and was buried there at St. George's Chapel.

Before he lost his mental faculties, King George III loved books, music and astronomy, and was a patron of the arts and sciences. His personal library became a nucleus around which the future British Library was built. He also intervened to afford a measure of justice to John Harrison (1693–1776), who had labored 50 years to develop an accurate chronometer, to measure time with accuracy at sea, and thereby determine longitude with some precision. Parliament had offered a prize of 20,000 pounds to any man who could accomplish this, but when Harrison did so, parliament reneged. With the personal aid of King George III, Harrison was awarded the bulk of the prize money, but he died on March 24, 1776, without appropriate recognition.

King George III was also admired by the astronomer William Herschel (1738–1822), who discovered the planet Uranus in 1781, and attempted to name it *Georgium Sidus* in honor of his King.

Thus King George III was not all bad, but it is more than a little puzzling how room could be found for him in a book just 124 pages long entitled *Great Rulers of History*. The work in question, by Theodore Rowland-Entwistle and Jean Cooke, was published in 1995.

43. *Queen Charlotte (1744–1818)*

Charlotte was Charlotte Sophia, or Sophie Charlotte (sources consulted are in conflict on the form of her name), a princess from Mecklenburg-Strelitz, a tiny principality in northern Germany. She was a daughter of the former Prince of Mirow and Duke of Mecklenburg-Strelitz, Charles Louis Frederick (1708–1752), and his wife, Elisabeth Albertina of Saxe-Hildburghausen (1713–1761).

Charlotte was born at Mirow, Germany, on May 19, 1744. In 1752 her father died and her brother came to rule as Duke Adolf Frederick IV of Mecklenburg-Strelitz (1738–1794).

She had not yet been accepted as an adult in her home when she was propelled to fame as the prospective bride of King George III (1738–1820) of England. She had never been allowed at an adult dinner party and her excitement in life consisted of dressing up in fancy clothes on Sundays to attend long, dreary Protestant religious services. Once a week, she was permitted something that was a bit more fun: a carriage ride.

Although Prince George was of strong moral character, he also was equipped with the strong Hanoverian sex drive. The 15-year-old Sarah Lennox (–1826) came into George's view just when his testosterone levels were peaking. Initially, Prince George panted and sighed about the 15-year-old beauty and felt that he must have her. Dutiful to a fault, even in sexual matters, George allowed himself to be persuaded by his mother and his primary advisor, John Stuart, Earl of Bute (1713–1792), that the Lennox girl was not a suitable candidate for George.

The 22-year-old King was of high moral character, and thus willing to wait for sex until he was married, but he insisted that a bride be found, and soon. To satisfy the two-fold need that the King's bride be both royal and Protestant, the list of potential mates was soon narrowed to German princesses. George, influenced by his mother's recommendation, selected Princess Charlotte, even though "she was not in every particular as I could wish...."

David Graeme was sent to Germany to negotiate the marriage in a preliminary way. Charlotte's dying mother readily agreed to the proposal to marry her 17-year-old daughter to the King of England. Graeme pointed out that the marriage contract would require Charlotte to join the Anglican Church of England. Charlotte was a Lutheran, but her mother agreed that the marriage contract's provisions concerning the Anglican Church were not a problem.

Charlotte was brought by her brother from the nursery to the drawing room to meet the important representative of the King of England, who had come to Mecklenburg-Strelitz to select her to be England's Queen Consort. Following what was apparently the custom of the era, Charlotte was asked to lie on a couch while the King's representative placed his foot on her to claim her for England. Charlotte was then sent back to the nursery, and the adults worked out the business matters.

The contract was written in Latin and specified that Charlotte must leave for England immediately, join the Anglican Church of England, be married according to Anglican rites, and refrain from participating in political matters. Charlotte's mother could scarcely have dreamed of a finer match for her daughter. She signed the proposed marriage contract for her daughter on her deathbed, and this was none too soon, because she then died on July 12, 1761.

About a week after Charlotte had been "footed" by the representative of the King of England, she and her ladies rushed to Cuxhaven, and then shipped out on an English royal yacht bound for Harwich, England. Several versions of the journey at sea are found in various sources and they all agree that the ride was stormy and rough, and that all, or almost all, of Charlotte's ladies grew seasick; but Charlotte did not. The interesting little detail on which they disagree concerns Charlotte's efforts to learn to play "God Save the King" on a musical instrument to please her husband-to-be. Most sources say that the instrument was a harpsichord, and it is true enough that the harpsichord would feature prominently in their later domestic life on evenings when King George played the flute accompanied by Queen Charlotte at the harpsichord. However, it is very difficult to picture a naval vessel of that era being stable enough to permit one to play a harpsichord while at sea. Petronelle Cook's *Queen Consorts of England: The Power Behind the Throne*, published in 1993, states that the musical instrument that Charlotte used during this voyage was "her guitar." This is certainly more plausible.

George and Charlotte did not meet until their wedding day. They were married by Thomas Secker (1693–1768), the Archbishop of Canterbury, on September 8, 1761, at St. James' Palace. Someone had made the unfortunate selection of Sarah Lennox for chief bridesmaid, and more than one source reports that King George had his eyes on Sarah during most of the ceremony. This testimony is credible. Sarah was a beauty, while Charlotte was not. The king's new wife had far more important assets and they would serve George and the marriage well in the years to come.

This was an age when large, buxom women were prized. Charlotte was neither. In 1761 she was described as "…not tall nor a beauty. Pale and very thin but looks sensible and genteel." Charlotte's life as Queen would be entirely domestic and she was happy with it. She had neither interest nor influence in political matters. The King became devoted to her, and she would love and be faithful to him.

King George III and his new Queen Consort were crowned at Westminster Abbey on September 22, 1761.

Charlotte and George were well suited toward one another in many ways. The first illustration of this was perhaps the moral high ground, which both of them sought. Among the adjectives used to describe the 22-year-old King George were solemn, priggish and censorious. They were no doubt true, but Queen Charlotte raised the bar for acceptable behavior a notch or two early in her reign as queen consort. Rex Whitworth's 1992 biography of an uncle of King George III entitled *William Augustus, Duke of Cumberland: A Life* tells us that the new Queen was very big on decorum and that "she immediately set about improving standards. Cards were abolished and no courts were held on Sundays." Both Prince William (1721–1765) and his rather eccentric spinster sister, Princess Amelia (1711–1786), beat a hasty retreat from the new "monotony of St. James'."

King George III had asserted that his only important wish in his bride was that she provide a fruitful marriage. This desire for fecundity in the royal marriage was fulfilled, early, and often. The first-born child, the future King George IV, arrived in August 1762. King George III and his Queen Consort were faithful to one another (a rare arrangement for English monarchs of that era). They had 15 named children, 13 of whom survived beyond infancy. The two who failed to survive were Prince Octavius (1779–1783) and Prince Alfred (1780–1782).

Two of their children would come to the throne of England as kings. A complete list of the 13 children that survived infancy is presented here:

Prince George, Prince of Wales, later King George IV (1762–1830)
Prince Frederick, Duke of York and Albany (1763–1827)
Prince William, Duke of Clarence and St. Andrews and Earl of Munster, later King
 William IV (1765–1837)
Princess Charlotte, Princess Royal (1766–1828)
Prince Edward, Duke of Kent (1767–1820)
Princess Augusta (1768–1840)
Princess Elizabeth (1770–1840)
Prince Ernest, Duke of Cumberland (1771–1851)
Prince Augustus, Duke of Sussex (1773–1843)
Prince Adolphus, Duke of Cambridge (1774–1850)
Princess Mary (1776–1857)
Princess Sophia (1777–1848)
Princess Amelia (1783–1810)

Both Queen Charlotte and her husband were fond of domestic life, and Charlotte had neither interest nor influence in political matters. While it must be admitted that King George III botched most political matters that he became involved with, and lost the English colonies in America, there is no reason to believe that Queen Charlotte would have improved matters had she tried to meddle. The marriage contract stipulated that she stay away from political matters, and she did so. This was in marked contrast to the Queen Consort who had preceded Charlotte. She was the artful politician, Queen Caroline (1683–1737), the consort of King George II (1683–1760).

David Williamson's work entitled *Brewer's British Royalty*, published in 1996, tells us that "George was a man of very simple habits and tastes and he and Queen Charlotte adopted a lifestyle far more akin to that of the rising middle class than to that of the nobility and gentry."

George and Charlotte came to favor Kew as a place of residence. In part, this was attributable to King George's mental instability. The peace and quiet of Kew were desirable from that standpoint, but the thoroughly domestic George and Charlotte also favored Kew over more majestic residences on account of their simple tastes. Charlotte, her husband, and their fast-growing family lived for a time at Dutch House, Kew Gardens. Soon construction of the now-demolished Kew Palace was completed and they moved there.

David Williamson tells us in his *Kings & Queens of Britain*, published in 1992, that "the Queen's life was tranquil and uneventful although she lived through stirring times." No doubt Williamson is referring to the American Revolution, the French Revolution and possibly the Napoleonic Wars. While it is true that she played no direct role in those dramatic events, they surely influenced the emotional health of Queen Charlotte's husband, and his several breakdowns and final insanity made her life anything but "tranquil and uneventful."

One gathers that the only domestic "fault" of Charlotte's was stinginess in money matters. Here again, her husband was a bird of a feather, being equally, if not more, penurious. Frances ("Fanny") Burney (1752–1840) was keeper of the queen's robes for about five years. Burney was a novelist, and from her pen we get glimpses of Queen Charlotte and her household. Burney mentioned that rations were short and dreariness was great. Cook's *Queen Consorts of England: The Power Behind the Throne* tells us, "From the pages of her (Burney's) journal we see a clear picture of the middle-aged George and Charlotte — kindly, considerate and undemanding people for their station in life, but terribly dull."

During the final illness of the King's mother, Augusta, Dowager Princess of Wales (1719–1772), both the King and Queen Charlotte visited her almost every day.

Both Charlotte and her husband loved music. They played their instruments together for their own enjoyment and also held musicales at court and gave fetes, with music.

Since the periodic physical and mental breakdowns of her husband affected Queen Charlotte greatly, a recap of the three primary breakdowns will be given here.

In 1764 King George III suffered his first attack of the illness which eventually led to his disabling insanity. Williamson's Brewer's *British Royalty* calls it "an illness now believed to have been porphyria, the 'royal malady' (though suspicion has also fallen on lead poisoning through the drinking vessels he used)." Queen Charlotte was the first to suspect that her husband's problem was primarily mental, and by the time the court physicians began to listen to her, the king was improving.

The King's second attack of his unfortunate illness occurred in 1788 and lasted into 1789. England's loss of the American colonies in the recent America Revolution may have contributed to the King's stress. Queen Charlotte did her best to keep him away from additional stress, and they stayed at Windsor during much of this period. This episode was particularly rough on Queen Charlotte. She was a prude, as was her husband, and to learn that the King was exposing himself in front of women of the court was shocking to her. She wept a lot and tried to prevent details of the King's insanity from leaking beyond the court. Sad to say, that the mad King mistreated even his beloved wife and children at times during this episode. In February 1789 the Regency Bill came close to passage. Since Charlotte disapproved of that bill, and since her husband's illness was abating, she began to take him into public to display his normalcy. The plan worked, the Regency Bill was put on hold, and when the king's recovery from this episode was full, in gratitude, Queen Charlotte and her husband attended a service of thanksgiving at St. Paul's Cathedral.

The third and final attack arrived in 1810. Initially it was assumed that there would again be a recovery, and Charlotte was assigned care of the King and the royal household. Williamson's Kings & *Queens of Britain* states, "When the King finally lapsed into insanity, the Queen was given the custody of his person, but could seldom bring herself to see him."

Even the loyal Queen Charlotte finally had to face the fact that her husband was no longer fit to reign over England. On February 5, 1811, their eldest son, George, Prince of Wales, was proclaimed Prince Regent of the United Kingdom.

In a sense, this must have been something of a relief to Queen Charlotte, for her trials during her husband's several mental disturbances had been great.

However, Charlotte did not approve of the new Regent, his morals or his manners. In fact she was hard pressed to find much that she did approve of among her surviving progeny. Her sons had produced almost a dozen illegitimate children and, as she approached death, there was only one legitimate grandchild alive. She was Princess Charlotte (1796–1817), and she had been named for Queen Charlotte. Sadly, she died in 1817 following the birth of a stillborn son.

Charlotte's final years were rather sad. She became extremely stout, but presided over some weddings of her children. After presiding at the wedding of her daughter, Princess Elizabeth (1770–1840), Cook's *Queen Consorts of England: The Power Behind the Throne* tells us that Queen Charlotte "…just gave up. She had done what she could, as well as she could, for as long as she could, and she was worn out."

Charlotte died at Kew Palace on November 17, 1818. She was buried in the then new Royal Tomb House at St. George's Chapel, Windsor Castle. Her death went unnoticed by her insane old husband.

While Charlotte prized high moral character and virtue, and thus found much to displease her among her progeny, had she lived long enough to see her in action, Charlotte's granddaughter, Queen Victoria (1819–1901), would have brought joy to Queen Charlotte's heart.

44. *Prince George, Prince of Wales, later King George IV (1762–1830)*

Prince George was the first child born to King George III (1738–1820) and his Consort, Queen Charlotte (1744–1818). The King had expressed the desire that his marriage be fruitful, and the birth of Prince George on August 12, 1762, at St. James' Palace, just eleven months after the royal wedding, was punctual indeed, and he would be followed by a host of brothers and sisters. Upon his birth, Prince George succeeded to several titles of nobility. Also, since King George III had waited until he was King to marry, baby George was, at birth, heir-apparent to the throne of England. Accordingly, he was made Prince of Wales with dispatch. This was done five days after his birth, on August 17, 1762.

Lady Charlotte Finch (1725–1813) was appointed as his governess. A sub-governess and both wet and dry nurses were also appointed. On September 18, 1762, the prince was christened as George Augustus Frederick by Thomas Secker (1693–1768), who was then Archbishop of Canterbury.

In 1763 a brother was produced for Prince George. He was Prince Frederick (1763–1827), who would be titled Duke of York and Albany. As youngsters, George and Frederick were raised together.

In 1764 King George III suffered his first attack of the illness that eventually led to his disabling insanity. David Williamson's *Brewer's British Royalty*, published in 1996, calls it "an illness now believed to have been porphyria, the 'royal malady' (though suspicion has also fallen on lead poisoning through the drinking vessels he used)."

In 1771 Robert D'Arcy, Earl of Holdernesse (1718–1778), was appointed as governor to the princes, with Leonard Smelt (–1800) as sub-governor. For tutors, they shared William Markham (1719–1807), Bishop of Chester, and Cyril Jackson (1746–1819). In 1772 the two princes were given their own establishment at Dutch House near their parents' royal residence.

In May 1776, when Prince George was almost 14 years old, Holdernesse resigned as governor, complaining that he had lost the respect of the two princes. Smelt, Markham and Jackson also left their positions. Thomas Brudenell-Bruce, Earl of Ailesbury (1729–1814), was appointed as the new governor of the princes, but he had hardly warmed the chair when he resigned. Both tutors were replaced. Markham's position as the lead tutor was given to Richard Hurd (1720–1808), Bishop of Lichfield and Coventry, while Jackson was replaced by William Arnold.

E. A. Smith's 1999 biography entitled *George IV* tells us that "George was an intelligent and perceptive pupil," and although the subjects on the Princes' syllabus looked impressive enough on paper, the studies were not in depth nor wholly successful. The index to Smith's biography summarizes Prince George's education as "unprepared for kingship."

Prince George developed into a handsome, intelligent young man with engaging manners. Saul David's 1998 biography of George entitled *Prince of Pleasure: The Prince of Wales and the Making of the Regency* quotes Richard Hurd's assessment of the Prince when he was a young man of 15: "'He will either be the most polished gentlemen or the most accomplished blackguard in Europe, possibly an admixture of both.' It was a particularly prescient remark."

Prince George was equipped with the strong Hanoverian sex drive, and by age 16 his hormones were raging. Some sources indicate that George seduced one of his mother's maids of honor. However the first woman with whom he fell in love was Mary Hamilton, a lady of 23. This would become a pattern with George; i.e., sexual fixation on older women. She sensibly declined his overtures, and Prince George was obliged to look elsewhere for sexual fulfillment.

The Prince of Wales next pursued a married lady, Mrs. Mary Robinson (1758–1800), an actress. In this case, Prince George was 17 and the object of his affections was 20. She was clearly beautiful enough to attract anyone in the market, and the Prince had sexual relations with her. Worse, he left a trail of compromising letters in Mrs. Robinson's hands, which King George III was obliged to purchase from her to avoid scandal to the royal family.

George would continue to lead a rather reckless life, vis-à-vis sexual matters, and E. A. Smith's biography has an appendix entitled "George IV's Children." George never acknowledged any child as his own except his legitimate daughter, Charlotte Augusta (1796–1817). This policy was not an unreasonable one, given the potential for fraud. However, Smith has done some digging and the results of his research are available in his book. That appendix, of course, mentions mistresses as well as possible illegitimate children. Presentation of that material here is beyond the intended scope of this biographical sketch.

However, mention will be made here of another woman with whom Prince George enjoyed sexual relations, because she was not merely a mistress. She was his first wife, Mary Anne (or Maria) Smythe Fitzherbert (1756–1837), a Roman Catholic, who had previously been twice married and twice widowed. The prince had not intended marriage, but she refused to grant sexual favors without benefit of matrimony, and he relented. Prince George and Mrs. Fitzherbert were married on December 15, 1785. The marriage was declared null and void on account of the provisions of the Royal Marriages Act of 1772. This was a lucky break for Prince George, since he was a man of limited attention span toward specific members of the opposite sex, and surely not one prepared to give up a throne for love of a woman, as King Edward VIII (1894–1972) later did. Had not the Marriages Act nullified Prince George's 1785 marriage, he never could have become King of England, because of the anti–Catholic provisions in the laws of the kingdom.

When Prince George had come of age in 1783, he had set up his own establishment at Carlton House. He was financially assisted in this venture by both parliament, who voted him funds to pay debts, and even his penurious father, King George III, who allowed him an annual allowance. However, George spent money recklessly, and soon could find nobody, not even his father, who would loan him money. Prince George sold his stud racehorses and dismissed a number of his servants. This impressed both king and parliament and they both provided him with additional monies.

Possibly upset by the stress of the American Revolution, King George III had a second attack of porphyria in 1788. Sad to say that the insane king mistreated even his beloved wife and children at times during this episode. In February 1789 the Regency Bill came close to passage. Since Queen Charlotte disapproved of that bill, and since her husband's illness was abating, she began to take him into public to display his normalcy. The plan worked, the Regency Bill was put on hold, and when the king's recovery from this episode was full, in gratitude, Queen Charlotte and her husband attended a service of thanksgiving at St. Paul's Cathedral.

In 1795 Prince George made what would prove to be the worst mistake of his life. He married his first cousin, Princess Caroline (1768–1821) of Brunswick-Wolfenbuttel (Germany). The bride's father was Charles William Ferdinand (1735–1806), Duke of Brunswick-Wolfenbuttel, and her mother was Duchess Augusta (1737–1813), a daughter of an earlier Prince of Wales of England, Prince Frederick (1707–1751). Although they were closely related by blood, they were completely incompatible in every way. Our Prince George was fastidious to a fault. Caroline was poorly groomed and rarely bathed. George was revolted, and Caroline was less than pleased with her husband-to-be. She considered him to be fat and far less handsome than his portrait.

Somehow the two stumbled through the wedding ceremony at St. James' on April 8, 1795. Prince George used alcohol to summon a drunken stupor adequate to carry him through the disastrous event, and he managed to remain drunk through his wedding night. History tells us that the marriage was actually consummated that night (and that they had very few, if any, further sexual relations the rest of their lives), but that this one encounter produced the legitimate child Princess Charlotte (1796–1817), who was born January 7, 1796, exactly nine months after her parents coupled. George and Charlotte became separated, and there was a custody battle over baby Princess Charlotte. King George III resolved that dispute by taking custody of the child himself. Princess Charlotte would later marry Leopold (1790–1865), a prince of Saxe-Coburg-Saalfeld, who later became King Leopold I of Belgium.

King George III's final recorded mental disturbance began in 1810. For a time there was hope that he would recover, but it was not to be. The Regency Act was invoked, and Prince George was made Prince Regent of the United Kingdom on February 5, 1811. He took over the duties of the crown, while the King lived his final years, essentially blind, deaf and insane, at Windsor.

There have been several regents in England's history, but the terms "The Regency" and "The Regency Period" have come to be associated with the time that Prince George ruled England as Regent, prior to the death of the insane King George III. This regency period was quite eventful:

• The War of 1812 was begun and ended. British sources refer to it as the Anglo-American War. Many American sources deem it America's Second War for Independence.

• Napoleon met his defeat at Waterloo in 1815 by troops commanded by England's Arthur Wellesley, Duke of Wellington (1769–1852).

• Prince George's daughter, Princess Charlotte (1796–1817), died. This was a major event in English history, and her death sent Prince George's unmarried brothers scrambling to find mates, to provide an heir to the throne.

On January 29, 1820, King George III died, and Prince George acceded to the throne of England as King George IV. The new King quickly introduced a Bill of Pains and Penalties to strip his estranged wife of any right to the title of Queen Consort of England. The proposal brought a mixed reaction in parliament and was withdrawn. However, at his coronation at Westminster Abbey on July 19, 1821, the King gave orders to refuse entry to his estranged wife, should she appear. Appear she did, and she was firmly refused entry, some say, "to her own coronation," but that is a bit of a stretch. In any event, she was heard from no more, since she died on August 7, 1821.

The new King visited Ireland, Hanover, and Scotland. The Scottish visit was a delicate matter, since it was the first visit of a Hanoverian king of England to Scotland. It was stage-managed by Scotland's own Sir Walter Scott (1771–1832), and was a splendid success.

Some hoped that the visit to Ireland would prove to be a prelude to emancipation of Roman Catholics, and indeed they were emancipated by an act passed in 1829, though no credit should be given to King George IV for this, since he tried to block its passage. The act gave Catholics the right to vote and fully participate in public and political life.

King George IV had become quite stout in his later years, as a result of rich food and drink and lack of exercise. He died at Windsor Castle on June 26, 1830, and was buried at St. George's Chapel, Windsor.

In his will the king acknowledged as his wife Mary Anne (or Maria) Smythe Fitzherbert (1756–1837), whom he had married in 1785. She was offered a dukedom by George's brother, King William IV (1765–1837), but she refused it. Following her death in 1837, she was buried at the Roman Catholic Church in Brighton. A monument to her there clearly displayed three wedding rings, the third representing her marriage to George, the Prince of Wales.

45. *Prince Frederick, Duke of York and Albany (1763–1827)*

Frederick was the second child born to King George III (1738–1820) and his consort, Queen Charlotte (1744–1818). He was born on August 16, 1763, at St. James' Palace, and was only six months old when he was elected Prince Bishop of Osnabruck on February 27, 1764, through the influence of his father, who still ruled Hanover, in Germany, as elector of Hanover.

Lady Charlotte Finch (1725–1813) was appointed as the initial governess of both Prince Frederick and his elder brother George, Prince of Wales (1762–1830). As youngsters, Frederick and George were raised together.

In 1764 King George III suffered his first attack of the illness that eventually led to his disabling insanity. David Williamson's *Brewer's British Royalty*, published in 1996, calls it "an illness now believed to have been porphyria, the 'royal malady' (though suspicion has also fallen on lead poisoning through the drinking vessels he used)."

In 1771 Robert D'Arcy, Earl of Holdernesse (1718–1778) was appointed as governor to the princes, with Leonard Smelt (–1800) as sub-governor. Also in 1771, Prince Frederick was made a knight of the garter.

For tutors, the two Princes shared William Markham (1719–1807), Bishop of Chester, and Cyril Jackson (1746–1819). In 1772 the pair of princes were given their own establishment at Dutch House near their parents' royal residence.

In May 1776 Holdernesse resigned as governor, complaining that he had lost the respect of the two Princes. Smelt, Markham and Jackson also left their positions. Thomas Brudenell-Bruce, Earl of Ailesbury (1729–1814), was appointed as the new governor of the Princes, but he had hardly warmed the chair when he resigned. Both tutors were replaced. Markham's position as the lead tutor was given to Richard Hurd (1720–1808), Bishop of Lichfield and Coventry, while Jackson was replaced by William Arnold.

John Van der Kiste's 1999 work entitled *George III's Children* tells us that, "The boys rose at six o'clock and began lessons at seven, studying Latin, French, German, Italian, mathematics, religion and morals; history, government and laws, natural philosophy or the 'liberal sciences', and 'polite literature' (mainly Greek and Latin) … fencing, music, and landscape drawing, were also taught." This syllabus sounds reasonably comprehensive, but E. A. Smith's 1999 biography entitled *George IV* tells us that although the subjects on the Princes' syllabus looked impressive enough on paper, the studies were not in depth nor wholly successful. The index to Smith's biography summarizes Prince George's education as "unprepared for kingship." Since Prince Frederick was educated together with his elder brother, his education was no doubt similarly limited.

In 1780 Prince Frederick was made a brevet-colonel in the army, and he was soon sent to Hanover in Germany to improve his knowledge of German and French, and to learn the minutiae of military maneuvers and tactics.

During this stay in Continental Europe, Prince Frederick made a favorable impression on the Austrians and Prussians. Specifically, he made a fine impression on the Prussian King, Frederick II (1712–1786), Frederick the Great. This mighty Prussian was a distant relative. The only daughter of our Prince Frederick's great-great-grandfather, King George I (1660–1727), was the mother of Prussia's Frederick the Great.

It seems likely that nepotism was at work when Prince Frederick was promoted to major general in 1782, and to lieutenant general in 1784. While on the continent, Prince Frederick had the even greater good fortune to avoid a marriage, which was bruited about as a possibility. The potential bride was Frederick's first cousin, Princess Caroline (1768–1821) of Brunswick-Wolfenbuttel (Germany). Princess Caroline's father was Charles William Ferdinand (1735–1806), Duke of Brunswick-Wolfenbuttel, and her mother was Duchess Augusta (1737–1813), a daughter of an early Prince of Wales of England, Prince Frederick (1707–1751). Our Prince Frederick kept his head and managed to avoid this union, although the marriage possibility must have sounded attractive. The Prince had been afforded little in the way of sexual fulfillment, and here was an opportunity to gain a full-time sexual partner, and a royal one at that.

Prince Frederick's good fortune in avoiding this marriage resulted in Princess Caroline being available to marry Frederick's elder brother, George, Prince of Wales. Marry they did, and a disaster it was. The tale of that disaster is told in the biographical sketch of Prince George, immediately above.

During November 1784 Frederick was made a peer of Great Britain when he was given the English dukedom of York and the Scottish dukedom of Albany. In the English royal family, the Duke of York has often simultaneously held the title Duke of Albany. Prince Frederick also joined the peerage of Ireland when he was ennobled in November 1784 as Earl of Ulster, an Irish title of nobility.

In 1787 Prince Frederick returned to England and took a seat in the House of Lords in parliament. In that body, Prince Frederick made a speech in 1788 concerning the regency question. This was an important topic at that time, on account of the bouts of mental illness suffered by Frederick's father, the King. It was assumed that Price Frederick's speech reflected the views of his brother, Prince George, the man who would in fact become Regent of the United Kingdom, some years later.

Charles Lennox (1764–1819), later Duke of Richmond, insulted Prince Frederick's brother, the Prince of Wales. It was inappropriate for the heir to the throne to fight a duel to defend his honor, so Prince Frederick arranged to fight in his stead. The duel was fought with pistols on Wimbledon Common. Lennox fired first, and nearly hit the Prince. Prince Frederick then contemptuously discharged his pistol harmlessly in the air, ending the duel.

In 1791 a wedding was arranged for Frederick. The bride-to-be was Princess Frederica Charlotte Ulrica Catherine (1767–1820). She was the eldest daughter of the Prussian King, Frederick William II (1744–1797), and his first wife, Elizabeth Christine of Brunswick-Wolfenbuttel (1746–1840). The couple was married twice, first in Berlin on September 29, 1791, and a second time in London on either November 23 or 24, 1791. (Sources consulted disagree on the date.) The marriage was not a success. Van der Kiste's work entitled *George III's Children* portrays the eventual breakup as a relatively amicable one: "The marriage was not a success. The Duke of York was unfaithful, but like his grandfather, he had at least chosen a wife who accepted such behaviour as natural. Less fortunate was her inability to bear children. Once it was evident that the marriage always would be childless, they spent much of their lives under separate roofs. Yet relations between them remained amicable enough and never caused any scandal." Princess Frederica eventually made her home at Oatlands Park, Weybridge, Surrey, where she surrounded herself with pet dogs.

On February 1, 1793, France declared war on Britain, Holland and Spain. Those countries, allied with the Holy Roman Empire, took to the field of battle against France. In 1793 Prince Frederick was placed at the head of British forces in Flanders. This would prove to be an unfortunate choice. However, some sources indicate that Frederick was the King's favorite son. Moreover, he also had earlier attained high military ranks in Germany.

Troops under Prince Frederick's command scored some initial victories, but it soon became apparent that he was not effective in high military command. He was recalled to England in November 1794. However, Frederick continued to advance in rank and was made field marshal in 1795 and commander-in-chief of the forces in Great Britain and Ireland in 1801.

Prince Frederick held that position until March 1809, when the House of Commons preferred charges against him. Although the prince's handling of military matters would likely support reduction in his high rank, it was not really a military matter that provoked the outburst. Rather, it was women scorned.

The women were Prince Frederick's wife and Mrs. Mary Anne Clarke (1776–

1852), who had been mistress to Prince Frederick for several years. Prince Frederick made the mistake of establishing a house for Mrs. Clarke at Weybridge, so she would be close to his residence at Oatlands. When Mrs. Clarke attended church one Sunday, Prince Frederick's wife spied Mrs. Clarke in her church, and she decided that too much was too much. The Duchess of York complained of this affront to Prime Minister William Pitt (1759–1806). Then Prince Frederick tired of Mrs. Clarke as his mistress and took up with a Mrs. Cary. Mrs. Clarke apparently took offense at this two-timing (or, perhaps in her mind, three-timing) and complained. The resulting sexual scandal was clouded under a charge that Prince Frederick had allowed his mistress (Mrs. Mary Anne Clarke) to influence his selection of men given army commissions. There was more smoke than fire to this particular allegation, and Prince Frederick was acquitted of impropriety, but he was obliged to resign his title as commander-in-chief. That title was soon restored by Frederick's elder brother, when he came to rule the United Kingdom as Prince Regent.

In 1818 Prince Frederick's mother died, and in 1819 the Prince was given at least nominal responsibility for the care of his insane father, King George III. In 1820 the king died, and Frederick's brother, the Prince Regent, came to the throne as King George IV. Since the new King's only legitimate child had died in 1817, Prince Frederick became heir-presumptive to the throne of England upon the accession of King George IV.

Prince Frederick was a strong opponent of the concept of Roman Catholic emancipation. Roger Fulford's 1933 work entitled *Royal Dukes: The Father & Uncles of Queen Victoria* explains that Frederick's position was both genuine and fervent concerning the Roman Catholic Emancipation Bill before parliament. While King George IV was opposed to it, he would yield if it passed parliament. "But with the Duke of York it was seen to be different. The invocation to God, the broken sentences about his father, the fervent striking of the breast, showed that he was deliberately encasing himself in that dynastic obstinacy against which the arrows of justice and reason had so often shivered themselves to no purpose. Many years later Lord Melbourne told Queen Victoria, 'Your uncle the Duke of York declared many times that he would have gone to the scaffold sooner than give way about the Roman Catholics.'"

Frederick's anti–Catholic hysteria seems puzzling. After all, there was no move to make Catholicism the state religion, merely a bill to emancipate Catholics and permit them to participate fully in the public and political life of the kingdom. Perhaps Prince Frederick's melodramatics delayed the bill, but it did pass and became law in 1829.

Prince Frederick, Duke of York and Albany died on January 5, 1827, at Rutland House, Arlington Street, London. He lay in state in St. James' Palace prior to burial at St. George's Chapel, Windsor.

46. *Prince William,* *Duke of Clarence and St. Andrews* *and Earl of Munster, later* *King William IV (1765–1837)*

Prince William was the third child born to King George III (1738–1820) and his consort, Queen Charlotte (1744–1818). Since the first two children had also been sons, there was little reason to suspect, at the time of William's birth on August 21, 1765, that he would one day be King of England. Prince William was born at Buckingham House, St. James' Park, and christened as William Henry by Thomas Secker (1693–1768), who was then Archbishop of Canterbury. The royal nursery grew rapidly as King George III and Queen Charlotte filled it with children. David Williamson's *Kings & Queens of Britain*, published in 1992, describes it as a very lively place, from which "a nursemaid had to be dismissed for losing her temper with Prince William and banging his head against the wall."

In 1772 Prince William's two elder brothers were removed from the royal nursery and given their own establishment at Dutch House, where they were raised and educated together. Prince William spent some years in the house now known as Kew Palace. There his tutors were Henry William Majendie (1754–1830) and a Colonel Bude. W. Gore Allen's 1960 biography of William entitled *King William IV* indicates that Colonel Bude was a dour Calvinist, who failed to move Prince William in that direction. On the contrary, Prince William is described during this period of his life as a jolly, natural boy. On a duty visit to one of his parents' elder friends, Dr. Thomas, Bishop of Winchester, who was then 82 years old, Prince William, then aged 12, made a very favorable impression and was described by Mrs. Chapone, the Bishop's niece, as "so sensible and engaging that he won the Bishop's heart" and that William stayed to talk to the old gentleman while his siblings ran playing around the house. This incident, as well as much other valuable and obscure details of Prince William's life, is described by John Van der Kiste in his 1999 work entitled *George III's Children*.

King George III had decided early on the career path he desired for his first three sons. The eldest, Prince George (1762–1830), would be King, the second, Prince Frederick (1763–1827), would make his career in the army, and Prince William would find a home in the navy. William would later claim that he was happy that his father had chosen a naval career for him. In June 1779, at the age of 14, Prince William was sent to sea as an ordinary seaman on the flagship of Admiral Robert Digby (1732–1815). The food was terrible, but because of his royal status, he was allowed to dine, on occasion, with the officers. Both Prince William and his father, the King, had been careful not to ask for special treatment. Aboard the ship with William was his tutor, Henry William Majendie. The kingdom was at war, and attacks from French and Spanish vessels were possible, but none occurred. William spent Christmas of 1779 with his parents at Windsor.

By 1780, Prince William, now a midshipman, was serving under Admiral George Rodney (1719–1792) off the coast of Spain. He again spent Christmas with his parents in 1780. He also fell in love and was sexually active with a 16-year-old girl, Julia Fortescue. The King learned of this and determined that Prince William's future assignments would be further away from home.

In 1782, during the American Revolution, Prince William served off the North American coast near the Delaware River, and also near England's rebellious colony of New York.

Along with the other sailors, Prince William was happy enough to take advantage of sexual opportunities when liberty from sea duty permitted.

In 1782 William was inducted into the order of the garter. He returned from sea in June 1783, and King George III decided to remove him from the corrupting influence of London society. The King sent Prince William to Hanover, in Germany, hoping, according to Van der Kiste's *George III's Children*, that after spending some time with his elder brother, Prince Frederick, William would emerge "the Prince, the gentleman and the officer." His early tutor, the military officer Bude, accompanied him to help insure favorable results.

Prince William found life in Hanover dull, and the daily inspection of the huge royal stables bored him. The King's hopes that a stay in Hanover would make him "the Prince, the gentleman and the officer" were sadly disappointed. Prince Frederick introduced his brother to gambling, and Prince William became a frequent customer at local brothels. Prince William also had some love affairs, and one of his sexual partners was Caroline von Linsingen, by whom some sources say Prince William had an illegitimate child. Queen Charlotte learned of at least some of these amorous adventures and, surprisingly, the strait-laced queen indicated that it was natural for a young man to sow some wild oats at the age that Prince William was industriously sowing them.

In 1785 William was back at sea as a third-lieutenant on the frigate *Hebe*, and in 1786 he served as captain of the *Pegasus*. At that time, he was under the command of Horatio Nelson (1758–1805). Prince William and Horatio Nelson had earlier formed a friendship, and in 1787, when Nelson married, Prince William had the honor of giving away the bride.

As a naval officer, William annoyed some of the more experienced officers under his command, who found it difficult to serve under him. One source says that several of these officers found his command to be "intolerable."

On May 20, 1789, King George III gave Prince William these titles of nobility: Duke of Clarence and St. Andrews, and Earl of Munster. With those titles of nobility, William took his seat in the House of Lords, and he was also soon promoted to rear admiral, but his duty was limited to home waters.

About the time that William entered the House of Lords, he became infatuated with an actress named Dorothy Jordan (1761–1816), and became determined to win her favors. She had earlier love affairs, some of which produced children, but the relationship between Prince William and Dorothy Jordan would become quite noteworthy for a number of reasons. Other members of the English royal family, of course, had engaged in affairs, but none of them was anything like that of William's and Dorothy's, in terms of duration, stability, domesticity, and the number of illegitimate offspring produced. There were ten, all of whom William acknowledged. They were given the surname FitzClarence, and after William became King he gave all of them titles of nobility.

In 1794 Prince William was promoted to vice-admiral, in 1799 to admiral, and in 1811 to admiral of the fleet. Also in 1811, Prince William broke off his relationship of some 20 years with Dorothy Jordan. The reasons are not clear. One source hints that Dorothy may have become an alcoholic, but this is not confirmed. William made some financial provision for her and her daughters, but Dorothy's life was an unhappy one at best after the separation. She died near Paris, France, in 1816.

The only legitimate child of Prince George, Prince of Wales, was Princess Charlotte (1796–1817). Princess Charlotte died on November 6, 1817, following a stillbirth. Under the law of primogeniture, which had governed the succession to the English throne since the era of the Norman Conquest, the throne passes not to the King's eldest surviving son, but to the eldest child of the King's first-born son. If there is no such child, then the throne passes to the eldest surviving son, and when that son dies, to the first-born child of that son, or, if there is none, to the next son in succession.

Accordingly, the death of Princess Charlotte had several enormously important consequences. It made Prince William next in line for the throne after the deaths of his elder brothers George and Frederick, since neither of them had produced a legitimate surviving heir. Prince Charlotte's death also sent all of the unmarried sons of King George III scrambling to find brides to impregnate with heirs to the throne. As events turned out, Princess Charlotte's death would result in the throne passing from King George IV (1762–1830) to Prince William, who ruled as King William IV, and from him to Princess Victoria (1819–1901), who reigned as Queen Victoria.

During the months immediately following Princess Charlotte's death, one would have thought Prince William to be perhaps the most eligible bachelor in Europe. Actually, he had a tough time finding a bride. He considered the possibility of marrying Sophia Elizabeth Wickham of Oxfordshire, but the Prince Regent was advised by the cabinet that she would not be acceptable. By the time Prince William found a suitable bride willing to marry him, he was 52 years old. The marriage was arranged by Prince William's mother, and the bride-to-be may have consented to marry a man twice her age, because, at 26, she herself was no longer a prime candidate for eligible bachelors. The bride was Princess Adelaide (1792–1849), a daughter of Duke George I (1761–1803) of the small German principality of Saxe-Meiningen. Adelaide's mother was Duchess Louisa Eleonora of Saxe-Meiningen (1763–1837). William and Adelaide were married at Kew Palace on July 11, 1818. It was a double wedding. The other couple was William's brother, Prince Edward, Duke of Kent (1767–1820), and Victoria Mary Louisa (1786–1861), a widow of Prince Emich Charles of Leiningen (1763–1814).

Skeptics of Prince William's marriage must be given their due. The marriage failed of its primary purpose and produced no heirs for the throne. All of the children of this marriage died prematurely. They were:

Princess Charlotte Augusta Louisa (1819–1819)
Princess Elizabeth Georgiana Adelaide (1820–1821)
Stillborn male twins, born April 23, 1822

However, William fell in love with his bride, who was only three years senior to his eldest illegitimate daughter, and she became devoted to him. Surprising as it now seems, and surprising as it must have seemed then, William and Adelaide were to become exactly the King and Queen Consort that England then needed. Adelaide was fond of her numerous illegitimate stepchildren and welcomed them in her home.

In January 1827, Prince Frederick, Duke of York and Albany (1763–1827), died, putting Prince William next in line for the throne. Not long after Prince Frederick's death, Prince William was given a high naval title by politicians anxious to curry favor with the heir presumptive to the throne of England. The title was Lord High Admiral, and it had not been used in more than a century. England's most recent Lord High Admiral had been consort to Queen Anne (1665–1714): George, Duke of Cumberland and Earl of Kendal (1653–1708). It was no doubt assumed by the politicians that the title would be merely ceremonial, but Prince William had other ideas.

William had become a rather garrulous old man. Van der Kiste's *George III's Children* tells us that the Prince took to poking "his head round the corners of the dockyards" and raising questions at the Admiralty "on matters which had not been bothered with since the battle of Trafalgar."

Prince William even took some matters dealing with actual naval operations into his own hands. While there were elements of farce in his tenure as Lord High Admiral, he also introduced some overdue reforms. However, the politicians prevailed on King George IV to have Prince William eased out of his naval position. In a style very typical of Prince William, he graciously resigned and invited his leading opponents to his birthday party. *George III's Children* reminds us that King George III had said of his son, William, that, "though he might have a sudden temper, he was just as quick to forgive and never bore a grudge."

When William had become heir to the throne, parliament raised his allowance. However, by that time Prince William had developed into a frugal man with an eye for detail. Perhaps some of his parents' previously dormant parsimonious genes had become active.

King George IV died on June 26, 1830, and Prince William acceded to the throne on that day. He initially mentioned a desire to rule with his title styled Henry IX. When it was pointed out to the new King that the title Henry IX had been used by a grandson of the Catholic King James II (1633–1701) as a symbol of the then continuing claim of the House of Stuart to the throne of England, Prince

William relented and agreed to rule as King William IV. The earlier "Henry IX" had been Henry Benedict Thomas Edward Maria Clement Francis Xavier Stuart (1725–1807). The Stuart claim to the British throne had been silent for quite some time, but since Prince William and his Hanoverian ancestors owed their claim to the English throne to the successful ouster of the Stuart line, it was probably appropriate that the suggested title Henry IX be rejected.

King William IV and his Consort, Queen Adelaide, were crowned at Westminster Abbey on September 8, 1831. William ordered that the coronation be simple and inexpensive and he got his wish. The coronation cost about one-seventh of that spent crowing King George IV, and in that ceremony only a King was crowned, with the "Queen Consort" excluded from the grounds. On a per capita basis, the 1831 coronation cost one-fourteenth that of King George IV.

King William IV continued to exhibit the garrulous nature that first appeared in prominence during his term as Lord High Admiral. However, he could also be a shrewd statesman when necessary, and it was a shrewd monarch that Britain needed to usher the Reform Act to passage. John Cannon points out in his *The Oxford Companion to British History*, published in 1997, that "the transition from the unreformed system of 1830 to full democracy in the 20th century was effected by seven franchise measures—the Acts of 1832...." Passage of that crucial first Reform Act of 1832 did not come easily, but come it did, and a large measure of the credit for accomplishing this milestone in British liberty belongs to King William IV.

This relatively obscure King, who could at times be crude and was regarded by many as a buffoon, spearheaded the enactment of one of the most important laws upon which England's democratic monarchy rests. The goal was elusive, but the King stayed the course and persisted in the face of repeated and strong obstacles, and Reform prevailed. Not only was this a milestone for British democracy, but it may well have been the step needed to preserve the monarchy itself, while others in Europe crumbled.

While the King was fighting and winning this important battle, his Queen Consort was moving the kingdom away from the disgraces of the Hanoverian era toward the modesty and decorum of the Victorian era next in line.

King William and Queen Adelaide were frustrated by their inability to produce an heir, but they harbored not the slightest resentment toward the young woman who became heir presumptive, Princess Victoria (1819–1901). Ironically, Princess Victoria was the product of the other marriage in the double wedding of July 11, 1818. King William IV loved this niece and only regretted that she did not spend more time visiting him. The ring leaders responsible for keeping young Princess Victoria apart from her aging uncle, the King, were Princess Victoria's mother, Princess Victoria Mary Louisa (1786–1861), and that mother's personal secretary, Sir John Conroy.

A host of petty issues were at play here, but the main issue was the impatience of Princess Victoria Mary Louisa about King William IV dragging his feet about dying. She wanted the King dead before her daughter reached age 18, so that she could rule as Regent. King William IV was basically blameless in this family feud, until the dinner held to celebrate his 71st birthday. On that occasion the King stood and gave a blistering speech, which praised his niece, the heir presumptive, and called attention to the incompetence and evil of Princess Victoria's mother and her close associates. In his speech, the King asked God to spare his life for another nine months so that Princess Victoria could accede to the throne in her own right. God granted that request, but didn't leave much safety margin. Princess Victoria turned 18 on May 24, 1837, and King William IV died at Windsor Castle less than one month later, on June 19 or June 20, 1837. (Sources consulted disagree on the date.) The King was buried at St. George's Chapel, Windsor.

Lord Charles Grey (1764–1845), a prime minister who had worked with King William IV to enact the Reform Act of 1832, eloquently summed up King William's character and contributions with these words quoted from Williamson's *Kings & Queens of Britain:* "A man more sincerely devoted to the interests of his country, and better understanding what was necessary for the attainment of that object, there never did exist; and if ever there was a sovereign entitled to the character, His Majesty may truly be styled a Patriot King."

47. *Princess Charlotte, Princess Royal (1766–1828)*

Charlotte was the fourth child born to King George III (1738–1820) and his Consort, Queen Charlotte (1744–1818). She was born on September 29, 1766, at Buckingham House, St. James' Park, and christened as Charlotte Augusta Matilda by Thomas Secker (1693–1768), who was then Archbishop of Canterbury.

Lady Charlotte Finch (1725–1813) was appointed as Princess Charlotte's governess. Lady Finch served in that capacity for several of the royal children and was employed by King George III and Queen Charlotte for more than 30 years.

Many valuable and obscure details of Princess Charlotte's life are described by John Van der Kiste in his 1999 work entitled *George III's Children*. One of them deals with the concerns that the King and Queen had about medical problems involving their children. Van der Kiste tells us that two doctors were always in residence to attend to medical needs of the royal children, and that the arsenal of medical ammunition employed by these doctors included both bleeding and blistering.

Van der Kiste also relates that Princess Charlotte and some of the other royal children were vaccinated against smallpox at an early age. Here Van der Kiste is a bit critical of the King and Queen for risking vaccination using smallpox itself for the vaccine. However, that criticism seems unjust. Smallpox at this time was a very real threat, and Dr. Edward Jenner (1749–1823) did not develop and announce his safer vaccination method, using cowpox vaccine, until 1798. Queen Caroline (1683–1737), the intellectual Consort of King George II (1683–1760), had conceived and executed a plan to vaccinate some of her royal children against smallpox. King George III and Queen Charlotte were very sensibly following Queen Caroline's aggressive footsteps to protect their children.

The royal family was fortunate to secure some of the services of the artist Thomas Gainsborough (1727–1788), who taught the Princesses a bit about drawing and art. Princess Charlotte and her younger sister, Princess Elizabeth (1770–1840), were the most active artists among the Princesses, and paintings from the youth of both of them survive today in the Royal Collection.

Princess Charlotte's childhood was governed by a variety of rules, most of which involved the schedule that she must follow, her manners, and, perhaps above all, the obsequious and deferential rituals she was required to adhere to with her parents, the King and Queen of England. One example, also taken from Van der Kiste's *George III's Children*, pertains to the period around 1776, when Princess Charlotte was about ten years old. "When summoned to be present at royal games of whist, they had to stand behind the Queen's chair, and sometimes fell asleep in that position. Unless offered a chair themselves, they were not allowed to sit down. When leaving their parents' presence, they had to walk backwards."

Princess Charlotte and her younger sisters, at times, chafed under the rigid routine at home, and delighted to visit those friends of the family who were a bit indulgent. The girls were overjoyed when circumstances permitted them to visit their gloriously eccentric, unmarried great-aunt, Princess Amelia (1711–1786).

Charlotte was the first daughter born to King George III and his Queen Consort, and because of that placement in the sequence of royal births, she was declared "Princess Royal." The date of that announcement was June 22, 1789. This brings us to a discussion of the term "princess royal" in our vocabulary dealing with the English royal family. The title is bestowed on some (but by no means all) first-born daughters of the King of England. The practice began with King Charles I (1600–1649), and, therefore, his first-born daughter, Princess Mary (1631–1660) was England's first Princess Royal. Geoffrey Wakeford's 1973 work entitled *The Princesses Royal* explains the decision to create this title with these words: "Charles I, or his advisers, devised the status of Princess Royal to distinguish his daughter Mary Stuart from the 'ordinary' foreign princesses who were not necessarily of the blood royal and some of whom were sadly tainted with morganatic blood." However, not all first daughters of English kings have been designated "Princess Royal." There are unwritten rules concerning the bestowing of the term "princess royal" that are beyond the scope of this biographical sketch. Perhaps this sample illustration will suffice. One of these unwritten rules came into play with Princess Mary (1662–1694), the first-born daughter of King James II (1633–1701). In her case, she was deliberately not termed "Princess Royal" because of the later likelihood that she would one day rule England as Queen, which would be sufficient honor. Mary did, in fact, become monarch of England, with the title Queen Mary II (1662–1694).

Princess Charlotte was described by a contemporary observer as possessing "excellent judgment, wonderful memory, and great application."

Van der Kiste's *George III's Children* tells us that Princess Charlotte and her unmarried sisters began to call their residence "the nunnery," and Van der Kiste quotes a contemporary observer, who saw much of the family during this period. He was Sir James Bland Burges (1752–1824), and Burges said that "there was probably not 'a more unhappy family in England than that of our good King.'"

By the time Princess Charlotte was about 30 years old, a variety of potential mates had been considered for her, but no marriage resulted. On the list of those considered were the emperor of Austria, the Crown Prince of Denmark, Prince Frederick of Orange, the King of Sweden's brother (the Duke of Ostrogothland), and Duke Ferdinand of Wurttemberg.

The sad fact was that, although Princess Charlotte was a desirable marriage candidate because she was the eldest daughter of the King of England, she was physically unattractive. Also, several sources have pointed out that King George III was unusually possessive toward his daughters, and concerning his eldest, the "Princess Royal," he was especially particular. This aspect of King George III's relationship with Princess Charlotte and her sisters is explored in depth in Lucille Iremonger's 1958 work entitled *Love and the Princesses: The Strange Lives of Mad King George III and His Daughters.*

Striking a marriage contract for an unattractive daughter of an overly possessive King of England is not easily accomplished. However, by 1796 Charlotte was finally betrothed. The groom-to-be was then the Crown Prince of Wurttemberg. He was Frederick William Charles (1754–1816). The marriage contract provided that the children of the marriage would be brought up in Wurttemberg, and that Princess Charlotte would continue to worship according to the rites of the Anglican Church of England.

The groom-to-be was a son of King Frederick Eugene (1732–1797) of Wurttemberg in Germany. Prince Frederick's mother was Frederica of Brandenburg-Schwedt (1736–1798).

Perhaps two facts help explain why Crown Prince Frederick was willing to marry the unattractive English princess: (1) He was rather unattractive himself, and (2) He had been married once before in a marriage which ended in clouded circumstances. He abandoned his first wife in Russia, charging her with licentious behavior and adultery. There she died under mysterious circumstances at a prison fortress.

Princess Charlotte and Prince Frederick were married on May 18, 1797, in the Chapel Royal of St. James' Palace. Included in Princess Charlotte's trousseau were two sets of children's clothing, one for a boy, and one for a girl. As things turned out, neither was ever needed. Her only pregnancy ended when a stillborn daughter was delivered.

In 1797 Charlotte's father-in-law died and her husband became ruler of Wurttemberg. When his title became King, in 1806, Charlotte became Queen Consort of Wurttemberg. There is some confusion concerning the proper style for her husband's name and title as ruler of Wurttemberg, and the confusion is compounded by the conquest of Wurttemberg during the Napoleonic Wars. Charlotte's husband then remained ruler of Wurttemberg (subservient to France for a time), but the titles of Charlotte's husband changed.

L. F. Wise and E. W. Egan have compiled an encyclopedic directory entitled *Kings, Rulers & Statesmen*, which was published in 1967. It has an excellent track record for accuracy concerning matters such as this. The titles of Charlotte's husband are presented here as listed in that work:

Period of rule	Title	Birth-death years
1797–1802	Duke Friedrich II	1754–1816
1802–1806	Elector Friedrich	1754–1816
1806–1816	King Friedrich	1754–1816

On December 26, 1805, the treaty of Pressburg was signed, which completed French domination of Austria. That treaty altered the map of Europe to enlarge Bavaria and Wurttemberg and make them kingdoms subservient to France. Charlotte was now technically an enemy of her father, the King of England. Charlotte certainly did not consider herself an enemy when she sent a whimsical letter to her mother addressed *"Ma très chère, Mère et Soeur."* Neither Queen Charlotte nor King George III saw any humor in the matter. The King ordered that none of his family call Charlotte "Queen of Wurttemberg," and Queen Charlotte stopped writing directly to Charlotte. After Prince George (1762–1830) became Prince Regent in 1811, there was a period when any letters from Queen Charlotte to her daughter were sent to the Prince Regent, to be forwarded by him.

It is certainly true that Queen Charlotte of Wurttemberg was not uncomfortable in her dealings with Napoleon. She even helped arrange a marriage between Napoleon's youngest brother, Jerome Bonaparte (1784–1860), and her stepdaughter, Princess Catherine (1783–1835).

King Frederick died at Stuttgart on October 30, 1816. He had become enormously obese, which perhaps contributed to his demise. His widow, Charlotte, now the Dowager Queen, was heartbroken. David Williamson's *Brewer's British Royalty*, published in 1996, tells us that Charlotte wrote to her trustee, Sir John Coxe Hippisley (1748–1825), expressing her great love for her husband and the desire for her own death, where she would meet him in the afterlife. Even Charlotte's mother had now gotten over her earlier petty anger and announced that she and her daughters would wear mourning clothes for a month in sympathy for the newly bereaved queen.

Dowager Queen Charlotte had, from time to time, been visited in Germany by various brothers and sisters, but Charlotte herself had never returned to England after her 1797 marriage. In 1827 Charlotte finally visited her native England. Charlotte, of course, was anxious to visit with surviving members of her family and to meet her niece, the future Queen Victoria (1819–1901), but she also had medical matters on her mind. Queen Charlotte had become extremely obese and she also suffered from dropsy. So a visit with England's renowned physician and surgeon, Sir Astley Cooper (1768–1841), was scheduled while she was in London.

Queen Charlotte was seen by Dr. Cooper and his associates while she was in England, but no miracles were worked. During Charlotte's return voyage to Germany, she fell ill, and Dowager Queen Charlotte died on October 6, 1828, just a few days after arriving back at her German home. Wakeford's *The Princesses Royal* tells us that she was "buried alongside her husband in the vault of Ludwigsburg and she was mourned in Stuttgart and throughout the kingdom."

48. *Prince Edward, Duke of Kent and Strathern and Earl of Dublin (1767–1820)*

Edward was the fifth child born to King George III (1738–1820) and his Consort, Queen Charlotte (1744–1818). He was born on November 2, 1767, at Buckingham House, St. James' Park, and christened on November 30 as Edward Augustus. He was named for his recently deceased uncle, Prince Edward Augustus, Duke of York (1739–1767), who died on September 17, 1767.

An early tutor of Prince Edward's was Reverend John Fisher (1748–1825), who afterward was Bishop of Exeter, which, in time, translated to Bishop of Salisbury. Roger Fulford's 1933 work entitled *Royal Dukes: The Father & Uncles of Queen Victoria* provides interesting details about Prince Edward and his brothers. In that work, Fulford indicates that Reverend Fisher provided a gentle buffer for Prince Edward, deflecting some of King George III's stern discipline. Fisher was Edward's tutor from 1780 to 1785.

In 1785 Prince Edward was sent to Continental Europe to continue his education. There, his tutor was Baron George von Wangenheim, who embezzled substantial amounts of money from the 5,000 pounds per annum sent by King George III to his son.

In February 1785 Prince Edward entered the Hanoverian Guards as a cadet and he received training at the College of Geneva. There, Prince Edward became an enthusiastic supporter of rigid military discipline. This enthusiasm would become a liability in his future military life. On more than one occasion, military men in his command committed mutiny on account of Edward's rigid military discipline.

When he was 18 years old, Prince Edward was made an army colonel. The date of his appointment to that rank was May 30, 1786.

After a visit to England, Edward was sent to Gibraltar to serve under Major-general Charles O'Hara (–1802). There, Edward's rigid command style triggered several mutinies by troops under his command. Fulford's *Royal Dukes* uses harsh terms indeed in describing Edward's leadership style: "He was completely inhuman and bestially severe with his troops." Perhaps his superiors disapproved of Prince Edward's military leadership in Gibraltar. For whatever reason, he was sent to serve in Canada in 1791. There, Prince Edward continued to infuriate his troops with his strict discipline, but he gained a bit of popularity with the local Canadian civilians.

By this time, Prince Edward had entered into a conjugal arrangement with Julie de St. Laurant. Their relationship was thoroughly domestic, and although they were never married, they lived together as if they were husband and wife for nearly thirty years. It is quite likely that the relationship would have endured still longer had it not been for the death of Princess Charlotte (1796–1817), discussed subsequently, which sent all unmarried sons of King George III scrambling to find wives to impregnate with heirs to the throne.

While serving in North America under General Charles Grey (1729–1807), later Earl Grey, Prince Edward performed ably in the West Indies, and in storming the French island of Martinique, contributing to British control of Martinique for a few years.

Prince Edward rose in military rank to major general in 1793 and to lieutenant-general in 1796. In May 1799 he was promoted to general, and in July 1799 he was made commander-in-chief of forces in North America. In 1805 Prince Edward was raised to the rank of field marshal. Prince Edward continued to see duty at Gibraltar, where he continued to fail miserably in winning any respect from the troops under his command. In March 1802 Prince Edward was even appointed governor-general of Gibraltar, but mutiny seemed to follow Edward as the night does the day, and he was recalled to England in May 1803. As a face-saving gesture, he was allowed to retain the governor-generalship of Gibraltar for the remainder of his life.

In April 1799 Prince Edward was awarded three titles of nobility: Duke of Kent and Strathern, and Earl of Dublin. There are discrepancies among sources consulted concerning these titles: (1) Some sources say that the titles were awarded on April 23, while others say April 24. (2) The spelling of the Strathern title is rendered in some accounts as Strathearn.

The only legitimate child of the heir apparent to the throne of England, Prince George, Prince of Wales (1762–1830), was Princess Charlotte (1796–1817). Princess Charlotte died on November 6, 1817, following a stillbirth. Under the law of primogeniture, which had governed the succession to the English throne since the era of the Norman Conquest, the throne passes not to the King's eldest surviving son, but to the eldest child of the King's first-born son. If there is no such child, then the throne passes to the eldest surviving son, and when that son dies, to the first-born child of that son, or, if there is none, to the next son in succession.

Accordingly, the death of Princess Charlotte had several enormously important consequences. It made Prince William (1765–1837) next in line for the throne after the deaths of his elder brothers, George and Frederick, since neither of them had produced a legitimate surviving heir. Princess Charlotte's death also sent all of the unmarried sons of King George III scrambling to find brides to impregnate with heirs to the throne.

As events turned out, Princess Charlotte's death would result in the throne passing from King George IV (1762–1830) to Prince William, who ruled as King William IV (1765–1837), and from him to our Prince Edward's daughter, Princess Victoria (1819–1901), who reigned as Queen Victoria. Thus the link between the modern English royal family, represented by Queen Victoria, to the earlier "English Royal Family of America, from Jamestown to the American Revolution," was none other than Prince Edward, the subject of this biographical sketch.

Since Edward was one of the unmarried sons of King George III, he was among those sent forth to marry and produce legitimate heirs. Toward that end, Edward left his mistress of almost thirty years, although he provided her with an income of 500 pounds per year.

Prince Edward found a suitable bride, and he was first wed to her in a Lutheran ceremony at Coburg, Germany, in late May 1818. A second ceremony (a double wedding) was held at Kew Palace on July 11, 1818. Edward's bride was Victoria Mary Louisa (1786–1861), a widow of Prince Ernest Charles of Leiningen (1763–1814). The widow came to the marriage with two children. The other couple was Edward's older brother, Prince William (1765–1837), and Princess Adelaide (1792–1849), who was a daughter of Duke George I (1761–1803) of the small German principality of Saxe-Meiningen.

The father of Prince Edward's bride was Duke Francis Frederick of Saxe-Coburg (1750–1806). Her mother was Countess Augusta Reuss-Ebersdorf (1757–1831).

After a few weeks residence in England, Prince Edward joined his bride in Leiningen, Germany. She had regency responsibilities there for her son, Prince Charles of Leiningen (1804–1856). However, when Victoria Mary Louisa became pregnant, the couple agreed that it was important to return to England for the birth. This was done, and on May 24, 1819, the only child of Prince Edward was born at Kensington Palace. She was baptized as Princess Alexandrina Victoria (1819–1901).

Later in 1819, the family moved to Sidmouth, and there Prince Edward leased Woolbrook Cottage for the family. He had two motives: (1) economy, and (2) a belief that the sea air there would be healthier than the air of London. While it is true that the air of London was of dubious quality, as things turned out, that air probably would have been safer for Prince Edward's health. Edward caught a cold and when he failed to take care of it, the illness developed into pneumonia. The medical emergency became only worse under the services of Dr. William Maton (1774–1835), who employed bleeding to treat the prince. Under this care Prince Edward died on January 23, 1820.

At the time of Prince Edward's death, there were still living several sons of King George III (1738–1820). In fact, the insane old King George III had six days left to live, himself. However, by June 1837, when King William IV (1765–1837) died, there was nobody left alive who had a superior claim to the throne than Prince Edward's daughter, Princess Victoria. Since Prince Edward died when his daughter, Princess Victoria, was only eight months old, she never remembered him. The father figure in Queen Victoria's life was King Leopold I (1790–1865) of Belgium.

Ironically, Leopold was the widowed husband of the woman who would have succeeded to England's throne had not a botched childbirth taken her life. She was Princess Charlotte (1796–1817), the only legitimate child of Prince George (1762–1830).

49. *Princess Augusta (1768–1840)*

Augusta was the sixth child, and second daughter, born to King George III (1738–1820) and his Consort, Queen Charlotte (1744–1818). She was born on November 8, 1768, at Buckingham House, St. James' Park, and christened as Augusta Sophia by the Archbishop of Canterbury.

Lady Charlotte Finch (1725–1813), who had earlier been appointed as governess to the royal couple's first daughter, Princess Charlotte (1766–1828), continued in that capacity for Princess Augusta, as well.

Because of a number of rather unique factors, most of the six daughters of King George III, including Princess Augusta, were never openly married, and their lives were rather uneventful. As a result, conventional sources on English history and the royal family of England yield little material for biographical sketches of the daughters of King George III. However, we are fortunate to have available two excellent books which delve into some of the details of the six girls' lives. These two sources are (1) Morris Marples' *Six Royal Sisters: Daughters of George III,* published in 1969, and (2) John Van der Kiste's *George III's Children*, published in 1999. Since there will be numerous references to these two books in this biographical sketch, they will be referred to here simply as Marples' work and Van der Kiste's work, although these authors have also written other books.

Perhaps a word or two is appropriate here about some of the "unique factors" in the lives of these six Princesses that left many of them largely isolated from society and from viable marriage prospects.

The first "unique factor" is that these girls were daughters of "*Mad* King George III." He experienced three principal bouts of his mental ailment, and the final bout left him insane for the remainder of his life. The second "unique factor" to be mentioned at this point is that the King was unusually possessive about his daughters and dreaded the thought of losing them to marriage. The third "unique factor," for now, is that King George III and his Consort, Queen Charlotte, deemed it "inappropriate" for any of the royal daughters to marry before the eldest daughter, the "Princess Royal," secured a husband. That might not have presented a serious obstacle to marriage of the younger sisters, had the eldest among them been married with dispatch, but the sad fact is that this eldest daughter was rather physically unattractive.

Striking a marriage contract for an unattractive daughter of an overly possessive King of England is not easily accomplished. That marriage did not occur until 1797, and by then at least two of the younger princesses, Princess Augusta (1768–

1840) and Princess Elizabeth (1770–1840), were no longer prime marriage candidates on account of their ages. (Marples tells us that the normal age for a royal female to marry in the late 18th century was about fifteen or sixteen.) The delay in getting the eldest princess married was particularly unfair for Augusta, who, in her prime, was the prettiest of all the daughters, and she later demonstrated that she was well suited for conjugal love and domesticity.

Princess Augusta was never openly married, and although there are ample grounds to suspect that she may have been secretly married, the secret was so well kept that we can't be sure.

Having taken this advanced peek at where Princess Augusta's life would lead her, let us now touch on some of the more important and interesting events of that life, borrowing largely from the works of Messrs. Marples and Van der Kiste.

Princess Augusta spent much of her childhood in the company of her elder sister, Charlotte, and her younger sister, Elizabeth. From eldest to youngest, the age difference was a few months less than four years. The three girls had naturally affectionate natures, and although most considered Augusta the prettiest, no rivalry on that score seems to have emerged.

Although the King and Queen had six daughters in total, three Princes were born immediately after Princess Elizabeth. The last three daughters didn't start arriving until 1776, enough of an age gap to present a rather different childhood scenario for Augusta than that experienced by the youngest three Princesses.

Marples tells us that Princess Augusta matured more quickly in childhood than her elder sister. "Her letters at eleven, dashed down in a disorderly scrawl, have none of her elder sister's interest in self. Lively, amusing and gossipy, they are full of snippets of news about people and clothes and hair styles, and already reveal that note of detached humorous comment which makes her adult correspondence so entertaining."

Augusta was an extrovert with spontaneous warmth for all. She loved her parents and siblings, and so much admired her brothers that she learned to play their games. Augusta became a genuine tomboy. Years later, when Princess Augusta was about 70 years old, she was overheard bragging to a little boy about her previous athletic skills.

While one does not immediately associate a tomboy personality with serious interest in music, this particular tomboy mastered the harpsichord. She composed some music and played for visitors.

Having learned of this early involvement in athletics and Augusta's skill at the harpsichord, the reader may begin to assume that she had the benefit of a well-rounded education. That was far from the case. In those days, royal students were segregated by sex for their education. The boys were generally given a classical education, while the girls devoted a lot of time to needlework and drawing. The royal family was fortunate to secure some of the services of the artist Thomas Gainsborough (1727–1788), who taught the Princesses a bit about drawing and art, but Princess Augusta did not master this skill as well as her two sisters. Somehow, Princess

Augusta emerged from the relatively shallow scholastic environment as something of an intellectual. In her old age she still had a zeal for learning. History and theology were of particular interest to her as her life began to draw to a close.

Princess Augusta and the other elder sisters began to complain of being confined in "the nunnery." Queen Charlotte had arranged the sleeping quarters for the princesses, princes and staff to minimize and even prevent chance meetings between the Princesses and members of the opposite sex. As a result, the Princesses called their home "the nunnery" and began to chafe under the restrictions. Van der Kiste tells us that the situation got so bad that one of the royal Princesses (not Augusta) had a son fathered by one of the King's equerries. "His age and ugliness put him at no disadvantage ... for ... (the) spinster sisters were so secluded from the world, and allowed to mix with so few people, that it was said that they were more than ready to fall into the arms of the first man outside the family who looked at them."

Although the sheltered atmosphere in which the Princesses were forced to live was perhaps the greatest cross that the girls had to bear, it was not the only one. King George III was parsimonious in the extreme, even during the sane periods of his life. His Consort, Queen Charlotte, a bird of a feather, was equally, if not more, penurious. The results of this royal frugality impacted Princess Augusta and her two eldest sisters in many ways. Augusta had to share a bedroom with a sister, and there was little, if any, room for privacy in it. Sir James Bland Burges (1752–1824), who saw much of the family during this period, noted that in 1794 each girl was provided an allowance of 2,000 pounds per annum. Marples and Van der Kiste are agreed that from this modest sum the Princesses were required to pay for their clothing, jewelry and servants' wages. Van der Kiste tells us that Princess Augusta managed to live within this stipend.

Although the King had deemed it unseemly for any of his daughters to marry before the eldest one did, there were some possibilities for marriage that were mentioned for Princess Augusta. One was the Prince Royal of Denmark and Norway. However King George III objected to that idea, and in this case he had a very good reason. In 1766 he had permitted his youngest sister, Princess Caroline Matilda (1751–1775), to marry King Christian VII (1749–1808) of Denmark and Norway. That man was extremely retarded, and the marriage proved disastrous. As a result, King George III wanted no more of the royal house of Denmark and Norway for his family.

Another marriage possibility for Princess Augusta was Prince Frederick of Orange. Reports of Augusta's beauty had reached Holland and intrigued him. In 1791 Prince Ferdinand of Wurttemberg came to England for the express purpose of pursuing the possibility of capturing Princess Augusta for a bride. However, Augusta's elder sister was then unmarried (and would remain so until 1797), and it was deemed that marriage for Princess Augusta before her elder sister was wed would be unseemly. This cost Augusta her last serious chance at a royal marriage.

Instead of entering into an arranged marriage, Princess Augusta fell in love.

Her lover was an older man, Sir Brent Spencer (–1828). The only men whom the Princesses met on any kind of social basis were equerries or aides-de-camp, and Spencer was among that group. He was born about 1760, so he was only about eight years older that Augusta. It was about 1800 that Princess Augusta and Brent Spencer entered into their love union. It was far more than a mere affair and there is more than a slight possibility that their union was blessed by some kind of marriage. If so, it was a secret one, and the secret has held for two centuries. (We find ourselves back at "unseemly" again. It would have been considered unseemly for Augusta to marry a man so far below her royal station.)

Spencer served in the British army as a brigadier-general and held important overseas commands. He was promoted in rank and status during England's Regency Period, when Princess Augusta's brother, Prince George (1762–1830), ruled as Prince Regent of the United Kingdom in place of his now insane father, King George III. Princess Augusta and Prince George were extremely fond of one another and kept few secrets between them. It seems safe to assume that General Spencer owed some of his advancement to good words from the Prince Regent.

The union between Princess Augusta and Brent Spencer lasted some 28 years, until his death in 1828. The couple had the satisfaction of mutual love and affection, and the union ended in grief for the survivor, Princess Augusta. Marples tells us that the only written comment by Augusta now extant said, "I respect grief: I have had my share."

Ironically, about 1804, when the princess and Spencer had become inseparable, Prince Frederick (1769–1829) of Hesse-Homburg expressed interest in Princess Augusta for a bride. Fortunately for everybody, the query was sent to King George III and, possibly on account of a temporary bout of his periodic insanity, the king never replied. Had Augusta been required to reply, her answer would have been "no," but difficult to explain since she was scrupulous about keeping her relationship with Spencer secret from almost everyone.

During Queen Charlotte's decline to death, Princess Augusta was among those who cared for her at Kew. In 1821 Princess Augusta visited her sister, Charlotte (1766–1828), now Dowager Queen of Wurttemberg, and in 1827 Charlotte returned the visit in England.

Princess Augusta had inherited Frogmore and she made serious business out of managing the farm there. In her old age, Augusta read a good deal of history and theology. On the latter subject Augusta made it known that she disapproved of all sects.

Augusta had been close to both of her brothers who came to England's throne, King George IV (1762–1830) and King William IV (1765–1837), and she entertained King William IV and his Consort, Queen Adelaide (1792–1849), at her home. When King William IV died, Princess Augusta comforted his grieving widow and spent two winters with her for that purpose.

Princess Augusta lived the last months of her life at Clarence House, and it was there that she died on September 22, 1840. One finds admiration aplenty for Princess Augusta, and the favorable remarks were not all saved for her death, but sprinkled generously throughout accounts of the life of this delightful English princess.

50. *Princess Elizabeth (1770–1840)*

Elizabeth was the seventh child and third daughter born to King George III (1738–1820) and his Consort, Queen Charlotte (1744–1818). She was born on May 22, 1770, at Queen's House, St. James' (now Buckingham Palace), and christened by the Archbishop of Canterbury at St. James' Palace on June 17, 1770.

Lady Charlotte Finch (1725–1813), who had earlier been appointed as governess to the royal couple's first two daughters, Princess Charlotte (1766–1828) and Princess Augusta (1768–1840), continued in that capacity for Princess Elizabeth, as well.

Because of a number of rather unique factors, most of the six daughters of King George III, including Princess Elizabeth, led rather uneventful lives. (Princess Elizabeth did not secure a royal husband until she was almost 48 years old, and he was only a Prince of a tiny German principality.) As a result, conventional sources on English history and the royal family of England yield little material for biographical sketches of the daughters of King George III. However, we are fortunate to have available two excellent books which delve into some of the details of the six girls' lives. These two sources are (1) Morris Marples' *Six Royal Sisters: Daughters of George III*, published in 1969, and (2) John Van der Kiste's *George III's Children*, published in 1999. Since there will be numerous references to these two books in this biographical sketch, they will be referred to here simply as Marples' work and Van der Kiste's work, although these authors have also written other books. In addition, for our Princess Elizabeth, reference material is available in E. Thornton Cook's *Royal Elizabeths: The Romances of Five Princesses 1464–1840*. That work was published in 1929.

The first "unique factor" is that these girls were daughters of "*Mad* King George III." He experienced three principal bouts of his mental ailment, and the final bout left him insane for the remainder of his life. The second "unique factor" to be mentioned at this point is that the King was unusually possessive about his daughters and dreaded the thought of losing them to marriage. The third "unique factor," for now, is that King George III and his Consort, Queen Charlotte, deemed it "inappropriate" for any of the royal daughters to marry before the eldest daughter, the "Princess Royal," secured a husband. That might not have presented a serious obstacle to marriage of the younger sisters, had the eldest among them been married with dispatch, but the sad fact is that this eldest daughter was rather physically unattractive.

Striking a marriage contract for an unattractive daughter of an overly possessive King of England is not easily accomplished. That marriage did not occur until 1797, and by then at least two of the younger Princesses, Princess Elizabeth (1770–

1840) and Princess Augusta (1768–1840), were no longer prime marriage candidates on account of their ages. (Marples tells us that the normal age for a royal female to marry in the late 18th century was about fifteen or sixteen.)

Princess Elizabeth spent much of her childhood in the company of her elder sisters, Charlotte (1766–1828) and Augusta (1768–1840). From eldest to youngest, the age difference was a few months less than four years. All three girls had naturally affectionate natures, but Cook's work on *Royal Elizabeths* stresses that Elizabeth was a particularly "lovable, sweet-tempered child." In *Brewer's British Royalty*, published in 1996, David Williamson says Elizabeth was "good-humoured, high-spirited, intelligent and a gifted artist and musician." Most observers considered Augusta to be the prettiest, but no rivalry on that score seems to have emerged. This was fortunate for our Princess Elizabeth, because she was chubby, perhaps even fat, from a very early age until her death.

Although the King and Queen had six daughters in total, three Princes were born immediately after Princess Elizabeth. The last three daughters didn't start arriving until 1776, enough of an age gap to present a rather different childhood scenario for Elizabeth than that experienced by the youngest three Princesses, Mary, Sophia and Amelia.

The royal family was fortunate to secure some of the services of the artist Thomas Gainsborough (1727–1788), who taught the Princesses a bit about drawing and art. Princess Elizabeth and Princess Charlotte were the most active artists among the Princesses, and paintings from the youth of both of them survive today in the Royal Collection. Van der Kiste tells us that Elizabeth later "published lithographs, etchings, and mezzotints...."

Having learned of this early benefit of instruction from the famous artist Gainsborough, the reader may begin to assume that Elizabeth and her two elder sisters had the benefit of a well-rounded education. That was far from the case. In those days, royal students were segregated by sex for their education. The boys were generally given a classical education, while the girls devoted a lot of time to needlework and drawing. Any instruction in foreign languages, which these girls received, was prompted by its perceived usefulness in social situations. Ironically, when Princess Elizabeth finally married, she hadn't mastered German to the satisfaction of her fellow citizens in the German principality of Hesse-Homburg, even though she had had 48 years to work on it and a German-born mother to help her with the language.

Queen Charlotte insisted that her three eldest daughters be strictly brought up and that the governesses never permit incivility or lightness in their behavior. Princess Elizabeth's childhood was governed by a variety of rules, most of which involved the schedule that she must follow, her manners, and, perhaps above all, the obsequious and deferential rituals she was required to adhere to with her parents, the King and Queen of England. One example, also taken from Van der Kiste's *George III's Children*, pertains to the period around 1776 when Princess Elizabeth was about six years old. "When summoned to be present at royal games of whist, they had to stand behind the Queen's chair, and sometimes fell asleep in that position. Unless offered a chair themselves, they were not allowed to sit down. When leaving their parents' presence, they had to walk backwards."

Princess Elizabeth and her elder sisters, at times, chafed under the rigid routine at home, and delighted to visit those friends of the family who were a bit indulgent. The girls were overjoyed when circumstances permitted them to visit their gloriously eccentric, unmarried great-aunt, Princess Amelia (1711–1786).

Princess Elizabeth and both of her elder sisters began to complain of being confined in "the nunnery." Queen Charlotte had arranged the sleeping quarters for the Princesses, Princes and staff, to minimize and even prevent chance meetings between the Princesses and members of the opposite sex. As a result, the Princesses called their home "the nunnery" and began to resent the restrictions. Van der Kiste tells us that the situation got so bad that one of the royal Princesses (not Elizabeth) had a son fathered by one of the King's equerries. "His age and ugliness put him at no disadvantage ... for ... (the) spinster sisters were so secluded from the world, and allowed to mix with so few people, that it was said that they were more than ready to fall into the arms of the first man outside the family who looked at them."

Having raised the subject of love affairs, mention should be made of the rumor that Princess Elizabeth had such an affair and that it produced a child. On page 14, Marples mentions the rumor (calling it "a secret marriage in adolescence"). On pages 58 and 59, Marples again mentions that rumor, this time in connection with an alleged illness, and says, "It was whispered at the time by gossips that Princess Elizabeth's withdrawal from the scene was not due to illness, but due to pregnancy; and indeed there is some documentary evidence indicating that she was secretly married as [sic] the age of sixteen to one of the King's pages named George Ramus, to whom she bore a daughter christened Eliza...." On page 60, Marples points out that, if there had been such a marriage, it would have been illegal under the Royal Marriages Act, since the king did not consent to it, but, also on that page, mention is made of six or seven members of the Ramus family, whom King George III employed at various times as pages, none of whom were named George. Further on page 60, Marples points out, "It remains extremely difficult to fit the requirements of a pregnancy into the circumstances of Princess Elizabeth's illness," and seems to conclude (here) that the rumor of a husband and a pregnancy resulting in childbirth are not to be given credence.

Van der Kiste's work is silent on this intriguing subject, and he dug extensively into the lives of the Georgian princesses, particularly those of King George III. Even the jolly muck-raker Nigel Cawthorne, in his *The Sex Lives of the Kings & Queens of England*, published in 1994, fails to hint that Princess Elizabeth may have escaped from "the nunnery" long enough to provide a bit of sexual intrigue. Just when it begins to seem safe to conclude that the rumor had no basis in fact, Marples comes back on page 93 with the statement about Princess Elizabeth, much stronger than the earlier vacillation: "who, as it seems we must accept, was in fact a married woman of some eight or ten years' standing, with a clandestine husband and daughter somewhere in the background." It is difficult to draw conclusions (concerning the alleged affair, husband, pregnancy or child-birth) from this conflicting source material. Perhaps none is needed, for it was as a middle-aged lady that Elizabeth finally found conjugal happiness, perhaps even bliss.

Van der Kiste provides a view through Princess Elizabeth's eyes of her bore-dom: "Mama sits in a very small green room which she is very fond of, reads, writes and Botanizes," Elizabeth wrote from Frogmore in July 1791. "Augusta and me remain in the room next to hers across a passage and employ ourselves much in the same way...."

Although the sheltered atmosphere in which the Princesses were forced to live was perhaps the greatest cross that the girls had to bear, it was not the only one. King George III was parsimonious in the extreme, even during the sane periods of his life. His Consort, Queen Charlotte, a bird of a feather, was equally, if not more, penurious. The results of this royal frugality impacted Princess Elizabeth and her two elder sisters in many ways. Sir James Bland Burges (1752–1824), who saw much of the family during this period, noted that in 1794 each girl was provided an allowance of 2,000 pounds per annum. Marples and Van der Kiste are agreed that from this modest sum the Princesses were required to pay for their clothing, jew-elry and servants' wages. Van der Kiste tells us that Princess Elizabeth called her-self "a bad economist," and says herself that she "must go to gaol very soon." (Presumably the jail that Elizabeth had in mind was debtors' prison.) Elizabeth was very close to her eldest brother George, Prince of Wales (1762–1830). On at least one occasion, Elizabeth borrowed a three-figure sum from him. Compared to his own debts, the amount was a trifling figure indeed.

Princess Elizabeth's brother Prince Edward, Duke of Kent and Strathern and Earl of Dublin (1767–1820), resided for a time in Nova Scotia, in North America. There he became acquainted with the Frenchman Louis Philippe, Duke of Orleans (1773–1850), and the idea of arranging a marriage between the Duke and Elizabeth was discussed in some detail. The Duke of Orleans was Catholic and, although he was Royal, the French Revolution had placed him in exile. There was no certainty that he would ever come to the throne of France. The idea of a marriage with him for Elizabeth was dropped. This was probably best for Elizabeth. The Duke of Orleans came to the throne of France in 1830, but he was forced to abdicate in 1848. The marriage that Elizabeth actually did later enter was excellent, one that she deserved, having waited 48 years for an arranged marriage to royalty in the con-ventional manner.

In 1810 King George III lapsed into the third and final phase of his illness. The King was seen no more, and the Prince of Wales was made Prince Regent of the United Kingdom in 1811. Queen Charlotte took this badly, and Princess Elizabeth became her mother's close companion. If this biographical sketch of Princess Eliz-abeth has not yet demonstrated the absurdity of the restrictions placed on the three eldest Princesses, this one ironic twist should do the trick. Elizabeth was now over 40 years old yet she was forbidden by her mother, the Queen, to correspond with her brothers! Now, as helpmate and secretary to her mother, one of her duties was to correspond with these brothers on the Queen's behalf. Of course this gave her an opportunity to surreptitiously slip in her own messages, but it is appalling that a 40-year-old Princess of England should have to resort to such subterfuge.

Princess Elizabeth, now in her late 40s, had probably given up thoughts of matrimony, but Prince Frederick (1769–1829), the hereditary Prince of Hesse-Homburg, a tiny German principality, came to England to seek Elizabeth's hand in marriage. Securing the Queen's agreement was a stumbling block for a while. If the marriage went forward, the Queen would lose her secretary and close companion. Fortunately, the groom-to-be was able to charm Queen Charlotte, and the wedding was held on April 7, 1818. It was a semi-private affair in the throne room. The bride was just one month short of age 48, so it was apparent that it would be a childless marriage.

After a honeymoon at Royal Lodge, Windsor, loaned to the newlyweds by the Prince Regent, the hereditary Prince and his new hereditary Princess lingered in England to soften the impact on the Queen, and they visited Queen Charlotte at Brighton. While they were there, the hereditary Prince received an angry letter from the Landrgrave of Hesse-Homburg, demanding the Prince's return. Marples tells us that Prince Frederick replied indicating that, because of his happiness with Elizabeth, he could not possibly leave without her.

But leave they finally did, via the royal yacht, departing from Hastings to cross to Continental Europe at Calais, France.

There were things about Elizabeth's new German home that displeased her, but she wisely revealed them only by letter to close friends in England. For their part, the Germans found some faults in Prince Frederick's bride. The fact that she could not speak German fluently surprised them.

But Elizabeth and her husband were delighted with each other, and their marriage was a huge success. Elizabeth came to love not only her husband, but Homburg itself. She charmed the citizens, and genuinely admired the White Tower, the ancient portion of their old castle.

An unexpected opportunity to win the hearts of her new countrymen came in 1820, upon the death of the landgrave, Frederick V (1748–1820) of Hesse-Homburg. Elizabeth's husband succeeded as the new landgrave, styled Landgrave Frederick VI of Hesse-Homburg (1769–1829). Elizabeth would have become landgravine to her husband, but there was a problem. The former landgravine, Caroline (1746–1821) of Hesse-Darmstadt, was reluctant to give up her place at court. Graciously, and ingeniously, Elizabeth stepped aside and waited to assume the title landgravine until the reigning landgravine's death, which came soon on September 18, 1821. This generosity endeared her to all her countrymen.

Marples tells us that Elizabeth was deeply in love with her husband. A visitor from England, Miss Cornelia Knight, who stayed with Elizabeth and Landgrave Frederick VI several times, wrote of the landgrave with admiration, and commented on his "noble frankness of character, his patriarchal manners—he was the father of his people ... his air of culture. He spoke beautiful French, possessed an excellent library...."

The marriage relationship was based on romantic love, but Elizabeth also made herself useful in matters of state and was able to relieve a serious financial difficulty for her husband.

When Elizabeth's husband died in 1829, she was heartbroken, but looked back on her eleven years of marriage as the happiest years of her life. Elizabeth, now the dowager landgravine, settled down in the German principality, and although she twice visited England, she gave no serious thought to moving there. As a German widow, she was happy to confine herself to domestic activities and leave political matters to others. When she visited spas, it was not to search for a new husband, but to find some relief from medical problems with her legs.

Elizabeth died on January 10, 1840, at Frankfort-am-Main, attended by a faithful English maid of long standing. She was buried at the mausoleum of the landgraves at Homburg.

51. *Prince Ernest, Duke of Cumberland (1771–1851)*

Ernest was the eighth child born to King George III (1738–1820) and his Consort, Queen Charlotte (1744–1818). He was born on June 5, 1771, at Queen's House, and christened as Ernest Augustus, on July 1, in the great council chamber, by Frederick Cornwallis, Archbishop of Canterbury (1713–1783).

King George and Queen Charlotte were producing royal children at a rapid rate. On account of space limitations as well as a desire to separate the royal children into subgroups (e.g., to facilitate different types of education for boys versus girls), the flavor of the childhood of each royal child was strongly influenced by the subgroup into which he or she fell. Prince Ernest was the first member of the last clump of male children born to the King and Queen. In 1776 some of the royal children's residences were changed, and Prince Ernest was moved, with his younger brother Prince Augustus (1773–1843), to the house next door to the one shared by Prince William (1765–1837) and Prince Edward (1767–1820). These houses were close to their parents and sisters.

Ernest, aged five, and Augustus, aged three, were housed on the south side of Kew Green. They were accompanied to their new residence by Mr. Powell, their page, and Miss Sorrel, their dresser. The governor of these young Princes was Mr. Hayes, formerly a captain of British forces in North America.

In 1777 Princess Sophia (1777–1848) was born, and to make room for her, Prince Adolphus (1774–1850) was moved to share quarters with Princes Ernest and Augustus. Princess Sophia will make a more prominent appearance later in this biographical sketch, because of the allegation, or at least rumor, that she and Prince Ernest had an incestuous love affair. At this point, the staff for the three Princes consisted of the governor, two instructors and some servants. King George III soon appointed two tutors to provide more rigorous education for these three Princes, and hopefully instill in them some Anglican piety and virtue. The chosen tutors were William Cookson (–1820) and Reverend Thomas Hughes (–1833).

At the age of 15, Prince Ernest was enrolled in the University of Gottingen in Hanover, Germany. (In 1837 this same Prince Ernest would come to the throne of Hanover, which by then was a kingdom.) Military subjects formed a major portion of the curriculum at Gottingen, and Prince Ernest trained with the Hanoverian army.

He was made an officer in the army of Hanover and served during the campaign in Flanders, during the Napoleonic Wars. In May 1794, at the first battle of Tournai, Prince Ernest was severely wounded. He recuperated in England, but returned to combat again on the European Continent.

Throughout this period, there was great tension between Prince Ernest and his father, King George III. Prince Ernest was a handsome young man, who had served with honor in the army against Napoleon's forces. Combat wounds cost him loss of sight from his left eye, and eventually led to loss of use of his left arm. He had all the normal testosterone-driven urges of a man in his early twenties, plus an extra dose as a result of his Hanoverian ancestry. At home in England, several of his brothers were enjoying themselves, and at the Prince of Wales' Carlton House, the gaiety was particularly rich. The king wanted to keep Ernest away from that atmosphere. Ernest wanted military promotions and high rank in the British army.

At one point, the Prince simply refused to remain in the Hanoverian service under General John Louis von Walmoden (1736–1811), stating that honor would not permit him to do so. General von Walmoden was an unacknowledged illegitimate son of King George II (1683–1760). However, Prince Ernest did later accept the rank of lieutenant general in von Walmoden's army.

In a letter to his brother George, Prince of Wales (1762–1830), Prince Ernest shared the secret that he intended to go AWOL (absent without leave), and when this news reached the King, he allowed Prince Ernest to come home to England.

Upon his return, honors were heaped upon Prince Ernest. Parliament granted him an allowance of 12,000 pounds per year, and in the spring of 1799 he was created Duke of Cumberland. That same year, two additional titles of nobility were bestowed upon him: Duke of Teviotdale in the peerage of Great Britain, and Earl of Armagh in the peerage of Ireland. In July 1799 (back-dated to May 1798) the very high rank of lieutenant general in the British army was bestowed on the new Duke of Cumberland. In 1804 parliament increased Prince Ernest's annual allowance to 18,000 pounds per year, a very generous sum, and Cumberland was also granted some highly lucrative military commands.

About this time, Prince Ernest, Duke of Cumberland, entered politics as a radical reactionary. From Christopher Hibbert's George *III: A Personal History*, published in 1998, we learn that as early as the mid–1790's the prince had become "a confirmed reactionary of the most vehement kind."

David Williamson's *Brewer's British Royalty*, published in 1996, tells us that

Prince Ernest "was the least popular of George III's sons, with an unprepossessing appearance heightened by the loss of an eye. He also enjoyed, probably unjustifiably, a very unsavory reputation, being allegedly involved in the murder of his valet, Sallis, and also accused of having an incestuous relationship with his sister Princess Sophia and being the father of her natural son." We shall now attempt to assess this parade of horribles from Williamson and sort the true from the false.

It is clear that Prince Ernest had an unattractive personality, and that even his brothers had little fondness for him. His "unprepossessing appearance" can certainly be seen as a glass half-full, rather than half-empty, if we but recall that the Prince had been a handsome young man and lost his eye in combat in honorable military service against Napoleon.

Finding Cumberland innocent of the murder charge is an easy matter. The man who died in this incident was one of Cumberland's valets, named Joseph Sellis (–1810). In his 445 page biography of Prince Ernest, entitled *Ernest Augustus: Duke of Cumberland & King of Hanover,* G. M. Willis provides a wealth of information about the incident in question and concludes that it was clearly the valet, Seliss (sic), who attempted to murder the Duke of Cumberland, and that while defending himself, the Duke cut Seliss' throat. Willis tells us that this interpretation was quite clear at the time of the incident, but, some years later, political opponents of Cumberland's reopened the discussion, calling Cumberland the murderer. Cumberland sued for libel and won. The following additional sources are unanimous in their view that Cumberland was the victim, not the perpetrator in the Joseph Sellis matter:

• *Dictionary of National Biography.* 1909.
• Fulford, Roger. *Royal Dukes: The Father & Uncles of Queen Victoria.* 1933.
• Van der Kiste, John. *George III's Children.* 1999.

Sources consulted are also unanimous in their view that the illegitimate child borne by Princess Sophia was not the product of incest, but a son of Thomas Garth (1744–1829). John Van der Kiste tells us in his *George III's Children,* published in 1999, that the daughters of King George III were confined under such tight restraints, in "the nunnery" as they called it, that Princess Sophia had a son fathered by one of the King's equerries. "His age and ugliness put him at no disadvantage … for … (the) spinster sisters were so secluded from the world, and allowed to mix with so few people, that it was said that they were more than ready to fall into the arms of the first man outside the family who looked at them."

By 1815 Prince Ernest had fallen in love and wished to marry. His intended bride was a German woman, Frederica (1778–1841), a daughter of Charles, Grand Duke of Mecklenburg-Strelitz and his Duchess, the former Princess Frederica of Hesse-Darmstadt. The bride that Ernest had chosen had been twice married and twice widowed. Her first husband was a Prussian Prince, while her second husband was Prince Frederick of Solms-Braunfels. On account of this second marriage, Ernest's bride is often referred to as Princess Frederica of Solms-Braunfels.

But no matter what name the woman used, the Queen of England detested her. In Queen Charlotte's perception, Frederica had received a proposal of marriage from one of the Queen's sons, Prince Adolphus (1774–1850), but had married Prince Frederick of Solms-Braunfels, instead. In Queen Charlotte's eyes, Frederica had jilted Prince Adolphus.

Actually, the water is a bit muddy on this point, and it is difficult to say whether the Queen's interpretation was correct or erroneous. We know that King George III had given his permission for Adolphus to marry Frederica, but the King asked that the wedding be delayed until the war was over. Time went by, passions cooled, and Frederica wed the Solms-Braunfels Prince.

Prince Ernest was almost universally unpopular in England, so the prevailing view there was against the marriage. There were those who went to the ridiculous extreme in pointing out that the deaths of Frederica's first two husbands had been just a bit too convenient.

In any event, the unpopular Prince Ernest and his now unpopular bride were married. The approval that they needed to do this (on the English side) was from Prince George, who was now the Prince Regent, and the Regent readily granted that approval.

Two ceremonies were held. The first ceremony was in Germany on May 29, 1815. After that German ceremony, Queen Charlotte began asking questions about Frederica's virtue. The Queen's questions and objections notwithstanding, since children born to the newlyweds might come in the line of succession to the English throne, the couple were wed a second time in England. That ceremony was held at Carlton House, London on August 29, 1815. The royal couple had just one child, Prince George (1819–1878).

Let us take a look at the cast of characters who were pertinent to the line of succession to the English throne in 1817. At that time, King George III was still alive, but insanity had driven him from the stage of active characters. The King's eldest son, Prince George, was now ruling as Prince Regent and would soon come to the throne as King George IV. Although King George III and Queen Charlotte had produced 13 children who survived beyond infancy, in 1817 Prince George's child, Princess Charlotte (1796–1817), was the only legitimate grandchild! To make matters worse, that only legitimate grandchild died in November 1817, during the birth of a stillborn baby.

In England, succession to the throne followed the law of primogeniture, which had governed succession since the era of the Norman Conquest. Under that law, the throne passes not to the King's eldest surviving son, but to the eldest child of the King's first-born son. If there is no such child, then the throne passes to the eldest surviving son, and when that son dies, to the first-born child of that son, or, if there is none, to the next son in succession. As a result, the English throne passed from King George III to his eldest son, King George IV (1762–1830), and from him to his eldest living brother, who ruled England as King William IV (1765–1837). But, because of the law of primogeniture, the baton never passed down as far as our Prince Ernest. Instead, the throne passed from King William

IV to the only child of the next eldest son, Prince Edward, Duke of Kent (1767–1820). That only child came to England's throne as Queen Victoria (1819–1901).

Cumberland's British political actions were generally faulty. *The Concise Dictionary of National Biography*, published by Oxford University Press in 1992, tells us that Cumberland "opposed all relaxation of the Catholic penal laws, 1808; voted against the Regency Bill 1810; …opposed the Reform Bill of 1832…." John Cannon points out in his *The Oxford Companion to British History*, published in 1997, that "the transition from the unreformed system of 1830 to full democracy in the 20th century was effected by seven franchise measures—the Acts of 1832…."

In Hanover Germany, the line of succession worked differently than in England, because women were barred from ruling there by Salic law. For more than a century since the death of England's Queen Anne (1665–1714), England and Hanover had been ruled by the same person (ignoring, for simplicity, the 1807–1813 period of Napoleonic rule). However, because women were excluded from ruling in Hanover, when King William IV died, our Prince Ernest came to the throne of Hanover, while Victoria came to the throne of England. King Ernest Augustus, as he was called in Hanover, ruled from 1837 until his death in 1851. King Ernest Augustus was relatively popular in Hanover. For more than a century, Hanover had been ruled by absentee rulers. King Ernest Augustus was not only on the local scene, but he genuinely cared about the welfare of the citizens of his new kingdom, and tried to become "father of his people." As King, he maintained peace with Prussia, and even established a degree of harmony with that kingdom. When King Ernest Augustus died in 1851, his only son, George (1819–1878), ruled Hanover as King George V until 1866 when Prussia annexed Hanover.

Prince Ernest, Duke of Cumberland, later King Ernest Augustus of Hanover, died on November 18, 1851. He was buried, together with the coffin of his Queen Consort, Frederica (1778–1841), at Herrenhausen.

52. *Prince Augustus, Duke of Sussex (1773–1843)*

Augustus was the ninth child born to King George III (1738–1820) and his Consort, Queen Charlotte (1744–1818). He was born on January 27, 1773, at Queen's House, and christened on February 25 as Augustus Frederick by Frederick Cornwallis, Archbishop of Canterbury (1713–1783).

King George and Queen Charlotte were producing royal children at a rapid rate. On account of space limitations, and a desire to separate the royal children into subgroups (e.g., to facilitate different types of education for boys versus girls), the flavor of the childhood of each royal child was strongly influenced by the subgroup into which he or she fell. In 1776 some of the royal children's residences were changed, and Prince Augustus was moved, with his next elder brother, Prince

Ernest (1771–1851), to the house next door to the one shared by Prince William (1765–1837) and Prince Edward (1767–1820). These houses were close to their parents and sisters.

Augustus, aged three, and Ernest, aged five, were housed on the south side of Kew Green. They were accompanied to their new residence by Mr. Powell, their page, and Miss Sorrel, their dresser. The governor of these young Princes was Mr. Hayes, formerly a captain of British forces in North America.

In 1777 Princess Sophia (1777–1848) was born, and to make room for her, Prince Adolphus (1774–1850) was moved to share quarters with Princes Augustus and Ernest. At this point, the staff for the three Princes consisted of the governor, two instructors and some servants. King George III soon appointed two tutors to provide more rigorous education for these three Princes, and hopefully instill in them some Anglican piety and virtue. The chosen tutors were William Cookson (–1820) and Reverend Thomas Hughes (–1833).

In 1786 Augustus was sent with his brothers, Prince Ernest and Prince Adolphus, to study at the University of Gottingen in Hanover, Germany. Mollie Gillen tells us in her work entitled *Royal Duke: Augustus Frederick, Duke of Sussex (1773–1843)*, published in 1976, that "for the British Princes the town bore an excitingly strange face. Fifty-odd years later it still had 'a decided look of the middle ages about it....'" The daily lecture and study schedule was an arduous one, and by 1787 or 1788 the health of Prince Augustus' began to fail. The King and other members of the royal family were given periodic updates on Augustus' health, and they were not reassuring. Prince Augustus enjoyed the scholarly pursuits at Gottingen. His illness was no sham to avoid the rigors of study. His ailments were very real and needed attention. King George III gave his permission for Prince Augustus to move to a warmer climate to improve his health. In the winter of 1792, Prince Augustus arrived in Rome.

Quoting again from Mollie Gillen's delightfully comprehensive biography: "The next five months were probably among the happiest of the Prince's whole life. To enjoy peaceful sleep at night, to be able to breathe freely, to be a Prince receiving, with modest pleasure, deferential respect of all his acquaintances, to be sixteen, with intelligence, and a curiosity that was fed by new scenes and experiences, what more could a boy ask?"

We learn from Roger Fulford's *Royal Dukes: The Father & Uncles of Queen Victoria*, published in 1933, that Prince Augustus exchanged compliments with Pope Pius VI (1717–1799), the leader of the Roman Catholic Church. Fulford also tells us that Prince Augustus ventured out onto even thinner ice when he paid a courtesy call on one of the Cardinals at Rome. The Cardinal was Henry Benedict Thomas Edward Maria Clement Francis Xavier Stuart (1725–1807), a grandson of England's King James II (1633–1701) and, to any surviving Jacobites, this Cardinal was the rightful King of England, titled King Henry IX. Apparently the meeting between the Prince and the Cardinal was cordial and dealt largely with what a fine place England was.

In the spring of 1793 Prince Augustus fell in love with an English lady who was visiting Rome. The object of Prince Augustus' affection was Lady Augusta Murray (1768–1830). In England, Lady Augusta had established a reputation as something of a flirt, but also was known as a lady of great beauty.

The Prince and Lady Augusta first chanced to meet at a church in Rome. There, Prince Augustus gallantly offered to fix a strap on Lady Augusta's shoe, and by the time the prince finished tying the shoe, he was her captive.

Quoting again from Mollie Gillen's delightful biography: "Augusta Murray was of impeccable lineage, her father John Murray, fourth Earl of Dunmore, her mother Lady Charlotte Stewart, daughter of the sixth Earl of Galloway, with a descent traceable (as the Prince's was also) from James II of Scotland and Edward IV of England and (through her father) from Charles VII of France."

Prince Augustus became convinced that he must possess Lady Augusta, but Lady Augusta was not willing to permit the Prince any sexual favors without benefit of matrimony. An Anglican priest, William Gunn, was found in Rome, and he agreed to perform a secret marriage ceremony for the couple. Prince Augustus made no attempt to secure the King's consent to the marriage. It was performed in Rome on April 4, 1793.

Here some irony sets in. Prince Augustus had offered, if not "aid and comfort," at least congeniality, to the enemy (the Jacobite claimants to the throne of England) when he visited Cardinal Henry Stuart (1725–1807), but suffered no consequences for that courtesy. In contrast, his action in 1793 seems harmless (to an American author writing in the early 21st century). What he did in 1793 was marry an English noblewoman, and the marriage was performed in accordance with the rites of the Anglican Church of England. This seemingly innocent act violated the Royal Marriages Act of 1772, which carried severe penalties. Since our Prince Augustus managed to violate the Royal Marriages Act a second time, later in his life, let us examine the background and results of the Royal Marriages Act.

The Royal Marriages Act had been prompted when two of the brothers of King George III married women whom the King felt were unsuitable. The King responded by securing passage in 1772 of the Royal Marriages Act. That act placed strict limitations on the rights of members of the royal family under age 25 to marry without the approval of the "sovereign in council." It also carried less restrictive limitations on the rights of royal family members aged 25 and older to marry. King George III was a prude, and the provisions of this act reflect that personality trait. The act declared null and void any marriages that were performed in conflict with the act. In addition to nullifying marriages prohibited by the act, the new law carried very stiff penalties, not only for those who were married in violation of the act, but also for those who assisted in such a marriage. At the time the bill was being debated in parliament, the press lampooned it and pointed out ridiculous ramifications that might result under various hypothetical situations. Neither King George III nor the press failed to foresee the very real hazard hidden in the act, and this hazard became a reality in 1817. The problem was that, although King George III and Queen Charlotte had produced 13 children who survived beyond infancy, by the year 1817 Prince George's (1762–1830) child, Princess Charlotte

(1796–1817), was the only legitimate grandchild! To make matters worse, that only legitimate grandchild died in November 1817, during the birth of a stillborn baby. The succession to the throne of England looked murky indeed, and the Royal Marriages Act of King George III contributed to the sparse supply of viable candidates for the throne.

Perhaps assuming that sanity would one day prevail in England (vis-à-vis the Royal Marriages Act), Prince Augustus and his bride decided to have the marriage ceremony performed a second time in England, since children born to the marriage might well be pertinent to the line of succession to the throne of England. To prepare for this, the banns of marriage were read in church in London on three consecutive Sundays, announcing the intention of a "Mr. Augustus Frederick and a Miss Augusta Murray" to wed. By the time that that English marriage ceremony was performed on December 5, 1793, the bride was quite obviously pregnant. The ceremony was performed at St. George's Hanover Square in London.

During the summer of 1794, the authorities in England found little trouble in voiding both the marriage in Rome, "a shew or effigy of a marriage pretended to have been had and solemnized," and the one in London. Two children were born to this union and they certainly were "legitimate children" under any reasonable definition of that term, although their birth contravened the Royal Marriages Act promoted by King George III.

The children of this marriage were both known as d'Este. They were:

Augustus Frederick d'Este (1794–1848)
Augusta Emma d'Este (1801–1866)

Prince Augustus was an affectionate father to both of his children and saw them frequently, even after his love for their mother had dwindled.

The second child was born on August 9, 1801, and about that time the relationship between Prince Augustus and his wife began to cool. A few years later, the Prince's wife took the surname of d'Ameland and is sometimes referred to as Countess Augusta d'Ameland (1768–1830). Prince Augustus did not marry another woman until 1831, after the death of his wife Augusta, but the relationship was cool for a quarter of a century. In John Van der Kiste's *George III's Children*, published in 1999, it is stated that the reason for the marriage rupture has never been established. "The Prince, it was thought, may have been told that she had been unfaithful to him; she may have precipitated a quarrel with him by taunting him with desertion ... [or he may have been] a frustrated, disappointed, frequently sick man unable to resist parental pressure any longer, particularly if his invalid marriage was the only barrier to a dukedom and regular allowance."

On November 27, 1801, Prince Augustus was created Duke of Sussex. On the same day, additional titles of nobility were awarded to him. They were Earl of Inverness and Baron Arklow. The new Duke of Sussex was granted an income of 12,000 pounds per year by parliament, and that sum was later raised to 18,000.

While Augustus' next eldest brother, Prince Ernest, Duke of Cumberland

(1771–1851), had been a radical reactionary opposed to all things progressive, our Prince Augustus was the opposite. He became grandmaster of the Freemasons, president of the Society of Arts, and president of the Royal Society, the oldest surviving scientific body in the world. In his *Brewer's British Royalty*, published in 1996, David Williamson tells us: "He was a steady friend and benefactor to art, science and literature…. Though not very learned himself, he valued learning and his library was very extensive."

By 1831 Prince Augustus, Duke of Sussex, was older, and one would have thought wiser, but he managed to marry for a second time in violation of the Royal Marriages Act. His second wife was Lady Cecilia Underwood (1793–1873). She was a widow of Sir George Buggin (–1825). She had resumed use of her maiden name, Underwood, upon her husband's death. They were married on May 2, 1831. The marriage was kept secret for a time. No children were born of this marriage.

Queen Victoria (1819–1901) acceded to the throne of England on June 20, 1837. Although her mother and some advisors were hostile to Prince Augustus, Duke of Sussex, Queen Victoria was particularly fond of this uncle. In December 1837 she made him grand master of the order of the Bath, and made him captain general of the Honourable Artillery Company. More significantly, when planning her wedding ceremony for marriage to Albert (1819–1861), the young Queen insisted that she be given away by Prince Augustus, acting for her now dead father, Prince Edward (1767–1820). There was a good deal of grumbling and maneuvering about this topic, but the young Queen insisted upon Prince Augustus. The Duke of Sussex was, of course, fond of his niece, Queen Victoria. Sussex found a method to tangibly display that fondness when he relinquished his place in the order of royal precedence in favor to the Queen's Consort, Prince Albert. Queen Victoria repaid that favor by honoring Prince Augustus' wife with the title Duchess of Inverness.

On April 21, 1843, Prince Augustus died at Kensington Palace. A black-bordered obituary in *The Times* of London commented, "No death in the royal family short of the actual demise of a monarch could have occasioned a stronger feeling of deprivation than in the case of the Duke of Sussex." At his own request, Prince Augustus was buried in the public cemetery at Kensal Green, rather than at Windsor, to be sure that his wife would later be allowed to be buried beside him.

53. *Prince Adolphus,*
Duke of Cambridge (1774–1850)

Adolphus was the tenth child born to King George III (1738–1820) and his Consort, Queen Charlotte (1744–1818). He was born on February 24, 1774, at Queen's House, and christened on March 24, 1774, in the great council chamber of St. James' Palace, as Adolphus Frederick.

King George and Queen Charlotte were producing royal children at a rapid rate. On account of space limitations, and a desire to separate the royal children into subgroups (e.g., to facilitate different types of education for boys versus girls), the flavor of the childhood of each royal child was strongly influenced by the subgroup into which he or she fell. In 1777 Princess Sophia (1777–1848) was born, and to make room for her, Prince Adolphus was moved to share quarters with Princes Augustus (1773–1843) and Ernest (1771–1851). At this point, the staff for the three Princes consisted of a governor, two instructors and some servants.

King George III soon appointed two tutors to provide more rigorous education for these three Princes, and hopefully instill in them some Anglican piety and virtue. The chosen tutors were William Cookson (–1820) and Reverend Thomas Hughes (–1833).

In 1786, then only age 12, Prince Adolphus was sent to Hanover in Germany, accompanied by his brothers, Princes Augustus and Ernest. There, they studied at the University of Gottingen. Mollie Gillen tells us in her work entitled *Royal Duke: Augustus Frederick, Duke of Sussex (1773–1843)*, published in 1976, that "for the British Princes the town bore an excitingly strange face. Fifty-odd years later it still had 'a decided look of the middle ages about it....'"

The daily lecture and study schedule was an arduous one. Lectures were held in the homes of the professors since classes were small, and they ran from early morning to perhaps 8:00 in the evening. Only Saturday afternoons and Sundays were free from the rigid lecture schedule.

Prince Adolphus was destined for a career in the army, and military tactics were emphasized at the university. In addition, Adolphus was sent to Prussia to sharpen his military skills, and afterwards, in 1793, he was made a colonel in the Hanoverian army. Our Adolphus saw active combat duty in 1793, 1794 and 1795 during the Napoleonic Wars. During much of that period he served under General John Louis von Walmoden (1736–1811), who was an unacknowledged illegitimate son of Adolphus' great-grandfather, England's King George II (1683–1760). During this combat period, Adolphus was promoted from colonel to major general in the Hanoverian army. He was also wounded in the shoulder in combat and was, for a short time, a prisoner of war. He was rescued and returned to England to recuperate. By 1798 Prince Adolphus had risen to lieutenant general in the Hanoverian army.

In November 1801 Prince Adolphus was made Duke of Cambridge. At the same time, he received two additional titles of nobility: Earl of Tipperary in the Irish nobility, and Baron of Culloden. On February 3, 1802, Prince Adolphus, Duke of Cambridge was sworn in as a member of Great Britain's privy council.

Christopher Hibbert's 1998 work entitled *George III: A Personal History* provides us with information about young Adolphus' interest in the opposite sex. As Hibbert tells it, the Prince "...wished to marry his cousin, Frederica of Mecklenburg-Strelitiz, his mother's niece, the young widow of Prince Frederick of Prussia. The King granted his permission, but suggested that the wedding should be delayed until after the war. Prince Adolphus dutifully agreed; but in the meantime Princess Frederica fell in love with the Prince of Solms-Braunfels, whom she married shortly before giving birth to their child. After her second husband's death, Princess Frederica was, in 1815, married, for a third time, to Prince Adolphus's brother the Duke of Cumberland."

In 1803 Prince Adolphus transferred from the army of Hanover to the British army. By 1807 Hanover had been conquered by France, and Napoleon elected to annex Hanover to the kingdom of Westphalia, in Germany. That period of French rule of Hanover ended in 1813, and at some point afterwards, Prince Adolphus, Duke of Cambridge, was sent to Hanover from England to represent Great Britain there. Sources consulted differ on the year that Prince Adolphus returned to Hanover (dates from 1813 to 1816 are mentioned), and these sources also differ on the title that Adolphus held in Hanover. (Both governor general and viceroy are mentioned). There is no conflict of opinion about the warm response that Adolphus received from his Hanoverian friends upon his return.

In 1808 Prince Adolphus, Duke of Cambridge, was promoted to full general in the British army, and in 1813 he was promoted again, this time to field marshal.

The year 1817 became very significant to England and the line of succession to the English throne. Although King George III and Queen Charlotte had produced 13 children who survived beyond infancy, as of 1817, Prince George's (1762–1830) only child, Princess Charlotte (1796–1817), was the only legitimate grandchild! To make matters worse, that only legitimate grandchild died in November 1817, during the birth of a stillborn baby.

Princess Charlotte's death sent all of the unmarried sons of King George III scrambling to find brides to impregnate with heirs to the throne. In England, succession to the throne followed the law of primogeniture, which had governed succession since the era of the Norman Conquest. Under that law, the throne passes not to the King's eldest surviving son, but to the eldest child of the king's first-born son. If there is no such child, then the throne passes to the eldest surviving son, and when that son dies, to the first-born child of that son, or, if there is none, to the next son in succession. As a result, the English throne passed from King George III to his eldest son, King George IV (1762–1830), and from him to his eldest living brother, who ruled England as King William IV (1765–1837).

Our Prince Adolphus found a very suitable bride in Germany, Princess Augusta of Hesse-Cassel (1797–1889). She was a daughter of Landgrave Frederick of Hesse-Cassel (–1837) and his wife, the former Caroline of Nassau-Usingen. The bride-to-be of Prince Adolphus was a granddaughter of England's King George II. Princess Augusta's mother, Princess Mary (1723–1772), was a daughter of King George II, who in 1740 had married Prince Frederick (1720–1785). This Frederick ruled Hesse-Cassel as Frederich II, Landgrave of Hesse-Cassel.

Adolphus and Augusta were wed in Cassel, Germany on May 7, 1818, and a second wedding ceremony was performed in England on June 1, 1818, at Queen's House. The marriage was a very happy one and produced three children:

Prince George, later Duke of Cambridge (1819–1904)
Princess Augusta (1822–1916), later wed Grand Duke Adolphus Frederick of

Mecklenburg-Strelitz (1848–1914), and thereby became grand duchess of Mecklenburg-Strelitz

Princess Mary Adelaide (1833–1897), later wed Francis, Duke of Teck (1837–1900), and thereby became duchess of Teck

For nearly a quarter of a century, ending in 1837, our Adolphus lived in, and devoted himself to, Hanover. Perhaps inevitably, he became rather out of touch with matters of importance in England. In 1831 Lord Charles Grey (1764–1845) wrote to Prince Adolphus to request that he come to England to cast his vote in the House of Lords for the Reform Bill. This was a tremendously important bill and its passage was a milestone for British democracy. However, Prince Adolphus did not make the trip to England to cast his vote; not because he opposed the bill, but because he preferred not to leave his activities in Hanover, and his wife, Princess Augusta (1797–1889), dreaded another channel crossing to England.

An elder brother of Adolphus had married and produced a child to succeed King William IV to the throne. That elder brother was Prince Edward, Duke of Kent (1767–1820). He died young, but it was Prince Edward's only child, Princess Victoria (1819–1901), who came to the throne after King William IV and ruled Great Britain as Queen Victoria. Thus Prince Adolphus, Duke of Cambridge, lost in the heir-production race set in motion by the death of Princess Charlotte (1796–1817). However, Adolphus' third child became important indeed to the royal throne of Great Britain. That third child, Princess Mary Adelaide (1833–1897), was the mother of Mary (1867–1953), who married on July 6, 1893, England's Prince George Frederick Ernest Albert (1865–1936), who came to England's throne as King George V (1865–1936). As Queen Consort, Queen Mary used her clout to arrange the burial sites of her maternal grandparents (Prince Adolphus and his wife) to her liking.

While England's law of primogeniture made it clear that Victoria would come to England's throne upon the death of King William IV in 1837, the situation in Hanover, Germany, was more opaque. In Hanover, the line of succession worked differently than in England, because women were barred from ruling there by Salic law. For more than a century since the death of England's Queen Anne (1665–1714), England and Hanover had been ruled by the same person (ignoring, for simplicity, the 1807–1813 period of Napoleonic rule). However, because women were excluded from ruling in Hanover, when King William IV died, Prince Ernest, Duke of Cumberland (1771–1851), came to the throne of Hanover, while Victoria came to the throne of England. King Ernest Augustus, as he was called in Hanover, ruled from 1837 until his death in 1851.

This left no suitable role in Hanover for Prince Adolphus, Duke of Cambridge. Although he had not borne the official title, he had been *de facto* king of Hanover. John Van der Kiste's *George III's Children*, published in 1999, tells us that Prince Adolphus "brought his family back to England within a few weeks of the new reign. They took up residence at Cambridge House, Piccadilly, and at their country retreat of Cambridge Cottage, Kew." This had to be a psychological letdown for Adolphus. In a matter of weeks, he had gone from being virtually a King to being just another one of the surviving children of King George III; and the England that he had come home to was far different than the one he had left a quarter-century earlier.

Compounding his difficulties in adjusting to life in England was the fact that Prince Adolphus had become very eccentric, perhaps even "strange." Adolphus also lost most of his hearing. The final thirteen years of his life were not very pleasant for this deaf, old eccentric man.

Prince Adolphus, Duke of Cambridge, died on July 8, 1850, at Cambridge House, his home at Piccadilly, London. He was buried in a mausoleum, which he had previously arranged to be built at the east end of Kew Parish Church. He made these arrangements so that when his wife died, she could be buried with him.

The widow of Prince Adolphus, Duke of Cambridge, Princess Augusta, lived a long life. When it ended in 1889, Augusta was buried adjacent to her husband at Kew Parish Church, as planned. However, in 1928, their granddaughter, Queen Mary (1867–1953), the Consort of England's King George V, used her influence to have her grandparents' coffins moved to the royal tomb house at Windsor.

54. *Princess Mary (1776–1857)*

Mary was the eleventh child born to King George III (1738–1820) and his Consort, Queen Charlotte (1744–1818). Princess Mary was born on April 25, 1776, at Queen's House, and christened on May 19 by Frederick Cornwallis (1713–1783), Archbishop of Canterbury.

Lady Charlotte Finch (1725–1813), who had previously been governess to all of the royal couple's daughters, was young Mary's governess. Other sub-governesses who were involved with the royal Princesses during this era were named Martha Goldsworthy, Mary Hamilton and Jane Gomm. The last named lady joined the royal service in 1786 and her duties, at least for a time, were largely associated with Princess Mary and Princess Sophia (1777–1848).

Because of a number of rather unique factors, most of the six daughters of King George III, including Princess Mary, led rather uneventful lives. (E. g., Princess Mary did not secure a husband until she was 40 years old, and he was her cousin, with a less than impeccable pedigree.) As a result, conventional sources on English history and the royal family of England yield little material for biographical sketches of the daughters of King George III. However, we are fortunate to have available two excellent books which delve into some of the details of the six girls' lives. These two sources are (1) Morris Marples' *Six Royal Sisters: Daughters of George III*, published in 1969, and (2) John Van der Kiste's *George III's Children*, published in 1999. Since there will be numerous references to these two books in this biographical sketch, they will be referred to here simply as Marples' work and Van der Kiste's work, although these authors have also written other books. In addition, for

Princess Mary, reference material is available in E. Thornton Cook's *Royal Marys: Princess Mary and Her Predecessors*. That work was published in 1930.

The first "unique factor" is that these girls were daughters of "*Mad* King George III." He experienced three principal bouts of his mental ailment, and the final bout left him insane for the remainder of his life. The second "unique factor" is that the king was unusually possessive about his daughters and dreaded the thought of losing them to marriage. The third "unique factor" is that King George III and his Consort, Queen Charlotte, deemed it "inappropriate" for any of the royal daughters to marry before the eldest daughter, the "Princess Royal," secured a husband. That might not have presented a serious obstacle to marriage of the younger sisters, had the eldest among them been married with dispatch, but the sad fact is that this eldest daughter was rather physically unattractive.

Striking a marriage contract for an unattractive daughter of an overly possessive King of England is not easily accomplished. That marriage did not occur until 1797, and by then some of the younger Princesses were no longer prime marriage candidates on account of their ages. (Marples tells us that the normal age for a royal female to marry in the late 18th century was about fifteen or sixteen.) Most of the daughters of King George III and Queen Charlotte, including Princess Mary, were obliged to settle for rather unsatisfactory marriages or messy affairs with inappropriate members of the opposite sex. Long after Princess Mary had reached a normal marriage age for a royal female, her mother had joined the King in becoming overly possessive and resisting sensible marriage possibilities for her daughters.

In capsule form, this biographical sketch of Princess Mary will disclose a childhood, a lengthy young-womanhood, extending well into middle-age; then a generally tiresome marriage of nearly two decades duration, ended only by the death of the husband and, finally, a long and relatively lively old age.

In her childhood, Mary was regarded by essentially all contemporaries as the most beautiful of the six sisters. She retained enough of that allure to be described, with sincerity, as "a beauty" when she came to the altar as a 40-year-old bride.

David Williamson's *Brewer's British Royalty*, published in 1996, tells us that Mrs. Delany, a friend of Queen Charlotte, described Princess Mary, when she was in her fourth year, "as a most sweet child.... She could not remember my name, but making me a very low curtsey said 'How do you do, Duchess of Portland's friend? And how does your little niece do? I wish you had brought her.'" Marples' work quotes Frances ("Fanny") Burney's (1752–1840) description of a typical (boring) evening in 1785 with the Queen and daughters sitting at a large round table amusing themselves with books, drawing paper and conversation.

Although some of the Princesses had occasional exposure to high culture (e.g., visits by Thomas Gainsborough [1727–1788], who taught the Princesses a bit about drawing and art), the Princesses' education was structured to be superficial. In those days, royal students were segregated by sex for their education. The boys were generally given a classical education, while the girls devoted a lot of time to needlework and drawing. Any instruction in foreign languages that these girls received was prompted by its perceived usefulness in social situations. Princess Mary apparently lacked any special skills, such as art or music, with which some of her sisters were gifted. Mary's special skills would appear later in her life in social skills and as a health care companion to close relatives.

From *Brewer's British Royalty* we learn that Princess Mary made her debut at court at a ball held on her father's birthday, June 4, 1791. "Fanny" Burney, who saw her, said, "She looked most interesting and unaffectedly lovely; she is a sweet creature, and perhaps, in point of beauty, the first of this truly beautiful race." Other authorities would be less than unanimous in rating the Hanovers in the English royal family a "truly beautiful race," but nonetheless we have one vote placing Princess Mary at the top of this beauty contest.

Princesses were deliberately housed separately from their brothers to facilitate appropriate educational environments for the two sexes, but also, far more importantly, to isolate the Princesses as much as possible from members of the opposite sex. Van der Kiste's work provides a view through Princess Elizabeth's (1770–1840) eyes of her boredom: "Mama sits in a very small green room which she is very fond of, reads, writes and Botanizes," Elizabeth wrote from Frogmore in July, 1791. "Augusta and me remain in the room next to hers across a passage and employ ourselves much in the same way...." (The reference to "Augusta and me" suggests that the daughters' instruction in grammar was perhaps not very rigorous.)

The king enjoyed bathing in salt water, and he and his immediate household spent several summers at Weymouth to enjoy the seaside atmosphere, bathe, and breathe good refreshing salt air. Princess Mary was bored by all this. Marples' work relates that, "Fortunately there was the theater" as a local distraction, and "she (the Queen) put no restriction on the attendance of the Princesses.... Occasionally the royal party went as often as five times a week if there was some special attraction, but this was more than some of them could stand. 'It was pleasant enough,' wrote Princess Mary in October 1798, after seeing Kemble and his company on five successive nights, 'but one may have *too much* of a *good thing*, and that is my case in regard to going so often to see a very bad set of actors. However it amuses the King and we have nothing to do but submit and admire his being so easily pleased.'"

We have already discussed the fact that King George III was "overly possessive" of his six daughters and reluctant to see any of them marry and leave him. This point is much stressed in literature dealing with King George III and his daughters, and a whole book was devoted primarily to this subject. That book is Lucille Iremonger's *Love and the Princesses: The Strange Lives of Mad King George III and His Daughters*, published in 1958. Since the book's thesis is essentially correct, it is easy to overlook the suffocating confinement imposed on the six Princesses by their mother, Queen Charlotte. Our Princess Mary was among the youngest of the daughters of King George III, so Mary was perhaps injured as much by her mother's possessive nature as by her father's. It certainly was the mother rather than the father who restricted the Princesses' access, even to other young girls.

As a result of this parental selfishness, all six Princesses were denied appropriate relief from their normal hormonal urges in one way or another. The only Princess to marry to an appropriate royal husband at anything approaching a sensible age was Princess Charlotte (1766–1828), who wed in 1797 to a German prince. She was then almost 31. All younger sisters were supposed to wait until the eldest had been married. Even after the eldest had wed and left England, for a variety of reasons, acceptable marriages were not accomplished with any dispatch for the remaining five, and each Princess had to find her own way out of the resulting sexual suffocation.

This aspect of the lives of the six Princesses is relatively clear from surviving records for all the girls, except Princess Mary. In Mary's case, the early sexual facts are impenetrable. What we do know is that she finally married in 1816, at age 40, to her first cousin, Prince William Frederick, Duke of Gloucester (1776–1834). What is suspected, but not known, is that Princess Mary and this same Prince William Frederick also carried on an illicit love affair for a decade or more prior to their marriage. As early as 1796, when Mary was a ripe twenty-year-old, the society page gossip-writers were hinting of romance between Mary and William Frederick.

The names of other men who expressed romantic interest in Princess Mary, in one way or another, are also mentioned, but from surviving records we must conclude that there are two most likely answers to our prurient question about Princess Mary's sex life as a young woman: (1) She may have been somewhat asexual, or at least far less interested in men than her sisters; or (2) Mary may indeed have pulled off an undetected, decade-long, illicit affair with Prince William Frederick. Because of his lineage (which will be discussed further) he appeared at court with some regularity, and his presence near Mary would have aroused minimum suspicion. The fact that her married life, when it came, with Prince William Frederick was described by one observer as "loveless" may be a clue to the lack of discernible sexual activity prior to marriage.

It was finally determined that Prince William Frederick, Duke of Gloucester (1776–1834), would make a suitable husband for Princess Mary. There were protracted negotiations between William Frederick and Mary's eldest brother, the Prince Regent, George (1762–1830). At Mary's insistence, the Prince Regent forced William Frederick to agree never to place any obstacles between himself and Mary's relatives in time of trouble. Writing these words early in the 21st century, it seems hard to imagine what Princess Mary feared that Gloucester might do, with her powerful royal family so physically close to the location where the bride and groom would wed and live. But this was early in the 19th century and a woman, even a member of the royal family, as a matter of law, had few rights not granted to her by some man (father, husband, etc.).

Since feminist writers harp on this very point so often and so stridently, an observer ignorant of the facts may conclude that there is more smoke than fire in the allegations. This conclusion would be incorrect. As one indication of how unimportant women were deemed to be, one may observe that in the multi-volume

Dictionary of National Biography, published in London by Smith, Elder & Company as recently as 1909, there is no entry at all for our Princess Mary, a daughter of the King of England. Rather, where her biographical sketch should appear there is a notation: "See under William Frederick, second Duke of Gloucester." Thus the work that in 1909 claimed to be the most comprehensive set of biographies of English persons of importance, failed to include the daughter of a recent King of England and mentioned her only in passing as part of a biography of a man, her husband.

Thus negotiations were necessary to establish what would now be considered Mary's fundamental right(s). After these negotiations, the Prince Regent gave his consent to the union, and Queen Charlotte even gave her assent. It was agreed that Princess Mary would finally wed. Having waited 40 years to marry, it developed that Princess Mary would have to wait just a bit longer. It seems that there were to be two royal weddings that season, and Princess Mary was obliged to yield precedence to Princess Charlotte (1796–1817), the only legitimate child of the Prince Regent. Charlotte was wed on May 2, 1816, and Mary was finally married two months later, in July 1816, at Queen's House. The groom, Prince William Frederick, Second Duke of Gloucester, was a son of Prince William Henry, First Duke of Gloucester (1743–1805), who had secretly married in 1766 to William Frederick's mother, Maria Waldegrave (1736–1807). Maria was a widow of James Waldegrave, Earl of Waldegrave (1715–1763), and she was an illegitimate daughter of Sir Edward Walpole.

The secret 1766 marriage mentioned above became an important event in English history. The Royal Marriages Act of 1772 was prompted by the marriage, in 1771, of King George III's brother, Prince Henry, Duke of Cumberland (1745–1790), to a woman of whom the King disapproved. The bill became law when, for a second time, a brother of King George III, Prince William, Duke of Gloucester, confessed that he had long been married to Maria Waldegrave (1736–1807), an illegitimate daughter of Sir Edward Walpole. The Royal Marriages Act is still in force and it requires marriages of members of the royal family under the age of 25 to be approved by the crown.

Clearly Princess Mary's husband lacked the pedigree that King George III would have deemed appropriate. The king was still alive, but insane and no longer fit to do any deeming.

The marriage produced no children and it was not a particularly happy one. On the other hand, it was not nearly as sour as some sources have suggested. The detached married life in their home at Bagshot Park suited the temperaments of both husband and wife. William Frederick was vain, pompous and arrogant, but hardly the tyrant that some sources imply. He was true to his word to permit his wife to attend to family emergencies, and even left England during one family crisis to give Princess Mary time and space to attend to her duties as she saw them. William Frederick was capable of petty tyranny against his wife, and the details of one colorful oppression have survived. Van der Kiste quotes Thomas Creevey (1768–1838) when he relates the following story: "When her sisters and friends called upon her they were surprised to be marched up to the top of the house. The

Duchess apologized to them as they sat down, exhausted and out of breath, explaining that it was 'owing to the cruel manner in which she was treated by the Duke.' Deciding that the rooms on the drawing room floor were not kept in good order, he had them locked up and pocketed the keys himself."

William Frederick alienated King George IV (1762–1830) with his less than perfect treatment of Princess Mary, but Mary, ever the diplomat, managed to repair that family rift. Both King George IV and his successor, King William IV (1765–1837), enjoyed the company of their sister, Princess Mary, and she spent ample time with them before and after her husband's death.

William Frederick became seriously ill in late 1834, and Princess Mary, true to her character, nursed him with care until his death in November 1834. Once he had departed, it might not be wide of the mark to guess that he was not missed very much by anybody, including his widow. She certainly devoted no lengthy period of time in fruitless mourning. At the time of her husband's death, Mary was 58 years old, but she still had 23 years of living to do. Old age, by its nature, is devoid of great excitement, but Princess Mary's 23 years as a widow were relatively interesting.

Earlier in her life, Princess Mary had rendered devoted and effective nursing care to her mother, and took it upon herself to visit her ailing father and provide daily bulletins on his condition. She also nursed and cared for her sisters, Princess Amelia (1783–1810), Princess Augusta (1768–1840) and Princess Sophia (1777–1848). As mentioned, Mary also nursed her husband, to the best of her ability, through his final illness.

Mary loved people, and in her older years a constant stream of visitors, from both high and low stations in life, paid her frequent visits. As Princess Mary reached the closing years of her life, whatever fondness she had for children increased dramatically. She improvised opportunities to have children in her house by arranging children's parties and dances. Among the children were some of Mary's nieces and nephews. The children of her brother Prince Adolphus, Duke of Cambridge (1774–1850), became her special favorites. One of these children, Princess Mary Adelaide (1833–1897), would become the mother of the Queen Consort to England's King George V (1865–1936).

When Princess Mary finally reached the end of her long life on April 30, 1857, she was the last surviving child of King George III. She died at Gloucester House, Piccadilly, London and was buried in the Gloucester vault at St. George's Chapel, Windsor.

An interesting photograph appears on page 185 of Van der Kiste's work. It shows an elderly lady (Princess Mary) with Queen Victoria (1819–1901) and others. The caption reads: "Queen Victoria, with Princess Mary, Duchess of Gloucester ... at Gloucester House, 30 June 1856, from daguerreotype by Antoine Claudet. This was probably the only occasion on which a child of King George III was photographed." (The reason, not mentioned, was that photography was a very new invention while the children of King George III were living, and Princess Mary, who died in 1857, was the last of those children to die.)

55. *Princess Sophia (1777–1848)*

Sophia was the twelfth child born to King George III (1738–1820) and his Consort, Queen Charlotte (1744–1818). Princess Sophia was born on November 3, 1777, at Queen's House, and christened on December 1.

Lady Charlotte Finch (1725–1813), who had previously been governess to all of the royal couple's daughters, was young Sophia's governess. Other sub-governesses who were involved with the royal princesses during this era were named Martha Goldsworthy, Mary Hamilton, and Jane Gomm. The last named lady joined the royal service in 1786, and her duties, at least for a time, were largely associated with Princess Sophia and Princess Mary (1776–1857).

The Queen instructed the governess and sub-governesses to bring the royal girls up strictly and never permit incivility or lightness.

During Sophia's early childhood, a whirlwind of changes occurred in those serving as assistant governesses of the royal girls, and among the new names to appear was Charlotte Montmollin, followed by her cousins, Julie and Marianne. Two Swiss sisters, Marianne Moula and Suzanne Moula, also served in this era.

Although some of the Princesses had occasional exposure to high culture (e.g., visits by Thomas Gainsborough [1727–1788], who taught the Princesses a bit about drawing and art), the Princesses' education was structured to be superficial. In those days, royal students were segregated by sex for their education. The boys were generally given a classical education, while the girls devoted a lot of time to needlework and drawing. Any instruction in foreign languages, which these girls received, was prompted by its perceived usefulness in social situations. The assistant governess, Marianne Moula, apparently had some spunk. She was heard to wonder aloud about the educational value of "all this stitchery."

Apparently Princess Sophia was something of an exception to this scheme to provide the royal girls with little solid education. By her old age, Sophia had become fluent in German, French and Italian, and probably had picked up some rudiments of classical Greek and Latin from Lady Charlotte Finch and Mary Hamilton. Also, young Sophia was fortunate to have, for a time, the gifted Charlotte Montmollin, who taught a variety of subjects including ancient history and French.

As a child, Princess Sophia was small for her age; some attribute this to her being weaned too early when her wet-nurse had to leave to attend to some family emergency. It appears that Sophia was pretty enough as a child, although not the greatest beauty among the six royal sisters, and that she developed a personality that seemed attractive to all whom she met. Princess Sophia, as a little girl, was, to many, the favorite among the young royal princesses.

Because of a number of rather unique factors, most of the six daughters of King George III, including Princess Sophia, led generally uneventful lives. (We shall soon learn, however, that in Sophia's case, we have a bit of romantic drama. Sophia was driven by a combination of pluck, passion and desperation to an affair with a royal equerry, and gave birth to his son.) But Sophia's case was the exception rather than the rule. Conventional sources on English history and on the royal family of England yield little material for biographical sketches of the daughters of King George III. However, we are fortunate to have available two excellent books which delve into some of the details of the six girls' lives. These two sources are: (1) Morris Marples' *Six Royal Sisters: Daughters of George III,* published in 1969, and (2) John Van der Kiste's *George III's Children,* published in 1999. Since there will be numerous references to these two books in this biographical sketch, they will be referred to here simply as Marples' work and Van der Kiste's work, although these authors have also written other books.

The first "unique factor" is that these girls were daughters of "*Mad* King George III." He experienced three principal bouts of his mental ailment, and the final bout left him insane for the remainder of his life. The second "unique factor" is that the King was unusually possessive about his daughters and dreaded the thought of losing them to marriage. The third "unique factor" is that King George III and his Consort, Queen Charlotte, deemed it "inappropriate" for any of the royal daughters to marry before the eldest daughter, the "Princess Royal," secured a husband. That might not have presented a serious obstacle to marriage of the younger sisters, had the eldest among them been married with dispatch, but the sad fact is that this eldest daughter was rather physically unattractive.

Striking a marriage contract for an unattractive daughter of an overly possessive King of England is not easily accomplished. That marriage did not occur until 1797, and by then some of her sisters were no longer prime marriage candidates on account of their ages. (Marples tells us that the normal age for a royal female to marry in the late 18th century was about fifteen or sixteen.) Most of the daughters of King George III and Queen Charlotte were obliged to settle for rather unsatisfactory marriages or messy affairs with inappropriate members of the opposite sex. Long after our Princess Sophia had reached a normal marriage age for a royal female to marry, her mother had joined the King in becoming overly possessive and resisting sensible marriage possibilities for her daughters.

David Williamson's *Brewer's British Royalty,* published in 1996, reports that "as a child, Princess Sophia was moved enough on being told about prisons and the hard lot of prisoners to offer to give her allowance 'to buy bread for the poor prisoners.' Her parents were so struck by her generous thought that they augmented the amount given." We know that both the King and Queen were extremely parsimonious, so this report of generosity is rather startling.

Princess Sophia was not only a small child, but also a delicate one with a tendency to illness that lasted essentially all her life. Marples tells us that "all her life she suffered off and on from unexplained spasms and cramps, accompanied by nerves and depression, which at times confined her to her room and even her bed," and that her eldest sister Princess Charlotte (1766–1828) referred to Sophia as "the hot-house-plant." That term refers to the delicate nature of flowers or other plants that are raised in comfort in greenhouses during winter and early spring. These "hot-house-plants" have high mortality rates when transplanted to the real world outside the greenhouse.

One year Princess Sophia and Princess Elizabeth (1770–1840) were ordered, for health reasons, to spend the summer at the seaside. On this particular occasion, the destination was Eastbourne. King George III was a great advocate of the benefits of bathing in the sea and breathing the nurturing salt air. When the King was involved, the family went to the seaside at Weymouth. Marples tells us that Princess Mary and Princess Sophia rebelled at one point about the seaside, and Mary declared that, "Sophia and me do not intend to honour the sea with *our charms* this year." Possibly the grammar never improved, but Sophia at least had a change of heart about the sea. Although she was a bit fearful of the sea in 1795, Sophia bathed in it of her own accord.

Princess Sophia became an accomplished horsewoman who rode in her father's company at times. In 1798, when news of Rear-Admiral Horatio Nelson's dramatic defeat of Napoleon's forces at the battle of the Nile reached the King, he was riding his horse in company with Princess Sophia. That particular excursion had been undertaken to fortify Sophia's ever-delicate health.

We have already discussed the fact that King George III was "overly possessive" of his six daughters and reluctant to see any of them marry and leave him. This point is much stressed in literature dealing with King George III and his daughters, and a whole book was devoted primarily to this subject. That book is Lucille Iremonger's *Love and the Princesses: The Strange Lives of Mad King George III and His Daughters*, published in 1958. Since the book's thesis is essentially correct, it is easy to overlook the suffocating confinement imposed on the six Princesses by their mother, Queen Charlotte. Princess Sophia was among the youngest of the daughters of King George III, so Sophia was perhaps injured as much or more by her mother's possessive nature than by her father's. It certainly was the mother rather than the father who restricted the Princesses' access even to other young girls.

As a result of this parental selfishness, all six Princesses were denied appropriate relief from their normal hormonal urges in one way or another. The only Princess to marry to an appropriate royal husband at anything approaching a sensible age was Princess Charlotte (1766–1828), who wed in 1797 to a German prince. She was then almost 31. All younger sisters were supposed to wait until the eldest had been married. Even after the eldest had wed and left England, for a variety of reasons, acceptable marriages were not accomplished with any dispatch for the remaining five, and each Princess had to find her own way out of the resulting sexual suffocation.

Princess Sophia used her reputation as a rather chronic invalid to escape from a trip that the King and Queen took, and she used her privacy to become impregnated by General Thomas Garth (1744–1829). John Van der Kiste explains that the daughters of King George III were confined under such tight restraints in "the nunnery," as they called it, that the frustrated Princess Sophia was driven to an affair with one of the king's equerries, General Garth. "His age and ugliness put him at no disadvantage, for Princess Sophia and her spinster sisters were so secluded from the world, and allowed to mix with so few people, that it was said that they were more than ready to fall into the arms of the first man outside the family who looked at them."

The consummation of this affair came as no surprise to junior members of the royal family who were still living at home, nor even to servants and other observers who watched with growing anxiety as Sophia's obvious infatuation with the old and ugly General Garth became increasingly obvious to all who had eyes to see. Strangely, however, the King never suspected. Although the King had severe mental lapses, at the time that Princess Sophia and General Garth ground out their sexual frustrations in congress with one another in 1799, King George was of sound mind. Given the King's personality, it is not too difficult to believe that he missed the warning signs all about him. The surprising thing is that Queen Charlotte also failed to tumble to what was going on until Princess Sophia was quite pregnant. When the Queen became aware of the truth, she deliberately withheld it from the King, because she feared it might drive him into another bout of insanity. Queen Charlotte may well have assessed this hazard accurately.

Princess Sophia and General Garth may have entered into some form of a secret marriage. However, there is no surviving record of it, and Sophia and the general never lived together in any domestic arrangement. Had there been such a marriage, it would have lacked legal standing on account of the provisions of the Royal Marriages Act, which required the sovereign's permission for marriages of members of the royal family under 25 years of age.

The child who was born at Weymouth in the summer of 1800 as a product of this coupling was a boy, and he was named Thomas Garth after both his father and grandfather. General Garth admitted that he was the father, and because of later accusations that the boy was the child of an incestuous union between Sophia and her brother, Prince Ernest, Duke of Cumberland (1771–1851), it is fortunate that General Garth stepped forward in this manner. Surprisingly, General Garth suffered no punishment, either in his service to the royal family or in his military career, on account of this case of the ultimate in fraternization.

Young Thomas Garth was raised in the house of Sir Herbert Taylor (1775–1839). There Princess Sophia visited him from time to time. Young Garth conceived a scheme to blackmail the royal family with certain papers which his father had given to him. The blackmail scheme failed, and in 1816 Thomas Garth entered the British military service. In spite of preferential treatment which his father, General Garth, pursued on his son's behalf, the younger Garth rose only to the rank of captain.

We cannot be certain that Sophia's affair with General Garth was her first sexual dalliance, but we do know that it was her last, and that she never was legally married.

Princess Sophia and her unmarried sisters lived a sheltered life under the watchful eye of Queen Charlotte. These Princesses had attained middle age, or would shortly reach it, without shaking off the yoke of oppression by their mother. King George III had suffered his final bout of insanity in 1810, and the Regency Act was invoked in February 1811. Under that act, Sophia's eldest brother George (1762–1830) became Prince Regent. George had sympathized with his sisters' plight for years. Now, as Prince Regent, he was in a position to match his feelings with some action.

Prince George was extremely deferential to his mother, so the path from "the nunnery" to a degree of independence for his sisters was oblique, but in the end Sophia and the other Princesses had sent their mother separate declarations of independence and had their allowances raised dramatically by parliament.

Sophia continued to live with her mother until 1818, when the queen died. Sophia inherited Lower Lodge, Windsor, from her mother.

Sophia's brother, Prince Frederick, Duke of York and Albany (1763–1827), directed in his last will and testament that, after settling his debts, the residue should go to his sister, Princess Sophia. Frederick had not been very good with financial matters, and it was soon disclosed that there was no residue to inherit. Sophia was not surprised: "Of course there is *nothing* to inherit, but the naming me in such a manner made me feel I am Heir in his *affection*, which is the most precious gift I could receive." Princess Sophia had good reason to adore her brother Frederick. He had acted as a go-between in her contacts with General Garth and their son.

Princess Sophia lived in close physical proximity to her niece, the future Queen Victoria (1819–1901), and her widowed mother, Princess Victoria Mary Louisa (1786–1861), Duchess of Kent. At this time the duchess of Kent was scheming to be named Regent, should King William IV (1765–1837) die before Princess Victoria (1819–1901) became 18 years old. While plotting this scheme, the duchess of Kent employed Sir John Conroy (–1854) to manage her financial affairs, and Princess Sophia fell into the same Conroy trap. Conroy purchased land and houses in both Berkshire and Wales, which we now know were well beyond his financial resources. We know that he defrauded Princess Sophia of large sums (she left an estate worth only 1,607 pounds). He may have charmed her out of her money, or simply stolen it. Perhaps he accomplished a similar con game with the Duchess of Kent's finances. One of Queen Victoria's first acts as Queen was to banish Conroy from the royal court.

But money was the least of Princess Sophia's worries. Marples and Van der Kiste tell us that Sophia went blind in the right eye about 1838, and not long afterward her left eye failed as well. According to Marples' work: "Sophia now moved to more convenient quarters at York House (now demolished), where she lived surrounded by her innumerable knick-knacks, all of which she knew by touch, winding silk or tearing paper for invalids' pillows, while the four readers she employed read to her successively in English, German, French and Italian. She had always been a good linguist and her French reader was one of the daughters of the Swiss governess, Marianne Montmollin, who had taught her so successfully half a century before, and with whose family she had kept in friendly contact ever since. She refused to have a lady-in-waiting, saying that not being able to see, she would always imagine the lady sitting opposite her looked bored. Visits from friends and relations, and drives in the park with Princess Mary (after 1840 her only surviving sister) were her chief recreation."

Princes Sophia died on May 27, 1848, at Vicarage Place, Kensington. She was buried, in accordance with her request, at the public cemetery at Kensal, instead of Windsor, the normal burial site for a member of England's royal family.

56. *Princess Amelia (1783–1810)*

Amelia was the fifteenth child born to King George III (1738–1820) and his Consort, Queen Charlotte (1744–1818). Princess Amelia was born on August 7, 1783, at Royal Lodge, Windsor, and christened on September 18 by the Archbishop of Canterbury. She was named for her delightfully eccentric, spinster great-aunt, Princess Amelia (1711–1786). Amelia's godfather was her eldest brother George, Prince of Wales (1762–1830), and her godmothers were her two eldest sisters, Charlotte, Princess Royal (1766–1828), and Princess Augusta (1768–1840).

King George III and Queen Charlotte, both of German ancestry, had produced an amazingly large brood of royal children, and most of them lived relatively long lives for that era in England. However, after the birth of Princess Sophia (1777–1848), the children produced by the King and Queen lacked the robust good health of the earlier arrivals. After Princess Sophia came the short-lived Prince Octavius (1779–1783), followed by the even shorter-lived Prince Alfred (1780–1782). Princess Amelia was born next and, although she survived well beyond infancy, at a fairly early age warning signs began to appear that her health was below par. Amelia was the last child born to King George III and Queen Charlotte, and she died at the early age of 27.

Lady Charlotte Finch (1725–1813), who had previously been governess to all of the royal couple's daughters, was young Amelia's governess. Other sub-governesses who were involved with the royal Princesses during this era were named Martha Goldsworthy, Mary Hamilton, and Jane Gomm. The last named lady joined the royal service in 1786. There were numerous changes in the ranks of assistant governesses during Princess Amelia's childhood. One of the newer ones was Marianne Moula, and we know that she was still an assistant governess when Amelia was about age ten.

The Queen instructed the governess and sub-governesses to bring the royal girls up strictly and never permit incivility or lightness.

The Princesses' education was structured to be superficial. In those days, royal students were segregated by sex for their education. The boys were generally given a classical education, while the girls devoted a lot of time to needlework and drawing. Any instruction in foreign languages that these girls received was prompted by its perceived usefulness in social situations. The assistant governess, Marianne Moula, apparently had some spunk. She was heard to wonder aloud about the educational value of "all this stitchery." Princess Amelia's education was superficial, even in comparison to her sisters. Sources consulted are vague on the reasons, but it would seem that her poor health contributed, as did her status as the pampered youngest child of the King and Queen.

By an early age, Princess Amelia had become her father's favorite child. Later, when her health deteriorated, her father further pampered and even spoiled her.

Because of a number of rather unique factors, most of the six daughters of King George III, including Princess Amelia, led generally uneventful lives. (We shall soon learn however, that in Amelia's case, we have a bit of romantic drama. Amelia was driven by passion and desperation to an affair with a royal equerry much older than she.) Conventional sources on English history and on the royal family of England yield little material for biographical sketches of the daughters of King George III. However, we are fortunate to have available two excellent books which delve into some of the details of the six girls' lives. These two sources are: (1) Morris Marples' *Six Royal Sisters: Daughters of George III*, published in 1969, and (2) John Van der Kiste's *George III's Children*, published in 1999. Since there will be numerous references to these two books in this biographical sketch, they will be referred to here simply as Marples' work and Van der Kiste's work, although these authors have also written other books.

The first "unique factor" is that these girls were daughters of "*Mad* King George III." He experienced three principal bouts of his mental ailment, and the final bout left him insane for the remainder of his life. The second "unique factor" is that the King was unusually possessive about his daughters and dreaded the thought of losing them to marriage. The third "unique factor" is that King George III and his Consort, Queen Charlotte, deemed it "inappropriate" for any of the royal daughters to marry before the eldest daughter, the "Princess Royal," secured a husband. That might not have presented a serious obstacle to marriage of the younger sisters, had the eldest among them been married with dispatch, but the sad fact is that this eldest daughter was rather physically unattractive.

Striking a marriage contract for an unattractive daughter of an overly possessive King of England is not easily accomplished. That marriage did not occur until 1797, and by then some of her sisters were no longer prime marriage candidates on account of their ages. (Marples tells us that the normal age for a royal female to marry in the late 18th century was about fifteen or sixteen.) Most of the daughters of King George III and Queen Charlotte were obliged to settle for rather unsatisfactory marriages or messy affairs with inappropriate members of the opposite sex. By the time our Princess Amelia had reached a normal age for a royal female to marry, her mother had joined the King in becoming overly possessive and resisting sensible marriage possibilities for her daughters.

Working then from the sources mentioned, and others, the following biographical sketch of Princess Amelia, in approximate chronological order, emerges.

By age three, little Amelia had learned the dignity of her royal position. Her fourth birthday was celebrated with a rather spectacular party (elaborate birthday celebrations were the custom of King George and Queen Charlotte), and one of Amelia's birthday gifts was an adorable spaniel puppy.

On April 23, 1789, Princess Amelia made her first state appearance. King George III had been suffering from the second of his three bouts with mental illness, and a thanksgiving celebration was held on April 23 to give thanks for the King's recovery. His recovery from this episode was full, and in gratitude the King, Queen, and family attended a service of thanksgiving at St. Paul's Cathedral.

In 1793 Princess Amelia was among the royal family members who attended a review of troops bound for the Netherlands and combat duty.

At age eleven Amelia had not yet shown signs of the series of terrible illnesses that she would suffer. She was still healthy and even robust. Lucille Iremonger's 1958 work entitled *Love and the Princesses: The Strange Lives of Mad King George III and His Daughters* supplies useful and interesting information about Amelia. At this stage of her life, Iremonger says that Amelia did not look frail. By the time she was fourteen, she looked seventeen, and "she was naturally high-spirited and cheerful." She was a large girl and became a good horsewoman.

David Williamson's *Brewer's British Royalty*, published in 1996, tells us that young Amelia was vivacious and sweet-tempered.

We have already discussed the fact that King George III was "overly possessive" of his six daughters and reluctant to see any of them marry and leave him. This point is much stressed in literature dealing with King George III and his daughters, and a whole book (Iremonger's) was devoted primarily to this subject. Since the book's thesis is essentially correct, it is easy to overlook the suffocating confinement imposed on the six Princesses by their mother, Queen Charlotte. Our Princess Amelia was the youngest of the daughters of King George III, so she was perhaps injured as much or more by her mother's possessive nature than by her father's.

In 1797 the eldest sister Charlotte, Princess Royal, was wed to a German Prince. She was then almost 31. All younger sisters had been obliged to wait until the eldest had been married. In Princess Elizabeth's (1770–1840) vocabulary, the five younger Princesses were now seeking their "settlements." Even after the eldest had wed and left England, for a variety of reasons, acceptable marriages were not accomplished with any dispatch for the remaining five, and each Princess had to find her own way out of the resulting sexual suffocation.

King George III and the family members living with him made it a practice to spend several months most summers at the seaside at Weymouth. (Because of health limitations, which we will soon discuss, Amelia did not accompany the rest of the family on all of these excursions to Weymouth.) But she was with them there at about age fifteen, when she complained of a most unusual health problem, which perhaps was a harbinger of more serious illnesses to follow. The unusual symptom at age fifteen, at Weymouth, was a complaint that the wind caused pain to the "drumsticks in my ears."

In 1798 Princess Amelia came down with tuberculosis of the knee. A trip to the seaside was decided upon for Amelia's health, but rather than send her to their usual haunt, Weymouth, she was sent to Worthing. A retinue of attendants went with Amelia to Worthing, but Queen Charlotte was afraid to risk infecting any family members and none of the royal family went to Worthing with Amelia. England was now at war with France, and the military authorities protested that they could not protect Princess Amelia at Worthing. Nevertheless, she remained there until about Christmas that year.

The time has come to introduce a key player in the biography of Princess Amelia. He was Charles FitzRoy (1762–1831), a military man, and one of King George's equerries. (His rank is given in various sources as captain, colonel and major general. Presumably he held all those ranks, but it isn't clear how high he had risen in rank when he first caught Princess Amelia's eye.)

This FitzRoy was descended from one of the illegitimate children of King Charles II (1630–1685) and one of his mistresses, Barbara Villiers (1641–1709).

FitzRoy was more than 20 years older than Princess Amelia. They began to show interest in one another for a period of time before luck fell Amelia's way and she was able to play her invalid card to advantage. When Amelia was eighteen, she was left behind by the family when they departed from Weymouth. An entourage of royal attendants was left with young Amelia and, as luck would have it, one of them was Charles FitzRoy (1762–1831). They made love during this interlude. Perhaps FitzRoy should have kept his distance, but the 18-year-old Princess was too alluring to resist, and it is clear that it was Amelia, not FitzRoy, who initiated the affair.

One of the attendants, Jane Gomm, eventually warned Queen Charlotte of these amorous activities, but Queen Charlotte was in an awkward position. It was largely her fault that Amelia had been repressed from expressing her sexual urges with more acceptable companions, but more importantly, the queen feared that if word were to leak to the King of the affair, it might drive him into permanent insanity. (Eventually, King George III was just about the only one at court who didn't know of Amelia's affair with FitzRoy.) An angered Princess Amelia requested her mother to dismiss Miss Gomm. The Queen refused and instead she favored Amelia with a homily about "circumspection." Princess Amelia suggested to her mother that she discontinue riding with FitzRoy, but the Queen demurred, fearing that the King would notice.

By 1804 it is possible that Princess Amelia and Charles FitzRoy had entered into some kind of secret marriage. (Six years after Amelia's death, when FitzRoy married, the new wife was among those who believed that there had been such a secret marriage.) Whether or not there actually was a secret marriage is rather wide of the point, because if there had been such a marriage it would have been illegal under the Royal Marriages Act; and whether there had been such a marriage or not, Amelia played the role of a married lady, signing many of her letters "AFR" (Amelia FitzRoy), and having silverware inscribed to carry the same message.

In 1804 Amelia met with her favorite brother and godfather George, Prince of Wales. Amelia came away from that meeting believing that if her brother George were declared Regent, he would give Amelia permission to marry FitzRoy; i.e., the permission required by the Royal Marriages Act.

We cannot be certain that Prince George made such a promise without restrictions, but even if he did, it marked the starting point in a vicious "Catch 22" circle. (The King did eventually enter a final bout of insanity and, on account of it, Prince

George was indeed declared Regent by parliament. But the incident that was the main factor in causing the King's final insanity was the death of his beloved daughter Princess Amelia.)

About this time, rumors were afloat that Amelia had given birth to a child of FitzRoy's. Mrs. George Villiers, who had become a close friend of Amelia's and was privy to just about all the facts, emphatically denied this scurrilous rumor.

The sad denouement came rapidly. In 1805, the last year that the royal family summered at Weymouth, a grand banquet and ball was held at the Royal Hotel to celebrate Amelia's 22nd birthday. In 1807 Queen Charlotte penned another homily for Amelia's edification, in the mistaken belief that the FitzRoy affair had ended. In 1808 Mrs. Villiers obtained a copy of the Royal Marriages Act for Amelia. Noting that the act required her to give notification of intent to marry, Amelia drafted some letters along those lines, in which she referred to her "late father." King George would outlive Amelia by ten years.

When measles struck Amelia in 1808, in her weakened condition, it drove her to invalid status. In 1809 King George III began the 50th year of his reign and a Jubilee was held to celebrate it. Princess Amelia was sent to Weymouth with two thoughts in mind: perhaps this final trip would actually bring a cure, but, more certainly, it would remove her from the Jubilee festivities, of which she was too ill to partake. Princess Mary (1776–1857) was allowed to accompany and nurse her sister.

By the spring of 1810, Princess Amelia's condition had become grave, and the doctors attempted to strictly regulate her visits to very brief encounters with her closest relatives. However, Amelia had a loyal support system at work that managed to smuggle Charles FitzRoy in for clandestine visits.

Princess Amelia died on November 2, 1810, at Augusta Lodge, Windsor, and was buried at St. George's Chapel.

Dramatic events did not die with Amelia. Van der Kiste's work tells us that Sir Herbert Taylor (1775–1839) had given the opinion that the King was resigned to his daughter's death, and that George Canning (1770–1827), "the Tory politician, thought that, once she was dead and he was over the shock, it would hasten his recovery; it was the lingering suspense that had 'irritated him into madness.' Neither verdict would prove to be accurate. Since the king's illness of 1801, the family had lived in dread" of another outbreak of insanity threatening his reason for good. He was now aged 72. "During the last week of October, his behaviour had again been peculiar, and worry about Amelia may have been a contributory factor. Not until nine days after her death did the family think him well enough to be told." His reaction seemed fairly normal at first, but signs of great mental unbalance soon appeared. "He assured people at court that he knew she could be brought to life again." The King later became convinced that Amelia was alive and living in Hanover. Soon, he told his family that Prince Octavius, the infant son on whom he had doted, was also living there. "The German ancestral home, which he had never visited, had become a synonym in his confused mind for Heaven. The king slipped into the insanity from which he would never recover."

A sad sequel to Princess Amelia's sad biography must be mentioned. When Princess Amelia realized that death was not far away, she prepared a will leaving essentially everything that she owned (not much) to her lover, Charles FitzRoy. The primary executor of Amelia's estate was her godfather and eldest brother, Prince George, who had become Prince Regent of the United Kingdom on February 5, 1811. FitzRoy was persuaded by the executors that Amelia's possessions should remain in the royal family. Perhaps there was some valid reason for this, perhaps not. What cannot easily be forgiven was the Prince Regent's behavior toward his beloved sister's lover. Marples work tells us that a few years later, when the Prince Regent encountered FitzRoy at some court function, he merely turned his back on him.

BIBLIOGRAPHY

Aikin, Lucy. *Memoirs of the Court of King Charles the First*. London, Longman, Rees, Orme, Brown, Green and Longman, 1833.

Allen, W. Gore. *King William IV*. London, Cresset Press, 1960.

Allstrom, C. M. *Dictionary of Royal Lineage in Europe and Other Countries*. Chicago, Press of S. Th. Almberg, 1902.

Anderson, William J. *The Life of F. M., H. R. H. Edward, Duke of Kent*. Ottawa, Hunter, Rose & Co., 1870.

Andrews, Allen. *The Royal Whore: Barbara Villiers, Countess of Castlemaine*. Philadelphia, Chilton Book Co., 1970.

Ashley, Maurice. *Charles II: The Man and the Statesman*. New York, Praeger Publishers, 1971.

_____. *James II*. London, J. M. Dent & Sons, Ltd., 1977.

_____. *The Stuarts in Love*. New York, Macmillan Co., 1964.

Ashley, Mike. *The Mammoth Book of British Kings and Queens*. New York, Carroll & Graf Publishers, Inc., 1999.

Asprey, Robert B. *Frederick the Great: The Magnificent Enigma*. New York, Ticknor & Fields, 1986.

Aubrey's Brief Lives. London, Secker & Warburg, 1950.

Ayling, Stanley. *George the Third*. New York, Alfred A. Knopf, 1972.

Baker-Smith, Veronica. *A Life of Anne of Hanover, Princess Royal*. Leiden, The Netherlands, E. J. Brill, 1995.

Barroll, Leeds. *Anna of Denmark, Queen of England*. Philadelphia, University of Pennsylvania Press, 2001.

Barton, John. *The Hollow Crown: The Follies, Foibles and Faces of the Kings and Queens of England*. New York, Dial Press, 1971.

Beatson, Robert. *A Political Index to the Histories of Great Britain and Ireland: Or Complete Register of the Hereditary Honours, Public Offices, and Persons in Office*. London, England, Longman, Hurst, Rees & Orme, 1806.

Beatty, Michael A. *County Name Origins of the United States*. Jefferson, North Carolina, McFarland & Company, Inc., 2001.

Beet, E. A. *Mathematical Astronomy for Amateurs.* New York, W. W. Norton & Co., Inc., 1972.

Bellew, George. *Britain's Kings and Queens.* London, England, Pitkin Pictorials, Ltd., 1974.

Belloc, Hilaire. *Charles the First: King of England.* Philadelphia, J. B. Lippincott Co., 1933.

Bergeron, David M. *Royal Family, Royal Lovers: King James of England and Scotland.* Columbia, University of Missouri Press, 1991.

Best, Nicholas. *The Kings and Queens of Scotland.* London, England, Weidenfeld & Nicolson, 1999.

Bevan, Bryan. *Charles II's Minette: Princess Henriette-Anne, Duchess of Orleans.* London, England, Ascent Books, Ltd., 1979.

_____. *King William III, Prince of Orange: The First European.* London, England, Rubicon Press, 1997.

Bigham, Clive. *The Kings of England: 1066–1901.* New York, E. P. Dutton & Co., 1929.

Billings, Warren M., et al. *Colonial Virginia: A History.* White Plains, New York, KTO Press, 1986.

Bobrick, Benson. *Wide As the Waters: The Story of the English Bible and the Revolution It Inspired.* New York, Simon & Schuster, 2001.

Boehrer, Bruce T. *Monarchy and Incest in Renaissance England.* Philadelphia, University of Pennsylvania Press, 1992.

Bone, Quentin. *Henrietta Maria: Queen of the Cavaliers.* Urbana, University of Illinois Press, 1972.

Bowle, John. *Charles I.* Boston, Little, Brown & Co., 1975.

Bridge, F. Maynard. *Princes of Wales.* London, England, H. F. W. Deane & Sons, The Year Book Press, Ltd., 1922.

Brooke, John. *King George III.* New York, McGraw-Hill Book Co., 1972.

Brooke-Little, John. *The British Monarchy in Colour.* Dorset, England, Blandford Press, Ltd., 1976.

Brown, Beatrice Curtis. *Anne Stuart: Queen of England.* London, England, Geoffrey Bles, 1929.

Brown, Craig, and Lesley Cunliffe. *The Book of Royal Lists.* London, Routledge & Kegan Paul, 1982.

Brown, Lloyd A. "The Longitude." *The World of Mathematics.* New York, 1956.

Bryant, Arthur. *King Charles II.* London, England, Collins Clear Type Press, 1931.

_____. *Makers of England.* New York, Barnes & Noble, Inc., 1993.

Burke's Guide to the Royal Family. London, Burke's Peerage, Ltd., 1973.

Burton, John H. *A History of the Reign of Queen Anne.* London, William Blackwood & Sons, 1880.

Callow, John. *The Making of King James II: The Formative Years of a Fallen King.* Gloucestershire, England, Sutton Publishing Ltd., 2000.

Cannon, John. *The Oxford Companion to British History.* Oxford, Oxford University Press, 1997.

Cannon, John, and Ralph Griffiths. *The Oxford Illustrated History of the British Monarchy.* Oxford, England, Oxford University Press, 1998.

Carlton, Charles. *Charles I: The Personal Monarch.* London, Routledge & Kegan Paul, 1983.

Carlyle, Thomas. *History of Frederick the Second, Called Frederick the Great*. New York, Harper & Brothers, 1800.

Carr's Dictionary of English Queens, Kings' Wives, Celebrated Paramours, Handfast Spouses and Royal Changelings, 1977.

Castleden, Rodney. *World History: A Chronological Dictionary of Dates*. New York, Shooting Star Press, Inc.

Castries, Duc de. *The Lives of the Kings and Queens of France*. New York, Alfred A. Knopf, 1979.

Cavendish, Richard. "Birth of William of Orange: November 4, 1650." *History Today*, Vol. 50, No. 11. London, England: November 2000.

Cawthorne, Nigel. *The Sex Lives of the Kings and Queens of England*. London, England, Multimedia Books, Ltd., 1994.

Chapman, Hester W. *Queen Anne's Son: A Memoir of William Henry, Duke of Gloucester: 1689–1700*. London, England, Andre Deutsch, Ltd., 1954.

Churchill, Winston S. *A History of the English-Speaking Peoples*. New York, Dodd, Mead & Co., 1965.

Clark, George. *The Later Stuarts: 1660–1714*. Oxford, England, Clarendon Press, 1972.

The Concise Dictionary of National Biography. Oxford, Oxford University Press, 1992.

Cook, E. Thornton. *Royal Elizabeths: The Romance of Five Princesses: 1464–1840*. New York, E. P. Dutton & Co., 1929.

_____. *Royal Marys: Princess Mary and Her Predecessors*. New York, E. P. Dutton & Co., 1930.

Cook, Petronelle. *Queen Consorts of England: The Power Behind the Throne*. New York, Facts On File, Inc., 1993.

Coote, Stephen. *Royal Survivor: A Life of Charles II*. New York, St. Martin's Press, 2000.

Court and Private Life in the Time of Queen Charlotte: Being the Journals of Mrs. Papendiek, Assistant Keeper of the Wardrobe and Reader to Her Majesty. Edited by Her Granddaughter, Mrs. Vernon Delves Broughton. London, Richard Bentley & Son, 1887.

Cowley, Robert. *The Rulers of Britain*. Chicago, Illinois, Stonehenge Press, Inc., 1982.

Creston, Dormer. *The Youthful Queen Victoria*. New York, G. P. Putnam's Sons, 1952.

Curtis, Gila. *The Life and Times of Queen Anne*. London, England, Weidenfeld & Nicolson, 1972.

Danstrup, John. *A History of Denmark*. Copenhagen, Wivel, 1948.

David, Saul. *Prince of Pleasure: The Prince of Wales and the Making of the Regency*. New York, Atlantic Monthly Press, 1998.

Davidson, Lillias C. *Catherine of Braganza: Infanta of Portugal and Queen-Consort of England*. London, John Murray, 1908.

Davies, Godfrey. *The Early Stuarts: 1603–1660*. Oxford, England, Clarendon Press, 1937.

De-la-Noy, Michael. *The King Who Never Was: The Story of Frederick, Prince of Wales*. London, Peter Owen, 1996.

Delderfield, Eric R. *Kings and Queens of England*. New York, Weathervane Books, 1972.

Delderfield, Eric R. *Kings and Queens of England and Great Britain*. New York, Facts On File, 1990.

Dick, Oliver L. *Aubrey's Brief Lives*. London, Secker & Warburg, 1950.

Dictionary of National Biography. London, Smith, Elder & Co., 1909.

The Dictionary of National Biography Founded in 1882 by George Smith. London, Oxford University Press, 1921.

Doran, John. *Lives of the Queens of England of the House of Hanover*. New York, Redfield, 1855.

Durant, Will, and Ariel Durant. *The Story of Civilization: Part VIII: The Age of Louis XIV*. New York, Simon & Schuster, 1963.

_____, and _____. *The Story of Civilization: Part XI: The Age of Napoleon*. New York, Simon & Schuster, 1975.

Durst, Paul. *Intended Treason: What Really Happened in the Gunpowder Plot*. Cranbury, New Jersey, A. S. Barnes & Co., Inc., 1970.

Dutton, Ralph. *English Court Life: From Henry VII to George II*. London, B. T. Batsford, Ltd., 1963.

Dwelle, Mary Myers. *A Sketch of the Life of Queen Charlotte, 1744–1818: A Bicentennial Tribute from Her Namesake*. Charlotte, Heritage Printers, Inc., 1968.

Edwards, Graham. *The Last Days of Charles I*. Gloucestershire, England, Thrupp, 1999.

Egan, Pamela. *Kings and Queens of England and Scotland*. Abingdon, England, Vineyard Books, 1996.   .

Erickson, Carolly. *Bonnie Prince Charlie: A Biography*. New York, William Morrow & Co., Inc., 1989.

Evan, John. *King Charles I*. London, Arthur Baker, Ltd., 1952.

Falkus, Christopher. *The Life and Times of Charles II*. Garden City, New York, Doubleday & Co., 1972.

Foster, Joseph. *The Peerage, Baronetage and Knightage of the British Empire for 1880*. London, England, Nichols & Sons, 1880.

Fraser, Antonia. *Faith and Treason: The Story of the Gunpowder Plot*. New York, Anchor Books, 1996.

_____. *King Charles II*. London, England, Weidenfeld & Nicolson, 1979.

_____. *King James I of England: VI of Scotland*. New York, Alfred A. Knopf, 1975.

_____. *The Lives of the Kings and Queens of England*. Berkeley, University of California Press, 1995.

_____. *Royal Charles: Charles II and the Restoration*. New York, Alfred A. Knopf, 1980.

_____. *The Wives of Henry VIII*. New York, Alfred A. Knopf, 1992.

Fraser, Flora. *The Unruly Queen: The Life of Queen Caroline*. London, England, Macmillan General Books, 1996.

Fritze, Ronald H., and William B. Robison. *Historical Dictionary of Stuart England: 1603–1689*. Westport, Connecticut, Greenwood Press, 1996.

Fritze, Ronald H., et al. *Historical Dictionary of Tudor England: 1485–1603*. Westport, Connecticut, Greenwood Press, 1991.

Fulford, Roger. *Royal Dukes: The Father and Uncles of Queen Victoria*. London, England, Gerald Duckworth & Co., Ltd., 1933.

Gasquet, F. A. *The Adventures of King James II of England*. London, Longmans, Green & Co., 1904.

Gaxotte, Pierre. *Frederick the Great*. New Haven, Yale University Press, 1942.

Gillen, Mollie. *Royal Duke: Augustus Frederick, Duke of Sussex (1773–1843)*. London, Sidgwick & Jackson, 1976.

Gooch, G. P. *Frederick the Great: The Ruler, the Writer, the Man.* New York, Dorset Press, 1947.

Gould, William. *Lives of the Georgian Age: 1714–1837.* New York, Barnes & Noble Books, 1978.

Green, David. *Queen Anne.* New York, Charles Scribner's Sons, 1970.

Green, Mary Anne Everett. *Lives of the Princesses of England from the Norman Conquest.* London, England, Hurst & Blackett, 1855.

Greenwood, Alice Drayton. *Lives of the Hanoverian Queens of England.* London, George Bell & Sons, 1909.

Gregg, Edward. *Queen Anne.* London, England, ARK Paperbacks, 1984.

Gregg, Pauline. *King Charles I.* Berkeley, University of California Press, 1984.

Guttmacher, Manfred S. *America's Last King: An Interpretation of the Madness of George III.* New York, Charles Scribner's Sons, 1941.

Hamilton, Elizabeth. *Henrietta Maria.* New York, Coward, McCann & Geoghegan, Inc., 1976.

_____. *William's Mary: A Biography of Mary II.* New York, Taplinger Publishing Co., 1972.

Hardy, Alan. *The Kings' Mistresses.* London, England, Evans Brothers, Ltd., 1980.

Haswell, Jock. *James II: Soldier and Sailor.* New York, St. Martin's Press, 1972.

Hatton, Ragnhild. *George I: Elector and King.* Cambridge, Massachusetts, Harvard University Press, 1978.

Haynes, Henrietta. *Henrietta Maria.* London, Methuen & Co., Ltd., 1912.

Hayward, John. *Annals of the First Four Years of the Reign of Queen Elizabeth.* New York, AMS Press, 1968.

Hervey, John. *Some Materials Towards Memoirs of the Reign of King George II.* London, 1931.

Hibbert, Christopher. *Charles I.* New York, Harper & Row, 1968.

_____. *The Court at Windsor: A Domestic History.* New York, Harper Row, 1964.

_____. *George III: A Personal History.* New York, Basic Books, 1998.

_____. *George IV, Prince of Wales: 1762–1811.* New York, Harper & Row, 1972.

Higham, F. M. G. *Charles I: A Study.* London, England, Hamish Hamilton, 1932.

_____. *King James the Second.* London, Hamish Hamilton, 1934.

Hill, Christopher. *The Century of Revolution: 1603–1714.* London, England, Thomas Nelson & Sons, Ltd., 1963.

Hilliam, David. *Kings, Queens, Bones and Bastards: Who's Who in the English Monarchy from Egbert to Elizabeth II.* Gloucestershire, England, Sutton Publishing, Ltd., 2000.

_____. *Monarchs, Murderers and Mistresses: A Book of Royal Days.* Gloucestershire, England, Sutton Publishing, Ltd., 2000.

Hindley, Geoffrey. *The Guinness Book of British Royalty.* London, England, Guinness Publishing, Ltd., 1989.

Hodges, Margaret. *Lady Queen Anne. A Biography of Queen Anne of England.* New York, Farrar, Straus & Giroux, 1969.

Holme, Thea. *Caroline: A Biography of Caroline of Brunswick.* New York, Atheneum, 1980.

Hopkinson, M. R. *Anne of England: The Biography of a Great Queen.* London, Constable & Co., Ltd., 1934.

Hopkirk, Mary. *Queen Over the Water: Mary Beatrice of Modena: Queen of James II*. London, England, John Murray, 1953.

Hume, Martin. *The Courtships of Queen Elizabeth*. New York, McClure, Phillips & Co., 1904.

Hutton, Ronald. *Charles the Second: King of England, Scotland and Ireland*. Oxford, England, Clarendon Press, 1989.

Imbert-Terry, H. M. *A Constitutional King: George the First*. London, John Murray, 1927.

Iremonger, Lucille. *Love and the Princesses: The Strange Lives of Mad King George III and His Daughters*. New York, Thomas Y. Crowell Co., 1958.

Israel, Jonathan I. *The Dutch Republic: Its Rise, Greatness and Fall: 1477–1806*. New York, Oxford University Press, 1998.

Jenner, Heather. *Royal Wives*. London, England, Gerald Duckworth & Co., Ltd., 1967.

Jesse, J. Heneage. *Memoirs of the Life and Reign of King George the Third*. London, Tinsley Brothers, 1867.

Joelson, Annette. *England's Princes of Wales*. New York, Dorset Press, 1966.

John, Evan. *King Charles I*. New York, Roy Publishers.

Johnson, James. *Place Names of England and Wales*. London, England, Bracken Books, 1994.

Jordan, Ruth. *Sophie Dorothea*. New York, George Braziller, Inc., 1971.

Kenyon, J. P. *A Dictionary of British History*. Hertfordshire, England, Wordsworth Editions, Ltd., 1992.

_____. *The Stuarts*. Glasgow, William Collins Sons & Co., Ltd., 1970.

_____. *The Stuarts: A Study in English Kingship*. New York. Macmillan Co., 1959.

_____. *The Wordsworth Dictionary of British History*. Hertfordshire, England, Wordsworth Editions, Ltd., 1981.

Kishlansky, Mark. *A Monarchy Transformed: Britain 1603–1714*. London, England, Penguin Books, Ltd., 1996.

Lees-Milne, James. *The Last Stuarts: British Royalty in Exile*. New York, Charles Scribner's Sons, 1984.

Lewis, W. H. *The Scandalous Regent: A Life of Philippe, Duc d'Orleans 1674–1723 and of His Family*. New York, Harcourt Brace & World, Inc., 1961.

Linklater, Eric. *The Royal House*. Garden City, New York, Doubleday & Co., Inc., 1970.

Lister, T. H. *Life and Administration of Edward, First Earl of Clarendon: With Original Correspondence and Authentic Papers Never Before Published*. London, Longman, Orme, Brown, Green & Longmans, 1838.

Lodge, Edmund. "Henry, Prince of Wales." *Portraits of Illustrious Personages of Great Britain: With Biographical and Historical Memoirs of Their Lives and Actions*, Vol. 3, London: 1850.

Loftis, John. *The Memoirs of Anne, Lady Halkett and Ann, Lady Fanshawe*. Oxford, England, Oxford University Press, 1979.

Lofts, Norah. *Queens of England*. Garden City, New York, Doubleday & Co., Inc., 1977.

Longford, Elizabeth. *The Oxford Book of Royal Anecdotes*. Oxford, England, Oxford University Press, 1991.

Loth, David. *Royal Charles: Ruler and Rake*. New York, Brentano's, Inc., 1930.

MacCracken, Henry N. *Old Dutchess Forever!* New York, Hastings House Publishers, 1956.

MacDonogh, Giles. *Frederick the Great: A Life in Deed and Letters*. New York, St. Martin's Press, 1999.

Mangan, J. J. *The King's Favour: Three Eighteenth-Century Monarchs and the Favourites Who Ruled Them*. Gloucestershire, England, Alan Sutton Publishing Ltd., 1991.

Marlow, Joyce. *The Life and Times of George I*. London, England, Book Club Associates, 1973.

Marples, Morris. *Princes in the Making: A Study of Royal Education*. London, England, Faber & Faber, Ltd., 1965.

_____. *Six Royal Sisters: Daughters of George III*. London, Michael Joseph, 1969.

Masters, Brian. *The Mistresses of Charles II*. London, England, Blond & Briggs, Ltd., 1979.

Mathew, David. *James I*. University, Alabama, University of Alabama Press, 1968.

McCarthy, Justin. *The Reign of Queen Anne*. London, England, Chatto & Windus, 1902.

The McGraw-Hill Encyclopedia of World Biography. New York, McGraw-Hill, Inc., 1973.

McNaughton, Arnold. *The Book of Kings: A Royal Genealogy*. New York Times Book Co., 1973.

Meany, Edmond S. *Vancouver's Discovery of Puget Sound*. New York, Macmillan Co., 1907.

Melville, Lewis. *The First George: In Hanover and England*. New York, Charles Scribner's Sons, 1909.

_____. *The Windsor Beauties*. Boston, Houghton Mifflin Co., 1928.

Miller, Peggy. *James*. New York, St. Martin's Press, 1971.

Montague-Smith, P. W. *The Royal Line of Succession*. London, England, Pitkins.

Morgan, Kenneth O. *The Oxford History of Britain*. Oxford, England, Oxford University Press, 1993.

Morrah, Patrick. *A Royal Family: Charles I and His Family*. London, Constable & Co., Ltd., 1982.

Morris, Richard B. *Encyclopedia of American History*. New York, Harper & Brothers, 1953.

Murray, Jane. *The Kings and Queens of England: A Tourist Guide*. New York, Charles Scribner's Sons, 1974.

Neale, J. E. *Queen Elizabeth I*. Chicago, Illinois, Academy Chicago Publishers, 1999.

_____. *Queen Elizabeth I: A Biography*. Garden City, New York, Doubleday & Co., Inc., 1957.

Nenner, Howard. *The Right to be King: The Succession to the Crown of England, 1603–1714*. Chapel Hill, University of North Carolina Press, 1995.

Newman, Gerald. *Britain in the Hanoverian Age: 1714–1837*. New York, Garland Publishing, Inc., 1997.

Oakley, Stewart. *The Story of Denmark*. London, Faber & Faber, 1972.

Ollard, Richard. *Clarendon and His Friends*. London, England, Hamish Hamilton, Ltd., 1987.

_____. *The Image of the King: Charles I and Charles II*. London, England, Pimlico, 1993.

Oman, Carola. *Henrietta Maria*. London, Hodder & Stoughton, Ltd., 1936.

_____. *Mary of Modena*. Bungay, Suffolk, England, Hodder & Stoughton, Ltd., 1962.

_____. *Princess Amelia*. New York, Duffield & Co., 1924.

_____. *The Winter Queen: Elizabeth of Bohemia*. London, England, Phoenix Press, 2000.

Ormond, Richard. *The Face of Monarchy: British Royalty Portrayed*. Oxford, England, Phaidon Press, Ltd., 1977.

Pares, Richard. *King George III and the Politicians*. London, Oxford University Press, 1967.

Parry, R. H. *The English Civil War and After: 1642–1658*. Berkeley, University of California Press, 1970.

Paul, Herbert. *Queen Anne*. London, J. M. Dent & Sons, Ltd., 1900.

Payne, William L. *Index to Defoe's Review*. New York, Columbia University Press, 1948.

Pearson, Hesketh. *Merry Monarch: The Life and Likeness of Charles II*. New York, Harper & Brothers, 1960.

Petrie, Charles. *The Stuarts*. London, Eyre & Spottiswoode, 1958.

Pine, L. G. *Princes of Wales*. Rutland, Vermont, Charles E. Tuttle Co., Inc., 1970.

Plowden, Alison. *Elizabeth Regina: The Age of Triumph: 1588–1603*. Gloucestershire, England, Sutton Publishing, Ltd., 2000.

_____. *Marriage With My Kingdom: The Courtships of Queen Elizabeth I*. Gloucestershire, England, Sutton Publishing, Ltd., 1999.

_____. *The Stuart Princesses*. Gloucestershire, England, Sutton Publishing, Ltd., 1996.

_____. *The Young Elizabeth: The First Twenty-Five Years of Elizabeth I*. Gloucestershire, England, Sutton Publishing, Ltd., 1999.

Plumb, J. H. *England in the Eighteenth Century*. London, England, Penguin Books, Ltd., 1987.

_____. *The First Four Georges*. Boston, Little, Brown & Co., 1975.

Porcelli, Ernest. *The White Cockade: The Lives and Adventures of James Francis Edward Stuart and His Sons "Bonnie Prince Charlie" and Cardinal York*. London, England, Hutchinson & Co., Ltd., 1949.

Potter, Jeremy. *Pretenders to the English Throne*. Totowa, New Jersey, Barnes & Noble Books, 1978.

Quennell, Peter. *Caroline of England*. New York, Viking Press, 1940.

Read, Conyers. *The Tudors: Personalities and Practical Politics in Sixteenth Century England*. New York, W. W. Norton & Co., 1969.

Reddaway, W. F. *Frederick the Great and the Rise of Prussia*. New York, G. P. Putnam's Sons, 1925.

Redman, Alvin. *The House of Hanover*. New York, Funk & Wagnalls, 1968.

Reiners, Ludwig. *Frederick the Great: A Biography*. New York, G. P. Putnam's Sons, 1960.

Rickards, Russ. Letter to the author dated April 15, 2002.

Ritter, Gerhard. *Frederick the Great: A Historical Profile*. Berkeley, University of California Press, 1968.

Robb, Nesca A. *William of Orange*. London, England, William Heinemann, Ltd., 1962.

_____. *William of Orange: A Personal Portrait: Volume 1: 1650–1673*. London, William Heinemann, Ltd., 1962.

_____. *William of Orange: A Personal Portrait: Volume 2: The Later Years 1674–1702*. New York, St. Martin's Press, 1966.

Rodger, N. A. M. *The Admiralty*. Lavenham, Suffolk, England, Terence Dalton, Ltd., 1979.

Ross, Josephine. *Kings and Queens of Britain*. London, England, Artus Publishing Co., Ltd., 1994.

_____. *Suitors to the Queen: The Men in the Life of Elizabeth I of England.* New York, Coward, McCann & Geoghegan, Inc., 1975.

_____. *The Winter Queen: The Story of Elizabeth Stuart.* New York, Dorset Press, 1979.

Rosten, Leo. *A Guide to the Religions of America.* New York, Simon & Schuster, 1955.

Rowland-Entwistle, Theodore, and Jean Cooke. *Great Rulers of History: A Biographical Dictionary.* New York, Barnes & Noble Books, 1995.

Rubincam, Milton. "Queen Henrietta Maria: Maryland's Royal Namesake." *Maryland Historical Magazine,* Vol. 54, No. 2. Baltimore: June 1959.

St. John Parker, Michael. *Britain's Kings and Queens.* Andover, England, Pitkin Pictorials, Ltd., 1990.

Schultz, Harold J. *History of England.* New York, Barnes & Noble, Inc., 1968.

Secord, Arthur W. *Defoe's Review: September 28, 1708 to March 31, 1709.* New York, Columbia University Press, 1938.

Sedillot, Rene. *An Outline of French History.* New York, Alfred A. Knopf, 1967.

Sheehan, James J. *German History: 1770–1866.* Oxford, Clarendon Press, 1989.

Simon, Edith. *The Making of Frederick the Great.* Boston, Little Brown & Co., 1960.

Sinclair-Stevenson, Christopher. *Blood Royal: The Illustrious House of Hanover.* Garden City, New York, Doubleday & Co., Inc., 1980.

Smith, E. A. *George IV.* New Haven, Yale University Press, 1999.

Sobel, Dava. *Longitude.* New York, Walker & Co., 1995.

Sousa, Manuel A. E. *Catherine of Braganza: Princess of Portugal: Wife to Charles II.* Lisbon, Marconi Global Communications, 1994.

Strickland, Agnes. *Lives of the Last Four Princesses of the Royal House of Stuart.* London, England, Bell & Daldy, 1872.

_____. *Lives of the Queens of England from the Norman Conquest.* Philadelphia, George Barrie & Sons, 1903.

_____. *Lives of the Queens of England from the Norman Conquest: With Anecdotes of Their Courts, Now First Published from Official Records and Other Authentic Documents, Private As Well As Public.* Vol. 10. Philadelphia, Lea & Blanchard, 1847.

_____. *Lives of the Queens of Scotland and the English Princesses Connected with the Regal Succession of Great Britain.* New York, Harper & Brothers, 1878.

Strong, Roy. *Henry, Prince of Wales and England's Lost Renaissance.* Thames & Hudson, 1986.

Stuart, Dorothy M. *Portrait of the Prince Regent.* London, Methuen & Co., Ltd., 1953.

Tomalin, Claire. *Mrs. Jordan's Profession.* New York, Alfred A. Knopf, 1995.

Townend, Peter. *Burke's Genealogical and Heraldic History of the Peerage, Baronetage and Knightage.* London, Burke's Peerage, Ltd., 1970.

Trease, Geoffrey. *Seven Kings of England.* New York, Vanguard Press, 1955.

_____. *The Seven Queens of England.* New York, Vanguard Press, Inc., 1953.

Treasure, Geoffrey. *Who's Who in Early Hanoverian Britain (1714–1789).* London, England, Shepheard-Walwyn, Ltd., 1991.

Trench, Charles C. *George II.* London, England, Penguin Books, Ltd., 1973.

Trevelyan, G. M. *England Under the Stuarts.* New York, Barnes & Noble, Inc., 1965.

_____. *History of England.* Garden City, New York, Doubleday & Co., Inc., 1952.

Trevelyan, George M. *England Under Queen Anne: Blenheim.* London, Longmans, Green & Co. 1931.

_____. *England Under Queen Anne: The Peace and the Protestant Succession*. London, Longmans, Green & Co. 1934.

_____. *England Under Queen Anne: Ramillies and the Union with Scotland*. London, Longmans, Green & Co. 1932.

Turner, F. C. *James II*. London, England, Eyre & Spottiswoode, Ltd., 1950.

Usherwood, Stephen. *Reign by Reign*. New York, W. W. Norton & Co., Inc., 1960.

Van der Kiste, John. *George III's Children*. Gloucestershire, England, Sutton Publishing Ltd., 1992.

_____. *The Georgian Princesses*. Gloucestershire, England, Sutton Publishing Ltd., 2000.

_____. *King George II and Queen Caroline*. Gloucestershire, England, Sutton Publishing Ltd., 1997.

Van der Zee, Henri, and Barbara Van der Zee. *William and Mary*. London, England, Macmillan London, Ltd., 1973.

Vierhaus, Rudolf. *Germany in the Age of Absolutism*. Cambridge, Cambridge University Press, 1988.

Virta, Alan. *Prince George's County: A Pictorial History*. Norfolk, Virginia, Donning Co., 1984.

Wakeford, Geoffrey. *The Princesses Royal*. London, England, Robert Hale & Co., 1973.

Walpole, Horace. *Memoirs of the Reign of King George the Second*. London, England, Henry Colburn, 1846.

Walter, David. *James I*. Sussex, England, Wayland, Ltd., 1975.

Walters, John. *The Royal Griffin: Frederick, Prince of Wales 1707–1751*. New York, Stein & Day, 1972.

Watson, D. R. *The Life and Times of Charles I*. London, England, George Weidenfeld, Nicolson. Ltd. & Book Club Associates, 1972.

Webster's Biographical Dictionary. Springfield, Massachusetts, G. & C. Merriam & Co., 1962.

Webster's New Geographical Dictionary. Springfield, Massachusetts, Merriam-Webster, Inc., 1988.

Wedgwood, C. V. *A Coffin for King Charles: The Trial and Execution of Charles I*. New York, TIME, Inc., 1966.

Weir, Alison. *The Life of Elizabeth I*. New York, Ballantine Books, 1998.

Whitworth, Rex. *William Augustus, Duke of Cumberland: A Life*. London, Leo Cooper, 1992.

Williams, Basil F. *The Whig Supremacy: 1714–1760*. Oxford, Clarendon Press, 1987.

Williams, E. N. *The Penguin Dictionary of English and European History: 1485–1789*. Middlesex, England, Penguin Books, 1980.

Williams, Neville. *All the Queen's Men: Elizabeth I and Her Courtiers*. New York, Macmillan Co., 1972.

Williamson, David. *Brewer's British Royalty*. Cassell, London, England, 1996.

_____. *Kings and Queens of Britain*. New York, Dorset Press, 1992.

Willis, G. M. *Ernest Augustus: Duke of Cumberland and King of Hanover*. London, Arthur Barker, 1954.

Willson, David H. *King James VI and I*. New York, Oxford University Press, 1967.

Wilson, Elkin C. *Prince Henry and English Literature*. Ithica, New York, Cornell University Press, 1946.

Wilson, John H. *Nell Gwyn: Royal Mistress*. New York, Pellegrini & Cudahy, 1952.

Wise, L. F., and E. W. Egan. *Kings, Rulers and Statesmen*. New York, Sterling Publishing Co., Inc., 1967.

Wright, Constance. *A Royal Affinity: The Story of Frederick the Great and His Sister, Wilhelmina of Bayreuth*. New York, Charles Scribner's Sons, 1965.

Wyon, Frederick W. *The History of Great Britain during the Reign of Queen Anne*. London, Chapman & Hall, 1876.

Zweig, Stefan. *Mary, Queen of Scotland and the Isles*. New York, Viking Press, 1935.

INDEX

References are to entry numbers